PROFESSIONAL TRAINING

murach's
SQL for
SQL Server

Bryan Syverson

MIKE MURACH & ASSOCIATES, INC.

2560 West Shaw Lane, Suite 101 • Fresno, CA 93711-2765
www.murach.com • murachbooks@murach.com

Author:	Bryan Syverson
Editor:	Anne Prince
Copy Editor:	Judy Taylor
Cover Design:	Zylka Design
Production:	Tom Murach

Four books for every .NET programmer

Murach's C#

Murach's Beginning Visual Basic .NET

Murach's VB.NET Database Programming with ADO.NET

Murach's ASP.NET Web Programming with VB.NET

Two books for every Java programmer

Murach's Beginning Java 2 JDK 5

Murach's Java Servlets and JSP

Four books for every IBM mainframe programmer

Murach's Mainframe COBOL

Murach's CICS for the COBOL Programmer

Murach's OS/390 and z/OS JCL

DB2 for the COBOL Programmer, Part 1

10 9 8 7 6 5 4 3
ISBN: 1-890774-16-2

Contents

Expanded contents

Section 1 An introduction to SQL

Section 2 The essential SQL skills

Chapter 3 How to retrieve data from a single table

Chapter 4 How to retrieve data from two or more tables

Chapter 5   How to code summary queries

Chapter 6   How to code subqueries

Section 3 Database design and implementation

Introduction

If you want to learn SQL, you've picked the right book. And if you want to learn the specifics of SQL for Microsoft SQL Server, you've made an especially good choice. Along the way, you'll learn a lot about database management systems in general and about SQL Server in particular.

Why learn SQL? First, because most database programmers would be better programmers if they knew more about SQL. Second, because SQL programming is a valuable specialty in itself. And third, because knowing SQL is the first step toward becoming a database administrator. In short, knowing SQL makes you more valuable on the job.

What you'll learn in this book

- In section 1, you'll learn the concepts and terms you need for working with any database. You'll also learn how to use the Microsoft SQL Server 2000 Desktop Engine (MSDE) and the client tools for SQL Server 2000 that come on the CD. Then, you'll be able to run SQL statements on your own PC. At that point, you'll be prepared for rapid progress as you learn SQL.

- In section 2, you'll learn all the skills for retrieving data from a database and for adding, updating, and deleting that data. These skills move from the simple to the complex so you won't have any trouble if you're a SQL novice. And they present skills like using outer joins, summary queries, and subqueries that will raise your SQL expertise if you do have SQL experience.

- In section 3, you'll learn how to design a database and how to implement that design by using either SQL DDL (Data Definition Language) statements or the Enterprise Manager that comes with SQL Server. When you're done, you'll be able to design and implement your own databases. But even if you're never called upon to do that, this section will give you perspective that will make you a better SQL programmer.

- To complete your SQL skills, section 4 presents the skills for working with database features like views, stored procedures, functions, triggers, cursors, and transactions. These are the features that give a database management system much of its power. So once you master them, you'll have a powerful set of SQL skills.

3 reasons why you'll learn faster with this book

- Unlike most SQL books, this one starts by showing you how to query an existing database rather than how to create a new database. Why? Because that's what you're most likely to need to do first on the job. Once you master those skills, you can learn how to design and implement a database...whenever you need to do that. Or, you can learn how to work with other database features like views and stored procedures...whenever you need to do that.

- Like all our books, this one includes hundreds of examples that range from the simple to the complex. That way, you can quickly get the idea of how a feature works from the simple examples, but you'll also see how the feature is used in real-world examples.

- If you page through this book, you'll see that all of the information is presented in "paired pages," with the essential syntax, guidelines, and examples on the right page and the perspective and extra explanation on the left page. This helps you learn faster by reading less...and this is the ideal reference format when you need to refresh your memory about how to do something.

Who this book is for

I think it's fair to say that most application programmers don't know enough about SQL and the database management system they're using. That's why they often code SQL statements that don't perform as efficiently as they ought to. That's why they aren't able to code some of the queries that they need for their programs. And that's why they don't take advantage of all the features that SQL Server has to offer.

That's why we believe that this book should be required reading for every application programmer who uses SQL Server. Beyond that, we believe that this is the right book for anyone who wants to become a SQL specialist. It's also the right first book for anyone who wants to become a database administrator. Note, however, that this book doesn't present the performance tuning skills that database administrators need.

Is this a useful book for those who want to learn SQL but aren't going to be using SQL Server? We think so. Because SQL is a standard language, 90% or more of the SQL code in this book will work with any database management system. So after you use this book to master standard SQL, you only need to learn the non-standard SQL for the database management system that you will be using.

What are the prerequisites for using this book? We think it will help if you have some application programming experience so you have a basic idea of how a database is used and how programming statements are coded. On the other hand, everything you need to know about databases and SQL is presented in this book so you should be able to learn SQL without any programming background.

Everything you need is on the CD

To make it easy for you to learn on your own, the CD that comes with this book provides everything you need. That includes:

- The Microsoft SQL Server 2000 Desktop Engine (MSDE) so you can run SQL statements on your own PC
- The client tools that come with the Enterprise Evaluation Edition of Microsoft SQL Server 2000
- The databases that we used for the examples in this book
- Selected examples from this book so you can run them on your own PC

In appendix A, you'll find complete information for installing these items on your PC. And in chapter 2, you'll learn how to use them.

If you're using this book in a class, though, the database may be set up differently. In particular, the database may reside on a server that is used by all the students. In that case, you may need to get instructions for accessing the database from your instructor.

Support materials for trainers and instructors

If you're a trainer or instructor who would like to use this book for a course, we want you to know that your students can download a Student Workbook in PDF format from our web site (www.murach.com). This workbook includes chapter summaries, behavioral objectives, self-study questions, and exercises that ask the students to run queries on their own. In other words, this workbook includes everything that you usually find at the ends of the chapters in college textbooks. As such, it makes an excellent study guide.

We also offer an Instructor's Guide on CD that includes: (1) a complete set of PowerPoint slides that you can use to review and reinforce the content of the book; (2) behavioral objectives that describe the skills that a student should have upon completion of each chapter; (3) exercises that help the student practice those skills; and (4) short-answer and multiple-choice tests that test those skills. The objectives and exercises are the same ones that are in the Student Workbook, but they're in Word format so you can easily modify them.

To download a sample of this Instructor's Guide and to find out how to get the complete Guide, please go to our web site at www.murach.com and click on the Instructors link. Or, if you prefer, you can call Karen at 1-800-221-5528 or email karen@murach.com.

Please let us know how this book works for you

When we started this book, our goals were (1) to provide a SQL book for application programmers that would help them work more effectively; (2) to present all the skills that SQL specialists need; (3) to cover the database design

xvi   Introduction

and implementation skills that programmers are most likely to use; and (4) to do all that in a way that helps you learn faster and better than you can with any other book. Now, we sincerely hope that we've succeeded.

So if you have any comments about this book, we would appreciate hearing from you. In particular, we would like to know whether this book has lived up to your expectations. To reply, you can e-mail us or send your comments to our street address.

Thanks for buying this book. And thanks for reading it. We sure hope that it will help you handle all your SQL-related projects more efficiently and confidently, starting today.

Bryan Syverson
Author
bryan@murach.com

Anne Prince
Editor
anne@murach.com

Section 1

An introduction to SQL

Before you begin to learn the fundamentals of programming in SQL, you need to understand the concepts and terms related to SQL and relational databases. That's what you'll learn in chapter 1. Then, in chapter 2, you'll learn about some of the tools you can use to work with a SQL Server database. That will prepare you for using the skills you'll learn in the rest of this book.

1

An introduction to relational databases and SQL

Before you can use SQL to work with a SQL Server database, you need to be familiar with the concepts and terms that apply to database systems. In particular, you need to understand what a relational database is and the benefits relational databases offer over other data models. That's what you'll learn in the first part of this chapter. Then, you'll learn about some of the basic SQL statements and features provided by SQL Server 2000.

An introduction to client/server systems

In case you aren't familiar with client/server systems, the first two topics that follow introduce you to their essential hardware and software components. These are the types of systems that you're most likely to use SQL with. Then, the last topic gives you an idea of how complex client/server systems can be.

The hardware components of a client/server system

Figure 1-1 presents the three hardware components of a client/server system: the clients, the network, and the server. The *clients* are usually the PCs that are already available on the desktops throughout a company. And the *network* is the cabling, communication lines, network interface cards, hubs, routers, and other components that connect the clients and the server.

The *server*, commonly referred to as a *database server*, is a computer that has enough processor speed, internal memory (RAM), and disk storage to store the files and databases of the system and provide services to the clients of the system. This computer is usually a high-powered PC, but it can also be a midrange system like an AS/400 or Unix system, or even a mainframe system. When a system consists of networks, midrange systems, and mainframe systems, often spread throughout the country or world, it is commonly referred to as an *enterprise system*.

To back up the files of a client/server system, a server usually has a tape drive or some other form of offline storage. It often has one or more printers or specialized devices that can be shared by the users of the system. And it can provide programs or services like e-mail that can be accessed by all the users of the system.

In a simple client/server system, the clients and the server are part of a *local area network* (*LAN*). However, two or more LANs that reside at separate geographical locations can be connected as part of a larger network such as a *wide area network* (*WAN*). In addition, individual systems or networks can be connected over the Internet.

A simple client/server system

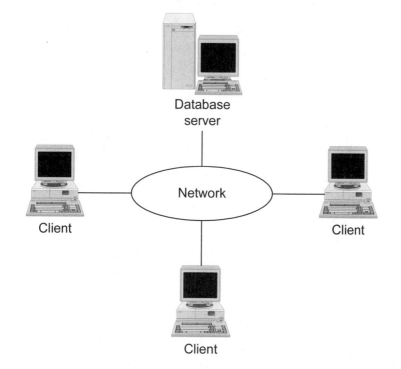

The three hardware components of a client/server system

- The *clients* are the PCs, Macintoshes, or workstations of the system.
- The *server* is a computer that stores the files and databases of the system and provides services to the clients. When it stores databases, it's often referred to as a *database server*.
- The *network* consists of the cabling, communication lines, and other components that connect the clients and the servers of the system.

Client/server system implementations

- In a simple *client/server system* like the one shown above, the server is typically a high-powered PC that communicates with the clients over a *local area network* (*LAN*).
- The server can also be a midrange system, like an AS/400 or a Unix system, or it can be a mainframe system. Then, special hardware and software components are required to make it possible for the clients to communicate with the midrange and mainframe systems.
- A client/server system can also consist of one or more PC-based systems, one or more midrange systems, and a mainframe system in dispersed geographical locations. This type of system is commonly referred to as an *enterprise system*.
- Individual systems and LANs can be connected and share data over larger private networks, such as a *wide area network* (*WAN*), or a public network like the Internet.

Figure 1-1   The hardware components of a client/server system

The software components of a client/server system

Figure 1-2 presents the software components of a typical client/server system. In addition to a *network operating system* that manages the functions of the network, the server requires a *database management system* (*DBMS*) like Microsoft SQL Server or Oracle. This DBMS manages the databases that are stored on the server.

In contrast to a server, each client requires *application software* to perform useful work. This can be a purchased software package like a financial accounting package, or it can be custom software that's developed for a specific application.

Although the application software is run on the client, it uses data that's stored on the server. To do that, it uses a *data access API* (*application programming interface*) such as ADO.NET. Since the technique you use to work with an API depends on the programming language and API you're using, you won't learn those techniques in this book. Instead, you'll learn about a standard language called *SQL*, or *Structured Query Language*, that lets any application communicate with any DBMS. (In conversation, SQL is pronounced as either *S-Q-L* or *sequel*.)

Once the software for both client and server is installed, the client communicates with the server via *SQL queries* (or just *queries*) that are passed to the DBMS through the API. After the client sends a query to the DBMS, the DBMS interprets the query and sends the results back to the client.

As you can see in this figure, the processing done by a client/server system is divided between the clients and the server. In this case, the DBMS on the server is processing requests made by the application running on the client. Theoretically, at least, this balances the workload between the clients and the server so the system works more efficiently. In contrast, in a file-handling system, the clients do all of the work because the server is used only to store the files that are used by the clients.

Client software, server software, and the SQL interface

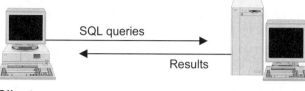

Client
Application software
Data access API

Database server
Database management system
Database

Server software

* To store and manage the databases of the client/server system, each server requires a *database management system* (*DBMS*) like Microsoft SQL Server.

* The processing that's done by the DBMS is typically referred to as *back-end processing*, and the database server is referred to as the *back end*.

Client software

* The *application software* does the work that the user wants to do. This type of software can be purchased or developed.

* The *data access API* (*application programming interface*) provides the interface between the application program and the DBMS. The newest data access API is ADO.NET, which can communicate directly with SQL Server. Older APIs required a data access model, such as ADO or DAO, plus a driver, such as OLE DB or ODBC.

* The processing that's done by the client software is typically referred to as *front-end processing*, and the client is typically referred to as the *front end*.

The SQL interface

* The application software communicates with the DBMS by sending *SQL queries* through the data access API. When the DBMS receives a query, it provides a service like returning the requested data (the *query results*) to the client.

* *SQL* stands for *Structured Query Language*, which is the standard language for working with a relational database.

Client/server versus file-handling systems

* In a client/server system, the processing done by an application is typically divided between the client and the server.

* In a file-handling system, all of the processing is done on the clients. Although the clients may access data that's stored in files on the server, none of the processing is done by the server. As a result, a file-handling system isn't a client/server system.

Figure 1-2   The software components of a client/server system

Other client/server system architectures

In its simplest form, a client/server system consists of a single database server and one or more clients. Many client/server systems today, though, include additional servers. In figure 1-3, for example, you can see two client/server systems that include an additional server between the clients and the database server.

The first illustration is for a simple Windows-based system. With this system, only the user interface for an application runs on the client. The rest of the processing that's done by the application is stored in one or more *business components* on the *application server*. Then, the client sends requests to the application server for processing. If the request involves accessing data in a database, the application server formulates the appropriate query and passes it on to the database server. The results of the query are then sent back to the application server, which processes the results and sends the appropriate response back to the client.

Similar processing is done by a web-based system, as illustrated by the second example in this figure. In this case, though, a *web browser* running on the client is used to send requests to a *web application* running on a *web server* somewhere on the Internet. The web application, in turn, can use *web services* to perform some of its processing. Then, the web application or web service can pass requests for data on to the database server.

Although this figure should give you an idea of how client/server systems can be configured, you should realize that they can be much more complicated than what's shown here. In a Windows-based system, for example, business components can be distributed over any number of application servers, and those components can communicate with databases on any number of database servers. Similarly, the web applications and services in a web-based system can be distributed over numerous web servers that access numerous database servers. In most cases, though, it's not necessary for you to know how a system is configured to use SQL.

Before I go on, you should know that client/server systems aren't the only systems that support SQL. For example, traditional mainframe systems and newer *thin client* systems also use SQL. Unlike client/server systems, though, most of the processing for these types of systems is done by a mainframe or another high-powered machine. The terminals or PCs that are connected to the system do little or no work.

A Windows-based system that uses an application server

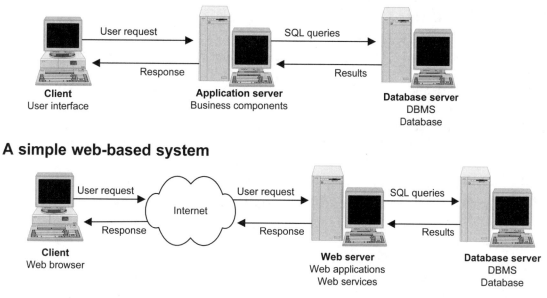

A simple web-based system

Description

- In addition to a database server and clients, a client-server system can include additional servers, such as *application servers* and *web servers*.

- Application servers are typically used to store *business components* that do part of the processing of the application. In particular, these components are used to process database requests from the user interface running on the client.

- Web servers are typically used to store *web applications* and *web services*. Web applications are applications that are designed to run on a web server. Web services are like business components, except that, like web applications, they are designed to run on a web server.

- In a web-based system, a *web browser* running on a client sends a request to a web server over the Internet. Then, the web server processes the request and passes any requests for data on to the database server.

- More complex system architectures can include two or more application servers, web servers, and database servers.

Figure 1-3   Other client/server system architectures

An introduction to the relational database model

In 1970, Dr. E. F. Codd developed a model for a new type of database called a *relational database.* This type of database eliminated some of the problems that were associated with standard files and other database designs. By using the relational model, you can reduce data redundancy, which saves disk storage and leads to efficient data retrieval. You can also view and manipulate data in a way that is both intuitive and efficient. Today, relational databases are the de facto standard for database applications.

How a database table is organized

The model for a relational database states that data is stored in one or more *tables.* It also states that each table can be viewed as a two-dimensional matrix consisting of *rows* and *columns.* This is illustrated by the relational table in figure 1-4. Each row in this table contains information about a single vendor.

In practice, the rows and columns of a relational database table are often referred to by the more traditional terms, *records* and *fields.* In fact, some software packages use one set of terms, some use the other, and some use a combination. In this book, I use the terms *rows* and *columns* because those are the terms used by SQL Server.

In general, each table is modeled after a real-word entity such as a vendor or an invoice. Then, the columns of the table represent the attributes of the entity such as name, address, and phone number. And each row of the table represents one instance of the entity. A value is stored at the intersection of each row and column, sometimes called a *cell.*

If a table contains one or more columns that uniquely identify each row in the table, you can define these columns as the *primary key* of the table. For instance, the primary key of the Vendors table in this figure is the VendorID column. In this example, the primary key consists of a single column. However, a primary key can also consist of two or more columns, in which case it's called a *composite primary key.*

In addition to primary keys, some database management systems let you define additional keys that uniquely identify each row in a table. If, for example, the VendorName column in the Vendors table contains unique data, it can be defined as a *non-primary key.* In SQL Server, this is called a *unique key.*

Indexes provide an efficient way of accessing the rows in a table based on the values in one or more columns. Because applications typically access the rows in a table by referring to their key values, an index is automatically created for each key you define. However, you can define indexes for other columns as well. If, for example, you frequently need to sort the Vendor rows by zip code, you can set up an index for that column. Like a key, an index can include one or more columns.

The Vendors table in an Accounts Payable database

Primary key   Columns

VendorID	VendorName	VendorAddress1	VendorAddress2	VendorCity
1	US Postal Service	Attn: Supt. Window Services	PO Box 7005	Madison
2	National Information Data Ctr	PO Box 96621	<NULL>	Washington
3	Register of Copyrights	Library Of Congress	<NULL>	Washington
4	Jobtrak	1990 Westwood Blvd Ste 260	<NULL>	Los Angeles
5	Newbrige Book Clubs	3000 Cindel Drive	<NULL>	Washington
6	California Chamber Of Commerce	3255 Ramos Cir	<NULL>	Sacramento
7	Towne Advertiser's Mailing Svcs	Kevin Minder	3441 W Macarthur Blvd	Santa Ana
8	BFI Industries	PO Box 9369	<NULL>	Fresno
9	Pacific Gas & Electric	Box 52001	<NULL>	San Francisco
10	Robbins Mobile Lock And Key	4669 N Fresno	<NULL>	Fresno
11	Bill Marvin Electric Inc	4583 E Home	<NULL>	Fresno
12	City Of Fresno	PO Box 2069	<NULL>	Fresno
13	Golden Eagle Insurance Co	PO Box 85826	<NULL>	San Diego
14	Expedata Inc	4420 N. First Street, Suite 108	<NULL>	Fresno
15	ASC Signs	1528 N Sierra Vista	<NULL>	Fresno
16	Internal Revenue Service	<NULL>	<NULL>	Fresno

Rows

Concepts

- A *relational database* consists of *tables*. Tables consist of *rows* and *columns*, which can also be referred to as *records* and *fields*.

- A table is typically modeled after a real-world entity, such as an invoice or a vendor.

- A column represents some attribute of the entity, such as the amount of an invoice or a vendor's address.

- A row contains a set of values for a single instance of the entity, such as one invoice or one vendor.

- The intersection of a row and a column is sometimes called a *cell*. A cell stores a single value.

- Most tables have a *primary key* that uniquely identifies each row in the table. The primary key is usually a single column, but it can also consist of two or more columns. If a primary key uses two or more columns, it's called a *composite primary key*.

- In addition to primary keys, some database management systems let you define one or more *non-primary keys*. In SQL Server, these keys are called *unique keys*. Like a primary key, a non-primary key uniquely identifies each row in the table.

- A table can also be defined with one or more *indexes*. An index provides an efficient way to access data from a table based on the values in specific columns. An index is automatically created for a table's primary and non-primary keys.

Figure 1-4   How a database table is organized

How the tables in a relational database are related

The tables in a relational database can be related to other tables by values in specific columns. The two tables shown in figure 1-5 illustrate this concept. Here, each row in the Vendors table is related to one or more rows in the Invoices table. This is called a *one-to-many relationship*.

Typically, relationships exist between the primary key in one table and the *foreign key* in another table. The foreign key is simply one or more columns in a table that refer to a primary key in another table. In SQL Server, relationships can also exist between a unique key in one table and a foreign key in another table.

Although one-to-many relationships are the most common, two tables can also have a one-to-one or many-to-many relationship. If a table has a *one-to-one relationship* with another table, the data in the two tables could be stored in a single table. Because of that, one-to-one relationships are used infrequently.

In contrast, a *many-to-many relationship* is usually implemented by using an intermediate table that has a one-to-many relationship with the two tables in the many-to-many relationship. In other words, a many-to-many relationship can usually be broken down into two one-to-many relationships.

The relationship between the Vendors and Invoices tables in the database

Primary key

VendorID	VendorName	VendorAddress1	VendorAddress2	VendorCity
114	Postmaster	Postage Due Technician	1900 E Street	Fresno
115	Roadway Package System, Inc	Dept La 21095	<NULL>	Pasadena
116	State of California	Employment Development Dept	PO Box 826276	Sacramento
117	Suburban Propane	2874 S Cherry Ave	<NULL>	Fresno
118	Unocal	P.O. Box 860070	<NULL>	Pasadena
119	Yesmed, Inc	PO Box 2061	<NULL>	Fresno
120	Dataforms/West	1617 W. Shaw Avenue	Suite F	Fresno
121	Zylka Design	3467 W Shaw Ave #103	<NULL>	Fresno
122	United Parcel Service	P.O. Box 505820	<NULL>	Reno
123	Federal Express Corporation	P.O. Box 1140	Dept A	Memphis

InvoiceID	VendorID	InvoiceNumber	InvoiceDate	InvoiceTotal
29	123	4-314-3057	5/2/2002	13.75
30	94	203339-13	5/2/2002	17.5
31	123	2-000-2993	5/3/2002	144.7
32	89	125520-1	5/5/2002	95
33	123	1-202-2978	5/6/2002	33
34	110	0-2436	5/7/2002	10976.06
35	123	1-200-5164	5/7/2002	63.4
36	110	0-2060	5/8/2002	23517.58
37	110	0-2058	5/8/2002	37966.19
38	123	963253272	5/9/2002	61.5

Foreign key

Concepts

* The tables in a relational database are related to each other through their key columns. For example, the VendorID column is used to relate the Vendors and Invoices tables above. The VendorID column in the Invoice table is called a *foreign key* because it identifies a related row in the Vendors table. A table may contain one or more foreign keys.

* When you define a foreign key for a table in SQL Server, you can't add rows to the table with the foreign key unless there's a matching primary key in the related table.

* The relationships between the tables in a database correspond to the relationships between the entities they represent. The most common type of relationship is a *one-to-many relationship* as illustrated by the Vendors and Invoices tables. A table can also have a *one-to-one relationship* or a *many-to-many relationship* with another table.

Figure 1-5   How the tables in a relational database are related

How the columns in a table are defined

When you define a column in a table, you assign properties to it as indicated by the design of the Invoices table in figure 1-6. The most critical property for a column is its data type, which determines the type of information that can be stored in the column. With SQL Server 2000, you can choose from the *data types* listed in this figure. As you define each column in a table, you generally try to assign the data type that will minimize the use of disk storage because that will improve the performance of the queries later.

In addition to a data type, you must identify whether the column can store a *null value*. A null represents a value that's unknown, unavailable, or not applicable. If you don't allow null values, then you must provide a value for the column or you can't store the row in the table.

You can also assign a *default value* to each column. Then, that value is assigned to the column if another value isn't provided. You'll learn more about how to work with nulls and default values later in this book.

Each table can also contain a numeric column whose value is generated automatically by the DBMS. In SQL Server, a column like this is called an *identity column*, and you establish it using the Identity, Identity Seed, and Identity Increment properties. You'll learn more about these properties in chapter 10. For now, just note that the primary key of both the Vendors and the Invoices tables—VendorID and InvoiceID—are identity columns.

The columns of the Invoices table

Column Name	Data Type	Length	Allow Nulls
InvoiceID	int	4	
VendorID	int	4	
InvoiceNumber	varchar	50	
InvoiceDate	smalldatetime	4	
InvoiceTotal	money	8	
PaymentTotal	money	8	
CreditTotal	money	8	
TermsID	int	4	
InvoiceDueDate	smalldatetime	4	
PaymentDate	smalldatetime	4	✓

Columns

Description	
Default Value	
Precision	10
Scale	0
Identity	Yes
Identity Seed	1
Identity Increment	1
Is RowGuid	No
Formula	
Collation	

Common SQL Server data types

Type	Description
bit	A value of 1 or 0 that represents a True or False value.
char, varchar, text	Any combination of letters, symbols, and numbers.
nchar, nvarchar, ntext	Unicode character data.
datetime, smalldatetime	Numeric data that represents a date and time.
decimal, numeric	Numeric data that is accurate to the least significant digit. The data can contain an integer and a fractional portion.
float, real	Floating-point values that contain an approximation of a decimal value.
bigint, int, smallint, tinyint	Numeric data that contains only an integer portion.
money, smallmoney	Monetary values that are accurate to four decimal places.

Description

- The *data type* that's assigned to a column determines the type of information that can be stored in the column. Depending on the data type, the column definition can also include its length, precision, and scale.

- Each column definition also indicates whether or not it can contain *null values*. A null value indicates that the value of the column is unknown.

- A column can also be defined with a *default value*. Then, that value is used if another value isn't provided when a row is added to the table.

- A column can also be defined as an *identity column*. An identity column is a numeric column whose value is generated automatically when a row is added to the table.

Figure 1-6   How the columns in a table are defined

How relational databases compare to other data models

Now that you understand how a relational database is organized, you're ready to learn how relational databases differ from other data models. Specifically, you should know how relational databases compare to conventional file systems, *hierarchical databases*, and *network databases*. Figure 1-7 presents the most important differences.

To start, you should realize that because the physical structure of a relational database is defined and managed by the DBMS, it's not necessary to define that structure within the programs that use the database. Instead, you can simply refer to the tables and columns you want to use by name and the DBMS will take care of the rest. In contrast, when you use a conventional file system, you have to define and control the files of the system within each application that uses them. That's because a conventional file system is just a collection of files that contain the data of the system. In addition, if you modify the structure of a file, you have to modify every program that uses it. That's not necessary with a relational database.

The hierarchical and network database models were predecessors to the relational database model. The hierarchical database model is limited in that it can only represent one-to-many relationships, also called *parent/child relationships*. The network database model is an extension of the hierarchical model that provides for all types of relationships.

Although hierarchical and network databases don't have the same drawbacks as conventional file systems, they still aren't as easy to use as relational databases. In particular, each program that uses a hierarchical or network database must navigate through the physical layout of the tables they use. In contrast, this navigation is automatically provided by the DBMS in a relational database system. In addition, programs can define ad hoc relationships between the tables of a relational database. In other words, they can use relationships that aren't defined by the DBMS. That's not possible with hierarchical and network databases.

Another type of database that's not mentioned in this figure is the *object-oriented database*. This type of database has all the features of a relational database, but the data is stored together with the *methods* that operate on it based on a concept called *encapsulation*. Although it's not important that you understand how this works, you should realize that object-oriented databases are becoming more and more popular.

A comparison of relational databases and conventional file systems

Feature	Conventional file system	Relational database
Definition	Each program that uses the file must define the file and the layout of the records within the file	Tables, rows, and columns are defined within the database and can be accessed by name
Maintenance	If the definition of a file changes, each program that uses the file must be modified	Programs can be used without modification when the definition of a table changes
Validity checking	Each program that updates a file must include code to check for valid data	Can include checks for valid data
Relationships	Each program must provide for and enforce relationships between files	Can enforce relationships between tables using foreign keys; ad hoc relationships can also be used
Data access	Each I/O operation targets a specific record in a file based on its relative position in the file or its key value	A program can use SQL to access selected data in one or more tables of a database

A comparison of relational databases and other database systems

Feature	Hierarchical database	Network database	Relational database
Supported relationships	One-to-many only	One-to-many, one-to-one, and many-to-many	One-to-many, one-to-one, and many-to-many; ad hoc relationships can also be used
Data access	Programs must include code to navigate through the physical structure of the database	Programs must include code to navigate through the physical structure of the database	Programs can access data without knowing its physical structure
Maintenance	New and modified relationships can be difficult to implement in application programs	New and modified relationships can be difficult to implement in application programs	Programs can be used without modification when the definition of a table changes

Description

- To work with any of the data models other than the relational database model, you must know the physical structure of the data and the relationships between the files or tables.
- Because relationships are difficult to implement in a conventional file system, redundant data is often stored in these types of files.
- The *hierarchical database* model provides only for one-to-many relationships, called *parent/child relationships*.
- The *network database* model can accommodate any type of relationship.
- Conventional files, hierarchical databases, and network databases are all more efficient than relational databases because they require fewer system resources. However, the flexibility and ease of use of relational databases typically outweighs this inefficiency.

Figure 1-7   How relational databases compare to other data models

An introduction to SQL and SQL-based systems

In the topics that follow, you'll learn how SQL and SQL-based database management systems evolved. In addition, you'll learn how some of the most popular SQL-based systems compare.

A brief history of SQL

Prior to the release of the first *relational database management system (RDBMS)*, each database had a unique physical structure and a unique programming language that the programmer had to understand. That all changed with the advent of SQL and the relational database management system.

Figure 1-8 lists the important events in the history of SQL. In 1970, Dr. E. F. Codd published an article that described the relational database model he had been working on with a research team at IBM. By 1978, the IBM team had developed a database system based on this model, called System/R, along with a query language called *SEQUEL* (*Structured English Query Language*). Although the database and query language were never officially released, IBM remained committed to the relational model.

The following year, Relational Software, Inc. released the first relational database management system, called *Oracle*. This RDBMS ran on a minicomputer and used SQL as its query language. This product was widely successful, and the company later changed its name to Oracle to reflect that success.

In 1982, IBM released its first commercial SQL-based RDBMS, called *SQL/DS* (*SQL/Data System*). This was followed in 1985 by *DB2* (*Database 2*). Both systems ran only on IBM mainframe computers. Later, DB2 was ported to other systems, including those that ran the Unix and Windows operating systems. Today, it continues to be IBM's premier database system.

During the 1980s, other SQL-based database systems, including SQL Server, were developed. Although each of these systems used SQL as its query language, each implementation was unique. That began to change in 1989, when the *American National Standards Institute* (*ANSI*) published its first set of standards for a database query language. These standards have been revised twice since then, most recently in 1999. As each database manufacturer has attempted to comply with these standards, their implementations of SQL have become more similar. However, each still has its own *dialect* of SQL that includes additions, or *extensions*, to the standards.

Although you should be aware of the SQL standards, they will have little effect on your job as a SQL programmer. The main benefit of the standards is that the basic SQL statements are the same in each dialect. As a result, once you've learned one dialect, it's relatively easy to learn another. On the other hand, porting applications that use SQL from one database to another isn't as easy as it should be. In fact, any non-trivial application will require at least modest modifications.

Important events in the history of SQL

Year	Event
1970	Dr. E. F. Codd developed the relational database model.
1978	IBM developed the predecessor to SQL, called Structured English Query Language (SEQUEL). This language was used on a database system called System/R, but neither the system nor the query language was ever released.
1979	Relational Software, Inc. (later renamed Oracle) released the first relational DBMS, Oracle.
1982	IBM released their first relational database system, SQL/DS (SQL/Data System).
1985	IBM released DB2 (Database 2).
1987	Microsoft released SQL Server.
1989	The American National Standards Institute (ANSI) published the first set of standards for a database query language, called ANSI/ISO SQL-89, or SQL1. These standards were similar to IBM's DB2 SQL dialect. Because they were not stringent standards, most commercial products could claim adherence.
1992	ANSI published revised standards (ANSI/ISO SQL-92, or SQL2) that were more stringent than SQL1 and incorporated many new features. These standards introduced levels of compliance that indicated the extent to which a dialect met the standards.
1999	ANSI published SQL3 (ANSI/ISO SQL-99). These standards incorporated new features, including support for objects. Levels of compliance were dropped and were replaced by a core specification along with specifications for nine additional packages.

Description

- SQL2 initially provided for three *levels of compliance*, or *levels of conformance*: entry, intermediate, and full. A transitional level was later added between the entry and intermediate levels because the jump between those levels was too great.

- SQL3 includes a *core specification* that defines the essential elements for compliance, plus nine *packages*. Each package is designed to serve a specific market niche.

- Most SQL databases are fully compliant with SQL-89, in transitional compliance with SQL-92, and core compliant with SQL-99. None are fully SQL-92 or SQL-99 compliant.

- Although SQL is a standard language, each vendor has its own *SQL dialect*, or *variant*, that may include extensions to the standards. SQL Server's SQL dialect is called *Transact-SQL*.

How knowing "standard SQL" helps you

- The most basic SQL statements are the same for all SQL dialects.
- Once you have learned one SQL dialect, you can learn other dialects easily.

How knowing "standard SQL" does not help you

- Any non-trivial application will require modification when moved from one SQL database to another.
- Standard SQL is a theoretical concept that's not available on any commercial system.

Figure 1-8   A brief history of SQL

A comparison of Oracle, DB2, and SQL Server

Although this book is about SQL Server, you may want to know about some of the other SQL-based relational database management systems. Figure 1-9 compares two of the most popular, Oracle and DB2, with SQL Server.

One of the main differences between SQL Server and the other database management systems is that SQL Server runs only under the Windows operating system. In contrast, Oracle and DB2 run under a variety of operating systems, including z/OS, Unix, and Windows. However, the fact that SQL Server was originally designed to run under Windows and it's inexpensive, fast, and easy to set up and maintain has made it the database of choice for small to medium network-based Windows systems.

DB2, on the other hand, was designed to run on IBM mainframe systems and continues to be the premier database for those systems. It also dominates in hybrid environments where IBM mainframes and newer servers must coexist. Although it's expensive, it's reliable and easy to maintain.

Oracle has a huge installed base of customers and continues to dominate the marketplace, especially for servers running the Unix operating system. Oracle works well in large companies and is the database of choice for Internet-based systems. It is extremely reliable, but is also expensive and difficult to maintain.

Other SQL-based systems

In addition to the three databases shown in figure 1-9, many other SQL-based systems are available. For example, Access is another RDBMS developed by Microsoft. It is intended for single-user or departmental databases. Other SQL-based databases include Ingres, which is owned by Computer Associates; Informix, which was one of the earliest systems to offer a significant set of development tools and is owned by IBM; Sybase, which is popular among financial institutions and is owned by the company of the same name; and Pervasive, which is a small and inexpensive database owned by Pervasive Software that's marketed to developers who want to integrate database function-ality into their products.

In addition to these proprietary systems, several *open source systems* are available. The source code for these systems is available to the public and can be used, rewritten, or sold without paying fees to the developers. Open source databases are commonly used for small web-based systems. Two of the most popular are MySQL and PostgreSQL. Both of these systems are used most often on Linux servers.

Features of Oracle, DB2, and SQL Server

Category	Oracle	IBM	Microsoft
Released	1979	1985	1987
Current version	Oracle 9i	DB2 Universal Database	SQL Server 2000
Platforms	Unix OS/390 Windows	OS/390, z/OS, and AIX Unix Windows	Windows
Strengths	Reliable Portable Internet support Huge market share Clustering support	Reliable Straightforward maintenance Integrates hybrid data sources Legacy support	Inexpensive Fast on small to medium systems Internet support Easy to manage and use
Weaknesses	Expensive Monolithic Requires expert tuning	Expensive Immature Internet support	Less reliable Not portable
Typical system	Medium to very large Network-based Mission-critical Enterprise-wide	Large to very large Centralized architecture Mission-critical Enterprise-wide	Small to medium Network-based

Description

- Oracle is the database of choice in Internet-based companies and those with homogeneous database systems. The company aggressively markets an all-Oracle suite of database, middleware, and applications.

- DB2 is the database of choice in large organizations with legacy IBM mainframe systems, especially those that work with a mix of data sources. IBM is now pursuing Internet-based businesses through Java support and encouraging installation on non-IBM hardware.

- SQL Server is the database of choice in small networked systems. Microsoft has recently added functionality to help it sell to larger enterprises and Internet-based businesses.

Figure 1-9   A comparison of Oracle, DB2, and SQL Server

The Transact-SQL statements

In the topics that follow, you'll learn about some of the SQL statements provided by SQL Server. As you'll see, you can use some of these statements to manipulate the data in a database, and you can use others to work with database objects. Although you may not be able to code these statements after reading these topics, you should have a good idea of how they work. Then, you'll be better prepared to learn the details of coding these statements when they're presented in sections 2 and 3 of this book.

An introduction to the SQL statements

Figure 1-10 summarizes some of the most common SQL statements. As you can see, these statements can be divided into two categories. The statements that work with the data in a database are called the *data manipulation language* (*DML*). These four statements are the ones that application programmers use the most. You'll see how these statements work later in this chapter, and you'll learn the details of using them in section 2 of this book.

The statements that work with the objects in a database are called the *data definition language* (*DDL*). On large systems, these statements are used exclusively by *database administrators*, or *DBAs*. It's the DBA's job to maintain existing databases, tune them for faster performance, and create new databases. On smaller systems, though, the SQL programmer may fill the role of the DBA. You'll see examples of some of these statements in the next figure, and you'll learn how to use them in chapter 10.

SQL statements used to work with data (DML)

Statement	Description
SELECT	Retrieves data from one or more tables.
INSERT	Adds one or more new rows to a table.
UPDATE	Changes one or more existing rows in a table.
DELETE	Deletes one or more existing rows from a table.

SQL statements used to work with database objects (DDL)

Statement	Description
CREATE DATABASE	Creates a new database.
CREATE TABLE	Creates a new table in a database.
CREATE INDEX	Creates a new index for a table.
ALTER TABLE	Changes the structure of an existing table.
DROP DATABASE	Deletes an existing database.
DROP TABLE	Deletes an existing table.
DROP INDEX	Deletes an existing index.

Description

- The SQL statements can be divided into two categories: the *data manipulation language (DML)* that lets you work with the data in the database and the *data definition language (DDL)* that lets you work with the objects in the database.
- SQL programmers typically work with the DML statements, while *database administrators (DBAs)* use the DDL statements.

Figure 1-10   An introduction to the SQL statements

Typical statements for working with database objects

To give you an idea of how you use the DDL statements you saw in the previous figure, figure 1-11 presents four sample statements. The first statement creates an accounts payable database named AP. This is the database that's used in many of the examples throughout this book.

The second example creates the Invoices table you saw earlier in this chapter. If you don't understand all of this code right now, don't worry. You'll learn how to code statements like this later in this book. For now, just realize that this statement defines each column in the table, including its data type, whether or not it allows null values, and its default value if it has one. In addition, it identifies identity columns, primary key columns, and foreign key columns.

The third statement in this figure changes the Invoices table by adding a column to it. Like the statement that created the table, this statement specifies all the attributes of the new column. Then, the fourth statement deletes the column that was just added.

The last statement creates an index on the Invoices table. In this case, the index is for the VendorID column, which is used frequently to access the table. Notice the name that's given to this index. This follows the standard naming conventions for indexes, which you'll learn about in chapter 10.

A statement that creates a new database

```
CREATE DATABASE AP
```

A statement that creates a new table

```
CREATE TABLE Invoices
(InvoiceID              INT             NOT NULL IDENTITY PRIMARY KEY,
VendorID                INT             NOT NULL
                        REFERENCES Vendors(VendorID),
InvoiceNumber           VARCHAR(50)     NOT NULL,
InvoiceDate             SMALLDATETIME   NOT NULL,
InvoiceTotal            MONEY           NOT NULL,
PaymentTotal            MONEY           NOT NULL DEFAULT 0,
CreditTotal             MONEY           NOT NULL DEFAULT 0,
TermsID                 INT             NOT NULL
                        REFERENCES Terms(TermsID),
InvoiceDueDate          SMALLDATETIME   NOT NULL,
PaymentDate             SMALLDATETIME   NULL)
```

A statement that adds a new column to the table

```
ALTER TABLE Invoices
ADD BalanceDue MONEY NOT NULL
```

A statement that deletes the new column

```
ALTER TABLE Invoices
DROP COLUMN BalanceDue
```

A statement that creates an index on the table

```
CREATE INDEX IX_Invoices_VendorID
    ON Invoices (VendorID)
```

Description

- The REFERENCES clause for a column indicates that the column contains a foreign key, and it names the table and column that contains the primary key. Because the Invoices table includes foreign keys to the Vendors and Terms tables, these tables must be created before the Invoices table.

- Because default values are specified for the PaymentTotal and CreditTotal columns, these values don't need to be specified when a row is added to the table.

- Because the PaymentDate column accepts nulls, a null value is assumed if a value isn't specified for this column when a row is added to the table.

Figure 1-11   Typical statements for working with database objects

How to query a single table

Figure 1-12 shows how to use a SELECT statement to query a single table in a database. At the top of this figure, you can see some of the columns and rows of the Invoices table. Then, in the SELECT statement that follows, the SELECT clause names the columns to be retrieved, and the FROM clause names the table that contains the columns, called the *base table*. In this case, six columns will be retrieved from the Invoices table.

Notice that the last column, BalanceDue, is calculated from three other columns in the table. In other words, a column by the name of BalanceDue doesn't actually exist in the database. This type of column is called a *calculated value*, and it exists only in the results of the query.

In addition to the SELECT and FROM clauses, this SELECT statement includes a WHERE clause and an ORDER BY clause. The WHERE clause gives the criteria for the rows to be selected. In this case, a row is selected only if it has a balance due that's greater than zero. And the returned rows are sorted by the InvoiceDate column.

This figure also shows the *result table*, or *result set*, that's returned by the SELECT statement. A result set is a logical table that's created temporarily within the database. When an application requests data from a database, it receives a result set.

The Invoices base table

InvoiceID	VendorID	InvoiceNumber	InvoiceDate	InvoiceTotal	PaymentTotal	CreditTotal	TermsID
1	34	QP58872	2/25/2002	116.54	116.54	0	4
2	34	Q545443	3/14/2002	1083.58	1083.58	0	4
3	110	P-0608	4/11/2002	20551.18	0	1200	5
4	110	P-0259	4/16/2002	26881.4	26881.4	0	3
5	81	MABO1489	4/16/2002	936.93	936.93	0	3
6	122	989319-497	4/17/2002	2312.2	0	0	4
7	82	C73-24	4/17/2002	600	600	0	2
8	122	989319-487	4/18/2002	1927.54	0	0	4
9	122	989319-477	4/19/2002	2184.11	2184.11	0	4
10	122	989319-467	4/24/2002	2318.03	2318.03	0	4
11	122	989319-457	4/24/2002	3813.33	3813.33	0	3
12	122	989319-447	4/24/2002	3689.99	3689.99	0	3
13	122	989319-437	4/24/2002	2765.36	2765.36	0	2
14	122	989319-427	4/25/2002	2115.81	2115.81	0	1
15	121	97/553B	4/26/2002	313.55	0	0	4

A SELECT statement that retrieves and sorts selected columns and rows from the Invoices table

```
SELECT InvoiceNumber, InvoiceDate, InvoiceTotal,
    PaymentTotal, CreditTotal,
    InvoiceTotal - PaymentTotal - CreditTotal AS BalanceDue
FROM Invoices
WHERE InvoiceTotal - PaymentTotal - CreditTotal > 0
ORDER BY InvoiceDate
```

The result set defined by the SELECT statement

InvoiceNumber	InvoiceDate	InvoiceTotal	PaymentTotal	CreditTotal	BalanceDue
P-0608	4/11/2002	20551.18	0	1200	19351.18
989319-497	4/17/2002	2312.2	0	0	2312.2
989319-487	4/18/2002	1927.54	0	0	1927.54
97/553B	4/26/2002	313.55	0	0	313.55
97/553	4/27/2002	904.14	0	0	904.14
97/522	4/30/2002	1962.13	0	200	1762.13
203339-13	5/2/2002	17.5	0	0	17.5
0-2436	5/7/2002	10976.06	0	0	10976.06

Concepts

- You use the SELECT statement to retrieve selected columns and rows from a *base table*. The result of a SELECT statement is a *result table*, or *result set*, like the one shown above.

- A result set can include *calculated values* that are calculated from columns in the table.

- The execution of a SELECT statement is commonly referred to as a *query*.

Figure 1-12   How to query a single table

How to join data from two or more tables

Figure 1-13 presents a SELECT statement that retrieves data from two tables. This type of operation is called a *join* because the data from the two tables is joined together into a single result set. For example, the SELECT statement in this figure joins data from the Invoices and Vendors tables.

An *inner join* is the most common type of join. When you use an inner join, rows from the two tables in the join are included in the result table only if their related columns match. These matching columns are specified in the FROM clause of the SELECT statement. In the SELECT statement in this figure, for example, rows from the Invoices and Vendors tables are included only if the value of the VendorID column in the Vendors table matches the value of the VendorID column in one or more rows in the Invoices table. If there aren't any invoices for a particular vendor, that vendor won't be included in the result set.

Although this figure shows only how to join data from two tables, you should know that you can extend this idea to join data from three or more tables. If, for example, you want to include line item data from a table named InvoiceLineItems in the results shown in this figure, you can code the FROM clause of the SELECT statement like this:

```
FROM Vendors
    INNER JOIN Invoices
        On Vendors.VendorID = Invoices.VendorID
    INNER JOIN InvoiceLineItems
        On Invoices.InvoiceID = InvoiceLineItems.InvoiceID
```

Then, in the SELECT clause, you can include any of the columns in the InvoiceLineItems table.

In addition to inner joins, SQL Server supports *outer joins* and *cross joins*. You'll learn more about the different types of joins in chapter 4.

A SELECT statement that joins data from the Vendors and Invoices tables

```
SELECT VendorName, InvoiceNumber, InvoiceDate, InvoiceTotal
FROM Vendors INNER JOIN Invoices
    ON Vendors.VendorID = Invoices.VendorID
WHERE InvoiceTotal >= 500
ORDER BY VendorName, InvoiceTotal DESC
```

The result set defined by the SELECT statement

VendorName	InvoiceNumber	InvoiceDate	InvoiceTotal
Bertelsmann Industry Svcs. Inc	509786	5/31/2002	6940.25
Cahners Publishing Company	587056	5/31/2002	2184.5
Computerworld	367447	5/31/2002	2433
Data Reproductions Corp	40318	7/18/2002	21842
Dean Witter Reynolds	75C-90227	6/6/2002	1367.5
Digital Dreamworks	P02-3772	6/3/2002	7125.34
Federal Express Corporation	963253230	5/15/2002	739.2
Ford Motor Credit Company	9982771	6/3/2002	503.2
Franchise Tax Board	RTR-72-3662-X	6/4/2002	1600
Fresno County Tax Collector	P02-88D77S7	6/6/2002	856.92
IBM	Q545443	3/14/2002	1083.58
Ingram	31359783	5/23/2002	1575
Ingram	31361833	5/23/2002	579.42
Malloy Lithographing Inc	0-2058	5/8/2002	37966.19
Malloy Lithographing Inc	P-0259	4/16/2002	26881.4
Malloy Lithographing Inc	0-2060	5/8/2002	23517.58
Malloy Lithographing Inc	P-0608	4/11/2002	20551.18

Concepts

- A *join* lets you combine data from two or more tables into a single result set.

- The most common type of join is an *inner join*. This type of join returns rows from both tables only if their related columns match.

- An *outer join* returns rows from one table in the join even if the other table doesn't contain a matching row.

Figure 1-13   How to join data from two or more tables

How to add, update, and delete data in a table

Figure 1-14 shows how you can use the INSERT, UPDATE, and DELETE statements to modify the data in a table. The first statement in this figure, for example, uses the INSERT statement to add a row to the Invoices table. To do that, the INSERT clause names the columns whose values are supplied in the VALUES clause. You'll learn more about specifying column names and values in chapter 7. For now, just realize that you have to specify a value for a column unless it's an identity column, a column that allows null values, or a column that's defined with a default value.

The two UPDATE statements in this figure illustrate how you can change the data in one or more rows of a table. The first statement, for example, assigns a value of 35.89 to the CreditTotal column of the invoice in the Invoices table with invoice number 367447. The second statement adds 30 days to the invoice due date for each row in the Invoices table whose TermsID column has a value of 4.

To delete rows from a table, you use the DELETE statement. The first DELETE statement in this figure, for example, deletes the invoice with invoice number 4-342-8069 from the Invoices table. The second DELETE statement deletes all invoices with a balance due of zero.

Before I go on, you should know that INSERT, UPDATE, and DELETE statements are often referred to as *action queries* because they perform an action on the database. In contrast, SELECT statements are referred to as *queries* since they simply query the database. When I use the term *query* in this book, then, I'm usually referring to a SELECT statement.

A statement that adds a row to the Invoices table

```
INSERT INTO Invoices (VendorID, InvoiceNumber, InvoiceDate,
    InvoiceTotal, TermsID, InvoiceDueDate)
VALUES (12, '3289175', '7/18/2002', 165, 3, '8/17/2002')
```

A statement that changes the value of the CreditTotal column for a selected row in the Invoices table

```
UPDATE Invoices
SET CreditTotal = 35.89
WHERE InvoiceNumber = '367447'
```

A statement that changes the values in the InvoiceDueDate column for all invoices with the specified TermsID

```
UPDATE Invoices
SET InvoiceDueDate = InvoiceDueDate + 30
WHERE TermsID = 4
```

A statement that deletes a selected invoice from the Invoices table

```
DELETE FROM Invoices
WHERE InvoiceNumber = '4-342-8069'
```

A statement that deletes all paid invoices from the Invoices table

```
DELETE FROM Invoices
WHERE InvoiceTotal - PaymentTotal - CreditTotal = 0
```

Concepts

- You use the INSERT statement to add rows to a table.
- You use the UPDATE statement to change the values in one or more rows of a table based on the condition you specify.
- You use the DELETE statement to delete one or more rows from a table based on the condition you specify.
- The execution of an INSERT, UPDATE, or DELETE statement is often referred to as an *action query*.

Warning

- Until you read chapter 7 and understand the effect that these statements can have on the database, do not execute the statements shown above.

Figure 1-14   How to add, update, and delete data in a table

SQL coding guidelines

SQL is a freeform language. That means that you can include line breaks, spaces, and indentation without affecting the way the database interprets the code. In addition, SQL is not case-sensitive like some languages. That means that you can use uppercase or lowercase letters or a combination of the two without affecting the way the database interprets the code.

Although you can code SQL statements with a freeform style, we suggest that you follow the coding recommendations presented in figure 1-15. First, you should start each clause of a statement on a new line. In addition, you should continue long clauses onto multiple lines and you should indent the continued lines. You should also capitalize the first letter of each keyword in a statement to make them easier to identify, and you should capitalize the first letter of each word in table and column names. Finally, you should use *comments* to document code that's difficult to understand.

The examples at the top of this figure illustrate these coding recommendations. The first example presents an unformatted SELECT statement. As you can see, this statement is difficult to read. In contrast, this statement is much easier to read after our coding recommendations are applied, as you can see in the second example.

The third example illustrates how to code a *block comment*. This type of comment is typically coded at the beginning of a statement and is used to document the entire statement. Block comments can also be used within a statement to describe blocks of code, but that's not common.

The fourth example in this figure includes a *single-line comment*. This type of comment is typically used to document a single line of code. A single-line comment can be coded on a separate line as shown in this example, or it can be coded at the end of a line of code. In either case, the comment is delimited by the end of the line.

Although many programmers sprinkle their code with comments, that shouldn't be necessary if you write your code so it's easy to read and understand. Instead, you should use comments only to clarify portions of code that are hard to understand. Then, if you change the code, you should be sure to change the comments too. That way, the comments will always accurately represent what the code does.

A SELECT statement that's difficult to read

```
select invoicenumber, invoicedate, invoicetotal,
invoicetotal - paymenttotal - credittotal as balancedue
from invoices where invoicetotal - paymenttotal -
credittotal > 0 order by invoicedate
```

A SELECT statement that's coded with a readable style

```
Select InvoiceNumber, InvoiceDate, InvoiceTotal,
    InvoiceTotal - PaymentTotal - CreditTotal As BalanceDue
From Invoices
Where InvoiceTotal - PaymentTotal - CreditTotal > 0
Order By InvoiceDate
```

A SELECT statement with a block comment

```
/*
Author: Bryan Syverson
Date: 8/22/02
*/
SELECT InvoiceNumber, InvoiceDate, InvoiceTotal,
    InvoiceTotal - PaymentTotal - CreditTotal AS BalanceDue
FROM Invoices
```

A SELECT statement with a single-line comment

```
SELECT InvoiceNumber, InvoiceDate, InvoiceTotal,
    InvoiceTotal - PaymentTotal - CreditTotal AS BalanceDue
    -- The fourth column calculates the balance due for each invoice
FROM Invoices
```

Coding recommendations

- Start each new clause on a new line.
- Break long clauses into multiple lines and indent continued lines.
- Capitalize the first letter of each keyword and each word in column and table names.
- Use *comments* only for portions of code that are difficult to understand. Then, make sure that the comments are correct and up-to-date.

How to code a comment

- To code a *block comment*, type /* at the start of the block and */ at the end.
- To code a *single-line comment*, type -- followed by the comment.

Description

- Line breaks, white space, indentation, and capitalization have no effect on the operation of a statement.
- Comments can be used to document what a statement does or what specific parts of a statement do. They are not executed by the system.

Note

- Throughout this book, SQL keywords are capitalized so they're easier to identify. However, it's not necessary or customary to capitalize SQL keywords in your own code.

Figure 1-15   SQL coding guidelines

How to work with other database objects

In addition to the tables you've already learned about, relational databases can contain other objects. In the two topics that follow, you'll be introduced to four of those objects: views, stored procedures, triggers, and user-defined functions. Then, in section 4, you'll learn more about how to code and use these objects.

How to work with views

A *view* is a predefined query that's stored in a database. To create a view, you use the CREATE VIEW statement as shown in figure 1-16. This statement causes the SELECT query you specify to be stored with the database. In this case, the CREATE VIEW statement creates a view named VendorsMin that retrieves three columns from the Vendors table.

Once you've created the view, you can refer to it instead of a table in most SQL statements. For this reason, a view is sometimes referred to as a *viewed table*. For example, the SELECT statement in this figure refers to the VendorsMin view rather than to the Vendors table. Notice that this SELECT statement makes use of the * operator, which causes all three of the columns defined by the view to be returned.

If you choose to, you can let a user query certain views but not query the tables on which the views are based. In this way, views can be used to restrict the columns and rows of a table that the user can see. In addition, you can simplify a user's access to one or more tables by coding complex SELECT queries as views.

A CREATE VIEW statement for a view named VendorsMin

```
CREATE VIEW VendorsMin AS
    SELECT VendorName, VendorState, VendorPhone
    FROM Vendors
```

The virtual table that's represented by the view

VendorName	VendorState	VendorPhone
US Postal Service	WI	(800) 555-1205
National Information Data Ctr	DC	(301) 555-8950
Register of Copyrights	DC	<NULL>
Jobtrak	CA	(800) 555-8725
Newbrige Book Clubs	NJ	(800) 555-9980
California Chamber Of Commerce	CA	(916) 555-6670
Towne Advertiser's Mailing Svcs	CA	<NULL>
BFI Industries	CA	(559) 555-1551
Pacific Gas & Electric	CA	(800) 555-6081

A SELECT statement that uses the VendorsMin view

```
SELECT * FROM VendorsMin
WHERE VendorState = 'CA'
ORDER BY VendorName
```

The result set that's returned by the SELECT statement

VendorName	VendorState	VendorPhone
Abbey Office Furnishings	CA	(559) 555-8300
American Express	CA	(800) 555-3344
ASC Signs	CA	<NULL>
Aztek Label	CA	(714) 555-9000
Bertelsmann Industry Svcs. Inc	CA	(805) 555-0584
BFI Industries	CA	(559) 555-1551
Bill Jones	CA	<NULL>
Bill Marvin Electric Inc	CA	(559) 555-5106
Blanchard & Johnson Associates	CA	(214) 555-3647

Description

- A *view* consists of a SELECT statement that's stored with the database. Because views are stored as part of the database, they can be managed independently of the applications that use them.

- A view behaves like a virtual table. Since you can code a view name anywhere you'd code a table name, a view is sometimes called a *viewed table*.

- Views can be used to restrict the data that a user is allowed to access or to present data in a form that's easy for the user to understand. In some databases, users may be allowed to access data only through views.

Figure 1-16   How to work with views

How to work with stored procedures, triggers, and user-defined functions

A *stored procedure* is a set of one or more SQL statements that are stored together in a database. To create a stored procedure, you use the CREATE PROCEDURE statement as shown in figure 1-17. Here, the stored procedure contains a single SELECT statement. To use the stored procedure, you send a request for it to be executed. One way to do that is to use the Transact-SQL EXEC statement as shown in this figure. You can also execute a stored procedure from an application program by issuing the appropriate statement. How you do that depends on the programming language and the API you're using to access the database.

When the server receives the request, it executes the stored procedure. If the stored procedure contains a SELECT statement like the one in this figure, the result set is sent back to the calling program. If the stored procedure contains INSERT, UPDATE, or DELETE statements, the appropriate processing is performed.

Notice that the stored procedure in this figure accepts an *input parameter* named @State from the calling program. The value of this parameter is then substituted for the parameter in the WHERE clause so that only vendors in the specified state are included in the result set. When it's done with its processing, a stored procedure can also pass *output parameters* back to the calling program. In addition, stored procedures can include *control-of-flow language* that determines the processing that's done based on specific conditions. You'll learn more about how to code stored procedures in chapter 14.

A *trigger* is a special type of stored procedure that's executed automatically when an insert, update, or delete operation is executed on a table. Triggers are used most often to validate data before a row is added or updated, but they can also be used to maintain the relationships between tables.

A *user-defined function*, or *UDF*, is also a special type of procedure. After it performs its processing, a UDF can return a single value or an entire table to the calling program. You'll learn how to code and use user-defined functions and triggers in chapter 14.

A CREATE PROCEDURE statement for a procedure named VendorsByState

```
CREATE PROCEDURE spVendorsByState @State char(2) AS
    SELECT VendorName, VendorState, VendorPhone
    FROM Vendors
    WHERE VendorState = @State
    ORDER BY VendorName
```

A statement that executes the VendorsByState stored procedure

```
EXEC spVendorsByState 'CA'
```

The result set that's created when the stored procedure is executed

VendorName	VendorState	VendorPhone
Abbey Office Furnishings	CA	(559) 555-8300
American Express	CA	(800) 555-3344
ASC Signs	CA	<NULL>
Aztek Label	CA	(714) 555-9000
Bertelsmann Industry Svcs. Inc	CA	(805) 555-0584
BFI Industries	CA	(559) 555-1551
Bill Jones	CA	<NULL>
Bill Marvin Electric Inc	CA	(559) 555-5106
Blanchard & Johnson Associates	CA	(214) 555-3647

Concepts

* A *stored procedure* is one or more SQL statements that have been compiled and stored with the database. A stored procedure can be started by application code on the client.

* Stored procedures can improve database performance because the SQL statements in each procedure are only compiled and optimized the first time they're executed. In contrast, SQL statements that are sent from a client to the server have to be compiled and optimized every time they're executed.

* In addition to SELECT statements, a stored procedure can contain other SQL statements such as INSERT, UPDATE, and DELETE. It can also contain *control-of-flow language*, which lets you perform conditional processing within the stored procedure.

* A *trigger* is a special type of procedure that's executed when rows are inserted, updated, or deleted from a table. Triggers are typically used to check the validity of the data in a row that's being updated or added to a table.

* A *user-defined function* (*UDF*) is a special type of procedure that can return a value or a table.

Figure 1-17   How to use stored procedures, triggers, and user-defined functions

Perspective

To help you understand how SQL is used from an application program, this chapter has introduced you to the hardware and software components of a client/server system. It has also described how relational databases are organized and how you use some of the basic SQL statements to work with the data in a relational database. With that as background, you're now ready to start using SQL Server. In the next chapter, then, you'll learn how to use some of the tools provided by SQL Server.

Terms

client	record	SQL dialect
server	field	extension
database server	cell	SQL variant
network	primary key	Transact-SQL
client/server system	composite primary key	open source system
local area network (LAN)	non-primary key	data manipulation
enterprise system	unique key	language (DML)
wide area network (WAN)	index	data definition
network operating system	foreign key	language (DDL)
database management	one-to-many relationship	database administrator
system (DBMS)	one-to-one relationship	(DBA)
back-end processing	many-to-many relationship	base table
back end	data type	result table
application software	null value	result set
data access API (application	default value	calculated value
programming interface)	identity column	query
front-end processing	hierarchical database	join
front end	parent/child relationship	inner join
SQL (Structured Query	network database	outer join
Language)	object-oriented database	cross join
SQL query	relational database manage-	action query
query results	ment system (RDBMS)	comment
application server	SEQUEL (Structured English	block comment
web server	Query Language)	single-line comment
business component	Oracle	view
web application	SQL/DS (SQL/Data System)	viewed table
web service	DB2 (Database 2)	stored procedure
web browser	ANSI (American National	input parameter
thin client	Standards Institute)	output parameter
relational database	levels of compliance	control-of-flow language
table	levels of conformance	trigger
row	core specification	user-defined function
column	package	(UDF)

2

How to work with a SQL Server database

In the last chapter, you learned about some of the SQL statements you can use to work with the data in a relational database. Before you learn the details of coding these statements, however, you need to become familiar with some of the tools that are available for working with a relational database. Since this book is about SQL Server, this chapter will teach you about some of the SQL Server tools. In addition, it will introduce you to some of the techniques you can use to work with SQL Server data from an application program. When you complete this chapter, you'll be ready to learn the essential skills for coding SQL statements that are presented in section 2 of this book.

An introduction to SQL Server 2000

The current version of SQL Server, Microsoft SQL Server 2000, is a complete database management system. It consists of a *database server* that provides the services for managing SQL Server databases and *client tools* that provide an interface for working with the databases. The two topics that follow will introduce you to these two components of SQL Server 2000.

Before I go on, you should know that this chapter assumes that you already have access to SQL Server 2000. If that's not the case, you can refer to appendix A of this book to learn how to install it from the CD that's provided. This appendix also shows you how to prepare the databases used in this book so you can work along with the book examples.

If you install SQL Server as described in appendix A, a desktop version of SQL Server, called the *Microsoft SQL Server 2000 Desktop Engine*, or *MSDE*, will be installed on your machine. Although this version of SQL Server restricts the number of users and the amount of data that SQL Server can manage, it provides a realistic testing environment that is 100% compatible with the full version of SQL Server 2000, called *SQL Server 2000 Enterprise Edition*. In fact, I used MSDE to create and test the statements you'll see throughout this book. Note, however, that MSDE is strictly a database server, or *database engine*. In other words, it doesn't provide the client tools you'll learn about in this chapter. To use these tools, you'll have to install them from the CD as described in appendix A.

The database engine

If you've installed MSDE on your own system, you'll want to know how to control the database engine. To do that, you use the SQL Server Service Manager presented in figure 2-1. You can access the Service Manager from the system tray in the Windows taskbar as illustrated in this figure or from the Windows Start menu. In either case, when you start the Service Manager, the dialog box shown in this figure is displayed.

As you can see, you can use the Service Manager to start and stop the database engine. By default, the database engine starts automatically when the operating system starts as indicated by the check box at the bottom of this dialog box. If that's not what you want, however, you can deselect this option and then use the Start and Stop buttons to start and stop the server manually.

By the way, if you simply want to find out if the database engine is running, you can do that by looking at the icon in the system tray. If it has a green triangle, it means that the engine is running. If it has a red square, it means that the engine is not running. And if it has two thick vertical lines, it means that the engine has been paused. Notice that these are the same symbols that are used on the Start/Continue, Pause, and Stop buttons in the SQL Server Service Manager dialog box.

The system tray with a SQL Server Service Manager icon

SQL Server Service Manager icon

```
⊲  ⊑  ⊳    4:10 PM
```

The SQL Server Service Manager dialog box

Description

- SQL Server consists of a *database server* that provides database management services and *client tools* that let you work with the database and the data it contains.

- If you don't have access to SQL Server on your school's or company's server, you can install the desktop version of SQL Server, called the *Microsoft SQL Server 2000 Desktop Engine*, or *MSDE*, on your own system. See appendix A of this book for details.

- After you install MSDE, the *SQL Server Service Manager* icon will be displayed in the system tray at the right side of the Windows taskbar as shown above. You can use the dialog box that's displayed when you double-click on this icon to control the database engine.

- If the database engine is running, you can click on the Pause or Stop button to stop it. Then, you can click on the Start/Continue button to restart the engine. Unless you start and stop the server manually, you probably won't ever use these buttons.

- If you want the database engine to start automatically each time you start your computer, you can select the Auto-start service when OS starts option. This is the default.

- To close the Service Manager dialog box, click the close button in the upper right corner (the one with an X on it). This closes the dialog box, but doesn't stop the database engine.

Figure 2-1   The database engine

The client tools

Figure 2-2 summarizes the client tools that are available with SQL Server 2000. In this book, you'll learn how to use three of these tools: Books Online, Enterprise Manager, and Query Analyzer. The other tools are used most often by database administrators and are beyond the scope of this book. To learn more about any of these tools, you can refer to the information in Books Online.

The Start menu with a list of the client tools

A summary of the client tools

Tool	Description
Books Online	Provides online help documentation.
Client Network Utility	Used to manage the client Net-Libraries that provide for communication with different network protocols and define server alias names.
Configure SQL XML Support in IIS	Used to define and register a new virtual directory on a web server running IIS (Internet Information Services) so that the SQL Server database can be accessed using HTTP (HyperText Transfer Protocol).
Enterprise Manager	Used to administer SQL Server databases.
Import and Export Data	Launches the Import/Export Wizard, which leads you through importing, exporting, and transforming data and objects from various sources.
Profiler	Captures SQL Server events so they can be analyzed to determine the cause of a problem or to improve query performance.
Query Analyzer	Used to design and test SQL statements and scripts interactively.

Description

- To work with a SQL Server database and the data it contains, you can use the SQL Server 2000 client tools.

- When you install the client tools, they'll appear in the Start→Programs→Microsoft SQL Server program group. To start any of these tools, just select it from that program group. You can also start Books Online by pressing F1 from one of the other client tools or by clicking on the Help button in a dialog box displayed by one of these tools. Then, Books Online displays context-sensitive help information.

Figure 2-2   The client tools

How to use the Enterprise Manager to view the definition of a database

Before you use SQL to work with a database, you need to know how the database is defined. In particular, you need to know how the columns in each table are defined and how the tables are related. To get this information, you can use the *Enterprise Manager*.

An introduction to the Enterprise Manager

Figure 2-3 presents the Enterprise Manager workspace. On the left side of the workspace is a *console tree* that lists the instances of SQL Server that you have access to. In most cases, you'll only have access to the instance of SQL Server on your own system. Then, you can expand the *node* for that instance to display the objects in the databases it manages.

If you expand the node for a database, you'll see the various types of objects it contains. And if you click on one of the object types, a list of the objects of that type appears in the right side of the workspace. In this figure, for example, you can see a list of the tables in the AP database. Notice that this list includes several system tables. You'll learn more about some of these tables later in this book.

To work with a specific object, you can right-click on it to display a shortcut menu or you can use the commands in the Action menu. To view the design of a table, for example, you can use the Design Table command. You'll learn how to use this command to view the definition of the columns in a table in just a moment. But first, the next figure shows you how to view the relationships between the tables in a database.

The Enterprise Manager workspace

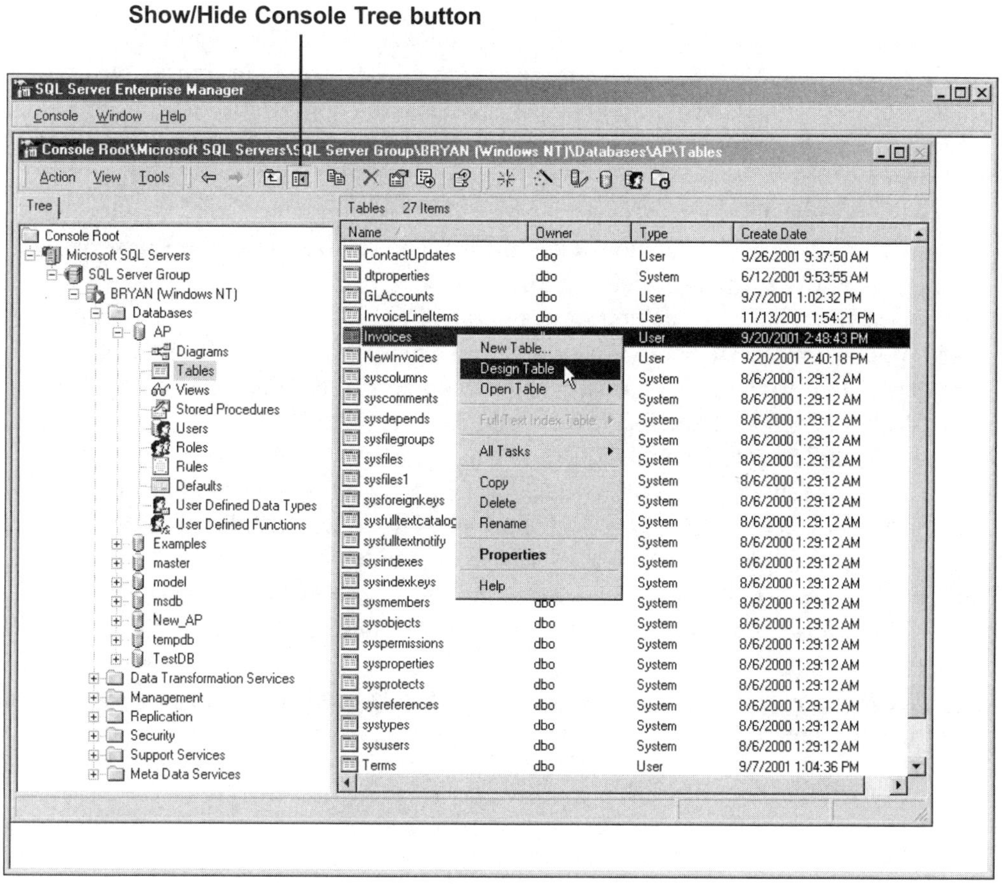

Show/Hide Console Tree button

Description

- The Enterprise Manager is a graphical tool that you can use to work with the objects in a database. It's particularly useful for defining and modifying database objects like tables, views, and stored procedures.

- The left side of the Enterprise Manager window displays installed instances of SQL Server in a tree structure, called the *console tree*. You can click on the plus (+) and minus (-) signs to the left of each *node* to expand or collapse the node.

- The right side of the Enterprise Manager window displays the items in the currently selected node. You can use the commands in the shortcut menu for an item or the commands in the Action menu to work with an item in this list.

- You can use the Show/Hide Console Tree button in the toolbar to hide or display the console tree.

Figure 2-3   An introduction to the Enterprise Manager

How to view the relationships between tables

The easiest way to view the relationships between the tables in a database is to display the *database diagrams* for the database as described in figure 2-4. Note, however, that database diagrams aren't created automatically when relationships are defined. Instead, they are typically created by the database designer to document the design. So if the person who designed the database you're working with didn't create database diagrams, you won't be able to use this technique to identify relationships. Instead, you'll have to use the Properties dialog box you'll learn about later in this chapter.

When you display a database diagram, the relationships between tables are displayed as links as shown in this figure. You can tell what type of relationship exists between two tables by looking at the endpoints of the link. The "one" side is represented by a key, and the "many" side is represented by an infinity symbol. In this diagram, all of the relationships are one-to-many.

As you review this diagram, notice that you can't tell which columns in each table form the relationship. However, you can see which columns are defined as primary key columns. As you may remember from chapter 1, these are the columns that are typically used on the "one" side of the relationships. From that information, you should be able to figure out which columns in the related tables identify the foreign keys. If not, you can review the relationships for each table by displaying that table's properties. You'll learn how to do that later in this chapter.

The relationships between the tables in the AP database

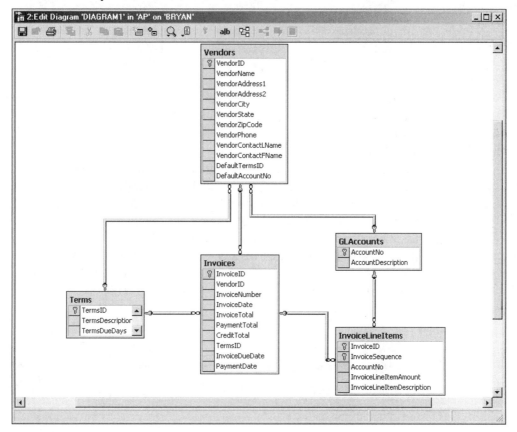

Description

- *Database diagrams* can be used to illustrate the relationships between the tables in a database. Reviewing the diagrams for an existing database is the easiest way to get an overall view of how the tables are related.

- To view a database diagram, select the Diagrams node for the database in the console tree, and then double-click on the diagram you want to display from the ones listed in the right pane. The diagram is displayed in a window like the one shown above.

- The relationships between the tables in the diagram appear as links, where the endpoints of the links indicate the type of relationship. A key indicates the "one" side of a relationship, and the infinity symbol (∞) indicates the "many" side of a relationship.

- To see more specific information about the relationships between tables, you can use the Properties dialog box. See figure 2-6 for more information.

Note

- When you first create a new database, it won't include any database diagrams. To create these types of diagrams, you can use the skills you'll learn in chapter 11.

Figure 2-4   How to view the relationships between tables

How to view the definition of the columns in a table

To display the definition of the columns in a table, you use the Design Table window shown in figure 2-5. You saw this window in the last chapter, so you should already be somewhat familiar with it.

The Design Table window is divided into two parts. At the top of the window, you can see the name and data type for each column, along with its length and an indication of whether or not it can contain null values. In addition, notice that a key symbol is displayed in the row selector to the left of the primary key column to make it easy to identify.

If you want to display additional information about a column, you can select the column by clicking on its row selector. Then, additional properties are displayed in the bottom part of the window. In this figure, for example, the properties for the DefaultTermsID column are displayed. As you can see, these properties indicate that this column has a default value of 3 and that it is not an identity column. Note that the properties that are available change depending on the data type of the column. For a decimal or numeric column, for example, the properties also indicate the precision and scale of the column. You'll learn more about that in chapter 8.

The columns in the Vendors table

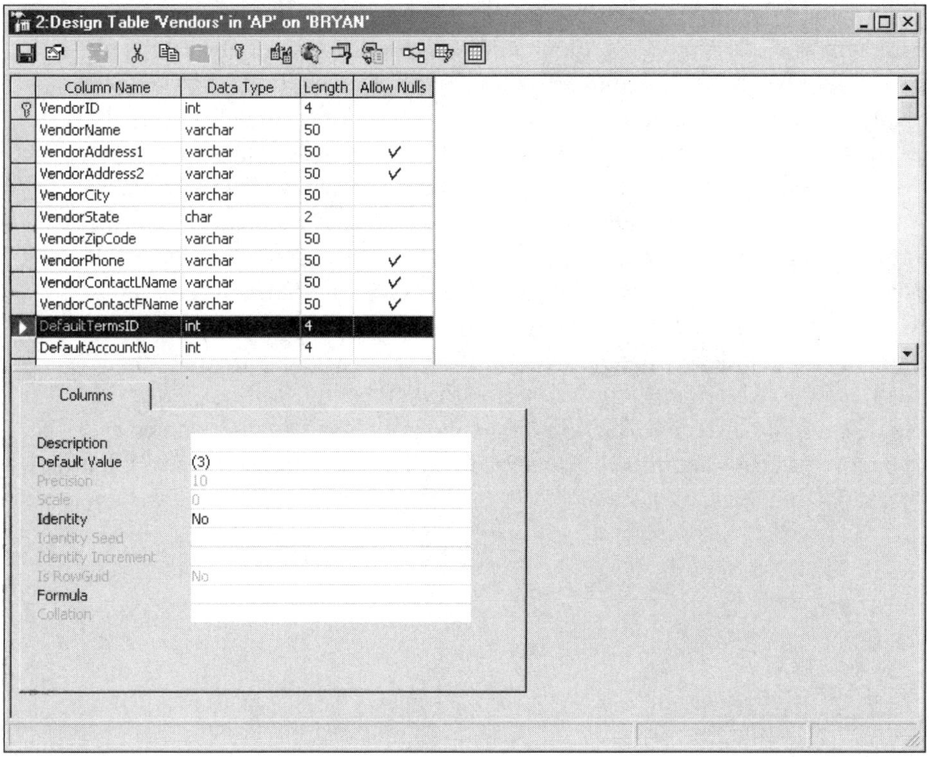

Description

- To view the definition of the columns in a table, select the Tables node in the console tree to display a list of tables in the right pane. Then, right-click on the table you want to display and select the Design Table command from the shortcut menu that's displayed.

- The Design Table window lists the name of each column in the table, along with its data type, its length, and whether or not it can contain null values.

- To display additional properties for a column, click on the row selector to the left of the column name to display its properties in the Columns tab at the bottom of the window.

Figure 2-5   How to view the definition of the columns in a table

How to view other table properties

Although you can learn a lot about a table by viewing its relationships in the database diagrams and its column definitions in the Design Table window, you can learn a lot more by viewing the table's properties. To do that, you can click on one of the buttons in the Design Table window as indicated in figure 2-6. Then, the Properties dialog box shown in this figure is displayed.

If you review the information in this figure, you'll see that each tab of the Properties dialog box presents information about a set of related properties. If you need more information about the foreign keys that are defined for a table, for example, you can display the Relationships tab. And if you need information about the keys and indexes that are defined for a table, you can display the Indexes/Keys tab. Although I won't describe these tabs in detail now, you'll want to take a look at the information they contain before you start working with a database. That way, you'll be better prepared to use the skills you'll learn in the next section of this book.

The Properties dialog box for the Vendors table

Table and Index
Properties button

Manage Relationships
button

Manage Indexes/Keys
button

Manage Constraints
button

Description

- You can use the Properties dialog box to view additional information about a table.

- You display the Properties dialog box from the Design Table window for a table. To do that, just click on one of the toolbar buttons shown above. The button you use determines the tab that's selected when the dialog box is first displayed.

- The Table tab contains some general information about the table, such as its owner and its identity column (if it contains one).

- The Relationships tab contains information about the foreign keys defined for the table and how the relationships between that table and the primary key table are enforced.

- The Indexes/Keys tab (shown above) contains information about the keys and indexes that have been defined for the table.

- The Check Constraints tab contains information about the *check constraints* defined for the table. Check constraints are used to restrict the values in a column. Because they're defined at the table level, they can refer to one or more columns in the table.

Figure 2-6   How to view other table properties

How to use the Query Analyzer

The *Query Analyzer* is an essential tool for working with the data in a SQL Server database. You'll want to use this tool to test the new skills you learn throughout this book. Fortunately, it's easy to use, as you'll see in the topics that follow.

How to connect to a database server

Unlike the Enterprise Manager, which lets you work with one or more instances of SQL Server, the Query Analyzer lets you work with a single instance. When you start the Query Analyzer, a dialog box like the one in figure 2-7 is displayed. This dialog box lets you select the instance of SQL Server you want to connect to, and it lets you enter the required connection information. You can also use this dialog box to start the selected server if it isn't already running.

As you can see in this figure, you can use one of two types of login authentication to connect to a server. In most cases, you can select the Windows authentication option to let Windows supply the appropriate login name and password for you. If you're using an older version of Windows, however, you'll have to use SQL Server authentication. Then, you have to enter the appropriate SQL Server login name and password. By default, each installation of SQL Server includes a user named "sa" with a null password. As a result, you can typically use this user name to connect to the server.

You may also need to use SQL Server authentication if you're accessing your school's or company's server. In that case, the server may have been set up with user names and passwords that are different from the ones you use to log on to Windows. Then, you'll need to find out what name and password to use.

How to connect using Windows authentication

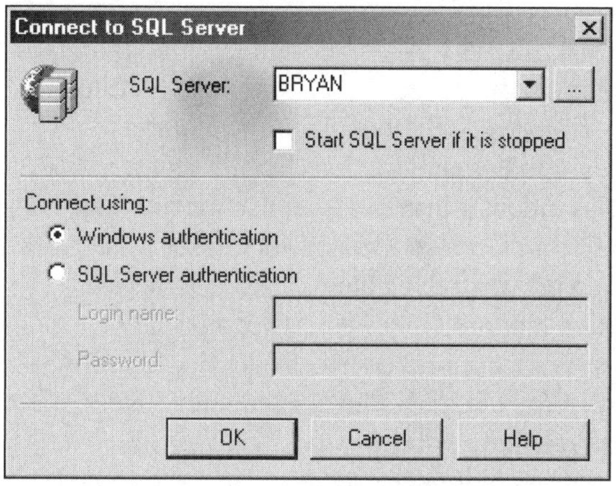

How to connect using SQL Server authentication

Description

- When you start the Query Analyzer, it displays a dialog box like the first one shown above. You can use this dialog box to connect to the database server you select using either Windows authentication or SQL Server authentication.

- If you select Windows authentication, SQL Server will use the login name and password that you use for your computer to verify that you are authorized to connect to the server. This type of authentication is available only with Windows NT or later versions of Windows.

- If you select SQL Server authentication, you'll need to enter an appropriate login name and password. This type of authentication is typically used only with older versions of the Windows operating system.

- If the database server hasn't been started, you can start it by selecting the Start SQL Server if it is stopped option. If you don't select this option and the server hasn't been started, you'll get an error message indicating that the server doesn't exist.

Figure 2-7   How to connect the Query Analyzer to a database server

How to enter and execute a query

After you connect to a database server, a Query Analyzer window like the one in figure 2-8 is displayed. The Query Analyzer provides a simple text editor that's specifically designed for writing Transact-SQL statements. To enter a statement, you simply click in the Query window and begin typing. To start a new line, you press the Enter key. And to indent a line, you can use the Tab key. You can also use the standard Windows commands in the Edit menu, such as Cut, Copy, Paste, Find, and Replace, to work with the statements you enter.

As you enter statements, you'll notice that the Query Analyzer automatically applies colors to various elements. For example, keywords are displayed in blue by default, and literal values are displayed in red. This makes your statements easier to read and understand and can help you identify coding errors.

Before you execute a query, you need to identify the database it uses. To do that, you select the database from the combo box in the toolbar. By default, a database named Master is selected, which usually isn't what you want.

To execute a query, you can click on the Execute Query button in the toolbar, press the F5 key, or select the Execute command from the Query menu. If the statement returns data, that data is displayed in the Grids tab of the results pane at the bottom of the Query window. In this figure, for example, the result set that's returned by the execution of a SELECT statement is displayed in the results pane. If you execute an action query, the Messages tab is displayed instead of the Grids tab. This tab will contain an indication of the number of rows that were affected by the query. The Messages tab is also used to provide error information, as you'll see in the next figure.

A SELECT statement and its results

Execute Query button

Select Database combo box

```
SQL Query Analyzer                                          _ □ ×
File  Edit  Query  Tools  Window  Help

     ▤ · ☞ ▣ 🖫  ✄ 🖹 🖺 🗗 🛤  ⌽  ▦ ·  ✓ ▶  ▪  ▯ AP          ▾  ⊟ 🐾 🔍  ☞ 🗃
```

Query window

```
Query · BRYAN.AP.BRYAN\bryan · Untitled1*                    _ □ ×

Select InvoiceNumber, InvoiceDate, InvoiceTotal, PaymentTotal, CreditTotal,
     InvoiceTotal - PaymentTotal - CreditTotal As BalanceDue
From Invoices
Where InvoiceTotal - PaymentTotal - CreditTotal > 0
Order By InvoiceDate
```

Results pane

	InvoiceNumber	InvoiceDate	InvoiceTotal	PaymentTotal	CreditTotal	BalanceDue
1	P-0608	2002-04-11 00:00:00	20551.1800	.0000	1200.0000	19351.1800
2	989319-497	2002-04-17 00:00:00	2312.2000	.0000	.0000	2312.2000
3	989319-487	2002-04-18 00:00:00	1927.5400	.0000	.0000	1927.5400
4	97/553B	2002-04-26 00:00:00	313.5500	.0000	.0000	313.5500
5	97/553	2002-04-27 00:00:00	904.1400	.0000	.0000	904.1400
6	97/522	2002-04-30 00:00:00	1962.1300	.0000	200.0000	1762.1300
7	203339-13	2002-05-02 00:00:00	17.5000	.0000	.0000	17.5000
8	0-2436	2002-05-07 00:00:00	10976.0600	.0000	.0000	10976.0600
9	963253272	2002-05-09 00:00:00	61.5000	.0000	.0000	61.5000
10	963253271	2002-05-09 00:00:00	158.0000	.0000	.0000	158.0000

▦ Grids 🗐 Messages

Query batch completed.   BRYAN (8.0) BRYAN\bryan (51) AP 0:00:00   40 rows Ln 2, Col 16

Connections: 1   NUM

Description

- To select the database that you want to work with, use the Select Database combo box in the toolbar.

- To enter a SQL statement, type it into the Query window. This window is a simple text editor, and you can use the standard Windows commands in the Edit menu to work with the text you enter.

- As you enter the text for a statement, the Query Analyzer applies color to various elements, such as SQL keywords and character strings, to make them easy to identify.

- To execute a SQL statement, press the F5 key, click the Execute Query button in the toolbar, or choose the Query→Execute command from the menu bar. If the statement retrieves data, the Query Analyzer opens the results pane and displays the results in the Grids tab as shown above. Otherwise, it displays the Messages tab, which indicates the number of rows that were affected by the statement.

- You can't modify the data that's displayed in the results pane.

Figure 2-8   How to enter and execute a query

How to handle errors

If an error occurs during the execution of a SQL statement, an error message is displayed in the Messages tab of the results pane as shown in figure 2-9. In this case, the error message indicates that the object name 'Invoices' is invalid. If you look at the combo box in the toolbar, you see that's because the Master database is selected, and this database doesn't contain a table named Invoices. This is a common mistake when you first start using the Query Analyzer. To correct it, simply select the appropriate database and execute the statement again.

This figure also lists some other common causes of errors. As you can see, most errors are caused by incorrect syntax. To prevent these types of errors, you can check the syntax of a statement before you execute it as described in the figure.

When an error is caused by invalid syntax or by being executed against the wrong database, you can usually identify and correct the problem without too much trouble. In some cases, though, you won't be able to figure out the cause of an error by the information that's provided in the Messages tab. Then, you can get additional information about the error by looking up the error number in Books Online. You'll learn how to use Books Online later in this chapter.

How the Query Analyzer displays an error message

Parse Query button

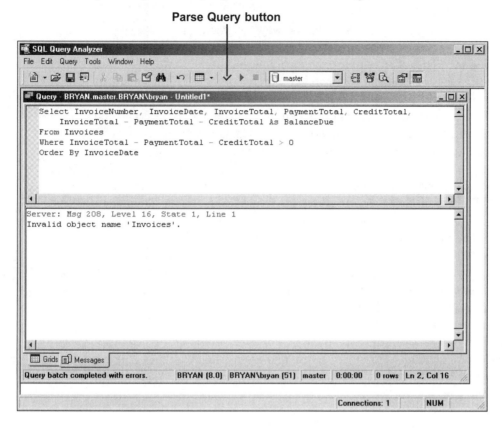

Common causes of errors

- Forgetting to select the correct database from the Select Database combo box
- Misspelling the name of a table or column
- Misspelling a keyword
- Omitting the closing quotation mark for a character string

Description

- If an error occurs during the execution of a SQL statement, the Query Analyzer displays an error message in the Messages tab of the results pane. To move to the line of code that caused the error, you can double-click on the first line of the error message.

- Most errors are caused by incorrect syntax and can be detected and corrected without any additional assistance. If not, you can look up a description of the error by its error number in the Books Online index under the *errors-SQL Server* or *system error messages-SQL Server* topic.

- If you want to check the syntax of a SQL statement before you execute it, you can click the Parse Query button or press Ctrl+F5. The results are displayed in the Messages tab.

Figure 2-9   How to handle errors

How to open and save queries

After you get a query working the way you want it to work, you may want to save it. Then, you can open it and run it again later or use it as the basis for a new query. To do that, you use the techniques in figure 2-10.

If you've used other Windows programs, you shouldn't have any trouble opening and saving query files. To save a new query, for example, or to save a modified query in the original file, you use the standard Save command. To save a modified query in a new file, you use the standard Save As command. And to open a query, you use the standard Open command. Note that when you save a query, it's saved with the file extension *sql*. This is illustrated in the Open Query File dialog box in this figure.

By default, the Query Analyzer saves queries in the My Document folder on your C drive. If that's not what you want, you can change the default using the Tools→Options command. When you select this command, an Options dialog box with several tabs is displayed. To change the default directory, change the Query file directory option in the General tab to the directory you want to use.

As you work with queries using the Query Analyzer, you may find it helpful to display two or more queries at the same time. To do that, you can open additional Query windows by clicking on the New Query button in the toolbar or pressing Ctrl+N. After you open two or more windows, you can use standard Windows techniques to move, resize, and arrange the windows. You can also use standard Windows techniques to cut, copy, and paste code from one window to another.

The Open Query File dialog box

New Query button

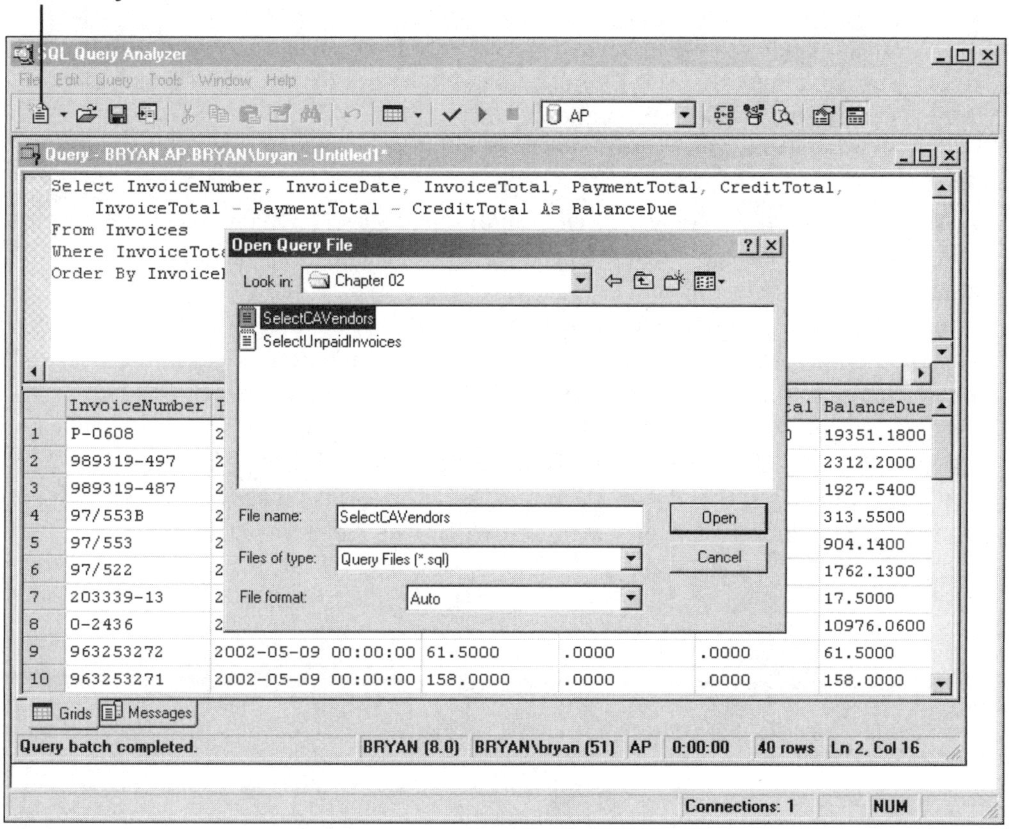

Description

- To save a query, select the File→Save or File→Save As command, click the Save button in the toolbar, or press Ctrl+S. Then, if necessary, use the Save Query dialog box to specify a file name for the query.

- To open a query, select the File→Open command, click the Open button in the toolbar, or press Ctrl+O. Then, use the Open Query File dialog box shown above to locate and open the query.

- If you try to open a query with an unsaved or modified query in the Query window, the Query Analyzer will display a dialog box that asks you if you want to save that query.

- You can work with two or more queries at the same time by opening a separate Query window for each one. To do that, click the New Query button in the toolbar or press Ctrl+N.

- The Query Analyzer's default directory for queries is C:\My Documents. To change the default directory, select the Tools→Options command and set the Query file directory option in the General tab of the dialog box that's displayed.

Figure 2-10   How to open and save queries

How to use the Object Browser

Another feature of the Query Analyzer is the *Object Browser*. The Object Browser lets you browse through the objects in a database as illustrated in figure 2-11. This is particularly useful for checking the names of tables and columns as you enter a query in a Query window.

The Object Browser also lets you work with some of the database objects. For example, you can use it to edit views, stored procedures, and functions. In addition, you can use it to display and modify the data in a table as illustrated in the figure. In this case, the data in the Invoices table is displayed. This can be useful when you're testing a query and you need to review the data in a table or you want to make some minor changes to the data in the table.

Before I go on, I want to point out the qualifier that's used on all of the object names in this figure: dbo. This qualifier indicates the owner of the objects. By default, any object that's created by a system administrator is listed as owned by dbo (database owner). That way, any user who has administrative privileges can access the object. In contrast, if an object is created by a user who doesn't have administrative privileges, only that user can access the object.

The Query Analyzer with the Object Browser window and the data in the Invoices table displayed

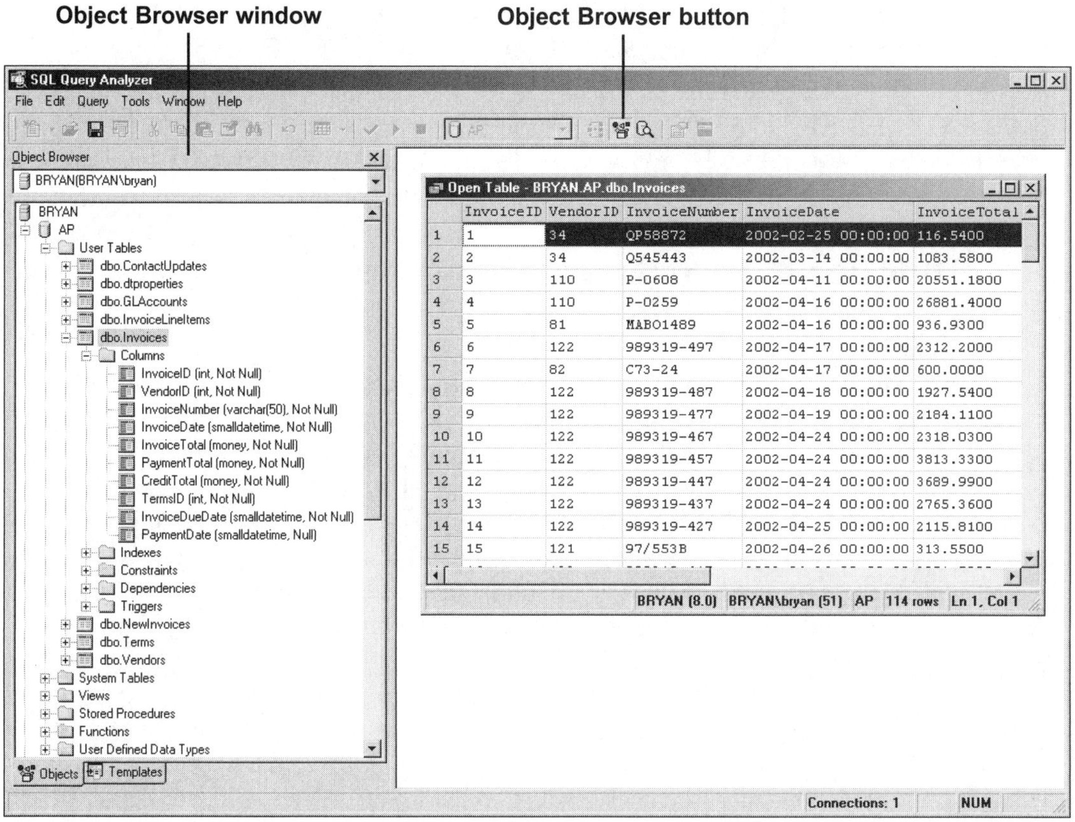

Object Browser window   Object Browser button

Description

- To display or hide the Object Browser window, click the Object Browser button or press F8.

- The Object Browser window displays the objects on the database server in a tree view, and you can click on the plus and minus buttons to expand and collapse the available nodes.

- You can use the Object Browser window to explore the objects on the database server. This is particularly helpful if you're entering a query and you don't remember the name of a column.

- You can also use the Object Browser to modify data and database objects. In particular, you can display and modify the data in a table as shown above. To display the data in a table, right-click on the table in the Object Browser and select the Open command from the shortcut menu that's displayed.

Figure 2-11   How to use the Object Browser

Other client tools

Although you'll typically use the Query Analyzer to code and execute SQL statements, you can also use the *Query Designer* to do that. The Query Designer is part of the Enterprise Manager, and you'll learn the details of using it in chapter 11. The topic that follows, though, introduces you to this tool so you'll have an idea of how and when to use it. Then, the next topic shows you how to use *Books Online*, which you'll use frequently as you learn SQL.

An introduction to the Query Designer

Figure 2-12 presents the Query Designer window. As you can see, this window helps you create queries using a graphical interface. In the diagram pane, you select the tables and columns that you want to use in the query. Then, the columns you select are listed in the grid pane, and you can use this pane to set the sort sequence and criteria for the query. As you work in the diagram and grid panes, the Query Designer generates a SQL statement and displays it in the SQL pane. When you have the statement the way you want it, you can execute it to display the results in the results pane. Unlike the results of a query that you execute using the Query Analyzer, you can modify the results displayed by the Query Designer.

When you first start working with a database, the Query Designer can help you become familiar with the tables and columns it contains. In addition, it can help you build simple queries quickly and easily. If you analyze the SQL statements that it generates, it can also help you learn SQL. Keep in mind, though, that the best way to learn SQL is to code it yourself. That's why this book emphasizes the use of the Query Analyzer. Plus, it can be difficult, and sometimes impossible, to create complex queries using the Query Designer. Because of that, you're usually better off writing complex queries yourself.

Although this figure shows how to use the Query Designer to create a SELECT statement, you should know that you can also use it to create INSERT, UPDATE, and DELETE statements. You'll learn more about how to do that in chapter 11.

The Query Designer window

Diagram pane

Grid pane

SQL pane

Results pane

The four panes in the Query Designer window

Pane	Description
Diagram pane	Displays the tables used by the query and lets you select the columns you want to include in the query.
Grid pane	Displays the columns selected in the diagram pane and lets you specify the sort order for the result set and the criteria you want to use to select the rows for the result set. You can also use this pane to select columns and create calculated values.
SQL pane	Displays the SQL statement built by the Query Designer based on the information in the diagram and grid panes.
Results pane	Displays the results of the query.

Description

- You can use the Query Designer to build simple queries quickly and easily. However, you may not be able to create more complex queries this way.

- In some cases, the Query Designer generates code that isn't as efficient as it could be or that includes unnecessary code.

- Although you'll typically use the Query Designer to build SELECT statements, you can also use it to build other SQL statements.

Figure 2-12 An introduction to the Query Designer

How to use Books Online

Figure 2-13 shows how to use another useful client tool: Books Online. You can use this tool to quickly look up a wide variety of information on SQL and SQL Server. For example, you can use it to look up information about SQL statements and functions or to get more information about an error message that's returned by SQL Server.

By default, Books Online displays information from all of the books in its reference library, which contain information about almost every aspect of SQL Server. If you're only interested in the books on a particular subject, however, you can limit the information that's displayed to a subset of books. For example, as you learn SQL, I think you'll find that the *SQL Programming: Transact-SQL* subset contains most of the information you'll need. To select a subset, you use the combo box near the top left corner of the Books Online window.

The first three tabs that are available from the Books Online window let you look for information in three different ways. You can use the Contents tab to select a topic from the table of contents for the selected books. You can use the Index tab to locate and select an index entry. And you can use the Search tab to search the available books for topics that contain the words you specify. When you select a topic or entry from any of these windows, it's displayed in the right pane of the window so you can review the information it contains.

If you know that you'll want to refer again to a topic that you've displayed, you can add it to the Favorites tab. To do that, display this tab, right-click in it, and select the Add command from the shortcut menu that's displayed. Then, you can display the topic by double-clicking on it in this tab.

After you've displayed two or more topics, you can use the Back and Forward buttons in the toolbar to move backward and forward between the topics. If you display a topic from the Contents tab or locate a displayed topic in the Contents tab using the Locate button, you can then use the Previous and Next buttons to move to the previous and next topics in the contents. And, of course, you can use the Print button to print a topic. These are the buttons you'll use most often, but you may want to experiment with the others as well as with the menu commands to find out how they work.

Books Online information for coding the Select statement

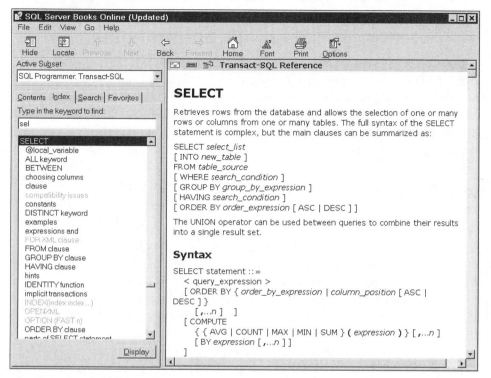

Description

- The Books Online application contains a complete set of SQL Server reference manuals.
- By default, information from all of the available manuals is displayed. To restrict a search to a subset of manuals, select that subset from the Active Subset combo box.
- The Contents tab lets you select a topic from the table of contents for the selected books. When you select a topic, it's displayed in the right pane of the window.
- The Index tab lets you locate an index entry by typing all or part of a keyword. As you type, the entries that match the keyword are listed. Then, you can double-click on an entry to display it in the right pane. If an entry refers to two or more topics, a dialog box is displayed that lets you choose a topic.
- The Search tab lets you search for information based on one or more words that you enter. When the results of the search are listed, you can double-click on an entry to display it in the right pane.
- You can use the Favorites tab to save topics that you refer to frequently. To add the currently displayed topic, right-click in this tab and select the Add command from the shortcut menu that's displayed. To display a topic from this tab, double-click on it.
- You can use the toolbar buttons to perform a variety of functions, including hiding and displaying the left pane, locating a topic in the Contents tab, moving to the previous or next topic in the contents, moving backward and forward through displayed topics, and printing the current topic.

Figure 2-13   How to use Books Online

How to use SQL from an application program

This book teaches you how to use SQL from within the SQL Server environment. As you learned in the last chapter, however, SQL is commonly used from application programs too. So in the topics that follow, you'll get a general idea of how that works. And you'll see that it's easy to recognize the SQL statements in an application program because they're coded just as they would be if they were running on their own.

Common data access models

Figure 2-14 shows three common ways for an application to access a SQL Server database. To access a SQL Server database from a Visual Basic .NET application, for example, you can use *ADO.NET*. This is Microsoft's newest *data access model*, and it can communicate directly with SQL Server.

To access SQL Server from a Visual Basic 6 or Access application, you can use an older data access model called *ADO*. This data access model was the predecessor to ADO.NET, and it's flexible and easy to use. Unlike ADO.NET, though, ADO requires additional software, called a *driver*, to communicate with SQL Server.

Although ADO is still in widespread use, ADO.NET is gaining in popularity, particularly for web-based applications. That's because web-based applications by necessity work with *disconnected data*. That means that once they've sent a response to the client, they don't maintain their connection to the database. And ADO.NET uses a *disconnected data architecture* that provides the functionality that's needed to accomplish this.

The third data access model shown in this figure is *JDBC*, which is used by Java applications. Like ADO, JDBC requires a driver to communicate with SQL Server.

Common options for accessing SQL Server data

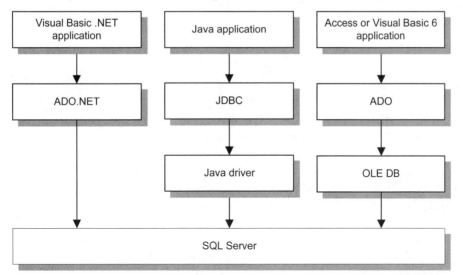

Description

- To work with the data in a SQL Server database, an application uses a *data access model*. For a Visual Basic .NET application, that model is typically *ADO.NET*. For a Java application, that model is typically *JDBC* (*Java Database Connectivity*). And for an Access or Visual Basic 6 application, that model is typically *ADO* (*ActiveX Data Objects*).

- Each data access model defines a set of objects you can use to connect to and work with a SQL Server database. For example, each of the three models shown above includes a Connection object that you can use to specify the information for connecting to a database.

- Some of the data access models require additional software, called *drivers*, to communicate with SQL Server. For example, ADO requires an OLE DB driver, and JDBC requires a Java driver.

- ADO.NET, which is Microsoft's newest data access model, includes its own driver so it can communicate directly with SQL Server.

Figure 2-14   Common data access models

How to use ADO.NET from a Visual Basic .NET program

To illustrate how you use a data access model, this topic introduces you to the basic ADO.NET objects that you use in a Visual Basic .NET application. Then, in the next topic, you'll see the actual Visual Basic code that creates and uses these objects. Keep in mind, though, that there's a lot more you need to know about Visual Basic and ADO.NET than what's presented here. To learn more, I recommend our book, *Murach's Beginning Visual Basic .NET*.

To start, the data used by an application is stored in a *dataset* that contains one or more *data tables*. To load data into a data table, you use a *data adapter*. The main function of the data adapter is to manage the flow of data between a dataset and a database. To do that, it uses *data commands* that define the SQL statements to be issued. The data command for retrieving data, for example, defines a SELECT statement. Then, the data command opens a connection to the database using a *data connection* and passes the SELECT statement to the database. After the SELECT statement is executed, the results are sent back to the data adapter, which stores them in the data table. Then, the data connection is closed.

To update the data in a database, the data adapter uses a data command that defines an INSERT, UPDATE, or DELETE statement for a data table. Then, the data command uses the data connection to connect to the database and perform the requested operation. When the operation is complete, the data connection is closed again until the next operation is performed on the database.

Basic ADO.NET objects in a Visual Basic .NET application

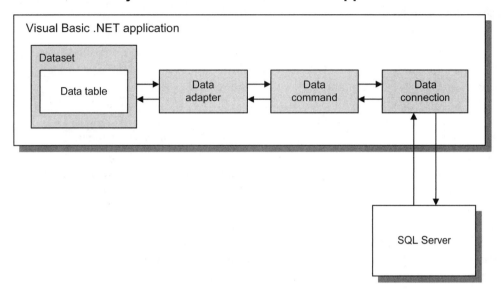

Description

- To work with the data in a SQL Server database from a Visual Basic .NET application, you use the ADO.NET objects shown above.

- The data used by an application is stored in a *data table* within a *dataset*. A data table has a row and column format like a table in a SQL Server database, and a dataset can contain one or more data tables.

- To retrieve data from a database and store it in a data table, a *data adapter* issues a SELECT statement that's stored in a *data command*. Next, the data command uses a *data connection* to connect to the database and retrieve the data. Then, the data is passed back to the data adapter, which stores the data in the dataset.

- To update the data in a database based on the data in a data table, the data adapter issues an INSERT, UPDATE, or DELETE statement that's stored in a data command. Then, the data command uses a data connection to connect to the database and update the database.

- After data is retrieved from a database or updated in a database, the connection is closed and the resources used by the connection are released. This is referred to as a *disconnected data architecture*.

Figure 2-15   How to use ADO.NET from a Visual Basic .NET program

Visual Basic code that retrieves data from a SQL Server database

Figure 2-16 presents Visual Basic code that uses the ADO.NET objects shown in the previous figure. This code is from a simple application that retrieves and displays information from the Vendors table. It creates the ADO.NET objects used by the application and then uses them to load the vendor data into a data table. Although I don't expect you to understand this code, I hope it will give you a feel for how you use SQL from an application program.

This code starts by creating the connection, data adapter, command, and dataset objects used by the application. At this point, these are generic objects, which means they don't contain any information that's specific to the application. That's taken care of by the statements that follow. The next statement, for example, sets the connection string for the connection object. The connection string provides ADO.NET with the information it needs to connect to the database.

Once the connection string is set, the next statement assigns the connection object to the command object. That means that when the command that this object will contain is executed, it will use the connection string in the connection object to connect to the database. Then, the next statement specifies the SELECT statement for the command object, and the statement after that assigns the command object to the data adapter, which will manage the retrieval operation.

The last three statements open the connection to the database, retrieve the data into the data table, and close the connection. Notice that the statement that retrieves the data refers to the data adapter, which contains a reference to the command object that contains the SELECT statement. Also notice that this statement names the table where the data that's retrieved by the SELECT statement will be stored. In this case, the data will be stored in a table named Vendors.

Now that you've reviewed this code, you can see that there's a lot involved in accessing a SQL Server database from an application program. However, you can also see that only one statement in this figure actually involves using SQL. That's the statement that specifies the SELECT statement to be executed. Of course, if the program also provided for updating the data in the Vendors table, it would include INSERT, UPDATE, and DELETE statements as well. With the skills that you'll learn in this book, though, you won't have any trouble coding the SQL statements you need.

Visual Basic code that defines ADO.NET objects used to retrieve data from the Vendors table

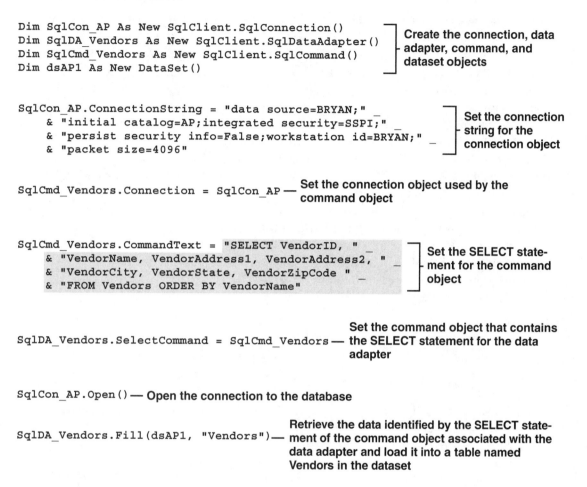

```
Dim SqlCon_AP As New SqlClient.SqlConnection()
Dim SqlDA_Vendors As New SqlClient.SqlDataAdapter()
Dim SqlCmd_Vendors As New SqlClient.SqlCommand()
Dim dsAP1 As New DataSet()
```
Create the connection, data adapter, command, and dataset objects

```
SqlCon_AP.ConnectionString = "data source=BRYAN;" _
    & "initial catalog=AP;integrated security=SSPI;" _
    & "persist security info=False;workstation id=BRYAN;" _
    & "packet size=4096"
```
Set the connection string for the connection object

```
SqlCmd_Vendors.Connection = SqlCon_AP
```
Set the connection object used by the command object

```
SqlCmd_Vendors.CommandText = "SELECT VendorID, " _
    & "VendorName, VendorAddress1, VendorAddress2, " _
    & "VendorCity, VendorState, VendorZipCode " _
    & "FROM Vendors ORDER BY VendorName"
```
Set the SELECT statement for the command object

```
SqlDA_Vendors.SelectCommand = SqlCmd_Vendors
```
Set the command object that contains the SELECT statement for the data adapter

```
SqlCon_AP.Open()
```
Open the connection to the database

```
SqlDA_Vendors.Fill(dsAP1, "Vendors")
```
Retrieve the data identified by the SELECT statement of the command object associated with the data adapter and load it into a table named Vendors in the dataset

```
SqlCon_AP.Close()
```
Close the connection to the database

Description

- Before you can issue a SQL statement from a Visual Basic program, you have to create the ADO.NET objects described in figure 2-15.

- After you create the ADO.NET objects, you have to set the properties of those objects that define how they work. For example, the ConnectionString property of a connection object contains information ADO.NET needs to connect to a database.

Figure 2-16   Visual Basic code that retrieves data from a SQL Server database

Perspective

In this chapter, you learned how to use the Enterprise Manager to view the definition of a database, you learned how to use the Query Analyzer to execute SQL statements, and you learned how to use Books Online to get information from the online reference manuals. With that as background, you're ready to go on to the next chapter where you'll start learning the details of coding your own SQL statements.

Before you go on to the next chapter, though, I recommend that you do the exercises that follow. The first exercise leads you through using the Enterprise Manager to look at the definition of the Accounts Payable (AP) database that's used throughout this book. The more familiar you are with this database, the easier it will be for you to understand the statements that use it. The second exercise leads you through using the Query Analyzer to enter and execute SQL statements. You'll want to use this tool as you learn the skills presented throughout the next section of this book. The third exercise leads you through using Books Online. That way, you'll be able to look up the information you need about any of the statements and features presented in this book.

Terms

database server
database engine
client tools
MSDE (Microsoft SQL Server
    Desktop Engine)
SQL Server Service Manager
Enterprise Manager
console tree
node
database diagram
check constraint
Query Analyzer
Object Browser
Query Designer

Books Online
data access model
ADO (ActiveX Data Objects)
JDBC (Java Database Connectivity)
ADO.NET
driver
data table
dataset
data adapter
data command
data connection
disconnected data
disconnected data architecture

Before you do the exercises for this chapter

The exercises that follow have been included to help you become familiar with the AP database that's used in the examples throughout this book. They also give you practice in using the SQL Server client tools to work with the database.

If you're working on your own PC, you'll need to set up your system before you can do these exercises. Specifically, you'll need to install SQL Server, you'll need to install the database and SQL files used by these exercises on your C drive, and you'll need to attach the database to the server. The procedures you'll use to do these tasks are described in appendix A, and the files you need are on the CD that comes with this book.

Exercise 2-1   Use the Enterprise Manager to view the AP database

In this exercise, you'll use the Enterprise Manager to view the definition of the AP database.

Start the Enterprise Manager and locate the AP database

1. Use the Windows Start menu to locate and start the Enterprise Manager.

2. When the Enterprise Manager workspace is displayed, expand the Microsoft SQL Servers node, the SQL Server Group node, and the node for the instance of SQL Server that contains the AP database. (If the database engine isn't currently running, this will start it.) At this point, you should see folders for all of the services provided by SQL Server.

3. Expand the Database node to display a list of the databases that the server manages. Then, expand the node for the AP database to display a list of the types of objects that can be stored in the database as shown in the left part of the window in figure 2-3.

View the relationships between the tables in the database

4. Select the Diagrams node to display the database diagrams for the AP database in the right side of the window. In this case, the database contains a single diagram.

5. Double-click on the diagram to display it. This diagram should look like the one shown in figure 2-4.

6. Review the information that's contained in each table, note the primary key of each table, and try to identify the relationships between the tables.

7. When you're done, close the window to return to the Enterprise Manager workspace.

View the table definitions

8. Select the Tables node to display the tables in the AP database. Then, locate the Vendors table, right-click on it, and select the Design Table command as shown in figure 2-3 (you may have to use the View menu to set the view to Detail to match the display in the figure). A window like the one in figure 2-5 should be displayed.

9. Review the definition of each column in this table. In particular, note the data type of each column, whether it allows null values, and whether it has a default value. Also note that the VendorID column is defined as an identity column.

10. Click on the Table and Index Properties button in the toolbar to display the Tables tab of the Properties dialog box. Note the owner of the database. (If you're using MSDE, it should be dbo.) Also notice that this dialog box indicates the identity column for the table.

11. Click on the Relationships tab to display the foreign keys for the table. Then, drop down the Selected relationship combo box to see that this table has three foreign keys. Notice that the names of these keys identify the table on the other side of the relationship. Select each of these foreign keys and note the columns in the primary key and foreign key table that form the relationship.

12. Click on the Indexes/Keys tab. Then, use the combo box at the top of the dialog box to display the settings for each key and index.

13. Click on the Check Constraints tab and note that no check constraints are defined for this table.

14. When you're done reviewing the properties for the Vendors table, close the Properties dialog box and then close the Design Table Window.

15. Repeat this procedure for the other tables in the AP database. Then, close the Enterprise Manager.

Exercise 2-2   Query the AP database

In this exercise, you'll use the Query Analyzer to enter and execute a SELECT statement against the AP database. Then, you'll save the query, open and execute another query, and correct any errors you encounter.

Enter, execute, and save a query

1. Start the Query Analyzer and connect to the database server as shown in figure 2-7. If you encounter problems, make sure that SQL Server is running and that you're using the proper authentication.

2. When the Query Analyzer window is displayed, select the AP database from the Select Database combo box in the toolbar.

3. Enter the query shown in figure 2-8, being careful to type each column name correctly. Use continuation lines and indentation as appropriate. Note how the Query Analyzer displays the keywords in blue as you enter them.

4. Press F5 to execute the query and display the results in the Grids tab of the results pane. If errors are detected or the results don't look like those in figure 2-8, correct the problem before you continue.

5. Click the Save button in the toolbar to display the Save Query dialog box. Then, navigate to the C:\Murach\SQL for SQL Server\Scripts\Chapter 02 folder on your computer. Enter SelectUnpaidInvoices for the file name, and then click on the Save button to save the statement.

Open another query and correct errors

6. Click on the New Query toolbar button to open another Query window, and select the Master database from the Select Database combo box. Then, use the Open command in the File menu to display the Open Query File dialog box, and open the query named FormatVendorAddress in the C:\Murach\SQL for SQL Server\Scripts\Chapter 02 folder.

7. Click the Parse Query toolbar button to see that the syntax of this statement is valid. Then, click the Execute Query toolbar button to execute it. When you do, an error message is displayed in the Messages tab of the results pane indicating that 'Vendors' isn't a valid object name. That's because this table isn't in the Master database. To fix this error, select the AP database.

8. Execute the query again. This time, you'll get a message indicating that 'VendorZip' isn't a valid column name. To find the correct column name, open the Object Browser window. Then, expand the AP database, the User Tables folder, the Vendors table, and the Columns folder. Locate the correct column name and modify the SELECT statement accordingly.

9. Execute the query one more time. If it works correctly, the result set will consist of 122 rows, starting with Computer Library in Phoenix, AZ. If it doesn't, correct the problem and execute the query again. Once you have it working, save it and close the Query Analyzer.

Exercise 2-3   Use Books Online

In this exercise, you'll use Books Online to search for and display information in the online manuals.

1. Start Books Online. When you do, the Entire Collection subset should be selected and the Contents tab should be displayed. If not, select this subset and tab.

2. Review the books that are available from the Contents tab and notice that most of them have little or nothing to do with coding SQL. Now, select *SQL Programmer: Transact-SQL* as the Active Subset to see what books it contains.

3. Expand the *Using the SQL Server Tools* book. Then, expand the *User Interface Reference* book and the *SQL Query Analyzer Help* book. Finally, click on the *Overview of SQL Query Analyzer* topic to display it in the right pane.

4. Click on the Favorites tab to display it. Then, right-click in this tab and select the Add command to add the Query Analyzer topic.

5. Click on the Contents tab to return to it. Then, click the Next toolbar button to display the next topic in this book.

6. Switch back to the Favorites tab and double-click on the topic you added to display it. Then, remove this topic from the tab by right-clicking on it and selecting Remove.

7. Click on the Index tab. Then, enter "object b" to highlight the Object Browser entry. Double-click on this entry to display a dialog box that lists the available topics. Select the *Using Object Browser* topic to display it in the right pane.

8. Click on the *Querying from Object Browser* link in the right pane to display that topic. Then, click on the Locate toolbar button to display the Contents tab with the currently displayed topic highlighted.

9. Click on the Search tab, enter *query file directory*, and click on the List Topics button. Double-click on the first topic in the list to display it in the right pane. Notice that all occurrences of the words *query*, *file*, and *directory* are highlighted.

10. Click the Back toolbar button one or more times to display previous topics. Then, click the Forward button to display subsequent topics.

11. Continue experimenting with the various features of Books Online until you feel comfortable with this tool. Then, close the program.

Section 2

The essential SQL skills

This section teaches you the essential SQL coding skills for working with the data in a SQL Server database. The first four chapters in this section show you how to retrieve data from a database using the SELECT statement. In chapter 3, you'll learn how to code the basic clauses of the SELECT statement to retrieve data from a single table. Then, in chapter 4, you'll learn how to get data from two or more tables. In chapter 5, you'll learn how to summarize the data that you retrieve. And in chapter 6, you'll learn how to code subqueries, which are SELECT statements coded within other statements.

Next, chapter 7 shows you how to use the INSERT, UPDATE, and DELETE statements to add, update, and delete rows in a table. Finally, chapter 8 shows you how to work with the various types of data that SQL Server supports and how to use some of the SQL Server functions for working with data in your SQL statements. When you complete these chapters, you'll have the skills you need to code most any SELECT, INSERT, UPDATE, or DELETE statement.

3

How to retrieve data from a single table

In this chapter, you'll learn how to code SELECT statements that retrieve data from a single table. You should realize, though, that the skills covered here are the essential ones that apply to any SELECT statement you code…no matter how many tables it operates on, no matter how complex the retrieval. So you'll want to be sure you have a good understanding of the material in this chapter before you go on to the chapters that follow.

An introduction to the SELECT statement

To help you learn to code SELECT statements, this chapter starts by presenting its basic syntax. Next, it presents several examples that will give you an idea of what you can do with this statement. Then, the rest of this chapter will teach you the details of coding this statement.

The basic syntax of the SELECT statement

Figure 3-1 presents the basic syntax of the SELECT statement. The syntax summary at the top of this figure uses conventions that are similar to those used in other programming manuals. Capitalized words are *keywords* that you have to type exactly as shown. In contrast, you have to provide replacements for the lowercase words. For example, you can enter a list of columns in place of *select_list*, and you can enter a table name in place of *table_source*.

Beyond that, you can choose between the items in a syntax summary that are separated by pipes (|) and enclosed in braces ({}) or brackets ([]). And you can omit items enclosed in brackets. If you have a choice between two or more optional items, the default item is underlined. And if an element can be coded multiple times in a statement, it's followed by an ellipsis (…). You'll see examples of pipes, braces, default values, and ellipses in syntax summaries later in this chapter. For now, if you compare the syntax in this figure with the coding examples in the next figure, you should easily see how the two are related.

The syntax summary in this figure has been simplified so that you can focus on the four main clauses of the SELECT statement: SELECT, FROM, WHERE, and ORDER BY. Most of the SELECT statements you code will contain all four of these clauses. However, only the SELECT and FROM clauses are required.

The SELECT clause is always the first clause in a SELECT statement. It identifies the columns that will be included in the result set. These columns are retrieved from the base tables named in the FROM clause. Since this chapter focuses on retrieving data from a single table, the FROM clauses in all of the statements you'll see in this chapter name a single base table. In the next chapter, though, you'll learn how to retrieve data from two or more tables.

The WHERE and ORDER BY clauses are optional. The ORDER BY clause determines how the rows in the result set are sorted, and the WHERE clause determines which rows in the base table are included in the result set. The WHERE clause specifies a search condition that's used to *filter* the rows in the base table. This search condition can consist of one or more *Boolean expressions*, or *predicates*. A Boolean expression is an expression that results in a value of True, False, or Unknown. When all the Boolean expressions in a search condition are true, the row is included in the result set.

In this book, I won't use the term "predicate" because I don't think it clearly describes the content of the WHERE clause. Instead, I'll use the term "search condition" or "Boolean expression" to refer to an expression that results in a True or False value.

The basic syntax of the SELECT statement

```
SELECT select_list
FROM table_source
[WHERE search_condition]
[ORDER BY order_by_list]
```

The four clauses of the SELECT statement

Clause	Description
SELECT	Describes the columns that will be included in the result set.
FROM	Names the table from which the query will retrieve the data.
WHERE	Specifies the conditions that must be met for a row to be included in the result set. This clause is optional.
ORDER BY	Specifies how the rows in the result set will be sorted. This clause is optional.

Description

- You use the basic SELECT statement shown above to retrieve the columns specified in the SELECT clause from the base table specified in the FROM clause and store them in a result set.

- The WHERE clause is used to *filter* the rows in the base table so that only those rows that match the search condition are included in the result set. If you omit the WHERE clause, all of the rows in the base table are included.

- The search condition of a WHERE clause consists of one or more *Boolean expressions*, or *predicates*, that result in a value of True, False, or Unknown. If the combination of all the expressions is True, the row being tested is included in the result set. Otherwise, it's not.

- If you include the ORDER BY clause, the rows in the result set are sorted in the specified sequence. Otherwise, the rows are returned in the same order as they appear in the base table. In most cases, that means that they're returned in primary key sequence.

Note

- The syntax shown above does not include all of the clauses of the SELECT statement. You'll learn about the other clauses later in this book.

Figure 3-1   The basic syntax of the SELECT statement

SELECT statement examples

Figure 3-2 presents five SELECT statement examples. All of these statements retrieve data from the Invoices table. If you aren't already familiar with this table, you should use the Enterprise Manager as described in the last chapter to review its definition.

The first statement in this figure retrieves all of the rows and columns from the Invoices table. Here, an asterisk (*) is used as a shorthand to indicate that all of the columns should be retrieved, and the WHERE clause is omitted so that there are no conditions on the rows that are retrieved. Notice that this statement doesn't include an ORDER BY clause, so the rows are in primary key sequence. You can see the results following this statement as they're displayed by the Query Analyzer. Notice that both horizontal and vertical scroll bars are displayed, indicating that the result set contains more rows and columns than can be displayed on the screen at one time.

The second statement retrieves selected columns from the Invoices table. As you can see, the columns to be retrieved are listed in the SELECT clause. Like the first statement, this statement doesn't include a WHERE clause, so all the rows are retrieved. Then, the ORDER BY clause causes the rows to be sorted by the InvoiceTotal column in descending sequence.

The third statement also lists the columns to be retrieved. In this case, though, the last column is calculated from two columns in the base table, CreditTotal and PaymentTotal, and the resulting column is given the name TotalCredits. In addition, the WHERE clause specifies that only the invoice whose InvoiceID column has a value of 17 should be retrieved.

The fourth SELECT statement includes a WHERE clause whose condition specifies a range of values. In this case, only invoices with invoice dates between 05/01/2002 and 05/31/2002 will be retrieved. In addition, the rows in the result set will be sorted by invoice date.

The last statement in this figure shows another variation of the WHERE clause. In this case, only those rows with invoice totals greater than 50,000 are retrieved. Notice that since none of the rows in the Invoices table satisfy this condition, the result set is empty.

A SELECT statement that retrieves all the data from the Invoices table

```
SELECT *
FROM Invoices
```

	InvoiceID	VendorID	InvoiceNumber	InvoiceDate	InvoiceTotal	PaymentTotal	CreditTotal
1	1	34	QP58872	2002-02-25 00:00:00	116.5400	116.5400	.0000
2	2	34	Q545443	2002-03-14 00:00:00	1083.5800	1083.5800	.0000
3	3	110	P-0608	2002-04-11 00:00:00	20551.1800	.0000	1200.0000
4	4	110	P-0259	2002-04-16 00:00:00	26881.4000	26881.4000	.0000

(114 rows)

A SELECT statement that retrieves three columns from each row, sorted in descending sequence by invoice total

```
SELECT InvoiceNumber, InvoiceDate, InvoiceTotal
FROM Invoices
ORDER BY InvoiceTotal DESC
```

	InvoiceNumber	InvoiceDate	InvoiceTotal
1	0-2058	2002-05-08 00:00:00	37966.1900
2	P-0259	2002-04-16 00:00:00	26881.4000
3	0-2060	2002-05-08 00:00:00	23517.5800
4	40318	2002-07-18 00:00:00	21842.0000

(114 rows)

A SELECT statement that retrieves two columns and a calculated value for a specific invoice

```
SELECT InvoiceID, InvoiceTotal, CreditTotal + PaymentTotal AS TotalCredits
FROM Invoices
WHERE InvoiceID = 17
```

	InvoiceID	InvoiceTotal	TotalCredits
1	17	356.4800	356.4800

A SELECT statement that retrieves all invoices between given dates

```
SELECT InvoiceNumber, InvoiceDate, InvoiceTotal
FROM Invoices
WHERE InvoiceDate BETWEEN '2002-05-01' AND '2002-05-31'
ORDER BY InvoiceDate
```

	InvoiceNumber	InvoiceDate	InvoiceTotal
6	7548906-20	2002-05-01 00:00:00	27.0000
7	4-314-3057	2002-05-02 00:00:00	13.7500
8	203339-13	2002-05-02 00:00:00	17.5000
9	2-000-2993	2002-05-03 00:00:00	144.7000

(70 rows)

A SELECT statement that returns an empty result set

```
SELECT InvoiceNumber, InvoiceDate, InvoiceTotal
FROM Invoices
WHERE InvoiceTotal > 50000
```

	InvoiceNumber	InvoiceDate	InvoiceTotal

Figure 3-2   SELECT statement examples

How to code the SELECT clause

Figure 3-3 presents an expanded syntax for the SELECT clause. The keywords shown in the first line allow you to restrict the rows that are returned by a query. You'll learn how to code them in a few minutes. First, though, you'll learn various techniques for identifying which columns are to be included in a result set.

How to code column specifications

Figure 3-3 summarizes the techniques you can use to code column specifications. You saw how to use some of these techniques in the previous figure. For example, you can code an asterisk in the SELECT clause to retrieve all of the columns in the base table, and you can code a list of column names separated by commas. Note that when you code an asterisk, the columns are returned in the order that they occur in the base table.

You can also code a column specification as an *expression*. For example, you can use an arithmetic expression to perform a calculation on two or more columns in the base table, and you can use a string expression to combine two or more string values. An expression can also include one or more functions. You'll learn more about each of these techniques in the topics that follow.

But first, you should know that when you code the SELECT clause, you should include only the columns you need. For example, you shouldn't code an asterisk to retrieve all the columns unless you need all the columns. That's because the amount of data that's retrieved can affect system performance. This is particularly important if you're developing SQL statements that will be used by application programs.

The expanded syntax of the SELECT clause

```
SELECT [ALL|DISTINCT] [TOP n [PERCENT] [WITH TIES]]
    column_specification [[AS] result_column]
    [, column_specification [[AS] result_column]] ...
```

Five ways to code column specifications

Source	Option	Syntax
Base table value	All columns	*
	Column name	column_name
Calculated value	Result of a calculation	Arithmetic expression (see figure 3-6)
	Result of a concatenation	String expression (see figure 3-5)
	Result of a function	Function (see figure 3-7)

Column specifications that use base table values

The * is used to retrieve all columns

```
SELECT *
```

Column names are used to retrieve specific columns

```
SELECT VendorName, VendorCity, VendorState
```

Column specifications that use calculated values

An arithmetic expression is used to calculate BalanceDue

```
SELECT InvoiceNumber,
    InvoiceTotal - PaymentTotal - CreditTotal AS BalanceDue
```

A string expression is used to calculate FullName

```
SELECT VendorContactFName + ' ' + VendorContactLName AS FullName
```

A function is used to calculate CurrentDate

```
SELECT InvoiceNumber, InvoiceDate,
    GETDATE() AS CurrentDate
```

Description

- Use SELECT * only when you need to retrieve all of the columns from a table. Otherwise, list the names of the columns you need.

- An *expression* is a combination of column names and operators that evaluate to a single value. In the SELECT clause, you can code arithmetic expressions, string expressions, and expressions that include one or more functions.

- After each column specification, you can code an AS clause to specify the name for the column in the result set. See figure 3-4 for details.

Note

- The other elements shown in the syntax summary above let you control the number of rows that are returned by a query. You can use the ALL and DISTINCT keywords to determine whether or not duplicate rows are returned. And you can use the TOP clause to retrieve a specific number or percent of rows. See figures 3-8 and 3-9 for details.

Figure 3-3   How to code column specifications

How to name the columns in a result set

By default, a column in a result set is given the same name as the column in the base table. However, you can specify a different name if you need to. You can also name a column that contains a calculated value. When you do that, the new column name is called a *column alias*. Figure 3-4 presents two techniques for creating column aliases.

The first technique is to code the column specification followed by the AS keyword and the column alias. This is the ANSI-standard coding technique, and it's illustrated by the first example in this figure. Here, a space is added between the two words in the name of the InvoiceNumber column, the InvoiceDate column is changed to just Date, and the InvoiceTotal column is changed to Total. Notice that because a space is included in the name of the first column, it's enclosed in brackets ([]). As you'll learn in chapter 10, any name that doesn't follow SQL Server's rules for naming objects must be enclosed in either brackets or double quotes. Column aliases can also be enclosed in single quotes.

The second example in this figure illustrates another technique for creating a column alias. Here, the column is assigned to an alias using an equal sign. This technique is available only on SQL Server and is included for compatibility with earlier versions of SQL Server. So although you may see this technique used in older code, I don't recommend it for new statements you write.

The third example in this figure illustrates what happens when you don't assign an alias to a calculated column. As you can see, no name is assigned to the column, which usually isn't what you want. So you should always be sure to assign a name to any column that's calculated from other columns in the base table.

Two SELECT statements that name the columns in the result set

A SELECT statement that uses the AS keyword (the preferred technique)

```
SELECT InvoiceNumber AS [Invoice Number], InvoiceDate AS Date,
    InvoiceTotal AS Total
FROM Invoices
```

A SELECT statement that uses the equal operator (an older technique)

```
SELECT [Invoice Number] = InvoiceNumber, Date = InvoiceDate,
    Total = InvoiceTotal
FROM Invoices
```

The result set for both SELECT statements

	Invoice Number	Date	Total
1	QP58872	2002-02-25 00:00:00	116.5400
2	Q545443	2002-03-14 00:00:00	1083.5800
3	P-0608	2002-04-11 00:00:00	20551.1800
4	P-0259	2002-04-16 00:00:00	26881.4000
5	MABO1489	2002-04-16 00:00:00	936.9300

A SELECT statement that doesn't provide a name for a calculated column

```
SELECT InvoiceNumber, InvoiceDate, InvoiceTotal,
    InvoiceTotal - PaymentTotal - CreditTotal
FROM Invoices
```

	InvoiceNumber	InvoiceDate	InvoiceTotal	(No column name)
1	QP58872	2002-02-25 00:00:00	116.5400	.0000
2	Q545443	2002-03-14 00:00:00	1083.5800	.0000
3	P-0608	2002-04-11 00:00:00	20551.1800	19351.1800
4	P-0259	2002-04-16 00:00:00	26881.4000	.0000
5	MABO1489	2002-04-16 00:00:00	936.9300	.0000

Description

- By default, a column in the result set is given the same name as the column in the base table. If that's not what you want, you can specify a *column alias* or *substitute name* for the column.

- One way to name a column is to use the AS phrase as shown in the first example above. Although the AS keyword is optional, I recommend you code it for readability.

- Another way to name a column is to code the name followed by an equal sign and the column specification as shown in the second example above. This syntax is unique to Transact-SQL.

- You should always specify an alias for a column that contains a calculated value. If you don't, no name is assigned to it as shown in the third example above.

- If an alias includes spaces or special characters, you must enclose it in double quotes or brackets ([]). That's true of all names you use in Transact-SQL. SQL Server also lets you enclose column aliases in single quotes for compatibility with earlier releases.

Figure 3-4   How to name the columns in a result set

How to code string expressions

A *string expression* consists of a combination of one or more character columns and *literal values*. To combine, or *concatenate*, the columns and values, you use the *concatenation operator* (+). This is illustrated by the examples in figure 3-5.

The first example shows how to concatenate the VendorCity and VendorState columns in the Vendors table. Notice that because no alias is assigned to this column, it doesn't have a name in the result set. Also notice that the data in the VendorState column appears immediately after the data in the VendorCity column in the results. That's because of the way VendorCity is defined in the database. Because it's defined as a variable-length column (the varchar data type), only the actual data in the column is included in the result. In contrast, if the column had been defined with a fixed length, any spaces following the name would have been included in the result. You'll learn about data types and how they affect the data in your result set in chapter 8.

The second example shows how to format a string expression by adding spaces and punctuation. Here, the VendorCity column is concatenated with a *string literal*, or *string constant*, that contains a comma and a space. Then, the VendorState column is concatenated with that result, followed by a string literal that contains a single space and the VendorZipCode column.

Occasionally, you may need to include a single quotation mark or an apostrophe within a literal string. If you simply type a single quote, however, the system will misinterpret it as the end of the literal string. As a result, you must code two quotation marks in a row. This is illustrated by the third example in this figure.

How to concatenate string data

```
SELECT VendorCity, VendorState, VendorCity + VendorState
FROM Vendors
```

	VendorCity	VendorState	(No column name)
1	Madison	WI	MadisonWI
2	Washington	DC	WashingtonDC
3	Washington	DC	WashingtonDC

How to format string data using literal values

```
SELECT VendorName,
    VendorCity + ', ' + VendorState + ' ' + VendorZipCode AS Address
FROM Vendors
```

	VendorName	Address
1	US Postal Service	Madison, WI 53707
2	National Information Data Ctr	Washington, DC 20090
3	Register of Copyrights	Washington, DC 20559
4	Jobtrak	Los Angeles, CA 90025

How to include apostrophes in literal values

```
SELECT VendorName + '''s Address: ',
    VendorCity + ', ' + VendorState + ' ' + VendorZipCode
FROM Vendors
```

	(No column name)	(No column name)
1	US Postal Service's Address:	Madison, WI 53707
2	National Information Data Ctr's Address:	Washington, DC 20090
3	Register of Copyrights's Address:	Washington, DC 20559
4	Jobtrak's Address:	Los Angeles, CA 90025
5	Newbrige Book Clubs's Address:	Delran, NJ 08370
6	California Chamber Of Commerce's Address:	Sacramento, CA 95827

Description

- A *string expression* can consist of one or more character columns, one or more *literal values*, or a combination of character columns and literal values.

- The columns specified in a string expression must contain string data (that means they're defined with the char or varchar data type).

- The literal values in a string expression also contain string data, so they can be called *string literals* or *string constants*. To create a literal value, enclose one or more characters within single quotation marks (').

- You can use the *concatenation operator* (+) to combine columns and literals in a string expression.

- You can include a single quote within a literal value by coding two single quotation marks as shown in the third example above.

Figure 3-5   How to code string expressions

How to code arithmetic expressions

Figure 3-6 shows how to code *arithmetic expressions*. To start, it summarizes the five *arithmetic operators* you can use in this type of expression. Then, it presents three examples that illustrate how you use these operators.

The SELECT statement in the first example includes an arithmetic expression that calculates the balance due for an invoice. This expression subtracts the PaymentTotal and CreditTotal columns from the InvoiceTotal column. The resulting column is given the name BalanceDue.

When SQL Server evaluates an arithmetic expression, it performs the operations from left to right based on the *order of precedence*. This order says that multiplication, division, and modulo operations are done first, followed by addition and subtraction. If that's not what you want, you can use parentheses to specify how you want an expression evaluated. Then, the expressions in the innermost sets of parentheses are evaluated first, followed by the expressions in outer sets of parentheses. Within each set of parentheses, the expression is evaluated from left to right in the order of precedence. Of course, you can also use parentheses to clarify an expression even if they're not needed for the expression to be evaluated properly.

To illustrate how parentheses and the order of precedence affect the evaluation of an expression, consider the second example in this figure. Here, the expressions in the second and third columns both perform the same operations. When SQL Server evaluates the expression in the second column, it performs the multiplication operation before the addition operation because multiplication comes before addition in the order of precedence. When SQL Server evaluates the expression in the third column, however, it performs the addition operation first because it's enclosed in parentheses. As you can see in the result set shown here, these two expressions result in different values.

Although you're probably familiar with the addition, subtraction, multiplication, and division operators, you may not be familiar with the modulo operator. This operator returns the remainder of a division of two integers. This is illustrated in the third example in this figure. Here, the second column contains an expression that returns the quotient of a division operation. Note that the result of the division of two integers is always an integer. You'll learn more about that in chapter 8. The third column contains an expression that returns the remainder of the division operation. If you study this example for a minute, you should quickly see how this works.

The arithmetic operators in order of precedence

*	Multiplication
/	Division
%	Modulo (Remainder)
+	Addition
–	Subtraction

A SELECT statement that calculates the balance due

```
SELECT InvoiceTotal, PaymentTotal, CreditTotal,
    InvoiceTotal - PaymentTotal - CreditTotal AS BalanceDue
FROM Invoices
```

	InvoiceTotal	PaymentTotal	CreditTotal	BalanceDue
1	116.5400	116.5400	.0000	.0000
2	1083.5800	1083.5800	.0000	.0000
3	20551.1800	.0000	1200.0000	19351.1800

A SELECT statement that uses parentheses to control the sequence of operations

```
SELECT InvoiceID,
    InvoiceID + 7 * 3 AS OrderOfPrecedence,
    (InvoiceID + 7) * 3 AS AddFirst
FROM Invoices
```

	InvoiceID	OrderOfPrecedence	AddFirst
1	1	22	24
2	2	23	27
3	3	24	30

A SELECT statement that uses the modulo operator

```
SELECT InvoiceID,
    InvoiceID / 10 AS Quotient,
    InvoiceID % 10 AS Remainder
FROM Invoices
```

	InvoiceID	Quotient	Remainder
9	9	0	9
10	10	1	0
11	11	1	1

Description

- Unless parentheses are used, the operations in an expression take place from left to right in the *order of precedence*. For arithmetic expressions, multiplication, division, and modulo operations are done first, followed by addition and subtraction.

- Whenever necessary, you can use parentheses to clarify or override the sequence of operations. Then, the operations in the innermost sets of parentheses are done first, followed by the operations in the next sets, and so on.

Figure 3-6   How to code arithmetic expressions

How to use functions

Figure 3-7 introduces you to *functions* and illustrates how you use them in column specifications. A function performs an operation and returns a value. For now, don't worry about the details of how the functions shown here work. You'll learn more about all of these functions in chapter 8. Instead, just focus on how they're used in column specifications.

To code a function, you begin by entering its name followed by a set of parentheses. If the function requires one or more *parameters*, you enter them within the parentheses and separate them with commas. When you enter a parameter, you need to be sure it has the correct data type. You'll learn more about that in chapter 8.

The first example in this figure shows how to use the LEFT function to extract the first character of the VendorContactFName and VendorContactLName columns. The first parameter of this function specifies the string value, and the second parameter specifies the number of characters to return. The results of the two functions are then concatenated to form initials as shown in the result set for this statement.

The second example shows how to use the CONVERT function to change the data type of a value. This function requires two parameters. The first parameter specifies the new data type, and the second parameter specifies the value to convert. In addition, this function accepts an optional third parameter that specifies the format of the returned value. The first CONVERT function shown here, for example, converts the PaymentDate column to a character value with the format mm/dd/yy. And the second CONVERT function converts the PaymentTotal column to a variable-length character value that's formatted with commas. These functions are included in a string expression that concatenates their return values with the InvoiceNumber column and three literal values.

The third example uses two functions that work with dates. The first one, GETDATE, returns the current date. Notice that although this function doesn't accept any parameters, the parentheses are still included. The second function, DATEDIFF, gets the difference between two date values. This function requires three parameters. The first one specifies the units in which the result will be expressed. In this example, the function will return the number of days between the two dates. The second and third parameters specify the start date and the end date. Here, the second parameter is the invoice date and the third parameter is the current date, which is obtained using the GETDATE function.

A SELECT statement that uses the LEFT function

```
SELECT VendorContactFName, VendorContactLName,
    LEFT(VendorContactFName, 1) +
    LEFT(VendorContactLName, 1) AS Initials
FROM Vendors
```

	VendorContactFName	VendorContactLName	Initials
1	Francesco	Alberto	FA
2	Ania	Irvin	AI
3	Lukas	Liana	LL

A SELECT statement that uses the CONVERT function

```
SELECT 'Invoice: #' + InvoiceNumber
    + ', dated ' + CONVERT(char(8), PaymentDate, 1)
    + ' for $' + CONVERT(varchar(9), PaymentTotal, 1)
FROM Invoices
```

	(No column name)
1	Invoice: #QP58872, dated 04/11/02 for $116.54
2	Invoice: #Q545443, dated 05/14/02 for $1,083.58

A SELECT statement that computes the age of an invoice

```
SELECT InvoiceDate,
    GETDATE() AS 'Today''s Date',
    DATEDIFF(day, InvoiceDate, GETDATE()) AS Age
FROM Invoices
```

	InvoiceDate	Today's Date	Age
1	2002-02-25 00:00:00	2002-09-12 12:27:52.827	199
2	2002-03-14 00:00:00	2002-09-12 12:27:52.827	182
3	2002-04-11 00:00:00	2002-09-12 12:27:52.827	154

Description

- An expression can include any of the *functions* that are supported by SQL Server. A function performs an operation and returns a value.

- A function consists of the function name, followed by a set of parentheses that contains any *parameters*, or *arguments*, required by the function. If a function requires two or more arguments, you separate them with commas.

- For more information on using functions, see chapter 8.

Figure 3-7   How to use functions

How to eliminate duplicate rows

By default, all of the rows in the base table that satisfy the search condition you specify in the WHERE clause are included in the result set. In some cases, though, that means that the result set will contain duplicate rows, or rows whose column values are identical. If that's not what you want, you can include the DISTINCT keyword in the SELECT clause to eliminate the duplicate rows.

Figure 3-8 illustrates how this works. Here, both SELECT statements retrieve the VendorCity and VendorState columns from the Vendors table. The first statement, however, doesn't include the DISTINCT keyword. Because of that, the same city and state can appear in the result set multiple times. In the results shown in this figure, for example, you can see that Anaheim CA occurs twice and Boston MA occurs three times. In contrast, the second statement includes the DISTINCT keyword, so each city/state combination is included only once.

A SELECT statement that returns all rows

```
SELECT VendorCity, VendorState
FROM Vendors
ORDER BY VendorCity
```

	VendorCity	VendorState	
1	Anaheim	CA	
2	Anaheim	CA	
3	Ann Arbor	MI	
4	Auburn Hills	MI	
5	Boston	MA	
6	Boston	MA	
7	Boston	MA	
8	Brea	CA	

(121 rows)

A SELECT statement that eliminates duplicate rows

```
SELECT DISTINCT VendorCity, VendorState
FROM Vendors
```

	VendorCity	VendorState	
1	Anaheim	CA	
2	Ann Arbor	MI	
3	Auburn Hills	MI	
4	Boston	MA	
5	Brea	CA	
6	Carol Stream	IL	
7	Charlotte	NC	
8	Chicago	IL	

(53 rows)

Description

- The DISTINCT keyword prevents duplicate (identical) rows from being included in the result set. It also causes the result set to be sorted by its first column.

- The ALL keyword causes all rows matching the search condition to be included in the result set, regardless of whether rows are duplicated. Since this is the default, you'll usually omit it.

- To use the DISTINCT or ALL keyword, code it immediately after the SELECT keyword as shown above.

Figure 3-8   How to eliminate duplicate rows

How to return a subset of selected rows

In addition to eliminating duplicate rows, you can limit the number of rows that are retrieved by a SELECT statement. To do that, you use the TOP clause. Figure 3-9 shows you how.

You can use the TOP clause in one of two ways. First, you can use it to retrieve a specific number of rows from the beginning, or top, of the result set. To do that, you code the TOP keyword followed by an integer value that specifies the number of rows to be returned. This is illustrated in the first example in this figure. Here, only five rows are returned. Notice that this statement also includes an ORDER BY clause that sorts the rows by the InvoiceTotal column in descending sequence. That way, the invoices with the highest invoice totals will be returned.

You can also use the TOP clause to retrieve a specific percent of the rows in the result set. To do that, you include the PERCENT keyword as shown in the second example. In this case, the result set includes six rows, which is five percent of the total of 122 rows.

By default, the TOP clause causes the exact number or percent of rows you specify to be retrieved. However, if additional rows match the values in the last row, you can include those additional rows by including WITH TIES in the TOP clause. This is illustrated in the third example in this figure. Here, the SELECT statement says to retrieve the top five rows from a result set that includes the VendorID and InvoiceDate columns sorted by the InvoiceDate column in descending sequence. As you can see, however, the result set includes six rows instead of five. That's because WITH TIES is included in the TOP clause, and the columns in the sixth row have the same values as the columns in the fifth row.

A SELECT statement with a TOP clause

```
SELECT TOP 5 VendorID, InvoiceTotal
FROM Invoices
ORDER BY InvoiceTotal DESC
```

	VendorID	InvoiceTotal
1	110	37966.1900
2	110	26881.4000
3	110	23517.5800
4	72	21842.0000
5	110	20551.1800

A SELECT statement with a TOP clause and the PERCENT keyword

```
SELECT TOP 5 PERCENT VendorID, InvoiceTotal
FROM Invoices
ORDER BY InvoiceTotal DESC
```

	VendorID	InvoiceTotal
1	110	37966.1900
2	110	26881.4000
3	110	23517.5800
4	72	21842.0000
5	110	20551.1800
6	110	10976.0600

A SELECT statement with a TOP clause and the WITH TIES keyword

```
SELECT TOP 5 WITH TIES VendorID, InvoiceDate
FROM Invoices
ORDER BY InvoiceDate DESC
```

	VendorID	InvoiceDate
1	72	2002-07-18 00:00:00
2	72	2002-06-20 00:00:00
3	102	2002-06-14 00:00:00
4	117	2002-06-11 00:00:00
5	95	2002-06-08 00:00:00
6	95	2002-06-08 00:00:00

Description

- You can use the TOP clause within a SELECT clause to limit the number of rows included in the result set. When you use this clause, the first n rows that meet the search condition are included, where n is an integer.

- If you include PERCENT, the first n percent of the selected rows are included in the result set.

- If you include WITH TIES, additional rows will be included if their values match, or *tie,* the values of the last row.

- You should include an ORDER BY clause whenever you use the TOP keyword. Otherwise, the rows in the result set will be in no particular sequence.

Figure 3-9   How to return a subset of selected rows

How to code the WHERE clause

Earlier in this chapter, I mentioned that to improve performance, you should code your SELECT statements so that they retrieve only the columns you need. That goes for retrieving rows too: The fewer rows you retrieve, the more efficient the statement will be. Because of that, you'll almost always include a WHERE clause on your SELECT statements with a search condition that filters the rows in the base table so that only the rows you need are retrieved. In the topics that follow, you'll learn a variety of ways to code this clause.

How to use comparison operators

Figure 3-10 shows you how to use the *comparison operators* in the search condition of a WHERE clause. As you can see in the syntax summary at the top of this figure, you use a comparison operator to compare two expressions. If the result of the comparison is True, the row being tested is included in the query results.

The examples in this figure show how to use some of the comparison operators. The first WHERE clause, for example, uses the equal operator (=) to retrieve only those rows whose VendorState column have a value of IA. Notice that because the state code is a string literal, it must be included in single quotes. In contrast, the numeric literal used in the second WHERE clause is not enclosed in quotes. This clause uses the greater than (>) operator to retrieve only those rows that have a balance due greater than zero.

The third WHERE clause illustrates another way to retrieve all the invoices with a balance due. Like the second clause, it uses the greater than operator. Instead of comparing the balance due to a value of zero, however, it compares the invoice total to the total of the payments and credits that have been applied to the invoice.

The fourth WHERE clause illustrates how you can use comparison operators other than equal with string data. In this example, the less than operator (<) is used to compare the value of the VendorName column to a literal string that contains the letter M. That will cause the query to return all vendors with names that begin with the letters A through L.

You can also use the comparison operators with date literals, as illustrated by the fifth and sixth WHERE clauses. The fifth clause will retrieve rows with invoice dates on or before May 31, 2002, and the sixth clause will retrieve rows with invoice dates on or after May 1, 2002. Notice that, like string literals, date literals must be enclosed in single quotes. Also notice that the two literals specify the dates using different formats. You'll learn more about the acceptable date formats in chapter 8.

The last WHERE clause shows how you can test for a not equal condition. To do that, you code a less than sign followed by a greater than sign. In this case, only rows with a credit total that's not equal to zero will be retrieved.

The syntax of the WHERE clause with comparison operators

```
WHERE expression_1 operator expression_2
```

The comparison operators

=	Equal
>	Greater than
<	Less than
<=	Less than or equal to
>=	Greater than or equal to
<>	Not equal

Examples of WHERE clauses that retrieve...

Vendors located in Iowa

```
WHERE VendorState = 'IA'
```

Invoices with a balance due (two variations)

```
WHERE InvoiceTotal - PaymentTotal - CreditTotal > 0
WHERE InvoiceTotal > PaymentTotal + CreditTotal
```

Vendors with names from A to L

```
WHERE VendorName < 'M'
```

Invoices on or before a specified date

```
WHERE InvoiceDate <= '2002-05-31'
```

Invoices on or after a specified date

```
WHERE InvoiceDate >= '5/1/02'
```

Invoices with credits that don't equal zero

```
WHERE CreditTotal <> 0
```

Description

- You can use a comparison operator to compare any two expressions that result in like data types. Although unlike data types may be converted to data types that can be compared, the comparison may produce unexpected results.

- If the result of a comparison results in a True value, the row being tested is included in the result set. If it's False or Unknown, the row isn't included.

- To use a string literal or a *date literal* in a comparison, enclose it in quotes. To use a numeric literal, enter the number without quotes.

- Character comparisons performed on SQL Server databases are not case-sensitive. So, for example, 'CA' and 'Ca' are considered equivalent.

Figure 3-10   How to use the comparison operators

Whenever possible, you should compare expressions that have similar data types. If you attempt to compare expressions that have different data types, SQL Server may implicitly convert the data type for you. Often, this implicit conversion is acceptable. However, implicit conversions will occasionally yield unexpected results. In that case, you can use the CONVERT function you saw earlier in this chapter or the CAST function you'll learn about in chapter 8 to explicitly convert data types so the comparison yields the results you want.

How to use the AND, OR, and NOT logical operators

Figure 3-11 shows how to use *logical operators* in a WHERE clause. You can use the AND and OR operators to combine two or more search conditions into a *compound condition*. And you can use the NOT operator to negate a search condition. The examples in this figure illustrate how these operators work.

The first two examples illustrate the difference between the AND and OR operators. When you use the AND operator, both conditions must be true. So, in the first example, only those vendors in New Jersey whose year-to-date purchases are greater than 200 are retrieved from the Vendors table (2 rows). When you use the OR operator, though, only one of the conditions must be true. So, in the second example, all the vendors from New Jersey and all the vendors whose year-to-date purchases are greater than 200 are retrieved (76 rows).

The third example shows a compound condition that uses two NOT operators. As you can see, this expression is somewhat difficult to understand. Because of that, and because using the NOT operator can reduce system performance, you should avoid using this operator. The fourth example in this figure, for instance, shows how the search condition in the third example can be rephrased to eliminate the NOT operator. Notice that the condition in the fourth example is much easier to understand.

The last two examples in this figure show how the order of precedence for the logical operators and the use of parentheses affect the result of a search condition. By default, the NOT operator is evaluated first, followed by AND and then OR. However, you can use parentheses to override the order of precedence or to clarify a logical expression, just as you can with arithmetic expressions. In the next to last example, for instance, no parentheses are used, so the two conditions connected by the AND operator are evaluated first. In the last example, though, parentheses are used so that the two conditions connected by the OR operator are evaluated first. If you take a minute to review the results shown in this figure, you should quickly see how these two conditions differ.

The syntax of the WHERE clause with logical operators

```
WHERE [NOT] search_condition_1 {AND|OR} [NOT] search_condition_2 ...
```

Examples of queries using logical operators

A search condition that uses the AND operator

```
WHERE VendorState = 'NJ' AND YTDPurchases > 200
```

A search condition that uses the OR operator

```
WHERE VendorState = 'NJ' OR YTDPurchases > 200
```

A search condition that uses the NOT operator

```
WHERE NOT (InvoiceTotal >= 5000 OR NOT InvoiceDate <= '2002-07-01')
```

The same condition rephrased to eliminate the NOT operator

```
WHERE InvoiceTotal < 5000 AND InvoiceDate <= '2002-07-01'
```

A compound condition without parentheses

```
WHERE InvoiceDate > '05/01/2002'
    OR InvoiceTotal > 500
    AND InvoiceTotal - PaymentTotal - CreditTotal > 0
```

	InvoiceNumber	InvoiceDate	InvoiceTotal	BalanceDue	
5	97/522	2002-04-30 00:00:00	1962.1300	1762.1300	
6	4-314-3057	2002-05-02 00:00:00	13.7500	.0000	
7	203339-13	2002-05-02 00:00:00	17.5000	17.5000	
8	2-000-2993	2002-05-03 00:00:00	144.7000	.0000	

(91 rows)

The same compound condition with parentheses

```
WHERE (InvoiceDate > '05/01/2002'
    OR InvoiceTotal > 500)
    AND InvoiceTotal - PaymentTotal - CreditTotal > 0
```

	InvoiceNumber	InvoiceDate	InvoiceTotal	BalanceDue	
5	97/522	2002-04-30 00:00:00	1962.1300	1762.1300	
6	203339-13	2002-05-02 00:00:00	17.5000	17.5000	
7	0-2436	2002-05-07 00:00:00	10976.0600	10976.0600	
8	963253272	2002-05-09 00:00:00	61.5000	61.5000	

(39 rows)

Description

- You can use the AND and OR *logical operators* to create *compound conditions* that consist of two or more conditions. You use the AND operator to specify that the search must satisfy both of the conditions, and you use the OR operator to specify that the search must satisfy at least one of the conditions.

- You can use the NOT operator to negate a condition. Because this operator can make the search condition unclear, you should rephrase the condition if possible so it doesn't use NOT.

- When SQL Server evaluates a compound condition, it evaluates the operators in this sequence: (1) NOT, (2) AND, and (3) OR. You can use parentheses to override this order of precedence or to clarify the sequence in which the operations will be evaluated.

Figure 3-11   How to use the AND, OR, and NOT logical operators

How to use the IN operator

Figure 3-12 shows how to code a WHERE clause that uses the IN operator. When you use this operator, the value of the test expression is compared with the list of expressions in the IN phrase. If the test expression is equal to one of the expressions in the list, the row is included in the query results. This is illustrated by the first example in this figure, which will return all rows whose TermsID column is equal to 1, 3, or 4.

You can also use the NOT operator with the IN phrase to test for a value that's not in a list of expressions. This is illustrated by the second example in this figure. In this case, only those vendors who are not in California, Nevada, or Oregon are retrieved.

If you look at the syntax of the IN phrase shown at the top of this figure, you'll see that you can code a *subquery* in place of a list of expressions. Subqueries are a powerful tool that you'll learn about in detail in chapter 6. For now, though, you should know that a subquery is simply a SELECT statement within another statement. In the third example in this figure, for instance, a subquery is used to return a list of VendorID values for vendors who have invoices dated May 1, 2002. Then, the WHERE clause retrieves a vendor row only if the vendor is in that list. Note that for this to work, the subquery must return a single column, in this case, VendorID.

The syntax of the WHERE clause with an IN phrase

```
WHERE test_expression [NOT] IN ({subquery|expression_1 [, expression_2]...})
```

Examples of the IN phrase

An IN phrase with a list of numeric literals

```
WHERE TermsID IN (1, 3, 4)
```

An IN phrase preceded by NOT

```
WHERE VendorState NOT IN ('CA', 'NV', 'OR')
```

An IN phrase with a subquery

```
WHERE VendorID IN
   (SELECT VendorID
    FROM Invoices
    WHERE InvoiceDate = '2002-05-01')
```

Description

- You can use the IN phrase to test whether an expression is equal to a value in a list of expressions. Each of the expressions in the list must evaluate to the same type of data as the test expression.

- The list of expressions can be coded in any order without affecting the order of the rows in the result set.

- You can use the NOT operator to test for an expression that's not in the list of expressions.

- You can also compare the test expression to the items in a list returned by a *subquery* as illustrated by the third example above. You'll learn more about coding subqueries in chapter 6.

Figure 3-12   How to use the IN operator

How to use the BETWEEN operator

Figure 3-13 shows how to use the BETWEEN operator in a WHERE clause. When you use this operator, the value of a test expression is compared to the range of values specified in the BETWEEN phrase. If the value falls within this range, the row is included in the query results.

The first example in this figure shows a simple WHERE clause that uses the BETWEEN operator. It retrieves invoices with invoice dates between May 1, 2002 and May 31, 2002. Note that the range is inclusive, so invoices with invoice dates of May 1 and May 31 are included in the results.

The second example shows how to use the NOT operator to select rows that are not within a given range. In this case, vendors with zip codes that aren't between 93600 and 93799 are included in the results.

The third example shows how you can use a calculated value in the test expression. Here, the PaymentTotal and CreditTotal columns are subtracted from the InvoiceTotal column to give the balance due. Then, this value is compared to the range specified in the BETWEEN phrase.

The last example shows how you can use calculated values in the BETWEEN phrase. Here, the first value is the result of the GETDATE function, and the second value is the result of the GETDATE function plus 30 days. So the query results will include all those invoices that are due between the current date and 30 days from the current date.

The syntax of the WHERE clause with a BETWEEN phrase

```
WHERE test_expression [NOT] BETWEEN begin_expression AND end_expression
```

Examples of the BETWEEN phrase

A BETWEEN phrase with literal values

```
WHERE InvoiceDate BETWEEN '2002-05-01' AND '2002-05-31'
```

A BETWEEN phrase preceded by NOT

```
WHERE VendorZipCode NOT BETWEEN 93600 AND 93799
```

A BETWEEN phrase with a test expression coded as a calculated value

```
WHERE InvoiceTotal - PaymentTotal - CreditTotal BETWEEN 200 AND 500
```

A BETWEEN phrase with the upper and lower limits coded as calculated values

```
WHERE InvoiceDueDate BETWEEN GetDate() AND GetDate() + 30
```

Description

- You can use the BETWEEN phrase to test whether an expression falls within a range of values. The lower limit must be coded as the first expression, and the upper limit must be coded as the second expression. Otherwise, the result set will be empty.

- The two expressions used in the BETWEEN phrase for the range of values are inclusive. That is, the result set will include values that are equal to the upper or lower limit.

- You can use the NOT operator to test for an expression that's not within the given range.

Figure 3-13   How to use the BETWEEN operator

How to use the LIKE operator

One final operator you can use in a search condition is the LIKE operator shown in figure 3-14. You use this operator along with the *wildcards* shown at the top of this figure to specify a *string pattern*, or *mask*, you want to match. The examples shown in this figure illustrate how this works.

In the first example, the LIKE phrase specifies that all vendors in cities that start with the letters SAN should be included in the query results. Here, the percent sign (%) indicates that any characters can follow these three letters. So San Diego and Santa Ana are both included in the results.

The second example selects all vendors whose vendor name starts with the letters COMPU, followed by any one character, the letters ER, and any characters after that. Two vendor names that match that pattern are Compuserve and Computerworld.

The third example searches the values in the VendorContactLName column for a name that can be spelled two different ways: Damien or Damion. To do that, the mask specifies the two possible characters in the fifth position, E and O, within brackets.

The fourth example uses brackets to specify a range of values. In this case, the VendorState column is searched for values that start with the letter N and end with any letter from A to J. That excludes states like Nevada (NV) and New York (NY).

The fifth example shows how to use the caret (^) to exclude one or more characters from the pattern. Here, the pattern says that the value in the VendorState column must start with the letter N, but must not end with the letters K through Y. This produces the same result as the previous statement.

The last example in this figure shows how to use the NOT operator with a LIKE phrase. The condition in this example tests the VendorZipCode column for values that don't start with the numbers 1 through 9. The result is all zip codes that start with the number 0.

The LIKE operator provides a powerful technique for finding information in a database that can't be found using any other technique. Keep in mind, however, that this technique requires a lot of overhead, so it can reduce system performance. For this reason, you should avoid using the LIKE operator in production SQL code whenever possible.

The syntax of the WHERE clause with a LIKE phrase

```
WHERE match_expression [NOT] LIKE pattern
```

Wildcard symbols

Symbol	Description
%	Matches any string of zero or more characters.
_	Matches any single character.
[ ]	Matches a single character listed within the brackets.
[-]	Matches a single character within the given range.
[^]	Matches a single character not listed after the caret.

WHERE clauses that use the LIKE operator

Example	Results that match the mask
WHERE VendorCity LIKE 'SAN%'	"San Diego" and "Santa Ana"
WHERE VendorName LIKE 'COMPU_ER%'	"Compuserve" and "Computerworld"
WHERE VendorContactLName LIKE 'DAMI[EO]N'	"Damien" and "Damion"
WHERE VendorState LIKE 'N[A-J]'	"NC" and "NJ" but not "NV" or "NY"
WHERE VendorState LIKE 'N[^K-Y]'	"NC" and "NJ" but not "NV" or "NY"
WHERE VendorZipCode NOT LIKE '[1-9]%'	"02107" and "08816"

Description

- You use the LIKE operator to retrieve rows that match a *string pattern*, called a *mask*. Within the mask, you can use special characters, called *wildcards*, that determine which values in the column satisfy the condition.

- You can use the NOT keyword before the LIKE keyword. Then, only those rows with values that don't match the string pattern will be included in the result set.

- Most LIKE phrases will significantly degrade performance compared to other types of searches, so use them only when necessary.

Figure 3-14   How to use the LIKE operator

How to use the IS NULL clause

In chapter 1, you learned that a column can contain a *null value*. A null isn't the same as zero, a blank string that contains one or more spaces (' '), or an empty string (''). Instead, a null value indicates that the information is not applicable, not available, or unknown. When you allow null values in one or more columns, you'll need to know how to test for them in search conditions. To do that, you use the IS NULL clause as shown in figure 3-15.

This figure uses a table named NullSample to illustrate how to search for null values. This table contains two columns. The first column, InvoiceID, is an identity column. The second column, InvoiceTotal, contains the total for the invoice, which can be a null value. As you can see in the first example, the invoice with InvoiceID 3 contains a null value.

The second example in this figure shows what happens when you retrieve all the invoices with invoice totals equal to zero. Notice that the row that has a null invoice total isn't included in the result set. Likewise, it isn't included in the result set that contains all the invoices with invoices totals that aren't equal to zero, as illustrated by the third example. Instead, you have to use the IS NULL clause to retrieve rows with null values, as shown in the fourth example.

You can also use the NOT operator with the IS NULL clause as illustrated in the last example in this figure. When you use this operator, all of the rows that don't contain null values are included in the query results.

The syntax of the WHERE clause with the IS NULL clause

```
WHERE expression IS [NOT] NULL
```

The contents of the NullSample table

```
SELECT *
FROM NullSample
```

	InvoiceID	InvoiceTotal
1	1	125.0000
2	2	.0000
3	3	NULL
4	4	2199.9900
5	5	.0000

A SELECT statement that retrieves rows with zero values

```
SELECT *
FROM NullSample
WHERE InvoiceTotal = 0
```

	InvoiceID	InvoiceTotal
1	2	.0000
2	5	.0000

A SELECT statement that retrieves rows with non-zero values

```
SELECT *
FROM NullSample
WHERE InvoiceTotal <> 0
```

	InvoiceID	InvoiceTotal
1	1	125.0000
2	4	2199.9900

A SELECT statement that retrieves rows with null values

```
SELECT *
FROM NullSample
WHERE InvoiceTotal IS NULL
```

	InvoiceID	InvoiceTotal
1	3	NULL

A SELECT statement that retrieves rows without null values

```
SELECT *
FROM NullSample
WHERE InvoiceTotal IS NOT NULL
```

	InvoiceID	InvoiceTotal
1	1	125.0000
2	2	.0000
3	4	2199.9900
4	5	.0000

Description

- A *null value* represents a value that's unknown, unavailable, or not applicable. It isn't the same as a zero, a blank space (' '), or an empty string ('').
- To test for a null value, you can use the IS NULL clause. You can also use the NOT keyword with this clause to test for values that aren't null.
- The definition of each column in a table indicates whether or not it can store null values. Before you work with a table, you should identify those columns that allow null values so you can accommodate them in your queries.

Note

- SQL Server provides an extension that lets you use = NULL to test for null values. For this to work, however, the ANSI_NULLS system option must be set to OFF. For more information on this option, see Books Online.

Figure 3-15   How to use the IS NULL clause

How to code the ORDER BY clause

The ORDER BY clause specifies the sort order for the rows in a result set. In most cases, you'll use column names from the base table to specify the sort order as you saw in some of the examples earlier in this chapter. However, you can also use other techniques to sort the rows in a result set, as described in the topics that follow.

How to sort a result set by a column name

Figure 3-16 presents the expanded syntax of the ORDER BY clause. As you can see, you can sort by one or more expressions in either ascending or descending sequence. This is illustrated by the three examples in this figure.

The first two examples show how to sort the rows in a result set by a single column. In the first example, the rows in the Vendors table are sorted in ascending sequence by the VendorName column. Notice that since ascending is the default sequence, the ASC keyword is omitted. In the second example, the rows are sorted by the VendorName column in descending sequence.

To sort by more then one column, you simply list the names in the ORDER BY clause separated by commas as shown in the third example. Here, the rows in the Vendors table are first sorted by the VendorState column in ascending sequence. Then, within each state, the rows are sorted by the VendorCity column in ascending sequence. Finally, within each city, the rows are sorted by the VendorName column in ascending sequence. This can be referred to as a *nested sort* because one sort is nested within another.

Although all of the columns in this example are sorted in ascending sequence, you should know that doesn't have to be the case. For example, I could have sorted by the VendorName column in descending sequence like this:

```
ORDER BY VendorState, VendorCity, VendorName DESC
```

Note that the DESC keyword in this example applies only to the VendorName column. The VendorState and VendorCity columns are still sorted in ascending sequence.

The expanded syntax of the ORDER BY clause

```
ORDER BY expression [ASC|DESC] [, expression [ASC|DESC]] ...
```

An ORDER BY clause that sorts by one column in ascending sequence

```
SELECT VendorName,
    VendorCity + ', ' + VendorState + ' ' + VendorZipCode AS Address
FROM Vendors
ORDER BY VendorName
```

	VendorName	Address
1	Abbey Office Furnishings	Fresno, CA 93722
2	American Booksellers Assoc	Tarrytown, NY 10591
3	American Express	Los Angeles, CA 90096

An ORDER BY clause that sorts by one column in descending sequence

```
SELECT VendorName,
    VendorCity + ', ' + VendorState + ' ' + VendorZipCode AS Address
FROM Vendors
ORDER BY VendorName DESC
```

	VendorName	Address
1	Zylka Design	Fresno, CA 93711
2	Zip Print & Copy Center	Fresno, CA 93777
3	Zee Medical Service Co	Washington, IA 52353

An ORDER BY clause that sorts by three columns

```
SELECT VendorName,
    VendorCity + ', ' + VendorState + ' ' + VendorZipCode AS Address
FROM Vendors
ORDER BY VendorState, VendorCity, VendorName
```

	VendorName	Address
1	AT&T	Phoenix, AZ 85062
2	Computer Library	Phoenix, AZ 85023
3	Wells Fargo Bank	Phoenix, AZ 85038
4	Aztek Label	Anaheim, CA 92807
5	Blue Shield of California	Anaheim, CA 92850
6	Diversified Printing & Pub	Brea, CA 92621
7	Abbey Office Furnishings	Fresno, CA 93722
8	ASC Signs	Fresno, CA 93703
9	BFI Industries	Fresno, CA 93792

Description

- The ORDER BY clause specifies how you want the rows in the result set sorted. You can sort by one or more columns, and you can sort each column in either ascending (ASC) or descending (DESC) sequence. ASC is the default.
- By default, in an ascending sort, nulls appear first in the sort sequence, followed by special characters, then numbers, then letters. Although you can change this sequence, that's beyond the scope of this book.
- You can sort by any column in the base table regardless of whether it's included in the SELECT clause. The exception is if the query includes the DISTINCT keyword. Then, you can only sort by columns included in the SELECT clause.

Figure 3-16   How to sort a result set by a column name

How to sort a result set by an alias, an expression, or a column number

Figure 3-17 presents three more techniques you can use to specify sort columns. First, you can use a column alias that's defined in the SELECT clause. The first SELECT statement in this figure, for example, sorts by a column named Address, which is an alias for the concatenation of the VendorCity, VendorState, and VendorZipCode columns. Notice that within the Address column, the result set is also sorted by the VendorName column.

You can also use an arithmetic or string expression in the ORDER BY clause, as illustrated by the second example in this figure. Here, the expression consists of the VendorContactLName column concatenated with the VendorContactFName column. Notice that neither of these columns is included in the SELECT clause. Although SQL Server allows this seldom-used coding technique, many other systems do not.

The last example in this figure shows how you can use column numbers to specify a sort order. To use this technique, you code the number that corresponds to the column of the result set, where 1 is the first column, 2 is the second column, and so on. In this example, the ORDER BY clause sorts the result set by the second column, which contains the concatenated address, then by the first column, which contains the vendor name. The result set returned by this statement is the same as the result set returned by the first statement. Notice, however, that the statement that uses column numbers is more difficult to read because you have to look at the SELECT clause to see what columns the numbers refer to. In addition, if you add or remove columns from the SELECT clause, you may also have to change the ORDER BY clause to reflect the new column positions. As a result, you should avoid using this technique.

An ORDER BY clause that uses an alias

```
SELECT VendorName,
    VendorCity + ', ' + VendorState + ' ' + VendorZipCode AS Address
FROM Vendors
ORDER BY Address, VendorName
```

	VendorName	Address
1	Aztek Label	Anaheim, CA 92807
2	Blue Shield of California	Anaheim, CA 92850
3	Malloy Lithographing Inc	Ann Arbor, MI 48106

An ORDER BY clause that uses an expression

```
SELECT VendorName,
    VendorCity + ', ' + VendorState + ' ' + VendorZipCode AS Address
FROM Vendors
ORDER BY VendorContactLName + VendorContactFName
```

	VendorName	Address
1	Dristas Groom & Mccormick	Fresno, CA 93720
2	Internal Revenue Service	Fresno, CA 93888
3	US Postal Service	Madison, WI 53707

An ORDER BY clause that uses column positions

```
SELECT VendorName,
    VendorCity + ', ' + VendorState + ' ' + VendorZipCode AS Address
FROM Vendors
ORDER BY 2, 1
```

	VendorName	Address
1	Aztek Label	Anaheim, CA 92807
2	Blue Shield of California	Anaheim, CA 92850
3	Malloy Lithographing Inc	Ann Arbor, MI 48106

Description

- The ORDER BY clause can include a column alias that's specified in the SELECT clause.

- The ORDER BY clause can include any valid expression. The expression can refer to any column in the base table, even if it isn't included in the result set.

- The ORDER BY clause can use numbers to specify the columns to use for sorting. In that case, 1 represents the first column in the result set, 2 represents the second column, and so on.

Figure 3-17   How to sort a result set by an alias, an expression, or a column number

Perspective

The goal of this chapter has been to teach you the basic skills for coding SELECT statements. You'll use these skills in almost every SELECT statement you code. As you'll see in the chapters that follow, however, there's a lot more to coding SELECT statements than what's presented here. In the next three chapters, then, you'll learn additional skills for coding SELECT statements. When you complete those chapters, you'll know everything you need to know about retrieving data from a SQL Server database.

Terms

keyword	literal value	comparison operator
filter	string literal	logical operator
Boolean expression	string constant	compound condition
predicate	arithmetic expression	subquery
expression	arithmetic operator	string pattern
column alias	order of precedence	mask
substitute name	function	wildcard
string expression	parameter	null value
concatenate	argument	nested sort
concatenation operator	date literal	

4

How to retrieve data from two or more tables

In the last chapter, you learned how to create result sets that contain data from a single table. Now, this chapter will show you how to create result sets that contain data from two or more tables. To do that, you can use either a join or a union.

How to work with inner joins

A *join* lets you combine columns from two or more tables into a single result set. In the topics that follow, you'll learn how to use the most common type of join, an *inner join*. You'll learn how to use other types of joins later in this chapter.

How to code an inner join

Figure 4-1 presents the *explicit syntax* for coding an inner join. As you'll see later in this chapter, SQL Server also provides an implicit syntax that you can use to code inner joins. However, the syntax shown in this figure is the one you'll use most often.

To join data from two tables, you code the names of the two tables in the FROM clause along with the JOIN keyword and an ON phrase that specifies the *join condition*. The join condition indicates how the two tables should be compared. In most cases, they're compared based on the relationship between the primary key of the first table and a foreign key of the second table. The SELECT statement in this figure, for example, joins data from the Vendors and Invoices tables based on the VendorID column in each table. Notice that because the equal operator is used in this condition, the value of the VendorID column in a row in the Vendors table must match the VendorID in a row in the Invoices table for that row to be included in the result set. In other words, only vendors with one or more invoices will be included. Although you'll code most inner joins using the equal operator, you should know that you can compare two tables based on other conditions, too.

In this example, the Vendors table is joined with the Invoices table using a column that has the same name in both tables: VendorID. Because of that, the columns must be qualified to indicate which table they come from. As you can see, you code a *qualified column name* by entering the table name and a period in front of the column name. Although this example uses qualified column names only in the join condition, you must qualify a name anywhere it appears in the statement if the same name occurs in both tables. If you don't, SQL Server will return an error indicating that the column name is ambiguous. Of course, you can also qualify column names that aren't ambiguous. However, I recommend you do that only if it clarifies your code.

The explicit syntax for an inner join

```
SELECT select_list
FROM table_1
    [INNER] JOIN table_2
        ON join_condition_1
    [[INNER] JOIN table_3
        ON join_condition_2]...
```

A SELECT statement that joins the Vendors and Invoices tables

```
SELECT InvoiceNumber, VendorName
FROM Vendors JOIN Invoices
    ON Vendors.VendorID = Invoices.VendorID
```

The result set

	InvoiceNumber	VendorName
1	QP58872	IBM
2	Q545443	IBM
3	P-0608	Malloy Lithographing Inc
4	P-0259	Malloy Lithographing Inc
5	MABO1489	Wang Laboratories, Inc.
6	989319-497	United Parcel Service
7	C73-24	Reiter's Scientific & Pro Books
8	989319-487	United Parcel Service

(114 rows)

Description

- A *join* is used to combine columns from two or more tables into a result set based on the *join conditions* you specify. For an *inner join*, only those rows that satisfy the join condition are included in the result set.

- A join condition names a column in each of the two tables involved in the join and indicates how the two columns should be compared. In most cases, you use the equal operator to retrieve rows with matching columns. However, you can also use any of the other comparison operators in a join condition.

- In most cases, you'll join two tables based on the relationship between the primary key in one table and a foreign key in the other table. However, you can also join tables based on relationships not defined in the database. These are called *ad hoc relationships*.

- If the two columns in a join condition have the same name, you have to qualify them with the table name so that SQL Server can distinguish between them. To code a *qualified column name*, type the table name, followed by a period, followed by the column name.

Notes

- The INNER keyword is optional and is seldom used.

- This syntax for coding an inner join can be referred to as the *explicit syntax*. It is also called the *SQL-92 syntax* because it was introduced by the SQL-92 standards.

- You can also code an inner join using the *implicit syntax*. See figure 4-7 for more information.

Figure 4-1   How to code an inner join

When and how to use correlation names

When you name the tables to be joined in the FROM clause, you can assign temporary names to the tables called *correlation names* or *table aliases*. To do that, you use the AS phrase just as you do when you assign a column alias. After you assign a correlation name, you must use that name in place of the original table name throughout the query. This is illustrated in figure 4-2.

The first SELECT statement in this figure joins data from the Vendors and Invoices table. Here, both tables have been assigned correlation names that consist of a single letter. Although short correlation names like this can reduce typing, they can also make a query more difficult to read and maintain. As a result, you should only use correlation names when they simplify or clarify the query.

The correlation name used in the second SELECT statement in this figure, for example, simplifies the name of the InvoiceLineItems table to just LineItems. That way, the shorter name can be used to refer to the InvoiceID column of the table in the join condition. Although this doesn't improve the query in this example much, it can have a dramatic effect on a query that refers to the InvoiceLineItems table several times.

The syntax for an inner join that uses correlation names

```
SELECT select_list
FROM table_1 [AS] n1
    [INNER] JOIN table_2 [AS] n2
        ON n1.column_name operator n2.column_name
    [[INNER] JOIN table_3 [AS] n3
        ON n2.column_name operator n3.column_name]...
```

An inner join with correlation names that make the query more difficult to read

```
SELECT InvoiceNumber, VendorName, InvoiceDueDate,
    InvoiceTotal - PaymentTotal - CreditTotal AS BalanceDue
FROM Vendors AS v JOIN Invoices AS i
    ON v.VendorID = i.VendorID
WHERE InvoiceTotal - PaymentTotal - CreditTotal > 0
ORDER BY InvoiceDueDate DESC
```

	InvoiceNumber	VendorName	InvoiceDueDate	BalanceDue
1	39104	Data Reproductions Corp	2002-07-20 00:00:00	85.3100
2	40318	Data Reproductions Corp	2002-07-20 00:00:00	21842.0000
3	0-2436	Malloy Lithographing Inc	2002-07-17 00:00:00	10976.0600

(40 rows)

An inner join with a correlation name that simplifies the query

```
SELECT InvoiceNumber, InvoiceLineItemAmount, InvoiceLineItemDescription
FROM Invoices JOIN InvoiceLineItems AS LineItems
    ON Invoices.InvoiceID = LineItems.InvoiceID
WHERE AccountNo = 540
ORDER BY InvoiceDate
```

	InvoiceNumber	InvoiceLineItemAmount	InvoiceLineItemDescription
1	97/553B	313.5500	Card revision
2	97/553	651.2900	DB2 Card decks
3	97/522	765.1300	SCMD Flyer

(8 rows)

Description

- *Correlation names* are temporary table names assigned in the FROM clause. You can use correlation names when long table names make qualified column names long or confusing. A correlation name can also be called a *table alias*.

- If you assign a correlation name to a table, you must use that name to refer to the table within your query. You can't use the original table name.

- Although the AS keyword is optional, I recommend you use it because it makes the FROM clause easier to read.

- You can use a correlation name for any table in a join without using correlation names for all of the other tables.

- Use correlation names whenever they simplify or clarify the query. Avoid using correlation names when they make a query more confusing or difficult to read.

Figure 4-2   When and how to use correlation names

How to work with tables from different databases

Although it's not common, you may occasionally need to join data from tables that reside in different databases, possibly even on different servers. To do that, you have to qualify one or more of the table names. Figure 4-3 shows you how.

To start, this figure presents the syntax of a *fully-qualified object name*. As you can see, a fully-qualified name consists of four parts: a server name, a database name, the name of the database owner, and the name of the object itself. In this chapter, you'll learn how to qualify table names. However, you should realize that you can use this syntax with other objects as well.

The first SELECT statement in this figure illustrates the use of fully-qualified object names. This statement joins data from two tables (Vendors and Customers) in two different databases (AP and ProductOrders). Both databases are on the same server (Bryan) and have the same owner (dbo). Notice that correlation names are assigned to both of these tables to make them easier to refer to in the join condition.

Although you can qualify all your table names this way, that's usually not necessary. Instead, you specify only the parts that are different from the current settings. When you start the Query Analyzer, for example, you connect to a specific server. As long as you work with databases in that server, then, you don't need to include the server name. Similarly, before you execute a statement, you select the database it uses. So as long as you work with tables in that database, you don't need to include the database name. You can also omit the owner name if it's the same as the user name that's associated with the user ID you used to log on to SQL Server. (If you used Windows authentication, that's your Windows user ID.) That's why all of the statements you've seen up to this point have included only the table name.

When you omit one or more parts from a fully-qualified object name, you create a *partially-qualified object name*. The second SELECT statement in this figure, for example, shows how the first statement can be rewritten using partially-qualified object names. Here, the server name, database name, and owner name are all omitted from the Vendors table since it resides in the current database (AP) on the current server (BRYAN) and is owned by dbo. The Customers table, however, must be qualified with the database name because it's not in the AP database. Notice that because the owner name falls between the database name and the table name, two periods were coded to indicate that this part of the name was omitted.

The syntax of a fully-qualified object name

```
server.database.owner_name.object_name
```

A join with fully-qualified table names

```
SELECT VendorName, CustLastName, CustFirstName,
    VendorState AS State, VendorCity AS City
FROM Bryan.AP.dbo.Vendors AS Vendors
    JOIN Bryan.ProductOrders.dbo.Customers AS Customers
    ON Vendors.VendorZipCode = Customers.CustZip
ORDER BY State, City
```

The same join with partially-qualified table names

```
SELECT VendorName, CustLastName, CustFirstName,
    VendorState AS State, VendorCity AS City
FROM Vendors
    JOIN ProductOrders..Customers AS Customers
    ON Vendors.VendorZipCode = Customers.CustZip
ORDER BY State, City
```

The result set

	VendorName	CustLastName	CustFirstName	State	City
1	Wells Fargo Bank	Marissa	Kyle	AZ	Phoenix
2	Aztek Label	Irvin	Ania	CA	Anaheim
3	Gary McKeighan Insurance	Neftaly	Thalia	CA	Fresno
4	Gary McKeighan Insurance	Holbrooke	Rashad	CA	Fresno
5	Shields Design	Damien	Deborah	CA	Fresno

(37 rows)

Description

- A *fully-qualified object name* is made up of four parts: the server name, the database name, the name of the database owner, and the name of the object (typically a table). This syntax can be used when joining tables from different databases or databases on different servers.

- If the server name, database name, or owner name is the same as the current server name, database name, or owner name, you can omit that part of the qualified name to create a *partially-qualified object name*. If the omitted name falls between two other parts of the name, code two periods to indicate that the name is omitted.

Figure 4-3   How to work with tables from different databases

How to use compound join conditions

Although a join condition typically consists of a single comparison, you can include two or more comparisons in a join condition using the AND and OR operators. Figure 4-4 illustrates how this works.

In the first SELECT statement in this figure, you can see that the Invoices and InvoiceLineItems tables are joined based on two comparisons. First, the primary key of the Invoices table, InvoiceID, is compared with the foreign key of the InvoiceLineItems table, also named InvoiceID. As in previous examples, this comparison uses an equal condition. Then, the InvoiceTotal column in the Invoices table is tested for a value greater than the value of the InvoiceLineItemAmount column in the InvoiceLineItems table. That means that only those invoices that have two or more line items will be included in the result set. You can see this result set in this figure.

Another way to code these conditions is to code the primary join condition in the FROM clause and the other condition in the WHERE clause. This is illustrated by the second SELECT statement in this figure.

When you use a WHERE clause to separate the join conditions, the join condition in the ON expression is performed before the tables are joined, and the search condition in the WHERE clause is performed after the tables are joined. Because of that, you might expect a SELECT statement to execute more efficiently if you code the search condition in the ON expression. However, SQL Server examines the join and search conditions in order to optimize the query. So you don't need to worry about which technique is most efficient. Instead, you should code the conditions so they're easy to understand. In most cases, your SELECT statements will be easier to read if you separate the conditions instead of coding them all in the ON expression.

An inner join with two conditions

```
SELECT InvoiceNumber, InvoiceDate,
    InvoiceTotal, InvoiceLineItemAmount
FROM Invoices JOIN InvoiceLineItems AS LineItems
    ON (Invoices.InvoiceID = LineItems.InvoiceID) AND
        (Invoices.InvoiceTotal > LineItems.InvoiceLineItemAmount)
ORDER BY InvoiceNumber
```

The same join with the second condition coded in a WHERE clause

```
SELECT InvoiceNumber, InvoiceDate,
    InvoiceTotal, InvoiceLineItemAmount
FROM Invoices JOIN InvoiceLineItems AS LineItems
    ON Invoices.InvoiceID = LineItems.InvoiceID
WHERE Invoices.InvoiceTotal > LineItems.InvoiceLineItemAmount
ORDER BY InvoiceNumber
```

The result set

	InvoiceNumber	InvoiceDate	InvoiceTotal	InvoiceLineItemAmount
1	97/522	2002-04-30 00:00:00	1962.1300	1197.0000
2	97/522	2002-04-30 00:00:00	1962.1300	765.1300
3	I77271-001	2002-06-05 00:00:00	662.0000	50.0000
4	I77271-001	2002-06-05 00:00:00	662.0000	75.6000
5	I77271-001	2002-06-05 00:00:00	662.0000	58.4000
6	I77271-001	2002-06-05 00:00:00	662.0000	478.0000

Description

- A join condition can include two or more conditions connected by AND or OR operators.

- In most cases, your code will be easier to read if you code the join condition in the ON expression and search conditions in the WHERE clause.

Figure 4-4   How to use compound join conditions

How to use a self-join

A *self-join* is a join where a table is joined with itself. Although self-joins are rare, there are some unique queries that are best solved using self-joins.

Figure 4-5 presents an example of a self-join that uses the Vendors table. Notice that since the same table is used twice, correlation names are used to distinguish between the two occurrences of the table. In addition, each column name used in the query is qualified by the correlation name since the columns occur in both tables.

The join condition in this example uses three comparisons. The first two match the VendorCity and VendorState columns in the two tables. As a result, the query will return rows for vendors that reside in the same city and state as another vendor. Because a vendor resides in the same city and state as itself, however, a third comparison is included to exclude rows that match a vendor with itself. To do that, this condition uses the not equal operator to compare the VendorID columns in the two tables.

Notice that the DISTINCT keyword is also included in this SELECT statement. That way, a vendor appears only once in the result set. Otherwise, it would appear once for each row with a matching city and state.

This example also shows how you can use columns other than key columns in a join condition. Keep in mind, however, that this is an unusual situation and you're not likely to code joins like this often.

A self-join that returns vendors from cities in common with other vendors

```
SELECT DISTINCT Vendors1.VendorName, Vendors1.VendorCity,
    Vendors1.VendorState
FROM Vendors AS Vendors1 JOIN Vendors AS Vendors2
    ON (Vendors1.VendorCity = Vendors2.VendorCity) AND
        (Vendors1.VendorState = Vendors2.VendorState) AND
        (Vendors1.VendorID <> Vendors2.VendorID)
ORDER BY Vendors1.VendorState, Vendors1.VendorCity
```

The result set

	VendorName	VendorCity	VendorState
1	Computer Library	Phoenix	AZ
2	AT&T	Phoenix	AZ
3	Wells Fargo Bank	Phoenix	AZ
4	Abbey Office Furnishings	Fresno	CA
5	California Business Machines	Fresno	CA

(84 rows)

Description

- A *self-join* is a join that joins a table with itself.
- When you code a self-join, you must use correlation names for the tables, and you must qualify each column name with the correlation name.
- Self-joins frequently include the DISTINCT keyword to eliminate duplicate rows.

Figure 4-5   How to use a self-join

Inner joins that join more than two tables

So far in this chapter, you've seen how to join data from two tables. However, SQL Server lets you join data from up to 256 tables. Of course, it's not likely that you'll ever need to join data from more than a few tables. In addition, each join requires additional system resources, so you should limit the number of joined tables whenever possible.

The SELECT statement in figure 4-6 joins data from four tables: Vendors, Invoices, InvoiceLineItems, and GLAccounts. Each of the joins is based on the relationship between the primary key of one table and a foreign key of the other table. For example, the AccountNo column is the primary key of the GLAccounts table and a foreign key of the InvoiceLineItems table.

Below the SELECT statement, you can see three tables. The first one presents the result of the join between the Vendors and Invoices tables. This table can be referred to as an *interim table* because it contains interim results. Similarly, the second table shows the result of the join between the first interim table and the InvoiceLineItems table. And the third table shows the result of the join between the second interim table and the GLAccounts table.

As you review the three tables in this figure, keep in mind that SQL Server may not actually process the joins as illustrated here. However, the idea of interim tables should help you understand how multi-table joins work.

A SELECT statement that joins four tables

```
SELECT VendorName, InvoiceNumber, InvoiceDate,
    InvoiceLineItemAmount AS LineItemAmount, AccountDescription
FROM Vendors
    JOIN Invoices ON Vendors.VendorID = Invoices.VendorID
    JOIN InvoiceLineItems
        ON Invoices.InvoiceID = InvoiceLineItems.InvoiceID
    JOIN GLAccounts ON InvoiceLineItems.AccountNo = GLAccounts.AccountNo
WHERE InvoiceTotal - PaymentTotal - CreditTotal > 0
ORDER BY VendorName, LineItemAmount DESC
```

The first interim table

	VendorName	InvoiceNumber	InvoiceDate	
1	Abbey Office Furnishings	203339-13	2002-05-02 00:00:00	
2	Blue Cross	547479217	2002-05-17 00:00:00	
3	Blue Cross	547480102	2002-05-19 00:00:00	
4	Blue Cross	547481328	2002-05-20 00:00:00	
5	Cardinal Business Media, Inc.	134116	2002-06-01 00:00:00	
6	Coffee Break Service	109596	2002-06-14 00:00:00	
7	Compuserve	2147483647	2002-05-09 00:00:00	
8	Computerworld	367447	2002-05-31 00:00:00	

(40 rows)

The second interim table

	VendorName	InvoiceNumber	InvoiceDate	LineItemAmount
1	Abbey Office Furnishings	203339-13	2002-05-02 00:00:00	17.5000
2	Blue Cross	547480102	2002-05-19 00:00:00	224.0000
3	Blue Cross	547481328	2002-05-20 00:00:00	224.0000
4	Blue Cross	547479217	2002-05-17 00:00:00	116.0000
5	Cardinal Business Media, Inc.	134116	2002-06-01 00:00:00	90.3600
6	Coffee Break Service	109596	2002-06-14 00:00:00	41.8000
7	Compuserve	2147483647	2002-05-09 00:00:00	9.9500
8	Computerworld	367447	2002-05-31 00:00:00	2433.0000

(44 rows)

The final result set

	VendorName	InvoiceNumber	InvoiceDate	LineItemAmount	AccountDescription
1	Abbey Office Furnishings	203339-13	2002-05-02 00:00:00	17.5000	Office Supplies
2	Blue Cross	547480102	2002-05-19 00:00:00	224.0000	Group Insurance
3	Blue Cross	547481328	2002-05-20 00:00:00	224.0000	Group Insurance
4	Blue Cross	547479217	2002-05-17 00:00:00	116.0000	Group Insurance
5	Cardinal Business Media, Inc.	134116	2002-06-01 00:00:00	90.3600	Card Deck Advertising
6	Coffee Break Service	109596	2002-06-14 00:00:00	41.8000	Meals
7	Compuserve	2147483647	2002-05-09 00:00:00	9.9500	Books, Dues, and Subscriptions
8	Computerworld	367447	2002-05-31 00:00:00	2433.0000	Card Deck Advertising

(44 rows)

Description

- You can think of a multi-table join as a series of two-table joins proceeding from left to right. The first two tables are joined to produce an *interim result set* or *interim table*. Then, the interim table is joined with the next table, and so on.

Figure 4-6   Inner joins that join more than two tables

How to use the implicit inner join syntax

Earlier in this chapter, I mentioned that SQL Server provides an *implicit syntax* for joining tables. This syntax was used prior to the SQL-92 standards. Although I recommend you use the explicit syntax, you should be familiar with the implicit syntax in case you ever need to maintain SQL statements that use it.

Figure 4-7 presents the implicit syntax for an inner join along with two statements that use it. As you can see, the tables to be joined are simply listed in the FROM clause. Then, the join conditions are included in the WHERE clause.

The first SELECT statement, for example, joins data from the Vendors and Invoices table. Like the SELECT statement you saw back in figure 4-1, these tables are joined based on an equal comparison between the VendorID columns in the two tables. In this case, though, the comparison in coded as the search condition of the WHERE clause. If you compare the result set shown in this figure with the one in figure 4-1, you'll see that they're identical.

The second SELECT statement uses the implicit syntax to join data from four tables. This is the same join you saw in figure 4-6. Notice in this example that the three join conditions are combined in the WHERE clause using the AND operator. In addition, an AND operator is used to combine the join conditions with the search condition.

Because the explicit syntax for joins lets you separate join conditions from search conditions, statements that use the explicit syntax are typically easier to read than those that use the implicit syntax. In addition, the explicit syntax helps you avoid a common coding mistake with the implicit syntax: omitting the join condition. As you'll learn later in this chapter, an implicit join without a join condition results in a cross join, which can return a large number of rows. For these reasons, I recommend you use the explicit syntax in all your new SQL code.

The implicit syntax for an inner join

```
SELECT select_list
FROM table_1, table_2 [,table_3]...
WHERE table_1.column_name operator table_2.column_name
    [AND table_2.column_name operator table_3.column_name]...
```

A SELECT statement that joins the Vendors and Invoices tables

```
SELECT InvoiceNumber, VendorName
FROM Vendors, Invoices
WHERE Vendors.VendorID = Invoices.VendorID
```

The result set

	InvoiceNumber	VendorName
1	QP58872	IBM
2	Q545443	IBM
3	P-0608	Malloy Lithographing Inc
4	P-0259	Malloy Lithographing Inc
5	MABO1489	Wang Laboratories, Inc.
6	989319-497	United Parcel Service
7	C73-24	Reiter's Scientific & Pro Books
8	989319-487	United Parcel Service

A statement that joins four tables

```
SELECT VendorName, InvoiceNumber, InvoiceDate,
    InvoiceLineItemAmount AS LineItemAmount, AccountDescription
FROM Vendors, Invoices, InvoiceLineItems, GLAccounts
WHERE Vendors.VendorID = Invoices.VendorID
  AND Invoices.InvoiceID = InvoiceLineItems.InvoiceID
  AND InvoiceLineItems.AccountNo = GLAccounts.AccountNo
  AND InvoiceTotal - PaymentTotal - CreditTotal > 0
ORDER BY VendorName, LineItemAmount DESC
```

The result set

	VendorName	InvoiceNumber	InvoiceDate	LineItemAmount	AccountDescription
1	Abbey Office Furnishings	203339-13	2002-05-02 00:00:00	17.5000	Office Supplies
2	Blue Cross	547480102	2002-05-19 00:00:00	224.0000	Group Insurance
3	Blue Cross	547481328	2002-05-20 00:00:00	224.0000	Group Insurance
4	Blue Cross	547479217	2002-05-17 00:00:00	116.0000	Group Insurance
5	Cardinal Business Media, Inc.	134116	2002-06-01 00:00:00	90.3600	Card Deck Advertising
6	Coffee Break Service	109596	2002-06-14 00:00:00	41.8000	Meals
7	Compuserve	2147483647	2002-05-09 00:00:00	9.9500	Books, Dues, and Subscriptions
8	Computerworld	367447	2002-05-31 00:00:00	2433.0000	Card Deck Advertising

Description

- Instead of coding a join condition in the FROM clause, you can code it in the WHERE clause along with any search conditions. Then, you simply list the tables you want to join in the FROM clause separated by commas.

- This syntax for coding joins is referred to as the *implicit syntax*, or the *theta syntax*. It was used prior to the SQL-92 standards, which introduced the explicit syntax.

- If you omit the join condition from the WHERE clause, a cross join is performed. You'll learn about cross joins later in this chapter.

Figure 4-7   How to use the implicit inner join syntax

How to work with outer joins

Although inner joins are the type of join you'll use most often, SQL Server also supports *outer joins*. Unlike an inner join, an outer join returns all of the rows from one or both tables involved in the join, regardless of whether the join condition is true. You'll see how this works in the topics that follow.

How to code an outer join

Figure 4-8 presents the explicit syntax for coding an outer join. Because this syntax is similar to the explicit syntax for inner joins, you shouldn't have any trouble understanding how it works. The main difference is that you include the LEFT, RIGHT, or FULL keyword to specify the type of outer join you want to perform. As you can see in the syntax, you can also include the OUTER keyword, but it's optional and is usually omitted.

The table in this figure summarizes the differences between left, right, and full outer joins. When you use a *left outer join*, the result set includes all the rows from the first, or left, table. Similarly, when you use a *right outer join*, the result set includes all the rows from the second, or right, table. And when you use a *full outer join*, the result set includes all the rows from both tables.

The example in this figure illustrates a left outer join. Here, the Vendors table is joined with the Invoices table. Notice that the result set includes vendor rows even if no matching invoices are found. In that case, null values are returned for the columns in the Invoices table.

When coding outer joins, it's a common practice to avoid using right joins. To do that, you can substitute a left outer join for a right outer join by reversing the order of the tables in the FROM clause and using the LEFT keyword instead of RIGHT. This often makes it easier to read statements that join more than two tables.

The explicit syntax for an outer join

```
SELECT select_list
FROM table_1
    {LEFT|RIGHT|FULL} [OUTER] JOIN table_2
        ON join_condition_1
    [{LEFT|RIGHT|FULL} [OUTER] JOIN table_3
        ON join_condition_2]...
```

What outer joins do

Joins of this type	Keep unmatched rows from
Left outer join	The first (left) table
Right outer join	The second (right) table
Full outer join	Both tables

A SELECT statement that uses a left outer join

```
SELECT VendorName, InvoiceNumber, InvoiceTotal
FROM Vendors LEFT JOIN Invoices
    ON Vendors.VendorID = Invoices.VendorID
ORDER BY VendorName
```

	VendorName	InvoiceNumber	InvoiceTotal
1	Abbey Office Furnishings	203339-13	17.5000
2	American Booksellers...	NULL	NULL
3	American Express	NULL	NULL
4	ASC Signs	NULL	NULL
5	Ascom Hasler Mailing...	NULL	NULL
6	AT&T	NULL	NULL
7	Aztek Label	NULL	NULL

(202 rows)

Description

- An *outer join* retrieves all rows that satisfy the join condition, plus unmatched rows in one or both tables.

- In most cases, you use the equal operator to retrieve rows with matching columns. However, you can also use any of the other comparison operators.

- When a row with unmatched columns is retrieved, any columns from the other table that are included in the result set are given null values.

Notes

- The OUTER keyword is optional and typically omitted.

- You can also code left outer joins and right outer joins using the implicit syntax. See figure 4-11 for more information.

Figure 4-8   How to code an outer join

Outer join examples

To give you a better understanding of how outer joins work, figure 4-9 presents three more examples. These examples use the Departments and Employees tables shown at the top of this figure. In each case, the join condition joins the tables based on the values in their DeptNo columns.

The first SELECT statement performs a left outer join on these two tables. In the result set produced by this statement, you can see that department number 3 is included in the result set even though none of the employees in the Employees table work in that department. Because of that, a null value is assigned to the LastName column from that table.

The second SELECT statement uses a right outer join. In this case, all of the rows from the Employees table are included in the result set. Notice, however, that two of the employees, Watson and Locario, are assigned to a department that doesn't exist in the Departments table. Of course, if the DeptNo column in this table had been defined as a foreign key to the Departments table, this would not have been allowed. In this case, though, a foreign key wasn't defined, so null values are returned for the DeptName column in these two rows.

The third SELECT statement in this figure illustrates a full outer join. If you compare the results of this query with the results of the queries that use a left and right outer join, you'll see that this is a combination of the two joins. In other words, each row in the Departments table is included in the result set, along with each row in the Employees table. Because the DeptNo column from both tables is included in this example, you can clearly identify the row in the Departments table that doesn't have a matching row in the Employees table and the two rows in the Employees table that don't have matching rows in the Departments table.

The Departments table

	DeptNo	DeptName
1	1	Accounting
2	2	Payroll
3	3	Operations
4	4	Personnel
5	5	Maintenance

The Employees table

	EmployeeID	LastName	FirstName	DeptNo
1	1	Smith	Cindy	2
2	2	Jones	Elmer	4
3	3	Simonian	Ralph	2
4	4	Hernandez	Olivia	1
5	5	Aaronsen	Robert	2
6	6	Watson	Denise	6
7	7	Brown	Dean	5
8	8	O'Leary	Rhea	4
9	9	Locario	Paulo	6

A left outer join

```
SELECT DeptName, Departments.DeptNo,
    LastName
FROM Departments LEFT JOIN Employees
    ON Departments.DeptNo =
        Employees.DeptNo
```

	DeptName	DeptNo	LastName
1	Accounting	1	Hernandez
2	Payroll	2	Smith
3	Payroll	2	Simonian
4	Payroll	2	Aaronsen
5	Operations	3	NULL
6	Personnel	4	Jones
7	Personnel	4	O'Leary
8	Maintenance	5	Brown

A right outer join

```
SELECT DeptName, Employees.DeptNo,
    LastName
FROM Departments RIGHT JOIN Employees
    ON Departments.DeptNo =
        Employees.DeptNo
```

	DeptName	DeptNo	LastName
1	Payroll	2	Smith
2	Personnel	4	Jones
3	Payroll	2	Simonian
4	Accounting	1	Hernandez
5	Payroll	2	Aaronsen
6	NULL	6	Watson
7	Maintenance	5	Brown
8	Personnel	4	O'Leary
9	NULL	6	Locario

A full outer join

```
SELECT DeptName, Departments.DeptNo,
    Employees.DeptNo, LastName
FROM Departments FULL JOIN Employees
    ON Departments.DeptNo =
        Employees.DeptNo
```

	DeptName	DeptNo	DeptNo	LastName
1	Accounting	1	1	Hernandez
2	Payroll	2	2	Simonian
3	Payroll	2	2	Smith
4	Payroll	2	2	Aaronsen
5	Operations	3	NULL	NULL
6	Personnel	4	4	O'Leary
7	Personnel	4	4	Jones
8	Maintenance	5	5	Brown
9	NULL	NULL	6	Watson
10	NULL	NULL	6	Locario

Description

- From these examples, you can see that none of the employees in the Employees table work in the Operations department, and two of the employees (Watson and Locario) work in a department that doesn't exist in the Departments table.

Figure 4-9   Outer join examples

Outer joins that join more than two tables

Like inner joins, you can use outer joins to join data from more than two tables. The two examples in figure 4-10 illustrate how this works. These examples use the Departments and Employees tables you saw in the previous figure, along with a Projects table. All three of these tables are shown at the top of this figure.

The first example in this figure uses left outer joins to join the data in the three tables. Here, you can see once again that none of the employees in the Employees table are assigned to the Operations department. Because of that, null values are returned for the columns in both the Employees and Projects tables. In addition, you can see that two employees, Brown and Jones, aren't assigned to a project.

The second example in this figure uses full outer joins to join the three tables. This result set includes unmatched rows from the Departments and Employees table just like the result set you saw in figure 4-9 that was created using a full outer join. In addition, the result set in this example includes an unmatched row from the Projects table: the one for project number P1014. In other words, none of the employees are assigned to this project.

The Departments table

	DeptNo	DeptName
1	1	Accounting
2	2	Payroll
3	3	Operations
4	4	Personnel
5	5	Maintenance

The Employees table

	EmployeeID	LastName	DeptNo
1	1	Smith	2
2	2	Jones	4
3	3	Simonian	2
4	4	Hernandez	1
5	5	Aaronsen	2
6	6	Watson	6
7	7	Brown	5
8	8	O'Leary	4
9	9	Locario	6

The Projects table

	ProjectNo	EmployeeID
1	P1011	8
2	P1011	4
3	P1012	3
4	P1012	1
5	P1012	5
6	P1013	6
7	P1013	9
8	P1014	10

A SELECT statement that joins the three tables using left outer joins

```
SELECT DeptName, LastName, ProjectNo
FROM Departments
    LEFT JOIN Employees
        ON Departments.DeptNo = Employees.DeptNo
    LEFT JOIN Projects
        ON Employees.EmployeeID = Projects.EmployeeID
ORDER BY DeptName, LastName, ProjectNo
```

The result set

	DeptName	LastName	ProjectNo
1	Accounting	Hernandez	P1011
2	Maintenance	Brown	NULL
3	Operations	NULL	NULL
4	Payroll	Aaronsen	P1012
5	Payroll	Simonian	P1012
6	Payroll	Smith	P1012
7	Personnel	Jones	NULL
8	Personnel	O'Leary	P1011

A SELECT statement that joins the three tables using full outer joins

```
SELECT DeptName, LastName, ProjectNo
FROM Departments
    FULL JOIN Employees
        ON Departments.DeptNo = Employees.DeptNo
    FULL JOIN Projects
        ON Employees.EmployeeID = Projects.EmployeeID
ORDER BY DeptName
```

The result set

	DeptName	LastName	ProjectNo
1	NULL	Watson	P1013
2	NULL	Locario	P1013
3	NULL	NULL	P1014
4	Accounting	Hernandez	P1011
5	Maintenance	Brown	NULL
6	Operations	NULL	NULL
7	Payroll	Aaronsen	P1012
8	Payroll	Simonian	P1012
9	Payroll	Smith	P1012
10	Personnel	Jones	NULL
11	Personnel	O'Leary	P1011

Figure 4-10   Outer joins that join more than two tables

How to use the implicit outer join syntax

Figure 4-11 presents the implicit syntax for coding outer joins. It's similar to the implicit syntax for coding inner joins. The difference is that you use the special operators shown in this figure to indicate whether you want to use a left or a right outer join. You can't code full outer joins using the implicit syntax.

The example in this figure shows how to use the implicit syntax to code a left outer join. This example joins data from the Vendors and Invoices tables just like the example you saw in figure 4-8. If you compare the result sets in these two examples, you'll see that they're identical.

Like inner joins, I don't recommend you use the implicit syntax for coding outer joins. However, you should be familiar with the implicit syntax so that you can maintain existing SQL code that uses this syntax. In fact, because Microsoft may not support the implicit syntax for outer joins in future releases of SQL Server, you may need to convert existing code to use the explicit syntax.

The implicit syntax for an outer join

```
SELECT select_list
FROM table_1, table_2 [, table 3]...
WHERE table_1.column_name {*=|=*} table_2.column_name
    [table_2.column_name {*=|=*} table_3.column_name]...
```

The implicit outer join operators

Operator	Description
*=	Left outer join
=*	Right outer join

A SELECT statement that joins two tables using a left outer join

```
SELECT VendorName, InvoiceNumber, InvoiceTotal
FROM Vendors, Invoices
WHERE Vendors.VendorID *= Invoices.VendorID
ORDER BY VendorName
```

	VendorName	InvoiceNumber	InvoiceTotal
1	Abbey Office Furnishings	203339-13	17.5000
2	American Booksellers...	NULL	NULL
3	American Express	NULL	NULL
4	ASC Signs	NULL	NULL
5	Ascom Hasler Mailing...	NULL	NULL
6	AT&T	NULL	NULL
7	Aztek Label	NULL	NULL

(202 rows)

Description

- You can use the join operators shown above to code an outer join condition in the WHERE clause instead of the FROM clause. Then, you simply list the tables you want to join in the FROM clause separated by commas.

- The syntax shown above is the implicit, or theta, syntax for outer joins. This was the only syntax in use prior to the SQL-92 standards.

- You can't perform a full outer join using the implicit syntax.

Figure 4-11   How to use the implicit outer join syntax

Other skills for working with joins

The two topics that follow present two additional skills for working with joins. In the first topic, you'll learn how to use inner and outer joins in the same statement. Then, in the second topic, you'll learn how to use another type of join, called a cross join.

How to combine inner and outer joins

Figure 4-12 shows how you can combine inner and outer joins. In this example, the Departments table is joined with the Employees table using an inner join. The result is an interim table that includes departments with one or more employees. Notice that the EmployeeID column is shown in this table even though it's not included in the final result set. That's because it's used by the join that follows.

After the Departments and Employees tables are joined, the interim table is joined with the Projects table using a left outer join. The result is a table that includes all of the departments that have employees assigned to them, all of the employees assigned to those departments, and the projects those employees are assigned. Here, you can clearly see that two employees, Brown and Jones, haven't been assigned projects.

The Departments table

	DeptNo	DeptName
1	1	Accounting
2	2	Payroll
3	3	Operations
4	4	Personnel
5	5	Maintenance

The Employees table

	EmployeeID	LastName	DeptNo
1	1	Smith	2
2	2	Jones	4
3	3	Simonian	2
4	4	Hernandez	1
5	5	Aaronsen	2
6	6	Watson	6
7	7	Brown	5
8	8	O'Leary	4
9	9	Locario	6

The Projects table

	ProjectNo	EmployeeID
1	P1011	8
2	P1011	4
3	P1012	3
4	P1012	1
5	P1012	5
6	P1013	6
7	P1013	9
8	P1014	10

A SELECT statement that combines an outer and an inner join

```
SELECT DeptName, LastName, ProjectNo
FROM Departments
    JOIN Employees
        ON Departments.DeptNo = Employees.DeptNo
    LEFT JOIN Projects
        ON Employees.EmployeeID = Projects.EmployeeID
ORDER BY DeptName
```

The interim table

	DeptName	LastName	EmployeeID
1	Payroll	Smith	1
2	Personnel	Jones	2
3	Payroll	Simonian	3
4	Accounting	Hernandez	4
5	Payroll	Aaronsen	5
6	Maintenance	Brown	7
7	Personnel	O'Leary	8

The result set

	DeptName	LastName	ProjectNo
1	Accounting	Hernandez	P1011
2	Maintenance	Brown	NULL
3	Payroll	Aaronsen	P1012
4	Payroll	Simonian	P1012
5	Payroll	Smith	P1012
6	Personnel	Jones	NULL
7	Personnel	O'Leary	P1011

Description

- You can combine inner and outer joins within a single SELECT statement using the explicit join syntax. You can't combine inner and outer joins using the implicit syntax.

Figure 4-12   How to combine inner and outer joins

How to use cross joins

A *cross join* produces a result set that includes each row from the first table joined with each row from the second table. The result set is known as the *Cartesian product* of the tables. Figure 4-13 shows how to code a cross join using either the explicit or implicit syntax.

To use the explicit syntax, you include the CROSS JOIN keywords between the two tables in the FROM clause. Notice that because of the way a cross join works, you don't include a join condition. The same is true when you use the implicit syntax. In that case, you simply list the tables in the FROM clause and omit the join condition from the WHERE clause.

The two SELECT statements in this figure illustrate how cross joins work. Both of these statements combine data from the Departments and Employees tables. As you can see, the result is a table that includes 45 rows. That's each of the five rows in the Departments table combined with each of the nine rows in the Employees table. Although this result set is relatively small, you can imagine how large it would be if the tables included hundreds or thousands of rows.

As you study these examples, you should realize that cross joins have few practical uses. As a result, you'll rarely, if ever, need to use one.

How to code a cross join using the explicit syntax

The explicit syntax for a cross join

```
SELECT select_list
FROM table_1 CROSS JOIN table_2
```

A cross join that uses the explicit syntax

```
SELECT Departments.DeptNo, DeptName, EmployeeID, LastName
FROM Departments CROSS JOIN Employees
ORDER BY Departments.DeptNo
```

How to code a cross join using the implicit syntax

The implicit syntax for a cross join

```
SELECT select_list
FROM table_1, table_2
```

A cross join that uses the implicit syntax

```
SELECT Departments.DeptNo, DeptName, EmployeeID, LastName
FROM Departments, Employees
ORDER BY Departments.DeptNo
```

The result set created by the statements above

	DeptNo	DeptName	EmployeeID	LastName
1	1	Accounting	1	Smith
2	1	Accounting	2	Jones
3	1	Accounting	3	Simonian
4	1	Accounting	4	Hernandez
5	1	Accounting	5	Aaronsen
6	1	Accounting	6	Watson
7	1	Accounting	7	Brown

(45 rows)

Description

- A *cross join* joins each row from the first table with each row from the second table. The result set returned by a cross join is known as a *Cartesian product*.

- To code a cross join using the explicit syntax, use the CROSS JOIN keywords in the FROM clause.

- To code a cross join using the implicit syntax, list the tables in the FROM clause and omit the join condition from the WHERE clause.

Figure 4-13   How to use cross joins

How to work with unions

Like a join, a *union* combines data from two or more tables. Instead of combining columns from base tables, however, a union combines rows from two or more result sets. You'll see how that works in the topics that follow.

The syntax of a union

Figure 4-14 shows how to code a union. As the syntax shows, you create a union by connecting two or more SELECT statements with the UNION operator. For this to work, the result of each SELECT statement must have the same number of columns, and the data types of the corresponding columns in each table must be compatible.

If you want to sort the result of a union operation, you can code an ORDER BY clause after the last SELECT statement. Note that the column names you use in this clause must be the same as those used in the first SELECT statement. That's because the column names you use in the first SELECT statement are the ones that are used in the result set.

By default, a union operation removes duplicate rows from the result set. If that's not what you want, you can include the ALL keyword. In most cases, though, you'll omit this keyword.

Unions that combine data from different tables

The example in this figure shows how to use a union to combine data from two different tables. In this case, the ActiveInvoices table contains invoices with outstanding balances, and the PaidInvoices table contains invoices that have been paid in full. Both of these tables have the same structure as the Invoices table you've seen in previous figures.

This union operation combines the rows in both tables that have an invoice date on or after 6/1/2002. Notice that the first SELECT statement includes a column named Source that contains the literal value "Active." The second SELECT statement includes a column by the same name, but it contains the literal value "Paid." This column is used to indicate which table each row in the result set came from.

Although this column is assigned the same name in both SELECT statements, you should realize that doesn't have to be the case. In fact, none of the columns have to have the same names. Corresponding columns do have to have compatible data types. But the corresponding relationships are determined by the order in which the columns are coded in the SELECT clauses, not by their names. When you use column aliases, though, you'll typically assign the same name to corresponding columns so that the statement is easier to understand.

The syntax for a union operation

```
    SELECT_statement_1
UNION [ALL]
    SELECT_statement_2
[UNION [ALL]
    SELECT_statement_3]...
[ORDER BY order_by_list]
```

A union that combines invoice data from two different tables

```
    SELECT 'Active' AS Source, InvoiceNumber, InvoiceDate, InvoiceTotal
    FROM ActiveInvoices
    WHERE InvoiceDate >= '06/01/2002'
UNION
    SELECT 'Paid' AS Source, InvoiceNumber, InvoiceDate, InvoiceTotal
    FROM PaidInvoices
    WHERE InvoiceDate >= '06/01/2002'
ORDER BY InvoiceTotal DESC
```

The result set

	Source	InvoiceNumber	InvoiceDate	InvoiceTotal
1	Active	40318	2002-07-18 00:00:00	21842.0000
2	Paid	P02-3772	2002-06-03 00:00:00	7125.3400
3	Paid	10843	2002-06-04 00:00:00	4901.2600
4	Paid	77290	2002-06-04 00:00:00	1750.0000
5	Paid	RTR-72-3662-X	2002-06-04 00:00:00	1600.0000
6	Paid	75C-90227	2002-06-06 00:00:00	1367.5000
7	Paid	P02-88D77S7	2002-06-06 00:00:00	856.9200
8	Active	I77271-001	2002-06-05 00:00:00	662.0000
9	Active	9982771	2002-06-03 00:00:00	503.2000
10	Paid	121897	2002-06-01 00:00:00	450.0000

(22 rows)

Description

- A *union* combines the result sets of two or more SELECT statements into one result set.
- Each result set must return the same number of columns, and the corresponding columns in each result set must have the same data type.
- By default, a union eliminates duplicate rows. If you want to include duplicate rows, code the ALL keyword.
- The column names in the final result set are taken from the first SELECT clause. Column aliases assigned by the other SELECT clauses have no effect on the final result set.
- To sort the rows in the final result set, code an ORDER BY clause after the last SELECT statement. This clause must refer to the column names assigned in the first SELECT clause.

Figure 4-14   How to combine data from different tables

Unions that combine data from the same table

Figure 4-15 shows how to use unions to combine data from a single table. In the first example, rows from the Invoices table that have a balance due are combined with rows from the same table that are paid in full. As in the example in the previous figure, a column named Source is added at the beginning of each interim table. That way, the final result set indicates whether each invoice is active or paid.

The second example in this figure shows how you can use a union with data that's joined from two tables. Here, each SELECT statement joins data from the Invoices and Vendors tables. The first SELECT statement retrieves invoices with totals greater than $10,000. Then, it calculates a payment of 33% of the invoice total. The two other SELECT statements are similar. The second one retrieves invoices with totals between $500 and $10,000 and calculates a 50% payment. And the third one retrieves invoices with totals less than $500 and sets the payment amount at 100% of the total. Although this is somewhat unrealistic, it helps illustrate the flexibility of union operations.

Notice in this example that the same column aliases are assigned in each SELECT statement. Although that's not required, I think you'll see that it makes the query easier to read. In particular, it makes it easy to see that the three SELECT statements have the same number and types of columns.

A union that combines information from the Invoices table

```
    SELECT 'Active' AS Source, InvoiceNumber, InvoiceDate, InvoiceTotal
    FROM Invoices
    WHERE InvoiceTotal - PaymentTotal - CreditTotal > 0
UNION
    SELECT 'Paid' AS Source, InvoiceNumber, InvoiceDate, InvoiceTotal
    FROM Invoices
    WHERE InvoiceTotal - PaymentTotal - CreditTotal <= 0
ORDER BY InvoiceTotal DESC
```

The result set

	Source	InvoiceNumber	InvoiceDate	InvoiceTotal
1	Paid	0-2058	2002-05-08 00:00:00	37966.1900
2	Paid	P-0259	2002-04-16 00:00:00	26881.4000
3	Paid	0-2060	2002-05-08 00:00:00	23517.5800
4	Active	40318	2002-07-18 00:00:00	21842.0000
5	Active	P-0608	2002-04-11 00:00:00	20551.1800

(114 rows)

A union that combines payment data from the same joined tables

```
    SELECT InvoiceNumber, VendorName, '33% Payment' AS PaymentType,
        InvoiceTotal AS Total, (InvoiceTotal * 0.333) AS Payment
    FROM Invoices JOIN Vendors
        ON Invoices.VendorID = Vendors.VendorID
    WHERE InvoiceTotal > 10000
UNION
    SELECT InvoiceNumber, VendorName, '50% Payment' AS PaymentType,
        InvoiceTotal AS Total, (InvoiceTotal * 0.5) AS Payment
    FROM Invoices JOIN Vendors
        ON Invoices.VendorID = Vendors.VendorID
    WHERE InvoiceTotal BETWEEN 500 AND 10000
UNION
    SELECT InvoiceNumber, VendorName, 'Full amount' AS PaymentType,
        InvoiceTotal AS Total, InvoiceTotal AS Payment
    FROM Invoices JOIN Vendors
        ON Invoices.VendorID = Vendors.VendorID
    WHERE InvoiceTotal < 500
ORDER BY PaymentType, VendorName, InvoiceNumber
```

The result set

	InvoiceNumber	VendorName	PaymentType	Total	Payment
6	P-0608	Malloy Lithographing Inc	33% Payment	20551.1800	6843.5429400
7	509786	Bertelsmann Industry Svcs. Inc	50% Payment	6940.2500	3470.1250000
8	587056	Cahners Publishing Company	50% Payment	2184.5000	1092.2500000
9	367447	Computerworld	50% Payment	2433.0000	1216.5000000

(113 rows)

Figure 4-15   Unions that combine data from the same table

Perspective

In this chapter, you learned a variety of techniques for combining data from two or more tables into a single result set. In particular, you learned how to use the SQL-92 syntax for combining data using inner joins. Of all the techniques presented in this chapter, this is the one you'll use most often. So you'll want to be sure you understand it thoroughly before you go on.

Terms

join	interim result set
join condition	interim table
inner join	implicit syntax
ad hoc relationship	theta syntax
qualified column name	outer join
explicit syntax	left outer join
correlation name	right outer join
table alias	full outer join
fully-qualified object name	cross join
partially-qualified object name	Cartesian product
self-join	union

5

How to code summary queries

In this chapter, you'll learn how to code queries that summarize data. For example, you can use summary queries to report sales totals by vendor or state, or to get a count of the number of invoices that were processed each day of the month. You'll also learn how to use a special type of function called an aggregate function. Aggregate functions allow you to easily do jobs like figure averages or totals, or find the highest value for a given column. So you'll use them frequently in your summary queries.

How to work with aggregate functions

In chapter 3, you were introduced to *scalar functions*, which operate on a single value and return a single value. In this chapter, you'll learn how to use *aggregate functions*, which operate on a series of values and return a single summary value. Because aggregate functions typically operate on the values in columns, they are sometimes referred to as *column functions*. A query that contains one or more aggregate functions is typically referred to as a *summary query*.

How to code aggregate functions

Figure 5-1 presents the syntax of the most common aggregate functions. Since the purpose of these functions is self-explanatory, I'll focus mainly on how you use them.

All of the functions but one operate on an expression. In the query in this figure, for example, the expression that's coded for the SUM function calculates the balance due of an invoice using the InvoiceTotal, PaymentTotal, and CreditTotal columns. The result is a single value that represents the total amount due for all the selected invoices. If you look at the WHERE clause in this example, you'll see that includes only those invoices with a balance due.

In addition to an expression, you can also code the ALL or DISTINCT keyword in these functions. ALL is the default, which means that all values are included in the calculation. The exceptions are null values, which are always excluded from these functions.

If you don't want duplicate values included, you can code the DISTINCT keyword. In most cases, you'll use DISTINCT only with the COUNT function. You'll see an example of that in the next figure. You won't use it with MIN or MAX because it has no effect on those functions. And it doesn't usually make sense to use it with the AVG and SUM functions.

Unlike the other aggregate functions, you can't use the ALL or DISTINCT keywords or an expression with COUNT(*). Instead, you code this function exactly as shown in the syntax. The value returned by this function is the number of rows in the base table that satisfy the search condition of the query, including rows with null values. The COUNT(*) function in the query in this figure, for example, indicates that the Invoices table contains 40 invoices with a balance due.

The syntax of the aggregate functions

Function syntax	Result
`AVG([ALL|DISTINCT] expression)`	The average of the non-null values in the expression.
`SUM([ALL|DISTINCT] expression)`	The total of the non-null values in the expression.
`MIN([ALL|DISTINCT] expression)`	The lowest non-null value in the expression.
`MAX([ALL|DISTINCT] expression)`	The highest non-null value in the expression.
`COUNT([ALL|DISTINCT] expression)`	The number of non-null values in the expression.
`COUNT(*)`	The number of rows selected by the query.

A summary query that counts unpaid invoices and calculates the total due

```
SELECT COUNT(*) AS NumberOfInvoices,
    SUM(InvoiceTotal - PaymentTotal - CreditTotal) AS TotalDue
FROM Invoices
WHERE InvoiceTotal - PaymentTotal - CreditTotal > 0
```

The result set

	NumberOfInvoices	TotalDue
1	40	66796.2400

Description

- *Aggregate functions*, also called *column functions*, perform a calculation on the values in a set of selected rows. You specify the values to be used in the calculation by coding an expression for the function's argument. In many cases, the expression is just the name of a column.

- A SELECT statement that includes an aggregate function can be called a *summary query*.

- The expression you specify for the AVG and SUM functions must result in a numeric value. The expression for the MIN, MAX, and COUNT functions can result in a numeric, date, or string value.

- By default, all values are included in the calculation regardless of whether they're duplicated. If you want to omit duplicate values, code the DISTINCT keyword. This keyword is typically used only with the COUNT function.

- All of the aggregate functions except for COUNT(*) ignore null values.

- Aggregate functions are often used with the GROUP BY clause of the SELECT statement, which is used to group the rows in a result set. See figure 5-3 for more information.

- If you code an aggregate function in the SELECT clause, that clause can't include non-aggregate columns from the base table.

Figure 5-1   How to code aggregate functions

Queries that use aggregate functions

Figure 5-2 presents four more queries that use aggregate functions. Before I describe these queries, you should know that with two exceptions, a SELECT clause that contains an aggregate function can contain only aggregate functions. The first exception is if the column specification results in a literal value. This is illustrated by the first column in the first two queries in this figure. The second exception is if the query includes a GROUP BY clause. Then, the SELECT clause can include any columns specified in the GROUP BY clause. You'll see how you use the GROUP BY clause later in this chapter.

The first two queries in this figure use the COUNT(*) function to count the number of rows in the Invoices table that satisfy the search condition. In both cases, only those invoices with invoice dates after 1/1/2002 are included in the count. In addition, the first query uses the AVG function to calculate the average amount of those invoices and the SUM function to calculate the total amount of those invoices. In contrast, the second query uses the MIN and MAX functions to calculate the minimum and maximum invoice amounts.

Although the MIN, MAX, and COUNT functions are typically used on columns that contain numeric data, they can also be used on columns that contain character or date data. In the third query, for example, they're used on the VendorName column in the Vendors table. Here, the MIN function returns the name of the vendor that's lowest in the sort sequence, the MAX function returns the name of the vendor that's highest in the sort sequence, and the COUNT function returns the total number of vendors. Note that since the VendorName column can't contain null values, the COUNT(*) function would have returned the same result.

The fourth query illustrates how using the DISTINCT keyword can affect the result of a COUNT function. Here, the first COUNT function uses the DISTINCT keyword to count the number of vendors that have invoices dated 1/1/2002 or later in the Invoices table. To do that, it looks for distinct values in the VendorID column. In contrast, because the second COUNT function doesn't include the DISTINCT keyword, it counts every invoice that's dated 1/1/2002 or later. Of course, you could accomplish the same thing using the COUNT(*) function. I used COUNT(VendorID) here only to illustrate the difference between coding and not coding the DISTINCT keyword.

A summary query that uses the COUNT, AVG, and SUM functions

```
SELECT 'After 1/1/2002' AS SelectionDate, COUNT(*) AS NumberOfInvoices,
    AVG(InvoiceTotal) AS AverageInvoiceAmount,
    SUM(InvoiceTotal) AS TotalInvoiceAmount
FROM Invoices
WHERE InvoiceDate > '2002-01-01'
```

	SelectionDate	NumberOfInvoices	AverageInvoiceAmount	TotalInvoiceAmount
1	After 1/1/2002	114	1879.7413	214290.5100

A summary query that uses the MIN and MAX functions

```
SELECT 'After 1/1/2002' AS SelectionDate, COUNT(*) AS NumberOfInvoices,
    MAX(InvoiceTotal) AS HighestInvoiceTotal,
    MIN(InvoiceTotal) AS LowestInvoiceTotal
FROM Invoices
WHERE InvoiceDate > '2002-01-01'
```

	SelectionDate	NumberOfInvoices	HighestInvoiceTotal	LowestInvoiceTotal
1	After 1/1/2002	114	37966.1900	6.0000

A summary query that works on non-numeric columns

```
SELECT MIN(VendorName) AS FirstVendor,
    MAX(VendorName) AS LastVendor,
    COUNT(VendorName) AS NumberOfVendors
FROM Vendors
```

	FirstVendor	LastVendor	NumberOfVendors
1	Abbey Office Furnishings	Zylka Design	122

A summary query that uses the DISTINCT keyword

```
SELECT COUNT(DISTINCT VendorID) AS NumberOfVendors,
    COUNT(VendorID) AS NumberOfInvoices,
    AVG(InvoiceTotal) AS AverageInvoiceAmount,
    SUM(InvoiceTotal) AS TotalInvoiceAmount
FROM Invoices
WHERE InvoiceDate > '2002-01-01'
```

	NumberOfVendors	NumberOfInvoices	AverageInvoiceAmount	TotalInvoiceAmount
1	34	114	1879.7413	214290.5100

Notes

- If you want to count all of the selected rows, you'll typically use the COUNT(*) function as illustrated by the first two examples above. An alternative is to code the name of any column in the base table that can't contain null values, as illustrated by the third example.
- If you want to count only the rows with unique values in a specified column, you can code the COUNT function with the DISTINCT keyword followed by the name of the column, as illustrated in the fourth example.

Figure 5-2   Queries that use aggregate functions

How to group and summarize data

Now that you understand how aggregate functions work, you're ready to learn how to group data and use aggregate functions to summarize the data in each group. To do that, you need to learn about two new clauses of the SELECT statement: GROUP BY and HAVING.

How to code the GROUP BY and HAVING clauses

Figure 5-3 presents the syntax of the SELECT statement with the GROUP BY and HAVING clauses. The GROUP BY clause determines how the selected rows are grouped, and the HAVING clause determines which groups are included in the final results. As you can see, these clauses are coded after the WHERE clause but before the ORDER BY clause. That makes sense because the search condition in the WHERE clause is applied before the rows are grouped, and the sort sequence in the ORDER BY clause is applied after the rows are grouped.

In the GROUP BY clause, you list one or more columns or expressions separated by commas. Then, the rows that satisfy the search condition in the WHERE clause are grouped by those columns or expressions in descending sequence. That means that a single row is returned for each unique set of values in the GROUP BY columns. This will make more sense when you see the examples in the next figure that group by two columns. For now, take a look at the example in this figure that groups by a single column.

This example calculates the average invoice amount for each vendor who has invoices in the Invoices table that average over $2,000. To do that, it groups the invoices by VendorID. Then, the AVG function calculates the average of the InvoiceTotal column. Because this query includes a GROUP BY clause, this function calculates the average invoice total for each group rather than for the entire result set. In that case, the aggregate function is called a *vector aggregate*. In contrast, aggregate functions like the ones you saw earlier in this chapter that return a single value for all the rows in a result set are called *scalar aggregates*.

The example in this figure also includes a HAVING clause. The search condition in this clause specifies that only those vendors with invoices that average over $2,000 should be included. Note that this condition must be applied after the rows are grouped and the average for each group has been calculated.

In addition to the AVG function, the SELECT clause includes the VendorID column. That makes sense since the rows are grouped by this column. However, you should know that the columns used in the GROUP BY clause don't have to be included in the SELECT clause.

The syntax of the SELECT statement with the GROUP BY and HAVING clauses

```
SELECT select_list
FROM table_source
[WHERE search_condition]
[GROUP BY group_by_list]
[HAVING search_condition]
[ORDER BY order_by_list]
```

A summary query that calculates the average invoice amount by vendor

```
SELECT VendorID, AVG(InvoiceTotal) AS AverageInvoiceAmount
FROM Invoices
GROUP BY VendorID
HAVING AVG(InvoiceTotal) > 2000
ORDER BY AverageInvoiceAmount DESC
```

	VendorID	AverageInvoiceAmount
1	110	23978.4820
2	72	10963.6550
3	104	7125.3400
4	99	6940.2500
5	119	4901.2600
6	122	2575.3288
7	86	2433.0000
8	100	2184.5000

Description

- The GROUP BY clause groups the rows of a result set based on one or more columns or expressions. It's typically used in SELECT statements that include aggregate functions.

- If you include aggregate functions in the SELECT clause, the aggregate is calculated for each set of values that result from the columns named in the GROUP BY clause.

- If you include two or more columns or expressions in the GROUP BY clause, they form a hierarchy where each column or expression is subordinate to the previous one.

- When a SELECT statement includes a GROUP BY clause, the SELECT clause can include aggregate functions, the columns used for grouping, and expressions that result in a constant value.

- A group-by list typically consists of the names of one or more columns separated by commas. However, it can contain any expression except for those that contain aggregate functions.

- The HAVING clause specifies a search condition for a group or an aggregate. This condition is applied after the rows that satisfy the search condition in the WHERE clause are grouped.

Figure 5-3   How to code the GROUP BY and HAVING clauses

Queries that use the GROUP BY and HAVING clauses

Figure 5-4 presents three more queries that group data. If you understood the query in the last figure, you shouldn't have any trouble understanding how the first query in this figure works. It groups the rows in the Invoices table by VendorID and returns a count of the number of invoices for each vendor.

The second query in this figure illustrates how you can group by more than one column. Here, a join is used to combine the VendorState and VendorCity columns from the Vendors table with a count and average of the invoices in the Invoices table. Because the rows are grouped by both state and city, a row is returned for each state and city combination. Then, the ORDER BY clause sorts the rows by city within state. Without this clause, the rows would be returned in no particular sequence.

The third query is identical to the second query except that it includes a HAVING clause. This clause uses the COUNT function to limit the state and city groups that are included in the result set to those that have two or more invoices. In other words, it excludes groups that have only one invoice.

A summary query that counts the number of invoices by vendor

```
SELECT VendorID, COUNT(*) AS InvoiceQty
FROM Invoices
GROUP BY VendorID
```

	VendorID	InvoiceQty
1	34	2
2	37	3
3	48	1
4	72	2
5	80	2

(34 rows)

A summary query that calculates the number of invoices and the average invoice amount for the vendors in each state and city

```
SELECT VendorState, VendorCity, COUNT(*) AS InvoiceQty,
    AVG(InvoiceTotal) AS InvoiceAvg
FROM Invoices JOIN Vendors
    ON Invoices.VendorID = Vendors.VendorID
GROUP BY VendorState, VendorCity
ORDER BY VendorState, VendorCity
```

	VendorState	VendorCity	InvoiceQty	InvoiceAvg
1	AZ	Phoenix	1	662.0000
2	CA	Fresno	19	1208.7457
3	CA	Los Angeles	1	503.2000
4	CA	Oxnard	3	188.0000
5	CA	Pasadena	5	196.1200

(20 rows)

A summary query that limits the groups to those with two or more invoices

```
SELECT VendorState, VendorCity, COUNT(*) AS InvoiceQty,
    AVG(InvoiceTotal) AS InvoiceAvg
FROM Invoices JOIN Vendors
    ON Invoices.VendorID = Vendors.VendorID
GROUP BY VendorState, VendorCity
HAVING COUNT(*) >= 2
ORDER BY VendorState, VendorCity
```

	VendorState	VendorCity	InvoiceQty	InvoiceAvg
1	CA	Fresno	19	1208.7457
2	CA	Oxnard	3	188.0000
3	CA	Pasadena	5	196.1200
4	CA	Sacramento	7	253.0014
5	CA	San Francisco	3	1211.0400

(12 rows)

Note

- You can use a join with a summary query to group and summarize the data in two or more tables.

Figure 5-4   Queries that use the GROUP BY and HAVING clauses

How the HAVING clause compares to the WHERE clause

As you've seen, you can limit the groups included in a result set by coding a search condition in the HAVING clause. In addition, you can apply a search condition to each row before it's included in a group. To do that, you code the search condition in the WHERE clause just as you would for any SELECT statement. To make sure you understand the differences between search conditions coded in the HAVING and WHERE clauses, figure 5-5 presents two examples.

In the first example, the invoices in the Invoices table are grouped by vendor name, and a count and average invoice amount are calculated for each group. Then, the HAVING clause limits the groups in the result set to those that have an average invoice total greater than $500.

In contrast, the second example includes a search condition in the WHERE clause that limits the invoices included in the groups to those that have an invoice total greater than $500. In other words, the search condition in this example is applied to every row. In the previous example, it was applied to each group of rows.

Beyond this, there are also two differences in the expressions that you can include in the WHERE and HAVING clauses. First, the HAVING clause can include aggregate functions as you saw in the first example in this figure, but the WHERE clause can't. That's because the search condition in a WHERE clause is applied before the rows are grouped. Second, although the WHERE clause can refer to any column in the base tables, the HAVING clause can only refer to columns included in the SELECT clause. That's because it filters the summarized result set that's defined by the SELECT, FROM, WHERE, and GROUP BY clauses. In other words, it doesn't filter the base tables.

A summary query with a search condition in the HAVING clause

```
SELECT VendorName, COUNT(*) AS InvoiceQty,
    AVG(InvoiceTotal) AS InvoiceAvg
FROM Vendors JOIN Invoices
    ON Vendors.VendorID = Invoices.VendorID
GROUP BY VendorName
HAVING AVG(InvoiceTotal) > 500
ORDER BY InvoiceQty DESC
```

	VendorName	InvoiceQty	InvoiceAvg
1	United Parcel Service	9	2575.3288
2	Zylka Design	8	714.8737
3	Malloy Lithographing Inc	5	23978.4820
4	Ingram	2	1077.2100
5	IBM	2	600.0600

(19 rows)

A summary query with a search condition in the WHERE clause

```
SELECT VendorName, COUNT(*) AS InvoiceQty,
    AVG(InvoiceTotal) AS InvoiceAvg
FROM Vendors JOIN Invoices
    ON Vendors.VendorID = Invoices.VendorID
WHERE InvoiceTotal > 500
GROUP BY VendorName
ORDER BY InvoiceQty DESC
```

	VendorName	InvoiceQty	InvoiceAvg
1	United Parcel Service	9	2575.3288
2	Malloy Lithographing Inc	5	23978.4820
3	Zylka Design	5	963.7600
4	Ingram	2	1077.2100
5	IBM	1	1083.5800

(20 rows)

Description

- When you include a WHERE clause in a SELECT statement that uses grouping and aggregates, the search condition is applied before the rows are grouped and the aggregates are calculated. That way, only the rows that satisfy the search condition are grouped and summarized.

- When you include a HAVING clause in a SELECT statement that uses grouping and aggregates, the search condition is applied after the rows are grouped and the aggregates are calculated. That way, only the groups that satisfy the search condition are included in the result set.

- A HAVING clause can only refer to a column included in the SELECT clause. A WHERE clause can refer to any column in the base tables.

- Aggregate functions can only be coded in the HAVING clause. A WHERE clause can't contain aggregate functions.

Figure 5-5   How the HAVING clause compares to the WHERE clause

How to code complex search conditions

You can code compound search conditions in a HAVING clause just as you can in a WHERE clause. This is illustrated by the first query in figure 5-6. This query groups invoices by invoice date and calculates a count of the invoices and the sum of the invoice totals for each date. In addition, the HAVING clause specifies three conditions. First, the invoice date must be between 5/1/2002 and 5/31/2002. Second, the invoice count must be greater than 1. And third, the sum of the invoice totals must be greater than $100.

Because the second and third conditions in the HAVING clause in this query include aggregate functions, they must be coded in the HAVING clause. The first condition, however, doesn't include an aggregate function, so it could be coded in either the HAVING or WHERE clause. The second statement in this figure, for example, shows this condition coded in the WHERE clause. Note that the query returns the same result set regardless of where you code this condition.

So how do you know where to code a search condition? In general, I think your code will be easier to read if you include all the search conditions in the HAVING clause. If, on the other hand, you prefer to code non-aggregate search conditions in the WHERE clause, that's OK, too.

Since a search condition in the WHERE clause is applied before the rows are grouped while a search condition in the HAVING clause isn't applied until after the grouping, you might expect a performance advantage by coding all search conditions in the HAVING clause. However, SQL Server takes care of this performance issue for you when it optimizes the query. To do that, it automatically moves search conditions to whichever clause will result in the best performance, as long as that doesn't change the logic of your query. As a result, you can code search conditions wherever they result in the most readable code without worrying about system performance.

A summary query with a compound condition in the HAVING clause

```
SELECT InvoiceDate, COUNT(*) AS InvoiceQty, SUM(InvoiceTotal) AS InvoiceSum
FROM Invoices
GROUP BY InvoiceDate
HAVING InvoiceDate BETWEEN '2002-05-01' AND '2002-05-31'
    AND COUNT(*) > 1
    AND SUM(InvoiceTotal) > 100
ORDER BY InvoiceDate DESC
```

The same query coded with a WHERE clause

```
SELECT InvoiceDate, COUNT(*) AS InvoiceQty, SUM(InvoiceTotal) AS InvoiceSum
FROM Invoices
WHERE InvoiceDate BETWEEN '2002-05-01' AND '2002-05-31'
GROUP BY InvoiceDate
HAVING COUNT(*) > 1
    AND SUM(InvoiceTotal) > 100
ORDER BY InvoiceDate DESC
```

The result set returned by both queries

	InvoiceDate	InvoiceQty	InvoiceSum
1	2002-05-31 00:00:00	3	11557.7500
2	2002-05-23 00:00:00	6	2761.1700
3	2002-05-22 00:00:00	2	442.5000
4	2002-05-20 00:00:00	3	308.6400
5	2002-05-19 00:00:00	2	266.6700
6	2002-05-18 00:00:00	5	208.6600
7	2002-05-17 00:00:00	3	156.7500
8	2002-05-14 00:00:00	3	374.7500
9	2002-05-13 00:00:00	5	574.7500
10	2002-05-11 00:00:00	4	216.5000

(15 rows)

Description

- You can use the AND and OR operators to code compound search conditions in a HAVING clause just as you can in a WHERE clause.

- If a search condition includes an aggregate function, it must be coded in the HAVING clause. Otherwise, it can be coded in either the HAVING or the WHERE clause.

- In most cases, your code will be easier to read if you code all the search conditions in the HAVING clause, but you can code non-aggregate search conditions in the WHERE clause, if you prefer.

Figure 5-6   How to code complex search conditions

How to summarize data using SQL Server extensions

So far, this chapter has discussed standard SQL keywords and functions. However, you should also know about two extensions SQL Server provides for summarizing data: the ROLLUP and CUBE operators. You'll learn how to use these operators in the topics that follow.

How to use the ROLLUP operator

You can use the ROLLUP operator to add one or more summary rows to a result set that uses grouping and aggregates. The two examples in figure 5-7 illustrate how this works.

The first example shows how the ROLLUP operator works when you group by a single column. Here, the invoices in the Invoices table are grouped by VendorID, and an invoice count and invoice total are calculated for each vendor. Notice that because the WITH ROLLUP phrase is included in the GROUP BY clause, an additional row is added at the end of the result set. This row summarizes all the aggregate columns in the result set. In this case, it summarizes the InvoiceCount and InvoiceTotal columns. Because the VendorID column can't be summarized, it's assigned a null value.

The second query in this figure shows how the ROLLUP operator works when you group by two columns. This query groups the vendors in the Vendors table by state and city and counts the number of vendors in each group. Notice that in addition to a summary row at the end of the result set, summary rows are included for each state.

You should also notice the ORDER BY clause in this query. It causes the rows in the result set to be sorted by city in descending sequence within state in descending sequence. The reason these columns are sorted in descending sequence is that the sort is performed after the summary rows are added to the result set, and those rows have null values in the VendorCity column. In addition, the final summary row has a null value in the VendorState column. So if you sorted these columns in ascending sequence, the rows with null values would appear before the rows they summarize, which isn't what you want.

You can also use another function, the GROUPING function, to work with null columns in a summary row. However, this function is typically used in conjunction with the CASE function, which you'll learn about in chapter 8. So I'll present the GROUPING function in that chapter.

A summary query that includes a final summary row

```
SELECT VendorID, COUNT(*) AS InvoiceCount,
    SUM(InvoiceTotal) AS InvoiceTotal
FROM Invoices
GROUP BY VendorID WITH ROLLUP
```

	VendorID	InvoiceCount	InvoiceTotal
30	117	1	16.6200
31	119	1	4901.2600
32	121	8	6940.2500
33	122	9	23177.9600
34	123	47	4378.0200
35	NULL	114	214290.5100	—— Summary row

A summary query that includes a summary row for each grouping level

```
SELECT VendorState, VendorCity, COUNT(*) AS QtyVendors
FROM Vendors
WHERE VendorState IN ('IA', 'NJ')
GROUP BY VendorState, VendorCity WITH ROLLUP
ORDER BY VendorState DESC, VendorCity DESC
```

	VendorState	VendorCity	QtyVendors
1	NJ	Washington	1
2	NJ	Fairfield	1
3	NJ	East Brunswick	2
4	NJ	NULL	4	—— Summary row for state 'NJ'
5	IA	Washington	1
6	IA	Fairfield	1
7	IA	NULL	2	—— Summary row for state 'IA'
8	NULL	NULL	6	—— Summary row for all rows

Description

- You can use the WITH ROLLUP phrase in the GROUP BY clause to add summary rows to the final result set. A summary is provided for each aggregate column included in the select list. All other columns, except the ones that identify which group is being summarized, are assigned null values.

- The ROLLUP operator adds a summary row for each group specified in the GROUP BY clause except for the rightmost group, which is summarized by the aggregate functions. It also adds a summary row to the end of the result set that summarizes the entire result set. If the GROUP BY clause specifies a single group, only the final summary row is added.

- The sort sequence in the ORDER BY clause is applied after the summary rows are added. Because of that, you'll want to sort grouping columns in descending sequence so that the summary row for each group, which can contain null values, appears after the other rows in the group.

- When you use the ROLLUP operator, you can't use the DISTINCT keyword in any of the aggregate functions.

- You can use the GROUPING function with the ROLLUP operator to determine if a summary row has a null value assigned to a given column. See chapter 8 for details.

Figure 5-7   How to use the ROLLUP operator

How to use the CUBE operator

Figure 5-8 shows you how to use the CUBE operator. This operator is similar to the ROLLUP operator, except that it adds summary rows for every combination of groups. This is illustrated by the two examples in this figure. As you can see, these examples are the same as the ones in figure 5-7 except that they use the CUBE operator instead of the ROLLUP operator.

In the first example, the result set is grouped by a single column. In this case, a single summary row is added at the end of the result set that summarizes all the groups. In other words, this works the same as it does with the ROLLUP operator.

In the second example, however, you can see how CUBE differs from ROLLUP when you group by two or more columns. In this case, the result set includes a summary row for each state just as it did when the ROLLUP operator was used. In addition, it includes a summary row for each city. The eighth row in this figure, for example, indicates that there are two vendors in cities named Washington. If you look at the first and fifth rows in the result set, you'll see that one of those vendors is in Washington, New Jersey and one is in Washington, Iowa. The same is true of the city named Fairfield. There are also two vendors in the city of East Brunswick, but both are in New Jersey.

Now that you've seen how the CUBE operator works, you may be wondering when you would use it. The fact is, you probably won't use it except to add a summary row to a result set that's grouped by a single column. And in that case, you could just as easily use the ROLLUP operator. In some unique cases, however, the CUBE operator can provide useful information that you can't get any other way.

A summary query that includes a final summary row

```
SELECT VendorID, COUNT(*) AS InvoiceCount,
    SUM(InvoiceTotal) AS InvoiceTotal
FROM Invoices
GROUP BY VendorID WITH CUBE
```

	VendorID	InvoiceCount	InvoiceTotal
30	117	1	16.6200
31	119	1	4901.2600
32	121	8	6940.2500
33	122	9	23177.9600
34	123	47	4378.0200
35	NULL	114	214290.5100

— **Summary row**

A summary query that includes a summary row for each set of groups

```
SELECT VendorState, VendorCity, COUNT(*) AS QtyVendors
FROM Vendors
WHERE VendorState IN ('IA', 'NJ')
GROUP BY VendorState, VendorCity WITH CUBE
ORDER BY VendorState DESC, VendorCity DESC
```

	VendorState	VendorCity	QtyVendors
1	NJ	Washington	1
2	NJ	Fairfield	1
3	NJ	East Brunswick	2
4	NJ	NULL	4
5	IA	Washington	1
6	IA	Fairfield	1
7	IA	NULL	2
8	NULL	Washington	2
9	NULL	Fairfield	2
10	NULL	East Brunswick	2
11	NULL	NULL	6

— **Summary row for state 'NJ'** (row 4)
— **Summary row for state 'IA'** (row 7)
— **Summary row for city 'Washington'** (row 8)
— **Summary row for city 'Fairfield'** (row 9)
— **Summary row for city 'East Brunswick'** (row 10)
— **Summary row for all rows** (row 11)

Description

- You can use the WITH CUBE phrase in the GROUP BY clause to add summary rows to the final result set. A summary is provided for each aggregate column included in the select list. All other columns, except the ones that identify which group is being summarized, are assigned null values.

- The CUBE operator adds a summary row for every combination of groups specified in the GROUP BY clause. It also adds a summary row to the end of the result set that summarizes the entire result set.

- The sort sequence in the ORDER BY clause is applied after the summary rows are added. Because of that, you'll want to sort grouping columns in descending sequence so that the summary row for each group, which can contain null values, appears after the other rows in the group.

- When you use the CUBE operator, you can't use the DISTINCT keyword in any of the aggregate functions.

- You can use the GROUPING function with the CUBE operator to determine if a summary row has a null value assigned to a given column. See chapter 8 for details.

Figure 5-8   How to use the CUBE operator

Perspective

In this chapter, you learned how to code queries that group and summarize data. In most cases, you'll be able to use the techniques presented here to get the summary information you need. If not, you may want to find out about another tool provided by SQL Server called *Analysis Services*. This tool provides a graphical interface that lets you build complex data models based on cubes. Then, you can use those models to analyze the database using complex patterns and correlations. You can find out more about this tool by referring to Books Online.

Terms

scalar function
aggregate function
column function
summary query
scalar aggregate
vector aggregate

6

How to code subqueries

A subquery is a SELECT statement that's coded within another SQL statement. As a result, you can use subqueries to build queries that would be difficult or impossible to do otherwise. In this chapter, you'll learn how to use subqueries within SELECT statements. Then, in the next chapter, you'll learn how to use them when you code INSERT, UPDATE, and DELETE statements.

An introduction to subqueries

Since you know how to code SELECT statements, you already know how to code a *subquery*. It's simply a SELECT statement that's coded within another SQL statement. The trick to using subqueries, then, is knowing where and when to use them. You'll learn the specifics of using subqueries throughout this chapter. The two topics that follow, however, will give you an overview of where and when to use them.

How to use subqueries

In figure 6-1, you can see that a subquery can be coded, or *introduced*, in the WHERE, HAVING, FROM, or SELECT clause of a SELECT statement. The SELECT statement in this figure, for example, illustrates how you can use a subquery in the search condition of a WHERE clause. When it's used in a search condition, a subquery can be referred to as a *subquery search condition* or a *subquery predicate*.

The statement in this figure retrieves all the invoices from the Invoices table that have invoice totals greater than the average of all the invoices. To do that, the subquery calculates the average of all the invoices. Then, the search condition tests each invoice to see if its invoice total is greater than that average.

When a subquery returns a single value as it does in this example, you can use it anywhere you would normally use an expression. However, a subquery can also return a single-column result set with two or more rows. In that case, it can be used in place of a list of values, such as the list for an IN operator. In addition, if a subquery is coded within a FROM clause, it can return a result set with two or more columns. You'll learn about all of these different types of subqueries in this chapter.

You can also code a subquery within another subquery. In that case, the subqueries are said to be nested. Because *nested subqueries* can be difficult to read and can result in poor performance, you should use them only when necessary.

Four ways to introduce a subquery in a SELECT statement

1. In a WHERE clause as a search condition
2. In a HAVING clause as a search condition
3. In the FROM clause as a table specification
4. In the SELECT clause as a column specification

A SELECT statement that uses a subquery in the WHERE clause

```
SELECT InvoiceNumber, InvoiceDate, InvoiceTotal
FROM Invoices
WHERE InvoiceTotal >
    (SELECT AVG(InvoiceTotal)
    FROM Invoices)
ORDER BY InvoiceTotal
```

The value returned by the subquery

```
1879.7413
```

The result set

	InvoiceNumber	InvoiceDate	InvoiceTotal
1	989319-487	2002-04-18 00:00:00	1927.5400
2	97/522	2002-04-30 00:00:00	1962.1300
3	989319-417	2002-04-26 00:00:00	2051.5900
4	989319-427	2002-04-25 00:00:00	2115.8100
5	989319-477	2002-04-19 00:00:00	2184.1100

(21 rows)

Description

- A *subquery* is a SELECT statement that's coded within another SQL statement.
- A subquery can return a single value, a result set that contains a single column, or a result set that contains one or more columns.
- A subquery that returns a single value can be coded, or *introduced*, anywhere an expression is allowed. A subquery that returns a single column can be introduced in place of a list of values, such as the values for an IN phrase. And a subquery that returns one or more columns can be introduced in place of a table in the FROM clause.
- The syntax for a subquery is the same as for a standard SELECT statement. However, a subquery doesn't typically include the GROUP BY or HAVING clause, and it can't include an ORDER BY clause unless the TOP phrase is used.
- A subquery that's used in a WHERE or HAVING clause is called a *subquery search condition* or a *subquery predicate*. This is the most common use for a subquery.
- Although you can introduce a subquery in a GROUP BY or ORDER BY clause, there is no practical application for doing that.
- Subqueries can be *nested* within other subqueries. However, subqueries that are nested more than two or three levels deep can be difficult to read and can result in poor performance.

Figure 6-1   How to use subqueries

How subqueries compare to joins

In the last figure, you saw an example of a subquery that returns an aggregate value that's used in the search condition of a WHERE clause. This type of subquery provides for processing that can't be done any other way. However, most subqueries can be restated as joins, and most joins can be restated as subqueries. This is illustrated by the SELECT statements in figure 6-2.

Both of the SELECT statements in this figure return a result set that consists of selected rows and columns from the Invoices table. In this case, only the invoices for vendors in California are returned. The first statement uses a join to combine the Vendors and Invoices table so that the VendorState column can be tested for each invoice. In contrast, the second statement uses a subquery to return a result set that consists of the VendorID column for each vendor in California. Then, that result set is used with the IN operator in the search condition so that only invoices with a VendorID in that result set are included in the final result set.

So if you have a choice, which technique should you use? In general, I recommend you use the technique that results in the most readable code. For example, I think that a join tends to be more intuitive than a subquery when it uses an existing relationship between two tables. That's the case with the Vendors and Invoices table used in the examples in this figure. On the other hand, a subquery tends to be more intuitive when it uses an ad hoc relationship.

As your queries get more complex, you may find that they're easier to code by using subqueries, regardless of the relationships that are involved. On the other hand, a query with an inner join typically performs faster than the same query with a subquery. So if system performance is an issue, you may want to use inner joins instead of queries.

You should also realize that when you use a subquery in a search condition, its results can't be included in the final result set. For instance, the second example in this figure can't be changed to include the VendorName column from the Vendors table. That's because the Vendors table isn't named in the FROM clause of the outer query. So if you need to include information from both tables in the result set, you need to use a join.

A query that uses an inner join

```
SELECT InvoiceNumber, InvoiceDate, InvoiceTotal
FROM Invoices JOIN Vendors
    ON Invoices.VendorID = Vendors.VendorID
WHERE VendorState = 'CA'
ORDER BY InvoiceDate
```

The same query restated with a subquery

```
SELECT InvoiceNumber, InvoiceDate, InvoiceTotal
FROM Invoices
WHERE VendorID IN
    (SELECT VendorID
    FROM Vendors
    WHERE VendorState = 'CA')
ORDER BY InvoiceDate
```

The result set returned by both queries

	InvoiceNumber	InvoiceDate	InvoiceTotal
1	QP58872	2002-02-25 00:00:00	116.5400
2	Q545443	2002-03-14 00:00:00	1083.5800
3	MABO1489	2002-04-16 00:00:00	936.9300
4	97/553B	2002-04-26 00:00:00	313.5500

(40 rows)

Advantages of joins

*   The result of a join operation can include columns from both tables. The result of a query that includes a subquery can only include columns from the table named in the outer query. It can't include columns from the table named in the subquery.
*   A join tends to be more intuitive when it uses an existing relationship between the two tables, such as a primary key to foreign key relationship.
*   A query with a join typically performs faster than the same query with a subquery, especially if the query uses only inner joins.

Advantages of subqueries

*   You can use a subquery to pass an aggregate value to the outer query.
*   A subquery tends to be more intuitive when it uses an ad hoc relationship between the two tables.
*   Long, complex queries can sometimes be easier to code using subqueries.

Description

*   Like a join, a subquery can be used to code queries that work with two or more tables.
*   Most subqueries can be restated as joins and most joins can be restated as subqueries.

Figure 6-2   How subqueries compare to joins

How to code subqueries in search conditions

You can use a variety of techniques to work with a subquery in a search condition. You'll learn about those techniques in the topics that follow. As you read these topics, keep in mind that although all of the examples illustrate the use of subqueries in a WHERE clause, all of this information applies to the HAVING clause as well.

How to use subqueries with the IN operator

In chapter 3, you learned how to use the IN operator to test whether an expression is contained in a list of values. One way to provide that list of values is to use a subquery. This is illustrated in figure 6-3.

The example in this figure retrieves the vendors from the Vendors table that don't have invoices in the Invoices table. To do that, it uses a subquery to retrieve the VendorID of each vendor in the Invoices table. The result is a result set like the one shown in this figure that contains just the VendorID column. Then, this result set is used to filter the vendors that are included in the final result set.

You should notice two things about this subquery. First, it returns a single column. That's a requirement when a subquery is used with the IN operator. Second, the subquery includes the DISTINCT keyword. That way, if more than one invoice exists for a vendor, the VendorID for that vendor will be included only once. Note, however, that when the query is analyzed by SQL Server, this keyword will be added automatically. So you can omit it if you'd like to.

In the previous figure, you saw that a query that uses a subquery with the IN operator can be restated using an inner join. Similarly, a query that uses a subquery with the NOT IN operator can typically be restated using an outer join. The first query shown in this figure, for example, can be restated as shown in the second query. In this case, though, I think the query with the subquery is more readable. In addition, a query with a subquery will sometimes execute faster than a query with an outer join. That of course, depends on a variety of factors. In particular, it depends on the sizes of the tables and the relative number of unmatched rows. So if performance is an issue, you may want to test your query both ways to see which one executes faster.

The syntax of a WHERE clause that uses an IN phrase with a subquery

```
WHERE test_expression [NOT] IN (subquery)
```

A query that returns vendors without invoices

```
SELECT VendorID, VendorName, VendorState
FROM Vendors
WHERE VendorID NOT IN
     (SELECT DISTINCT VendorID
      FROM Invoices)
```

The result of the subquery

	VendorID ▲
1	34
2	37
3	48
4	72
5	80
6	81

(34 rows)

The result set

	VendorID	VendorName	VendorState ▲
32	33	Nielson	OH
33	35	Cal State Termite	CA
34	36	Graylift	CA
35	38	Venture Communications Int'l	NY
36	39	Custom Printing Company	MO
37	40	Nat Assoc of College Stores	OH

(88 rows)

The query restated without a subquery

```
SELECT Vendors.VendorID, VendorName, VendorState
FROM Vendors LEFT JOIN Invoices
     ON Vendors.VendorID = Invoices.VendorID
WHERE Invoices.VendorID IS NULL
```

Description

- You can introduce a subquery with the IN operator to provide the list of values that are tested against the test expression.

- When you use the IN operator, the subquery must return a single column of values.

- A query that uses the NOT IN operator with a subquery can typically be restated using an outer join.

Figure 6-3   How to use subqueries with the IN operator

How to compare the result of a subquery with an expression

Figure 6-4 illustrates how you can use the comparison operators to compare an expression with the result of a subquery. In the example in this figure, the subquery returns the average balance due of the invoices in the Invoices table that have a balance due greater than zero. Then, it uses that value to retrieve all the invoices that have a balance due that's less than the average.

When you use a comparison operator as shown in this figure, the subquery must return a single value. In most cases, that means that it uses an aggregate function. However, you can also use the comparison operators with subqueries that return two or more values. To do that, you use the SOME, ANY, or ALL keyword to modify the comparison operator. You'll learn more about these keywords in the next two topics.

The syntax of a WHERE clause that compares an expression with the value returned by a subquery

```
WHERE expression comparison_operator [SOME|ANY|ALL] (subquery)
```

A query that returns invoices with a balance due less than the average

```
SELECT InvoiceNumber, InvoiceDate, InvoiceTotal,
    InvoiceTotal - PaymentTotal - CreditTotal AS BalanceDue
FROM Invoices
WHERE InvoiceTotal - PaymentTotal - CreditTotal  > 0
    AND InvoiceTotal - PaymentTotal - CreditTotal <
    (SELECT AVG(InvoiceTotal - PaymentTotal - CreditTotal)
    FROM Invoices
    WHERE InvoiceTotal - PaymentTotal - CreditTotal > 0)
ORDER BY InvoiceTotal DESC
```

The value returned by the subquery

```
1669.9060
```

The result set

	InvoiceNumber	InvoiceDate	InvoiceTotal	BalanceDue
1	31359783	2002-05-23 00:00:00	1575.0000	1575.0000
2	97/553	2002-04-27 00:00:00	904.1400	904.1400
3	I77271-001	2002-06-05 00:00:00	662.0000	662.0000
4	31361833	2002-05-23 00:00:00	579.4200	579.4200
5	9982771	2002-06-03 00:00:00	503.2000	503.2000

(33 rows)

Description

- You can use a comparison operator in a search condition to compare an expression with the results of a subquery.

- If you code a search condition without the ANY, SOME, and ALL keywords, the subquery must return a single value.

- If you include the ANY, SOME, or ALL keyword, the subquery can return a list of values. See figures 6-5 and 6-6 for more information on using these keywords.

Figure 6-4   How to compare the result of a subquery with an expression

How to use the ALL keyword

Figure 6-5 shows you how to use the ALL keyword. This keyword modifies the comparison operator so that the condition must be true for all the values returned by a subquery. This is equivalent to coding a series of conditions connected by AND operators. The table at the top of this figure describes how this works for some of the comparison operators.

If you use the greater than operator (>), the expression must be greater than the maximum value returned by the subquery. Conversely, if you use the less than operator (<), the expression must be less than the minimum value returned by the subquery. If you use the equal operator (=), the expression must be equal to all of the values returned by the subquery. And if you use the not equal operator (<>), the expression must not equal any of the values returned by the subquery. Note that a not equal condition could be restated using a NOT IN condition.

The query in this figure illustrates the use of the greater than operator with the ALL keyword. Here, the subquery selects the InvoiceTotal column for all the invoices with a VendorID value of 34. This results in a table with two rows, as shown in this figure. Then, the outer query retrieves the rows from the Invoices table that have invoice totals greater than all of the values returned by the subquery. In other words, this query returns all the invoices that have totals greater than the largest invoice for vendor number 34.

When you use the ALL operator, you should realize that if the subquery doesn't return any rows, the comparison operation will always be true. In contrast, if the subquery returns only null values, the comparison operation will always be false.

In many cases, a condition with the ALL keyword can be rewritten so it's easier to read and maintain. For example, the condition in the query in this figure could be rewritten to use the MAX function like this:

```
WHERE InvoiceTotal >
    (SELECT MAX(InvoiceTotal)
    FROM Invoices
    WHERE VendorID = 34)
```

Whenever you can, then, I recommend you replace the ALL keyword with an equivalent condition.

How the ALL keyword works

Condition	Equivalent expression	Description
x > ALL (1, 2)	x > 2	x must be greater than all the values returned by the subquery, which means it must be greater than the maximum value.
x < ALL (1, 2)	x < 1	x must be less than all the values returned by the subquery, which means it must be less than the minimum value.
x = ALL (1, 2)	(x = 1) AND (x = 2)	This condition can evaluate to True only if the subquery returns a single value or if all the values returned by the subquery are the same. Otherwise, it evaluates to False.
x <> ALL (1, 2)	(x <> 1) AND (x <> 2)	This condition is equivalent to: x NOT IN (1, 2)

A query that returns invoices larger than the largest invoice for vendor 34

```
SELECT VendorName, InvoiceNumber, InvoiceTotal
FROM Invoices JOIN Vendors ON Invoices.VendorID = Vendors.VendorID
WHERE InvoiceTotal > ALL
    (SELECT InvoiceTotal
    FROM Invoices
    WHERE VendorID = 34)
ORDER BY VendorName
```

The result of the subquery

	InvoiceTotal
1	116.5400
2	1083.5800

The result set

	VendorName	InvoiceNumber	InvoiceTotal
1	Bertelsmann Industry Svcs. Inc	509786	6940.2500
2	Cahners Publishing Company	587056	2184.5000
3	Computerworld	367447	2433.0000
4	Data Reproductions Corp	40318	21842.0000
5	Dean Witter Reynolds	75C-90227	1367.5000

(25 rows)

Description

- You can use the ALL keyword to test that a comparison condition is true for all of the values returned by a subquery. This keyword is typically used with the comparison operators <, >, <=, and >=.

- If no rows are returned by the subquery, a comparison that uses the ALL keyword is always true.

- If all of the rows returned by the subquery contain a null value, a comparison that uses the ALL keyword is always false.

Figure 6-5   How to use the ALL keyword

How to use the ANY and SOME keywords

Figure 6-6 shows how to use the ANY and SOME keywords. You use these keywords to test if a comparison is true for any, or some, of the values returned by a subquery. This is equivalent to coding a series of conditions connected with OR operators. Because these keywords are equivalent, you can use whichever one you prefer. The table at the top of this figure describes how these keywords work with some of the comparison operators.

The example in this figure shows how you can use the ANY keyword with the less than operator. This statement is similar to the one you saw in the previous figure, except that it retrieves invoices with invoice totals that are less than at least one of the invoice totals for a given vendor. Like the statement in the previous figure, this condition could be rewritten using the MAX function like this:

```
WHERE InvoiceTotal <
    (SELECT MAX(InvoiceTotal)
    FROM Invoices
    WHERE VendorID = 115)
```

Because you can usually replace an ANY condition with an equivalent condition that's more readable, you probably won't use ANY often.

How the ANY and SOME keywords work

Condition	Equivalent expression	Description
x > ANY (1, 2)	x > 1	*x* must be greater than at least one of the values returned by the subquery list, which means that it must be greater than the minimum value returned by the subquery.
x < ANY (1, 2)	x < 2	*x* must be less than at least one of the values returned by the subquery list, which means that it must be less than the maximum value returned by the subquery.
x = ANY (1, 2)	(x = 1) OR (x = 2)	This condition is equivalent to: **x IN (1, 2)**
x <> ANY (1, 2)	(x <> 1) OR (x <> 2)	This condition will evaluate to True for any non-empty result set containing at least one non-null value that isn't equal to *x*.

A query that returns invoices smaller than the largest invoice for vendor 115

```
SELECT VendorName, InvoiceNumber, InvoiceTotal
FROM Vendors JOIN Invoices ON Vendors.VendorID = Invoices.InvoiceID
WHERE InvoiceTotal < ANY
    (SELECT InvoiceTotal
    FROM Invoices
    WHERE VendorID = 115)
```

The result of the subquery

	InvoiceTotal
1	6.0000
2	25.6700
3	6.0000
4	6.0000

The result set

	VendorName	InvoiceNumber	InvoiceTotal
1	California Data Marketing	4-342-8069	10.0000
2	Rich Advertising	4-321-2596	10.0000
3	Vision Envelope & Printing	4-314-3057	13.7500
4	Costco	203339-13	17.5000
5	Shields Design	963253267	23.5000

(17 rows)

Description

- You can use the ANY or SOME keyword to test that a condition is true for one or more of the values returned by a subquery.
- ANY and SOME are equivalent keywords. SOME is the ANSI-standard keyword, but ANY is more commonly used.
- If no rows are returned by the subquery or all of the rows returned by the subquery contain a null value, a comparison that uses the ANY or SOME keyword is always false.

Figure 6-6   How to use the ANY and SOME keywords

How to code correlated subqueries

The subqueries you've seen so far in this chapter have been subqueries that are executed only once for the entire query. However, you can also code subqueries that are executed once for each row that's processed by the outer query. This type of query is called a *correlated subquery* (it's similar to using a loop to do repetitive processing in a programming language).

Figure 6-7 illustrates how correlated subqueries work. The example in this figure retrieves rows from the Invoices table for those invoices that have an invoice total that's greater than the average of all the invoices for the same vendor. To do that, the search condition in the WHERE clause of the subquery refers to the VendorID value of the current invoice. That way, only the invoices for the current vendor will be included in the average.

Each time a row in the outer query is processed, the value in the VendorID column for that row is substituted for the column reference in the subquery. Then, the subquery is executed based on the current value. If the VendorID value is 95, for example, this subquery will be executed:

```
SELECT AVG(InvoiceTotal)
FROM Invoices AS Inv_Sub
WHERE Inv_Sub.VendorID = 95
```

After this subquery is executed, the value it returns is used to determine whether the current invoice is included in the result set. For example, the value returned by the subquery for vendor 95 is 28.5016. Then, that value is compared with the invoice total of the current invoice. If the invoice total is greater than that value, the invoice is included in the result set. Otherwise, it's not. This process is repeated until each of the invoices in the Invoices table has been processed.

As you study this example, notice how the column names in the WHERE clause of the inner query are qualified to indicate whether they refer to a column in the inner query or the outer query. In this case, the same table is used in both the inner and outer queries, so aliases, or correlation names, have been assigned to the tables. Then, those correlation names are used to qualify the column names. Although you have to qualify a reference to a column in the outer query, you don't have to qualify a reference to a column in the inner query. However, it's common practice to qualify both names, particularly if they refer to the same table.

Because correlated subqueries can be difficult to code, you may want to test a subquery separately before using it within another SELECT statement. To do that, however, you'll need to substitute a constant value for the variable that refers to a column in the outer query. That's what I did to get the average invoice total for vendor 95. Once you're sure that the subquery works on its own, you can replace the constant value with a reference to the outer query so you can use it within a SELECT statement.

A query that uses a correlated subquery to return each invoice that's higher than the vendor's average invoice

```
SELECT VendorID, InvoiceNumber, InvoiceTotal
FROM Invoices AS Inv_Main
WHERE InvoiceTotal >
    (SELECT AVG(InvoiceTotal)
    FROM Invoices AS Inv_Sub
    WHERE Inv_Sub.VendorID = Inv_Main.VendorID)
ORDER BY VendorID, InvoiceTotal
```

The value returned by the subquery for vendor 95

```
28.5016
```

The result set

	VendorID	InvoiceNumber	InvoiceTotal
5	80	133560	175.0000
6	83	31359783	1575.0000
7	95	111-92R-10095	32.7000
8	95	111-92R-10093	39.7700
9	95	111-92R-10092	46.2100
10	110	P-0259	26881.4000
11	110	0-2058	37966.1900
12	115	24946731	25.6700

`(36 rows)`

Description

- A *correlated subquery* is a subquery that is executed once for each row processed by the outer query. In contrast, a *noncorrelated subquery* is executed only once. All of the subqueries you've seen so far have been noncorrelated subqueries.

- A correlated subquery refers to a value that's provided by a column in the outer query. Because that value varies depending on the row that's being processed, each execution of the subquery returns a different result.

- To refer to a value in the outer query, a correlated subquery uses a qualified column name that includes the table name from the outer query. If the subquery uses the same table as the outer query, an alias, or *correlation name*, must be assigned to one of the tables to remove ambiguity.

Note

- Because a correlated subquery is executed once for each row processed by the outer query, a query with a correlated subquery typically takes longer to run than a query with a noncorrelated subquery.

Figure 6-7   How to code correlated subqueries

How to use the EXISTS operator

Figure 6-8 shows you how to use the EXISTS operator with a subquery. This operator tests whether or not the subquery returns a result set. In other words, it tests whether the result set exists. When you use this operator, the subquery doesn't actually return a result set to the outer query. Instead, it simply returns an indication of whether any rows satisfy the search condition of the subquery. Because of that, queries that use this operator execute quickly.

You typically use the EXISTS operator with a correlated subquery as illustrated in this figure. This query retrieves all the vendors in the Vendors table that don't have invoices in the Invoices table. Notice that this query returns the same vendors as the two queries you saw in figure 6-3 that use the IN operator with a subquery and an outer join. However, the query in this figure executes more quickly than either of the queries in figure 6-3.

In this example, the correlated subquery selects all of the invoices that have the same VendorID value as the current vendor in the outer query. Because the subquery doesn't actually return a result set, it doesn't matter what columns are included in the SELECT clause. So it's customary to just code an asterisk. That way, SQL Server will determine what columns to select for optimum performance.

After the subquery is executed, the search condition in the WHERE clause of the outer query uses NOT EXISTS to test whether any invoices were found for the current vendor. If not, the vendor row is included in the result set. Otherwise, it's not.

The syntax of a subquery that uses the EXISTS operator

```
WHERE [NOT] EXISTS (subquery)
```

A query that returns vendors without invoices

```
SELECT VendorID, VendorName, VendorState
FROM Vendors
WHERE NOT EXISTS
    (SELECT *
    FROM Invoices
    WHERE Invoices.VendorID = Vendors.VendorID)
```

The result set

	VendorID	VendorName	VendorState
32	33	Nielson	OH
33	35	Cal State Termite	CA
34	36	Graylift	CA
35	38	Venture Communications Int'l	NY
36	39	Custom Printing Company	MO
37	40	Nat Assoc of College Stores	OH

```
(88 rows)
```

Description

- You can use the EXISTS operator to test that one or more rows are returned by the subquery. You can also use the NOT operator along with the EXISTS operator to test that no rows are returned by the subquery.

- When you use the EXISTS operator with a subquery, the subquery doesn't actually return any rows. Instead, it returns an indication of whether any rows meet the specified condition.

- Because no rows are returned by the subquery, it doesn't matter what columns you specify in the SELECT clause. So you typically just code an asterisk (*).

- Although you can use the EXISTS operator with either a correlated or a noncorrelated subquery, it's used most often with correlated subqueries. That's because it's usually better to use a join than a noncorrelated subquery with EXISTS.

Figure 6-8   How to use the EXISTS operator

Other ways to use subqueries

Although you'll typically use subqueries in the WHERE or HAVING clause of a SELECT statement, you can also use them in the FROM and SELECT clauses. You'll learn how to do that in the topics that follow.

How to code subqueries in the FROM clause

Figure 6-9 shows you how to code a subquery in a FROM clause. As you can see, you can code a subquery in place of a table specification. In this example, the results of the subquery, called a *derived table*, are joined with another table. When you use a subquery in this way, it can return any number of rows and columns.

Subqueries are typically used in the FROM clause to create derived tables that provide summarized data to a summary query. The subquery in this figure, for example, creates a derived table that contains the VendorID values and the average invoice totals for the five vendors with the top invoice averages. To do that, it groups the invoices by VendorID, sorts them in descending sequence by average invoice total, and then returns the top five rows. The derived table is then joined with the Invoices table, and the resulting rows are grouped by VendorID. Finally, the maximum invoice date and average invoice total are calculated for the grouped rows, and the results are sorted by the maximum invoice date in descending sequence.

You should notice four things about this query. First, the derived table is assigned a table alias so that it can be referred to from the outer query. Second, the result of the AVG function in the subquery is assigned a column alias. This is because a derived table can't have unnamed columns. Third, since the subquery uses a TOP phrase, it also includes an ORDER BY clause. Fourth, although you might think that you could use the average invoice totals calculated by the subquery in the select list of the outer query, you can't. That's because the outer query includes a GROUP BY clause, so only aggregate functions, columns named in the GROUP BY clause, and constant values can be included in this list. Because of that, the AVG function is repeated in the select list.

When used in the FROM clause, a subquery is similar to a view. As you learned in chapter 1, a view is a predefined SELECT statement that's saved with the database. Because it's saved with the database, a view typically performs more efficiently than a derived table. However, it's not always practical to use a view. In those cases, derived tables can be quite useful. In addition, derived tables can be useful for testing possible solutions before creating a view. Then, once the derived table works the way you want it to, you can define the view based on the subquery you used to create the derived table.

A query that uses a derived table to retrieve the top 5 vendors by average invoice total

```
SELECT Invoices.VendorID, MAX(InvoiceDate) AS LatestInv,
    AVG(InvoiceTotal) AS AvgInvoice
FROM Invoices JOIN
    (SELECT TOP 5 VendorID, AVG(InvoiceTotal) AS AvgInvoice
    FROM Invoices
    GROUP BY VendorID
    ORDER BY AvgInvoice DESC) AS TopVendor
    ON Invoices.VendorID = TopVendor.VendorID
GROUP BY Invoices.VendorID
ORDER BY LatestInv DESC
```

The derived table generated by the subquery

	VendorID	AvgInvoice
1	110	23978.4820
2	72	10963.6550
3	104	7125.3400
4	99	6940.2500
5	119	4901.2600

The result set

	VendorID	LatestInv	AvgInvoice
1	72	2002-07-18 00:00:00	10963.6550
2	119	2002-06-04 00:00:00	4901.2600
3	104	2002-06-03 00:00:00	7125.3400
4	99	2002-05-31 00:00:00	6940.2500
5	110	2002-05-08 00:00:00	23978.4820

Description

- A subquery that's coded in the FROM clause returns a result set called a *derived table*. When you create a derived table, you must assign an alias to it. Then, you can use the derived table within the outer query just as you would any other table.
- When you code a subquery in the FROM clause, you must assign names to any calculated values in the result set.
- Derived tables are most useful when you need to further summarize the results of a summary query.
- A derived table is like a view in that it retrieves selected rows and columns from one or more base tables. Because views are stored as part of the database, they're typically more efficient to use than derived tables. However, it may not always be practical to construct and save a view in advance.

Figure 6-9   How to code subqueries in the FROM clause

How to code subqueries in the SELECT clause

Figure 6-10 shows you how to use subqueries in the SELECT clause. As you can see, you can use a subquery in place of a column specification. Because of that, the subquery must return a single value.

In most cases, the subqueries you use in the SELECT clause will be correlated subqueries. The subquery in this figure, for example, calculates the maximum invoice date for each vendor in the Vendors table. To do that, it refers to the VendorID column from the Invoices table in the outer query.

Because subqueries coded in the SELECT clause are difficult to read, and because correlated subqueries are typically inefficient, you shouldn't use them unless you can't find another solution. In most cases, though, you can replace the subquery with a join. The first query shown in this figure, for example, could be restated as shown in the second query. This query joins the Vendors and Invoices tables, groups the rows by VendorName, and then uses the MAX function to calculate the maximum invoice date for each vendor. As you can see, this query is much easier to read than the one with the subquery. It will also execute more quickly.

A query that uses a correlated subquery in its SELECT clause to retrieve the most recent invoice for each vendor

```
SELECT DISTINCT VendorName,
    (SELECT MAX(InvoiceDate) FROM Invoices
    WHERE Invoices.VendorID = Vendors.VendorID) AS LatestInv
FROM Vendors
ORDER BY LatestInv DESC
```

The result set

	VendorName	LatestInv
1	Data Reproductions Corp	2002-07-18 00:00:00
2	Coffee Break Service	2002-06-14 00:00:00
3	Suburban Propane	2002-06-11 00:00:00
4	Pacific Bell	2002-06-08 00:00:00
5	Postmaster	2002-06-07 00:00:00

(122 rows)

The same query restated using a join

```
SELECT VendorName, MAX(InvoiceDate) AS LatestInv
FROM Vendors JOIN Invoices ON Vendors.VendorID = Invoices.VendorID
GROUP BY VendorName
ORDER BY LatestInv DESC
```

Description

- When you code a subquery for a column specification in the SELECT clause, the subquery must return a single value.

- A subquery that's coded within a SELECT clause is typically a correlated subquery.

- A query that includes a subquery in its SELECT clause can typically be restated using a join instead of the subquery. Because a join is usually faster and more readable, subqueries are seldom coded in the SELECT clause.

Figure 6-10   How to code subqueries in the SELECT clause

Guidelines for working with complex queries

So far, the examples you've seen of queries that use subqueries have been relatively simple. However, these types of queries can get complicated in a hurry, particularly if the subqueries are nested. Because of that, you'll want to be sure that you plan and test these queries carefully. You'll learn a procedure for doing that in a moment. But first, you'll see a complex query that illustrates the type of query I'm talking about.

A complex query that uses subqueries

Figure 6-11 presents a query that uses three subqueries. The first subquery is used in the FROM clause of the outer query to create a derived table that contains the state, name, and total invoice amount for each vendor in the Vendors table. The second subquery is also used in the FROM clause of the outer query to create a derived table that's joined with the first table. This derived table contains the state and total invoice amount for the vendor in each state that has the largest invoice total. To create this table, a third subquery is nested within the FROM clause of the subquery. This subquery is identical to the first subquery.

After the two derived tables are created, they're joined based on the columns in each table that contain the state and the total invoice amount. The final result set includes the state, name, and total invoice amount for the vendor in each state with the largest invoice total. This result set is sorted by state.

As you can see, this query is quite complicated and difficult to understand. In fact, you might be wondering if there isn't an easier solution to this problem. For example, you might think that you could solve the problem simply by joining the Vendors and Invoices table and creating a grouped aggregate. If you grouped by vendor state, however, you wouldn't be able to include the name of the vendor in the result set. And if you grouped by vendor state and vendor name, the result set would include all the vendors, not just the vendor from each state with the largest invoice total. If you think about how else you might solve this query, I think you'll see that the solution presented here is the most straightforward.

A query that uses three subqueries

```
SELECT Summary1.VendorState, Summary1.VendorName, TopInState.SumOfInvoices
FROM
        (SELECT V_Sub.VendorState, V_Sub.VendorName,
            SUM(I_Sub.InvoiceTotal) AS SumOfInvoices
        FROM Invoices AS I_Sub JOIN Vendors AS V_Sub
            ON I_Sub.VendorID = V_Sub.VendorID
        GROUP BY V_Sub.VendorState, V_Sub.VendorName) AS Summary1
    JOIN
        (SELECT Summary2.VendorState,
            MAX(Summary2.SumOfInvoices) AS SumOfInvoices
        FROM
            (SELECT V_Sub.VendorState, V_Sub.VendorName,
                SUM(I_Sub.InvoiceTotal) AS SumOfInvoices
            FROM Invoices AS I_Sub JOIN Vendors AS V_Sub
                ON I_Sub.VendorID = V_Sub.VendorID
            GROUP BY V_Sub.VendorState, V_Sub.VendorName) AS Summary2
        GROUP BY Summary2.VendorState) AS TopInState
    ON Summary1.VendorState = TopInState.VendorState AND
        Summary1.SumOfInvoices = TopInState.SumOfInvoices
ORDER BY Summary1.VendorState
```

The result set

	VendorState	VendorName	SumOfInvoices
1	AZ	Wells Fargo Bank	662.0000
2	CA	Digital Dreamworks	7125.3400
3	DC	Reiter's Scientific & Pro Books	600.0000
4	MA	Dean Witter Reynolds	1367.5000
5	MI	Malloy Lithographing Inc	119892.4100
6	NV	United Parcel Service	23177.9600
7	OH	Edward Data Services	207.7800
8	PA	Cardinal Business Media, Inc.	265.3600

`(10 rows)`

How the query works

- This query retrieves the vendor from each state that has the largest invoice total. To do that, it uses three subqueries: Summary1, Summary2, and TopInState. The Summary1 and TopInState subqueries are joined together in the FROM clause of the outer query, and the Summary2 subquery is nested within the FROM clause of the TopInState subquery.

- The Summary1 and Summary2 subqueries are identical. They join data from the Vendors and Invoices tables and produce a result set that includes the sum of invoices for each vendor grouped by vendor name within state.

- The TopInState subquery produces a result set that includes the vendor state and the largest sum of invoices for any vendor in that state. This information is retrieved from the results of the Summary2 subquery.

- The columns listed in the SELECT clause of the outer query are retrieved from the result of the join between the Summary1 and TopInState subqueries, and the results are sorted by state.

Figure 6-11   A complex query that uses subqueries

A procedure for building complex queries

To build a complex query like the one in the previous figure, you can use a procedure like the one in figure 6-12. To start, you should state the problem to be solved so that you're clear about what you want the query to accomplish. In this case, the question is, "Which vendor in each state has the largest invoice total?"

Once you're clear about the problem, you should outline the query using *pseudocode*. Pseudocode is simply code that represents the intent of the query, but doesn't necessarily use SQL code. The pseudocode shown in this figure, for example, uses part SQL code and part English. Notice that this pseudocode identifies the two main subqueries. Because these subqueries define derived tables, the pseudocode also indicates the alias that will be used for each: Summary1 and TopInState. That way, you can use these aliases in the pseudocode for the outer query to make it clear where the data it uses comes from.

If it's not clear from the pseudocode how each subquery will be coded, or, as in this case, if a subquery is nested within another subquery, you can also write pseudocode for the subqueries. For example, the pseudocode for the TopInState query is presented in this figure. Because this subquery has a subquery nested in its FROM clause, that subquery is identified in this pseudocode as Summary2.

The next step in the procedure is to code and test the actual subqueries to be sure they work the way you want them to. For example, the code for the Summary1 and Summary2 queries is shown in this figure, along with the results of these queries and the results of the TopInState query. Once you're sure that the subqueries work the way you want them to, you can code and test the final query.

If you follow the procedure presented in this figure, I think you'll find it easier to build complex queries that use subqueries. Before you can use this procedure, of course, you need to have a thorough understanding of how subqueries work and what they can do. So you'll want to be sure to experiment with the techniques you learned in this chapter before you try to build a complex query like the one shown here.

A procedure for building complex queries

1. State the problem to be solved by the query in English.
2. Use pseudocode to outline the query. The pseudocode should identify the subqueries used by the query and the data they return. It should also include aliases used for any derived tables.
3. If necessary, use pseudocode to outline each subquery.
4. Code the subqueries and test them to be sure that they return the correct data.
5. Code and test the final query.

The problem to be solved by the query in figure 6-11

Which vendor in each state has the largest invoice total?

Pseudocode for the query

```
SELECT Summary1.VendorState, Summary1.VendorName, TopInState.SumOfInvoices
FROM (Derived table returning VendorState, VendorName, SumOfInvoices)
        AS Summary1
    JOIN (Derived table returning VendorState, MAX(SumOfInvoices))
        AS TopInState
    ON Summary1.VendorState = TopInState.VendorState AND
        Summary1.SumOfInvoices = TopInState.SumOfInvoices
ORDER BY Summary1.VendorState
```

Pseudocode for the TopInState subquery

```
SELECT Summary2.VendorState, MAX(Summary2.SumOfInvoices)
FROM (Derived table returning VendorState, VendorName, SumOfInvoices)
    AS Summary2
GROUP BY Summary2.VendorState
```

The code for the Summary1 and Summary2 subqueries

```
SELECT V_Sub.VendorState, V_Sub.VendorName,
    SUM(I_Sub.InvoiceTotal) AS SumOfInvoices
FROM Invoices AS I_Sub JOIN Vendors AS V_Sub
    ON I_Sub.VendorID = V_Sub.VendorID
GROUP BY V_Sub.VendorState, V_Sub.VendorName
```

The result of the Summary1 and Summary2 subqueries

	VendorState	VendorName	SumOfInvoices
19	CA	Coffee Break Service	41.8000
20	MA	Dean Witter Reynolds	1367.5000
21	CA	Digital Dreamworks	7125.3400
22	CA	Dristas Groom & McCormick	220.0000

(34 rows)

The result of the TopInState subquery

	VendorState	SumOfInvoices
1	AZ	662.0000
2	CA	7125.3400
3	DC	600.0000
4	MA	1367.5000

(10 rows)

Figure 6-12   A procedure for building complex queries

Perspective

As you've seen in this chapter, subqueries provide a powerful tool for solving difficult problems. Before you use a subquery, however, remember that a subquery can often be restated more clearly by using a join. In addition, a query with a join often executes more quickly than a query with a subquery. Because of that, you'll typically use a subquery only when it can't be restated as a join or when it makes the query easier to understand without slowing it down significantly.

Terms

subquery
introduce a subquery
subquery search condition
subquery predicate
nested subquery
correlated subquery
noncorrelated subquery
derived table
pseudocode

7

How to insert, update, and delete data

In the last four chapters, you learned how to code the SELECT statement to
retrieve and summarize data. Now, you'll learn how to code the INSERT,
UPDATE, and DELETE statements to modify the data in a table. When you're
done with this chapter, you'll know how to code the four statements that are
used every day by professional SQL programmers.

How to create test tables

As you learn to code INSERT, UPDATE, and DELETE statements, you need to make sure that your experimentation won't affect "live" data or a classroom database that is shared by other students. Two ways get around that are presented next.

How to use the SELECT INTO statement to create test tables

Figure 7-1 shows how to use the SELECT INTO statement to create test tables that are derived from the tables in a database. Then, you can experiment all you want with the test tables, and delete them when you're done. When you use the SELECT INTO statement, the result set that's defined by the SELECT statement is simply copied into a new table.

The three examples in this figure show some of the ways you can use this statement. Here, the first example copies all of the columns from all of the rows in the Invoices table into a new table named InvoiceCopy. The second example copies all of the columns in the Invoices table into a new table, but only for rows where the balance due is zero. And the third example creates a table that contains summary data from the Invoices table.

For the examples in the rest of this chapter, I used the SELECT INTO statement to make copies of the Vendors and Invoices tables, and I named these tables VendorCopy and InvoiceCopy. If you do the same, you'll avoid corrupting the original database. Then, when you're done experimenting, you can use the DROP TABLE statement that's shown in this figure to delete the test tables.

When you use this technique to create tables, though, only the column definitions and data are copied, which means that definitions like those of primary keys, foreign keys, and default values aren't retained. As a result, the test results that you get with the copied tables may be slightly different than the results you would get with the original tables. You'll understand that better after you read chapters 9 and 10.

How to use the book's database for testing

If you installed the book's database from the CD to your own PC, you can do your testing on that database without worrying about how much you change it. Then, when you're through experimenting with the INSERT, UPDATE, and DELETE statements, you can decide whether or not you want to restore the database to its original data. If you do, you can use the procedure in appendix A.

When you test this way, though, remember that the definitions of primary keys, foreign keys, and default values are retained so the results may be slightly different than the ones shown in the examples. If, for example, you try to add a record with an invalid foreign key, SQL Server won't let you do that. You'll learn more about that in chapters 9 and 10.

The syntax of the SELECT INTO statement

```
SELECT select_list
INTO table_name
FROM table_source
[WHERE search_condition]
[GROUP BY group_by_list]
[HAVING search_condition]
[ORDER BY order_by_list]
```

A statement that creates a complete copy of the Invoices table

```
SELECT *
INTO InvoiceCopy
FROM Invoices
```

```
(122 row(s) affected)
```

A statement that creates a partial copy of the Invoices table

```
SELECT *
INTO OldInvoices
FROM Invoices
WHERE InvoiceTotal - PaymentTotal - CreditTotal = 0
```

```
(74 row(s) affected)
```

A statement that creates a table with summary rows from the Invoices table

```
SELECT VendorID, SUM(InvoiceTotal) AS SumOfInvoices
INTO VendorBalances
FROM Invoices
WHERE InvoiceTotal - PaymentTotal - CreditTotal <> 0
GROUP BY VendorID
```

```
(16 row(s) affected)
```

A statement that deletes a table

```
DROP TABLE InvoiceCopy
```

Description

- The INTO clause is a SQL Server extension that lets you create a new table based on the result set defined by the SELECT statement. Since the definitions of the columns in the new table are based on the columns in the result set, the column names assigned in the SELECT clause must be unique.

- You can code the other clauses of the SELECT INTO statement just as you would for any other SELECT statement. That includes grouping, aggregates, joins, and subqueries.

- If you use calculated values in the select list, you must name the column since that name is used in the definition of the new table.

- The table you name in the INTO clause must not exist. If it does, you must delete the table by using the DROP TABLE statement before you execute the SELECT INTO statement.

Warning

- When you use the SELECT INTO statement to create a table, only the column definitions and data are copied. That means that definitions of primary keys, foreign keys, indexes, default values, and so on are not included in the new table.

Figure 7-1   How to use the SELECT INTO statement to create test tables

How to insert new rows

To add new rows to a table, you use the INSERT statement. This statement lets you insert a single row with the values you specify or selected rows from another table. You'll see how to use both forms of the INSERT statement in the topics that follow. In addition, you'll learn how to work with default values and null values when you insert new rows.

How to insert a single row

Figure 7-2 shows how to code an INSERT statement to insert a single row. The two examples in this figure insert a row into the InvoiceCopy table. The data this new row contains is defined near the top of this figure.

In the first example, you can see that you name the table in which the row will be inserted in the INSERT clause. Then, the VALUES clause lists the values to be used for each column. You should notice three things about this list. First, it includes a value for every column in the table except for the InvoiceID column. This value is omitted because the InvoiceID column is defined as an identity column. Because of that, its value will be generated by SQL Server. Second, the values are listed in the same sequence that the columns appear in the table. That way, SQL Server knows which value to assign to which column. And third, a null value is assigned to the last column, PaymentDate, using the NULL keyword. You'll learn more about using this keyword in the next topic.

The second INSERT statement in this figure includes a column list in the INSERT clause. Notice that this list doesn't include the PaymentDate column since it allows a null value. In addition, the columns aren't listed in the same sequence as the columns in the InvoiceCopy table. When you include a list of columns, you can code the columns in any sequence you like. Then, you just need to be sure that the values in the VALUES clause are coded in the same sequence.

When you specify the values for the columns to be inserted, you must be sure that those values are compatible with the data types of the columns. You'll learn more about data types and how to work with them in the next chapter. For now, just realize that if any of the values aren't compatible with the data types of the corresponding columns, an error will occur and the row won't be inserted.

The syntax of the INSERT statement for inserting a single row

```
INSERT [INTO] table_name [(column_list)]
[DEFAULT] VALUES (expression_1 [, expression_2]...)
```

The values for a new row to be added to the Invoices table

Column	Value	Column	Value
InvoiceID	(Next available unique ID)	PaymentTotal	0
VendorID	97	CreditTotal	0
InvoiceNumber	456789	TermsID	1
InvoiceDate	8/01/2002	InvoiceDueDate	8/31/2002
InvoiceTotal	8,344.50	PaymentDate	null

An INSERT statement that adds the new row without using a column list

```
INSERT INTO InvoiceCopy
VALUES (97, '456789', '2002-08-01', 8344.50, 0, 0, 1, '2002-08-31', NULL)
```

An INSERT statement that adds the new row using a column list

```
INSERT INTO InvoiceCopy
    (VendorID, InvoiceNumber, InvoiceTotal, PaymentTotal, CreditTotal,
    TermsID, InvoiceDate, InvoiceDueDate)
VALUES
    (97, '456789', 8344.50, 0, 0, 1, '2002-08-01', '2002-08-31')
```

The response from the system

```
(1 row(s) affected)
```

Description

- You use the INSERT statement to add a new row to a table.

- In the INSERT clause, you specify the name of the table that you want to add a row to, along with an optional column list. The INTO keyword is optional and can be omitted.

- You specify the values to be inserted in the VALUES clause. The values you specify depend on whether you include a column list.

- If you don't include a column list, you must specify the column values in the same order as they appear in the table, and you must code a value for each column in the table. The exception is an identity column, which must be omitted.

- If you include a column list, you must specify the column values in the same order as they appear in the column list. You can omit columns with default values and columns that accept null values, and you must omit identity columns.

- To insert a null value into a column, you can use the NULL keyword. To insert a default value, you can use the DEFAULT keyword. And to insert a default row, you can code the DEFAULT keyword at the beginning of the VALUES clause. See figure 7-3 for more information on using these keywords.

Figure 7-2   How to insert a single row

How to insert default values and null values

If a column allows null values, you'll want to know how to insert a null value into that column. Similarly, if a column is defined with a default value, you'll want to know how to insert that value. The technique you use depends on whether the INSERT statement includes a column list, as shown by the examples in figure 7-3.

All of these INSERT statements use a table named ColorSample. This table contains the three columns shown at the top of this figure. The first column, ID, is defined as an identity column. The second column, ColorNumber, is defined with a default value of 0. And the third column, ColorName, is defined so that it allows null values.

The first two statements illustrate how you assign a default value or a null value using a column list. To do that, you simply omit the column from the list. In the first statement, for example, the column list names only the ColorNumber column, so the ColorName column is assigned a null value. Similarly, the column list in the second statement names only the ColorName column, so the ColorNumber is assigned its default value.

The next three statements show how you assign a default or null value to a column without including a column list. As you can see, you do that by using the DEFAULT and NULL keywords. For example, the third statement specifies a value for the ColorName column, but uses the DEFAULT keyword for the ColorNumber column. Because of that, SQL Server will assign a value of zero to this column. The fourth statement assigns a value of 808 to the ColorNumber column, and it uses the NULL keyword to assign a null value to the ColorName column. The fifth statement uses both the DEFAULT and NULL keywords.

Finally, in the sixth statement, the DEFAULT keyword is coded in front of the VALUES clause. When you use the DEFAULT keyword this way, any column that has a default value will be assigned that value, and all other columns (except the identity column) will be assigned a null value. Because of that, you can use this technique only when every column in the table is defined as either an identity column, a column with a default value, or a column that allows null values.

The definition of the ColorSample table

Column name	Data Type	Length	Identity	Allow Nulls	Default Value
ID	Int	4	Yes	No	No
ColorNumber	Int	4	No	No	0
ColorName	VarChar	10	No	Yes	No

Six INSERT statements for the ColorSample table

```
INSERT INTO ColorSample (ColorNumber)
VALUES (606)

INSERT INTO ColorSample (ColorName)
VALUES ('Yellow')

INSERT INTO ColorSample
VALUES (DEFAULT, 'Orange')

INSERT INTO ColorSample
VALUES (808, NULL)

INSERT INTO ColorSample
VALUES (DEFAULT, NULL)

INSERT INTO ColorSample
DEFAULT VALUES
```

The ColorSample table after the rows are inserted

	ID	ColorNumber	ColorName
1	1	606	NULL
2	2	0	Yellow
3	3	0	Orange
4	4	808	NULL
5	5	0	NULL
6	6	0	NULL

Description

- If a column is defined so that it allows null values, you can use the NULL keyword in the list of values to insert a null value into that column.
- If a column is defined with a default value, you can use the DEFAULT keyword in the list of values to insert the default value for that column.
- If all of the columns in a table are defined as either identity columns, columns with default values, or columns that allow null values, you can code the DEFAULT keyword at the beginning of the VALUES clause and then omit the list of values.
- If you include a column list, you can omit columns with default values and null values. Then, the default value or null value is assigned automatically.

Figure 7-3   How to insert default values and null values

How to insert rows selected from another table

Instead of using the VALUES clause of the INSERT statement to specify the values for a single row, you can use a subquery to select the rows you want to insert from another table. Figure 7-4 shows you how to do that.

Both examples in this figure retrieve rows from the InvoiceCopy table and insert them into a table named InvoiceArchive. This table is defined with the same columns as the InvoiceCopy table. However, the InvoiceID column isn't defined as an identity column, and the PaymentTotal and CreditTotal columns aren't defined with default values. Because of that, you must include values for these columns.

The first example in this figure shows how you can use a subquery in an INSERT statement without coding a column list. In this example, the SELECT clause of the subquery is coded with an asterisk so that all the columns in the InvoiceCopy table will be retrieved. Then, after the search condition in the WHERE clause is applied, all the rows in the result set are inserted into the InvoiceArchive table.

The second example shows how you can use a column list in the INSERT clause when you use a subquery to retrieve rows. Just as when you use the VALUES clause, you can list the columns in any sequence. However, the columns must be listed in the same sequence in the SELECT clause of the subquery. In addition, you can omit columns that are defined with default values or that allow null values.

Notice that the subqueries in these statements aren't coded within parentheses as a subquery in a SELECT statement is. That's because they're not coded within a clause of the INSERT statement. Instead, they're coded in place of the VALUES clause.

Before you execute INSERT statements like the ones shown in this figure, you'll want to be sure that the rows and columns retrieved by the subquery are the ones you want to insert. To do that, you can execute the SELECT statement by itself. Then, when you're sure it retrieves the correct data, you can add the INSERT clause to insert the rows in the derived table into another table.

The syntax of the INSERT statement for inserting rows selected from another table

```
INSERT [INTO] table_name [(column_list)]
SELECT column_list
FROM table_source
[WHERE search_condition]
```

An INSERT statement that inserts paid invoices in the InvoiceCopy table into the InvoiceArchive table

```
INSERT INTO InvoiceArchive
SELECT *
FROM InvoiceCopy
WHERE InvoiceTotal - PaymentTotal - CreditTotal = 0

(74 row(s) affected)
```

The same INSERT statement with a column list

```
INSERT INTO InvoiceArchive
    (InvoiceID, VendorID, InvoiceNumber, InvoiceTotal, CreditTotal,
    PaymentTotal, TermsID, InvoiceDate, InvoiceDueDate)
SELECT
    InvoiceID, VendorID, InvoiceNumber, InvoiceTotal, CreditTotal,
    PaymentTotal, TermsID, InvoiceDate, InvoiceDueDate
FROM InvoiceCopy
WHERE InvoiceTotal - PaymentTotal - CreditTotal = 0

(74 row(s) affected)
```

Description

- To insert rows selected from one or more tables into another table, you can code a subquery in place of the VALUES clause. Then, the rows in the derived table that result from the subquery are inserted into the table.

- If you don't code a column list in the INSERT clause, the subquery must return values for all the columns in the table where the rows will be inserted, and the columns must be returned in the same order as they appear in that table. The exception is an identity column, which must be omitted.

- If you include a column list in the INSERT clause, the subquery must return values for those columns in the same order as they appear in the column list. You can omit columns with default values and columns that accept null values, and you must omit identity columns.

Figure 7-4   How to insert rows selected from another table

How to modify existing rows

To modify the data in one or more rows of a table, you use the UPDATE statement. Although most of the UPDATE statements you code will perform simple updates like the ones you'll see in the next figure, you can also code more complex UPDATE statements that include subqueries and joins. You'll learn how to use these features after you learn how to perform a basic update operation.

How to perform a basic update operation

Figure 7-5 presents the syntax of the UPDATE statement. As you can see in the examples, most UPDATE statements include just the UPDATE, SET, and WHERE clauses. The UPDATE clause names the table to be updated, the SET clause names the columns to be updated and the values to be assigned to those columns, and the WHERE clause specifies the condition a row must meet to be updated. Although the WHERE clause is optional, you'll almost always include it. If you don't, all of the rows in the table will be updated, which usually isn't what you want.

The first UPDATE statement in this figure modifies the values of two columns in the InvoiceCopy table: PaymentDate and PaymentTotal. Because the WHERE clause in this statement identifies a specific invoice number, only the columns in that invoice will be updated. Notice in this example that the values to be assigned to the two columns are coded as literals. You should realize, however, that you can assign any valid expression to a column as long as it results in a value that's compatible with the data type of the column. You can also use the NULL keyword to assign a null value to a column that allows nulls, and you can use the DEFAULT keyword to assign the default value to a column that's defined with one.

The second UPDATE statement modifies a single column in the InvoiceCopy table: TermsID. This time, however, the WHERE clause specifies that all the rows for vendor 95 should be updated. Because this vendor has six rows in the InvoiceCopy table, all six rows will be updated.

The third UPDATE statement illustrates how you can use an expression to assign a value to a column. In this case, the expression increases the value of the CreditTotal column by 100. Like the first UPDATE statement, this statement updates a single row.

Before you execute an UPDATE statement, you'll want to be sure that you've selected the correct rows. To do that, you can execute a SELECT statement with the same search condition. Then, if the SELECT statement returns the correct rows, you can change it to an UPDATE statement.

In addition to the UPDATE, SET, and WHERE clauses, an UPDATE statement can also include a FROM clause. This clause is an extension to the SQL standards, and you'll see how to use it in the next two figures.

The syntax of the UPDATE statement

```
UPDATE table_name
SET column_name_1 = expression_1 [, column_name_2 = expression_2]...
[FROM table_source [[AS] table_alias]
[WHERE search_condition]
```

An UPDATE statement that assigns new values to two columns of a single row in the InvoiceCopy table

```
UPDATE InvoiceCopy
SET PaymentDate = '2002-09-21',
    PaymentTotal = 19351.18
WHERE InvoiceNumber = '97/522'

(1 row(s) affected)
```

An UPDATE statement that assigns a new value to one column of all the invoices for a vendor

```
UPDATE InvoiceCopy
SET TermsID = 1
WHERE VendorID = 95

(6 row(s) affected)
```

An UPDATE statement that uses an arithmetic expression to assign a value to a column

```
UPDATE InvoiceCopy
SET CreditTotal = CreditTotal + 100
WHERE InvoiceNumber = '97/522'

(1 row(s) affected)
```

Description

- You use the UPDATE statement to modify one or more rows in the table named in the UPDATE clause.
- You name the columns to be modified and the value to be assigned to each column in the SET clause. You can specify the value for a column as a literal or an expression.
- You can provide additional criteria for the update operation in the FROM clause, which is a SQL Server extension. See figures 7-6 and 7-7 for more information.
- You can specify the conditions that must be met for a row to be updated in the WHERE clause.
- You can use the DEFAULT keyword to assign the default value to a column that has one, and you can use the NULL keyword to assign a null value to a column that allows nulls.
- You can't update an identity column.

Warning

- If you omit the WHERE clause, all the rows in the table will be updated.

Figure 7-5   How to perform a basic update operation

How to use subqueries in an update operation

Figure 7-6 presents four more UPDATE statements that illustrate how you can use subqueries in an update operation. In the first statement, a subquery is used in the SET clause to retrieve the maximum invoice due date from the InvoiceCopy table. Then, that value is assigned to the InvoiceDueDate column for invoice number 97/522.

In the second statement, a subquery is used in the WHERE clause to identify the invoices to be updated. This subquery returns the VendorID value for the vendor in the VendorCopy table with the name "Pacific Bell." Then, all the invoices with that VendorID value are updated.

The third UPDATE statement also uses a subquery in the WHERE clause. This subquery returns a list of the VendorID values for all the vendors in California, Arizona, and Nevada. Then, the IN operator is used to update all the invoices with VendorID values in that list. Note that although the subquery returns 80 vendors, many of these vendors don't have invoices. As a result, the UPDATE statement only affects 51 invoices.

The fourth example in this figure shows how you can use a subquery in the FROM clause of an UPDATE statement to create a derived table. In this case, the subquery returns a table that contains the InvoiceID values of the ten invoices with the largest balances of $100 or more. (Because this UPDATE statement will apply a credit of $100 to these invoices, you don't want to retrieve invoices with balances less than that amount.) Then, the WHERE clause specifies that only those invoices should be updated. You can also use a column from a derived table in an expression in the SET clause to update a column in the base table.

An UPDATE statement that assigns the maximum due date in the InvoiceCopy table to a specific invoice

```
UPDATE InvoiceCopy
SET CreditTotal = CreditTotal + 100,
    InvoiceDueDate = (SELECT MAX(InvoiceDueDate) FROM InvoiceCopy)
WHERE InvoiceNumber = '97/522'

(1 row(s) affected)
```

An UPDATE statement that updates all the invoices for a vendor based on the vendor's name

```
UPDATE InvoiceCopy
SET TermsID = 1
WHERE VendorID =
    (SELECT VendorID
     FROM VendorCopy
     WHERE VendorName = 'Pacific Bell')

(6 row(s) affected)
```

An UPDATE statement that changes the terms of all invoices for vendors in three states

```
UPDATE InvoiceCopy
SET TermsID = 1
WHERE VendorID IN
    (SELECT VendorID
     FROM VendorCopy
     WHERE VendorState IN ('CA', 'AZ', 'NV'))

(51 row(s) affected)
```

An UPDATE statement that applies a $100 credit to the 10 largest invoices that have a balance due of $100 or more

```
UPDATE InvoiceCopy
SET CreditTotal = CreditTotal + 100
FROM
    (SELECT TOP 10 InvoiceID
     FROM InvoiceCopy
     WHERE InvoiceTotal - PaymentTotal - CreditTotal >= 100
     ORDER BY InvoiceTotal - PaymentTotal - CreditTotal DESC) AS TopInvoices
WHERE InvoiceCopy.InvoiceID = TopInvoices.InvoiceID

(10 rows(s) affected)
```

Description

- You can code a subquery in the SET, FROM, or WHERE clause of an UPDATE statement.
- You can use a subquery in the SET clause to return the value that's assigned to a column.
- You can use a subquery in the FROM clause to identify the rows that are available for update. Then, you can refer to the derived table in the SET and WHERE clauses.
- You can code a subquery in the WHERE clause to provide one or more values used in the search condition.

Figure 7-6   How to use subqueries in an update operation

How to use joins in an update operation

In addition to subqueries, you can use joins in the FROM clause of an UPDATE statement. Joins provide an easy way to base an update on data in a table other than the one that's being updated. The two examples in figure 7-7 illustrate how this works.

The first example in this figure updates the TermsID column in all the invoices in the InvoiceCopy table for the vendor named "Pacific Bell." This is the same update operation you saw in the second example in the previous figure. Instead of using a subquery to retrieve the VendorID value for the vendor, however, this UPDATE statement joins the InvoiceCopy and VendorCopy tables on the VendorID column in each table. Then, the search condition in the WHERE clause uses the VendorName column in the VendorCopy table to identify the invoices to be updated.

The second example in this figure shows how you can use the columns in a table that's joined with the table being updated to specify values in the SET clause. Here, the VendorCopy table is joined with a table named ContactUpdates. As you can see in the figure, this table includes VendorID, LastName, and FirstName columns. After the two tables are joined on the VendorID column, the SET clause uses the LastName and FirstName columns from the ContactUpdates table to update the VendorContactLName and VendorContactFName columns in the VendorCopy table.

An UPDATE statement that changes the terms of all the invoices for a vendor

```
UPDATE InvoiceCopy
SET TermsID = 1
FROM InvoiceCopy JOIN VendorCopy
    ON InvoiceCopy.VendorID = VendorCopy.VendorID
WHERE VendorName = 'Pacific Bell'
(6 row(s) affected)
```

An UPDATE statement that updates contact names in the VendorCopy table based on data in the ContactUpdates table

```
UPDATE VendorCopy
SET VendorContactLName = LastName,
    VendorContactFName = FirstName
FROM VendorCopy JOIN ContactUpdates
    ON VendorCopy.VendorID = ContactUpdates.VendorID
(8 row(s) affected)
```

The ContactUpdates table

	VendorID	LastName	FirstName
1	5	Davison	Michelle
2	12	Mayteh	Kendall
3	17	Onandonga	Bruce
4	44	Antavius	Anthony
5	76	Bradlee	Danny
6	94	Suscipe	Reynaldo
7	101	O'Sullivan	Geraldine
8	123	Bucket	Charles

Description

- If you need to specify column values or search conditions that depend on data in a table other than the one named in the UPDATE clause, you can use a join in the FROM clause.

- You can use columns from the joined tables in the values you assign to columns in the SET clause or in the search condition of a WHERE clause.

Figure 7-7   How to use joins in an update operation

How to delete existing rows

To delete one or more rows from a table, you use the DELETE statement. Just as you can with the UPDATE statement, you can use subqueries and joins in a DELETE statement to help identify the rows to be deleted. You'll learn how to use subqueries and joins after you learn how to perform a basic delete operation.

How to perform a basic delete operation

Figure 7-8 presents the syntax of the DELETE statement along with three examples that illustrate some basic delete operations. As you can see, you specify the name of the table that contains the rows to be deleted in the DELETE clause. You can also code the FROM keyword in this clause, but this keyword is optional and is usually omitted.

To identify the rows to be deleted, you code a search condition in the WHERE clause. Although this clause is optional, you'll almost always include it. If you don't, all of the rows in the table are deleted. This is a common coding mistake, and it can be disastrous.

You can also include a FROM clause in the DELETE statement to join additional tables with the base table. Then, you can use the columns of the joined tables in the search condition of the WHERE clause. The FROM clause is an extension to the standard SQL syntax. You'll see how to use it in the next figure.

The first DELETE statement in this figure deletes a single row from the InvoiceCopy table. To do that, it specifies the InvoiceID value of the row to be deleted in the search condition of the WHERE clause. The second statement is similar, but it deletes all the invoices with a VendorID value of 37. In this case, three rows are deleted.

The third DELETE statement shows how you can use an expression in the search condition of the WHERE clause. In this case, the InvoiceTotal, PaymentTotal, and CreditTotal columns are used to calculate the balance due. Then, if the balance due is zero, the row is deleted. You might use a statement like this after inserting the paid invoices into another table as shown in figure 7-4.

Finally, the fourth DELETE statement shows how easy it is to delete all the rows from a table. Because the WHERE clause has been omitted from this statement, all the rows in the InvoiceCopy table will be deleted, which probably isn't what you want.

Because you can't restore rows once they've been deleted, you'll want to be sure that you've selected the correct rows. One way to do that is to issue a SELECT statement with the same search condition. Then, if the correct rows are retrieved, you can be sure that the DELETE statement will work as intended.

The syntax of the DELETE statement

```
DELETE [FROM] table_name
[FROM table_source]
[WHERE search_condition]
```

A DELETE statement that removes a single row from the InvoiceCopy table

```
DELETE InvoiceCopy
WHERE InvoiceID = 115
```

```
(1 row(s) affected)
```

A DELETE statement that removes all the invoices for a vendor

```
DELETE InvoiceCopy
WHERE VendorID = 37
```

```
(3 row(s) affected)
```

A DELETE statement that removes all paid invoices

```
DELETE InvoiceCopy
WHERE InvoiceTotal - PaymentTotal - CreditTotal = 0
```

```
(74 row(s) affected)
```

A DELETE statement that removes all the rows from the InvoiceCopy table

```
DELETE InvoiceCopy
```

```
(114 row(s) affected)
```

Description

- You can use the DELETE statement to delete one or more rows from the table you name in the DELETE clause.

- You specify the conditions that must be met for a row to be deleted in the WHERE clause.

- You can specify additional criteria for the delete operation in the FROM clause. See figure 7-9 for more information.

Warning

- If you omit the WHERE clause from a DELETE statement, all the rows in the table will be deleted.

Figure 7-8   How to perform a basic delete operation

How to use subqueries and joins in a delete operation

The examples in figure 7-9 illustrate how you can use subqueries and joins in a DELETE statement. Because you've seen code like this in other statements, you shouldn't have any trouble understanding these examples.

The first two examples delete all the invoices from the InvoiceCopy table for the vendor named "Blue Cross." To accomplish that, the first example uses a subquery in the WHERE clause to retrieve the VendorID value from the VendorCopy table for this vendor. In contrast, the second example joins the InvoiceCopy and VendorCopy tables. Then, the WHERE clause uses the VendorName column in the VendorCopy table to identify the rows to be deleted.

The third DELETE statement deletes all vendors that don't have invoices. To do that, it uses a subquery to return a list of the VendorID values in the InvoiceCopy table. Then, it deletes all vendors that aren't in that list.

The fourth DELETE statement shows how you can use the FROM clause to join the base table named in the DELETE clause with a derived table. Here, the subquery creates a derived table based on the InvoiceCopy table. This subquery groups the invoices in this table by vendor and calculates the total invoice amount for each vendor. Then, after the derived table is joined with the VendorCopy table, the results are filtered by the total invoice amount. Because of that, only those vendors that have invoices totaling $100 or less will be deleted from the VendorCopy table.

A DELETE statement that deletes all invoices for a vendor based on the vendor's name

```
DELETE InvoiceCopy
WHERE VendorID =
    (SELECT VendorID
     FROM VendorCopy
     WHERE VendorName = 'Blue Cross')
(3 row(s) affected)
```

The same DELETE statement using a join

```
DELETE InvoiceCopy
FROM InvoiceCopy JOIN VendorCopy
    ON InvoiceCopy.VendorID = VendorCopy.VendorID
WHERE VendorName = 'Blue Cross'
(3 row(s) affected)
```

A DELETE statement that deletes vendors that don't have invoices

```
DELETE VendorCopy
WHERE VendorID NOT IN
    (SELECT DISTINCT VendorID FROM InvoiceCopy)
(88 row(s) affected)
```

A DELETE statement that deletes vendors whose invoices total $100 or less

```
DELETE VendorCopy
FROM VendorCopy JOIN
        (SELECT VendorID, SUM(InvoiceTotal) AS TotalOfInvoices
         FROM InvoiceCopy
         GROUP BY VendorID) AS InvoiceSum
    ON VendorCopy.VendorID = InvoiceSum.VendorID
WHERE TotalOfInvoices <= 100
(6 row(s) affected)
```

Description

- You can use subqueries and joins in the FROM clause of a DELETE statement to base the delete operation on the data in tables other than the one named in the DELETE clause.
- You can use any of the columns returned by a subquery or a join in the WHERE clause of the DELETE statement.
- You can also use subqueries in the WHERE clause to provide one or more values used in the search condition.

Note

- The FROM clause is a SQL Server extension.

Figure 7-9   How to use subqueries and joins in a delete operation

Perspective

In this chapter, you learned how to use the INSERT, UPDATE, and DELETE statements to modify the data in a database. Now, if you want to practice using these statements, please use one of the two options presented at the start of this chapter so you won't corrupt a live database or a database shared by others.

In chapters 9 and 10, you'll learn more about the table definitions that can affect the way these statements work. If, for example, you delete a row in a Vendors table that has related rows in an Invoices table, SQL Server may delete all of the related rows in the Invoices table. But that depends on how the relationship is defined. So, to complete your understanding of the INSERT, UPDATE, and DELETE statements, you need to read chapters 9 and 10.

8

How to work with data types and functions

In chapter 3, you were introduced to some of the scalar functions that you can use in a SELECT statement. Now, this chapter expands on that coverage by presenting many of the scalar functions. Because most of these functions are intended for use on a particular data type, this chapter also describes the data types that are available with SQL Server. When you complete this chapter, you'll have a thorough understanding of the data types and the functions that you can use with them.

A review of the SQL data types

A column's *data type* specifies the kind of information the column is intended to store. In addition, a column's data type determines the operations that can be performed on the column. You'll learn about the data types you're most likely to use in the topics that follow.

Data type overview

The SQL Server data types can be divided into the four categories shown in the first table in figure 8-1. The *string data types* are intended for storing a string of one or more characters, which can include letters, numbers, symbols, or special characters. The terms *character*, *string*, and *text* are used interchangeably to describe this type of data.

The *numeric data types* are intended for storing numbers that can be used for mathematical calculations. As you'll see in the next topic, SQL Server can store numbers in a variety of formats.

The *temporal data types* are used to store dates and times. These data types are typically referred to as *date/time*, or *date*, *data types*.

The other data types are used to store a variety of data items. For example, some are used to store *binary large objects* (*BLOBs*) like image files. Others are used to store pointers to system objects. Because these data types are used infrequently, I don't present them in this book.

Most of the SQL Server data types correspond to the ANSI-standard data types. These data types are listed in the second table in this figure. Here, the second column lists the SQL Server data type names, and the first column lists the synonyms SQL Server provides for the ANSI-standard data types. Although you can use these synonyms instead of the SQL Server data types, you're not likely to do that. If you do, SQL Server simply maps the synonyms to the corresponding SQL Server data types.

The only synonym I recommend you use is rowversion, which is a synonym for the timestamp data type. This data type is used to store unique numbers that are generated by SQL Server and that are typically used to identify various versions of a row in a table. Microsoft plans to modify the timestamp data type in a future release so that it's compatible with the timestamp data type defined by the standards. When it does that, it will also replace the current timestamp data type with a new rowversion data type. Because of that, you'll want to use the rowversion synonym instead of the timestamp data type.

The four data type categories

Category	Description
String	Strings of character data
Numeric	Integers, floating point numbers, currency, and other numeric data
Temporal (date/time)	Dates, times, or both
Other	Binary data or system pointers

ANSI-standard data types and SQL Server equivalents

Synonym for ANSI-standard data type	SQL Server data type used
binary varying	varbinary
char varying character varying	varchar
character	char
dec	decimal
double precision	float
float	real or float
integer	int
national char national character	nchar
national char varying national character varying	nvarchar
national text	ntext
rowversion	timestamp

Description

- SQL Server defines 26 unique *data types* that are divided into the four categories shown above.
- The *temporal data types* are typically referred to as *date/time data types*, or simply *date data types*.
- SQL Server supports most, but not all, of the ANSI-standard data types.
- SQL Server provides a synonym for each of the supported ANSI-standard data types. Although you can use these synonyms, I recommend you use the SQL Server data types instead. The exception is rowversion, which you should use instead of timestamp.
- When you use the synonym for an ANSI data type, it's mapped to the appropriate SQL Server data type indicated in the table above.

Figure 8-1   Data type overview

The numeric data types

Figure 8-2 presents the numeric data types supported by SQL Server. As you can see, these can be divided into three groups: integer, decimal, and real.

Integer data types store whole numbers, which are numbers with no digits to the right of the decimal point. The five integer data types differ in the amount of storage they use and the range of values they can store. Notice that the bigint, int, and smallint data types can store positive or negative numbers. In contrast, the tinyint and bit data types can store only positive numbers or zero.

To store numbers with digits to the right of the decimal point, you use the *decimal data types*. These data types have a fixed decimal point, which means that the number of digits to the right of the decimal point doesn't vary. The number of digits a value has to the right of the decimal point is called its *scale*, and the total number of digits is called its *precision*. Notice that the money and smallmoney data types have a fixed precision and scale. These data types are intended for storing units of currency. In contrast, you can customize the precision and scale of the decimal and numeric data types so they're right for the data to be stored. Although the decimal and numeric data types are synonymous, decimal is more commonly used.

In contrast to the *fixed-point numbers* stored by the decimal data types, the *real data types* are used to store *floating-point numbers*. These data types provide for very large and very small numbers, but with a limited number of *significant digits*. The real data type can be used to store a *single-precision number*, which provides for numbers with up to 7 significant digits. And the float data type can be used to store a *double-precision number*, which provides for numbers with up to 15 significant digits. Because the real data type is equivalent to float(24), the float data type is typically used for floating-point numbers.

To express the value of a floating-point number, you can use *scientific notation*. To use this notation, you type the letter E followed by a power of 10. For instance, 3.65E+9 is equal to 3.65 x 10^9, or 3,650,000,000. If you have a mathematical background, of course, you're already familiar with this notation.

Because the precision of all the integer and decimal data types is exact, these data types are considered *exact numeric data types*. In contrast, the real data types are considered *approximate numeric data types* because they may not represent a value exactly. That can happen, for example, when a number is rounded to the appropriate number of significant digits. For business applications, you will most likely use only the exact numeric types, as there's seldom the need to work with the very large and very small numbers that the real data types are designed for.

The integer data types

Type	Bytes	Description
bigint	8	Large integers from -9,223,372,036,854,775,808 through 9,223,372,036,854,775,807.
int	4	Integers from -2,147,483,648 through 2,147,483,647.
smallint	2	Small integers from -32,768 through 32,767.
tinyint	1	Very small positive integers from 0 through 255.
bit	1	Integers with a value of 1 or 0.

The decimal data types

Type	Bytes	Description
decimal[(p[,s])]	5-17	Decimal numbers with fixed precision (*p*) and scale (*s*) from $-10^{38}+1$ through $10^{38}-1$. The precision can be any number between 1 and 38; the default is 18. The scale can be any number between 0 and the precision; the default is 0.
numeric[(p[,s])]	5-17	Synonymous with decimal.
money	8	Monetary values with four decimal places from -922,337,203,685,477.5808 through 922,337,203,685,477.5807. Synonymous with decimal(19,4).
smallmoney	4	Monetary values with four decimal places from -214,748.3648 through 214,748.3647. Synonymous with decimal(10,4).

The real data types

Type	Bytes	Description
float[(n)]	4 or 8	Double-precision floating-point numbers from -1.79×10^{308} through 1.79×10^{308}. *n* represents the number of bits used to store the decimal portion of the number (the mantissa): n=24 is single-precision; n=53 is double-precision. The default is 53.
real	4	Single-precision floating point numbers from -3.4×10^{38} through 3.4×10^{38}. Synonymous with float(24).

Description

- The *integer data types* are used to store whole numbers, which are numbers without any digits to the right of the decimal point.

- The *decimal data types* are used to store decimal values, which can include digits to the right of the decimal point. The *precision* of a decimal value indicates the total number of digits that can be stored, and the *scale* indicates the number of digits that can be stored to the right of the decimal point.

- The integer and decimal data types are considered *exact numeric data types* because their precision is exact.

- The *real data types* are used to store *floating-point numbers*, which have a limited number of *significant digits*. These data types are considered *approximate numeric data types* because they may not represent a value exactly.

Figure 8-2   The numeric data types

The string data types

Figure 8-3 presents the four most common string data types supported by SQL Server. The char and varchar data types store strings of standard characters using one byte per character. The nchar and nvarchar data types store strings of *Unicode characters* that require two bytes per character. You'll learn more about the *Unicode specification* in a moment. In the ANSI standards, two-byte characters are known as *national characters*, hence the prefix *n* on the data types.

You use the char and nchar data types to store *fixed-length strings*. Data stored using these data types always occupies the same number of bytes regardless of the actual length of the string. These data types are typically used to define columns that have a fixed number of characters. For example, the VendorState column in the Vendors table is defined with the char(2) data type because it always contains two characters.

You use the varchar and nvarchar data types to store *variable-length strings*. Data stored using these data types occupies only the number of bytes needed to store the string. They're typically used to define columns whose lengths vary from one row to the next. In general, variable-length strings are more efficient than fixed-length strings.

Although you typically store numeric values using numeric data types, the string data types may be a better choice for some numeric values. For example, you typically store zip codes, telephone numbers, and social security numbers in string columns even if they contain only numbers. That's because their values aren't used in arithmetic operations. In addition, if you stored these numbers in numeric columns, leading zeroes would be stripped, which isn't what you want.

As I said, when you use the char and varchar data types, each character is stored in a single byte. Because a byte consists of eight *bits* and because eight bits can be combined in 256 different ways, each byte can represent one of 256 different characters. These characters are assigned numeric codes from 0 to 255. Most systems use the same codes for the first 128 characters. These are the codes defined by the *ASCII* (*American Standard Code for Information Interchange*) system. The other codes, however, may be unique on your system.

When you use the nchar and nvarchar data types to store Unicode characters, each character is stored in two bytes, which provides for 63,536 different characters. That allows for all of the characters used by most of the world's languages, and all systems associate the same numeric codes with the same characters. Because of that, you should use the nchar and nvarchar data types if your database will be used in a multi-language environment. Otherwise, you should use the char and varchar data types to keep storage requirements to a minimum.

The string data types used to store standard characters

Type	Bytes	Description
char[(n)]	n	Fixed-length strings of character data. *n* is the number of characters between 1 and 8000. The default is 1.
varchar[(n)]		Variable-length strings of character data. *n* is the maximum number of characters between 1 and 8000. The default is 1. The number of bytes used to store the string depends on the actual length of the string.

The string data types used to store Unicode characters

Type	Bytes	Description
nchar(n)	2×n	Fixed-length strings of Unicode character data. *n* is the number of characters between 1 and 4000. The default is 1.
nvarchar(n)		Variable-length strings of Unicode character data. *n* is the maximum number of characters between 1 and 4000. The default is 1. The number of bytes used to store the string depends on the actual length of the string. Two bytes are needed to store each character.

Description

- The string data types can be used to store standard characters that use a single byte of storage or *Unicode characters* that use two bytes of storage.

- The char and nchar data types are typically used for *fixed-length strings*. These data types use the same amount of storage regardless of the actual length of the string.

- The varchar and nvarchar data types are typically used for *variable-length strings*. These data types use only the amount of storage needed for a given string.

- Unless your system is used in a multi-language environment, you should use the char and varchar data types rather than nchar and nvarchar data types.

Note

- The *Unicode specification* is a scheme that's used to encode characters used in languages around the world. This reduces the possibility that a receiving system will translate the characters incorrectly. The Unicode data types support a wider range of characters than the standard character data types, but they require twice as much space per character.

Figure 8-3   The string data types

The date/time data types

Figure 8-4 presents the two date/time data types supported by SQL Server. These data types differ by the amount of storage they use and the range of values they can store. Both date/time data types reserve half of their storage space for the date and half for the time. As you'll see, the integer portion of the number stores the date, and the fractional portion of the number stores the time.

For a value with the datetime data type, the date is represented as the number of days before or after January 1, 1900. For example, September 2, 2002 is represented as 37,499, and December 1, 1899 is represented as -31.

The time portion of a datetime value is represented as a fraction equal to the number of milliseconds that have elapsed since 12 midnight divided by the number of milliseconds in a day. For example, 3:49 p.m. is represented as 0.65902777778 (56,940,000 divided by 86,400,000), and 1:45:30.5 a.m. is represented as 0.073269675922.

For a value with the smalldatetime data type, the date is represented as the number of days after January 1, 1900. The time portion is represented as the number of minutes that have elapsed since midnight divided by the number of minutes in a day. So September 2, 2002 is still represented as 37,499 and 3:49 p.m. is still represented as 0.65902777778. However, December 1, 1899 can't be represented because it is out of range. And 1:45:30.5 a.m. is represented as 0.073611111111, which is equivalent to 1:46:00 a.m., because the time is rounded to the nearest minute.

Note that SQL Server doesn't provide data types for storing just the date or just the time. Instead, if you store a date/time value without an explicit time, the time component is set to 00:00:00, which represents midnight. Similarly, if you store a date/time value without an explicit date, the date component is set to January 1, 1900.

When you work with date/time values, you need to know how to code date and time literals. This figure presents some of the most common formats for dates and times. All SQL Server systems recognize dates in the yyyy-mm-dd format, which is why I've used this format in most of the examples in this book. Most systems recognize the other date and time formats shown here as well. Since the supported formats depend on system settings, however, you may need to check and see which ones are acceptable on your system.

You also need to be aware of the two-digit year cutoff that's defined on your system when you work with date literals. When you code a two-digit year, the two-digit year cutoff determines whether the year is interpreted as a year in the 20th or the 21st century. By default, SQL Server interprets the years 00 through 49 as 2000 through 2049, and it interprets the years 50 through 99 as 1950 through 1999. Because the two-digit year cutoff can be modified, however, you'll want to find out what it is on your system before you use date literals with two-digit years. Then, if you code a date literal outside the range, you'll have to use a four-digit year. Of course, you can always code all of your date literals with four-digit years, just to be sure.

The temporal (date/time) data types

Type	Bytes	Description
datetime	8	Dates and times from January 1, 1753 through December 31, 9999, with an accuracy af 3.33 milliseconds.
smalldatetime	4	Dates and times from January 1, 1900 through June 6, 2079, with an accuracy of one minute.

Common date formats

Format	Example
yyyy-mm-dd	2002-08-15
mm/dd/yyyy	8/15/2002
mm-dd-yy	8-15-02
Month dd, yyyy	August 15, 2002
Mon dd, yy	Aug 15, 02
dd Mon yy	15 Aug 02

Common time formats

Format	Example
hh:mi	16:20
hh:mi am/pm	4:20 pm
hh:mi:ss	4:20:36
hh:mi:ss:mmm	4:20:36:12

Description

- Datetime values are stored internally as an 8-byte number that represents the number of days before or after January 1, 1900 and the number of milliseconds after midnight.

- Smalldatetime values are stored internally as a 4-byte number that represents the number of days after January 1, 1900 and the number of minutes after midnight.

- You can specify a date/time value by coding a date/time literal. To code a date/time literal, enclose the date/time value in single quotes. You can use any of the formats shown above as well as others.

- If you don't specify a time when storing a date value, the time defaults to 12:00 a.m. If you don't specify a date when storing a time value, the date defaults to January 1, 1900.

- If you specify a two-digit year, the century is determined based on a system configuration option that establishes the two-digit year cutoff. By default, the two-digit year cutoff is 50, which means that years from 00 to 49 are interpreted as 2000 to 2049, and the years 50 through 99 are interpreted as 1950 through 1999.

- You can specify a time using either a 12-hour or a 24-hour clock. For a 12-hour clock, am is the default if am or pm isn't specified.

- The date/time data types are considered approximate numeric data types because not all values can be represented precisely.

Figure 8-4   The date/time data types

How to convert data

As you work with the various data types, you'll find that you frequently need to convert a value with one data type to another data type. Although SQL Server does many conversions automatically, it doesn't always do them the way you want. Because of that, you need to be aware of how data conversion works, and you need to know when and how to specify the type of conversion you want to do.

How data conversion works

Before SQL Server can operate on two values, it must convert those values to the same data type. To do that, it converts the value that has the data type with the lowest precedence to the data type of the other value. Figure 8-5 presents the order of precedence for some common SQL Server data types.

To illustrate how this works, consider the three expressions shown in this figure. The first expression multiplies the InvoiceTotal column, which is defined with the money data type, by a decimal value. Because the decimal data type has a higher precedence than the money data type, the value in the InvoiceTotal column is converted to a decimal before the multiplication is performed. Then, the result of the operation is also a decimal value. Similarly, the integer literal in the second expression is converted to the money data type before it's subtracted from the PaymentTotal column, and the result of the operation is a money value.

The third example shows that implicit conversion is also used when a value is assigned to a column. In this case, a date literal is assigned to the PaymentDate column. Because this column is defined with the smalldatetime data type, the literal must be converted to this data type before it can be assigned to the column.

When SQL Server performs a conversion automatically, it's called an *implicit conversion*. However, not all conversions can be done implicitly. Some of the conversions that can't be done implicitly are listed in this figure. These conversions must be done explicitly. To perform an *explicit conversion*, you use the CAST and CONVERT functions you'll learn about in the next two topics.

Before I go on, you should realize that you won't usually code expressions with literal values like the ones shown in this figure. Instead, you'll use column names that contain the appropriate values. I used literal values here and in many of the examples throughout this chapter so that it's clear what data types are being evaluated.

Order of precedence for common SQL Server data types

Precedence	Category	Data type
Highest	Date/time	datetime
		smalldatetime
	Numeric	float
		real
		decimal
		money
		smallmoney
		int
		smallint
		tinyint
		bit
	String	nvarchar
		nchar
		varchar
Lowest		char

Conversions that can't be done implicitly

From data type	To data type
char, varchar, nchar, nvarchar	money, smallmoney
datetime, smalldatetime	decimal, numeric, float, real, bigint, int, smallint, tinyint, money, smallmoney, bit
money, smallmoney	char, varchar, nchar, nvarchar

Expressions that use implicit conversion

```
InvoiceTotal * .0775         -- InvoiceTotal (money) converted to decimal
PaymentTotal - 100           -- Numeric literal converted to money
PaymentDate = '2002-08-05'   -- Date literal converted to smalldatetime value
```

Description

- If you assign a value with one data type to a column with another data type, SQL Server converts the value to the data type of the column using *implicit conversion*. Not all data types can be converted implicitly to all other data types.

- SQL Server also uses implicit conversion when it evaluates an expression that involves values with different data types. In that case, it converts the value whose data type has lower precedence to the data type that has higher precedence. The result of the expression is returned in this same data type.

- Each combination of precision and scale for the decimal and numeric values is considered a different data type, with higher precision and scale taking precedence.

- If you want to perform a conversion that can't be done implicitly or you want to convert a data type with higher precedence to a data type with lower precedence, you can use the CAST or CONVERT functions to perform an *explicit conversion*.

Figure 8-5   How data conversion works

How to convert data using the CAST function

Figure 8-6 presents the syntax of the CAST function. This function lets you convert, or *cast*, an expression to the data type you specify.

The SELECT statement in this figure illustrates how this works. Here, the third column in the result set shows what happens when the smalldatetime values that are stored in the InvoiceDate column are cast as varchar values. As you can see, this conversion causes the date to be displayed in an alphanumeric format. The fourth column in the result set shows what happens when the money values in the InvoiceTotal column are cast as integer values. Before the digits to the right of the decimal point are dropped, the numbers are rounded to the nearest whole number. Finally, the last column in the result set shows the values from the InvoiceTotal column cast as varchar values. In this case, only two digits are displayed to the right of the decimal point.

This figure also illustrates a problem that can occur when you perform integer division without explicit conversion. In the first example, the number 50 is divided by the number 100 giving a result of 0. This happens because the result of the division of two integers must be an integer. For this operation to return an accurate result, then, you must explicitly convert one of the numbers to a decimal. Then, because the data type of the other value will be lower in the order of precedence, that value will be converted to a decimal value as well and the result will be a decimal. This is illustrated in the second example, where the value 100 is converted to a decimal. As you can see, the result is .5, which is what you want.

The syntax of the CAST function

```
CAST(expression AS data_type)
```

A SELECT statement that uses the CAST function

```
SELECT InvoiceDate, InvoiceTotal,
    CAST(InvoiceDate AS varchar) AS varcharDate,
    CAST(InvoiceTotal AS int) AS integerTotal,
    CAST(InvoiceTotal AS varchar) AS varcharTotal
FROM Invoices
```

	InvoiceDate	InvoiceTotal	varcharDate	integerTotal	varcharTotal
1	2002-02-25 00:00:00	116.5400	Feb 25 2002 12:00AM	117	116.54
2	2002-03-14 00:00:00	1083.5800	Mar 14 2002 12:00AM	1084	1083.58
3	2002-04-11 00:00:00	20551.1800	Apr 11 2002 12:00AM	20551	20551.18
4	2002-04-16 00:00:00	26881.4000	Apr 16 2002 12:00AM	26881	26881.40

How to convert data when performing integer division

Operation	Result
50/100	0
50/CAST(100 AS decimal(3))	.500000

Description

- You can use the CAST function to explicitly convert, or *cast*, an expression from one data type to another.

- When you perform a division operation on two integers, the result is an integer. To get a more accurate result, you can cast one of the integer values as a decimal. That way, the result will be a decimal.

- CAST is an ANSI-standard function and is used more frequently than CONVERT, which is unique to SQL Server. You should use CONVERT when you need the additional formatting capabilities it provides. See figure 8-7 for details.

Figure 8-6   How to convert data using the CAST function

How to convert data using the CONVERT function

In most cases, you'll use the CAST function to convert a value from one data type to another since it's an ANSI-standard function. However, SQL Server provides another function you can use to convert data: CONVERT. Figure 8-7 shows you how to use this function.

In the syntax at the top of this figure, you can see that the CONVERT function provides an optional style argument. You can use this argument to specify the format you want to use when you convert date/time, real, or money data to character data. Some of the common style codes are presented in this figure. For a complete list of codes, please refer to Books Online.

The SELECT statement in this figure shows several examples of the CONVERT function. The first thing you should notice here is that if you don't code a style argument, the CONVERT function works just like CAST. This is illustrated by the first and fourth columns in the result set. Because of that, you'll probably use CONVERT only when you need to use one of the formats provided by the style argument.

The second and third columns both use the CONVERT function to format the InvoiceDate column. The second column uses a style code of 1, so the date is returned in the mm/dd/yy format. In contrast, the third column uses a style code of 107, so the date is returned in the Mon dd, yyyy format. Notice that neither of these formats includes a time. Finally, the fifth column uses the CONVERT function to format the InvoiceTotal column with two digits to the right of the decimal point and commas to the left.

The syntax of the CONVERT function

```
CONVERT(data_type, expression [, style])
```

A SELECT statement that uses the CONVERT function

```
SELECT CONVERT(varchar, InvoiceDate) AS varcharDate,
    CONVERT(varchar, InvoiceDate, 1) AS varcharDate_1,
    CONVERT(varchar, InvoiceDate, 107) AS varcharDate_107,
    CONVERT(varchar, InvoiceTotal) AS varcharTotal,
    CONVERT(varchar, InvoiceTotal, 1) AS varcharTotal_1
FROM Invoices
```

	varcharDate	varcharDate_1	varcharDate_107	varcharTotal	varcharTotal_1
1	Feb 25 2002 12:00AM	02/25/02	Feb 25, 2002	116.54	116.54
2	Mar 14 2002 12:00AM	03/14/02	Mar 14, 2002	1083.58	1,083.58
3	Apr 11 2002 12:00AM	04/11/02	Apr 11, 2002	20551.18	20,551.18
4	Apr 16 2002 12:00AM	04/16/02	Apr 16, 2002	26881.40	26,881.40

Common style codes for converting date/time data to character data

Code	Output format
0 or 100 (default)	Mon dd yyyy hh:miAM/PM
1 or 101	mm/dd/yy or mm/dd/yyyy
7 or 107	Mon dd, yy or Mon dd, yyyy
8 or 108	hh:mi:ss
10 or 110	mm-dd-yy or mm-dd-yyyy
12 or 112	yymmdd or yyyymmdd
14 or 114	hh:mi:ss:mmm (24-hour clock)

Common style codes for converting real data to character data

Code	Output
0 (default)	6 digits maximum
1	8 digits; must use scientific notation
2	16 digits; must use scientific notation

Common style codes for converting money data to character data

Code	Output
0 (default)	2 digits to the right of the decimal point; no commas to the left
1	2 digits to the right of the decimal point; commas to the left
2	4 digits to the right of the decimal point; no commas to the left

Description

- You can use the CONVERT function to explicitly convert an expression from one data type to another.

- You can use the optional style argument to specify the format to be used for date/time, real, and money values converted to character data.

- See the *Cast and Convert* topic in Books Online for a complete list of style codes.

Figure 8-7   How to convert data using the CONVERT function

How to use other data conversion functions

Although CAST and CONVERT are the two conversion functions you'll use most often, SQL Server provides some additional functions to perform special types of conversions. These functions are presented in figure 8-8.

You can use the first function, STR, to convert a floating-point value to a character value. You can think of this function as two conversion functions combined into one. First, it converts a floating-point value to a decimal value with the specified length and number of digits to the right of the decimal point. Then, it converts the decimal value to a character value. The function in this figure, for example, converts the number 1234.5678 to a string with a maximum length of seven characters and one digit to the right of the decimal point. Notice that the decimal digits are rounded rather than truncated.

The other four functions are used to convert characters to their equivalent numeric code and vice versa. CHAR and ASCII work with standard character strings that are stored one byte per character. The CHAR function shown in this figure, for example, converts the number 79 to its equivalent ASCII code, the letter O. Conversely, the ASCII function converts the letter O to its numeric equivalent of 79. Notice that although the string in the ASCII function can include more than one character, only the first character is converted.

CHAR is frequently used to output ASCII control characters that can't be typed on your keyboard. The three most common control characters are presented in this figure. These characters can be used to format output so it's easy to read. The SELECT statement in this figure, for example, uses the CHAR(13) and CHAR(10) control characters to start new lines after the vendor name and vendor address in the output.

The NCHAR and UNICODE functions convert Unicode characters to and from their numeric equivalents. You can see how these functions work in the examples. Notice in the last example that to code a Unicode character as a literal value, you have to precede the literal with the letter N.

Other data conversion functions

Function	Description
STR(float[,length[,decimal]])	Converts a floating-point number to a character string with the given length and number of digits to the right of the decimal point. The length must include one character for the decimal point and one character for the sign. The sign is blank if the number is positive.
CHAR(integer)	Converts the ASCII code represented by an integer between 0 and 255 to its character equivalent.
ASCII(string)	Converts the leftmost character in a string to its equivalent ASCII code.
NCHAR(integer)	Converts the Unicode code represented by an integer between 0 and 65535 to its character equivalent.
UNICODE(string)	Converts the leftmost character in a UNICODE string to its equivalent UNICODE code.

Examples that use the data conversion functions

Function	Result
STR(1234.5678, 7, 1)	1234.6
CHAR(79)	O
ASCII('Orange')	79
NCHAR(332)	Ō
UNICODE(N'Ōr')	332

ASCII codes for common control characters

Control character	Value
Tab	Char(9)
Line feed	Char(10)
Carriage return	Char(13)

A SELECT statement that uses the CHAR function to format output

```
SELECT VendorName + CHAR(13) + CHAR(10)
    + VendorAddress1 + CHAR(13) + CHAR(10)
    + VendorCity + ', ' + VendorState + ' ' + VendorZipCode
FROM Vendors
WHERE VendorID = 1
```

```
US Postal Service
Attn:  Supt. Window Services
Madison, WI 53707
```

Description

- The CHAR function is typically used to insert control characters into a character string.

- To code a Unicode value as a literal, precede the value with the character N.

Figure 8-8   How to use other data conversion functions

How to work with string data

SQL Server provides a number of functions for working with string data. You'll learn how to use some of those functions in the topics that follow. In addition, you'll learn how to solve two common problems that can occur when you work with string data.

A summary of the string functions

Figure 8-9 summarizes the string functions that are available with SQL Server. Most of these functions are used to perform string manipulation. For example, you can use the LEN function to get the number of characters in a string. Note that this function counts spaces at the beginning of the string (leading spaces), but not spaces at the end of the string (trailing spaces). If you want to remove leading or trailing spaces from a string, you can use the LTRIM or RTRIM function.

You can use the LEFT and RIGHT functions to get the specified number of characters from the beginning and end of a string. You can use the SUBSTRING function to get the specified number of characters from anywhere in a string. You can use the REPLACE function to replace a substring within a string with another substring. And you can use the REVERSE function to reverse the order of the characters in a string.

The CHARINDEX function lets you locate the first occurrence of a substring within another string. The return value is a number that indicates the position of the substring. Note that you can start the search at a position other than the beginning of the string by including the start argument.

The PATINDEX function is similar to CHARINDEX. Instead of locating a string, however, it locates a string pattern. Like the string patterns you learned about in chapter 3 for use with the LIKE operator, the string patterns you use with the PATINDEX function can include wildcard characters. You can refer back to chapter 3 if you need to refresh your memory on how to use these characters.

The last three functions should be self-explanatory. You use the LOWER and UPPER functions to convert the characters in a string to lower or upper case. And you use the SPACE function to return a string that has the specified number of spaces.

Some of the string functions

Function	Description
`LEN(string)`	Returns the number of characters in the string. Leading spaces are included, but trailing spaces are not.
`LTRIM(string)`	Returns the string with any leading spaces removed.
`RTRIM(string)`	Returns the string with any trailing spaces removed.
`LEFT(string,length)`	Returns the specified number of characters from the beginning of the string.
`RIGHT(string,length)`	Returns the specified number of characters from the end of the string.
`SUBSTRING(string,start,length)`	Returns the specified number of characters from the string starting at the specified position.
`REPLACE(search,find,replace)`	Returns the search string with all occurrences of the find string replaced with the replace string.
`REVERSE(string)`	Returns the string with the characters in reverse order.
`CHARINDEX(find,search[,start])`	Returns an integer that represents the position of the first occurrence of the find string in the search string starting at the specified position. If the starting position isn't specified, the search starts at the beginning of the string. If the string isn't found, the function returns zero.
`PATINDEX(find,search[,start])`	Returns an integer that represents the position of the first occurrence of the find pattern in the search string starting at the specified position. If the starting position isn't specified, the search starts at the beginning of the string. If the pattern isn't found, the function returns zero. The find pattern can include wildcard characters. If the pattern begins with a wildcard, the value returned is the position of the first non-wildcard character.
`LOWER(string)`	Returns the string converted to lowercase letters.
`UPPER(string)`	Returns the string converted to uppercase letters.
`SPACE(integer)`	Returns a string with the specified number of space characters (blanks).

Notes

- The start argument must be an integer from 1 to the length of the string.
- The ANSI standards specify a TRIM function that removes both leading and trailing spaces from a string. Although this function isn't supported by SQL Server, you can get the same result by combining LTRIM and RTRIM (see the example in figure 8-10).

Figure 8-9   A summary of the string functions

Examples that use string functions

Figure 8-10 presents examples of most of the string functions. If you study the examples at the top of this figure, you shouldn't have any trouble figuring out how they work. If you're confused by any of them, though, you can refer back to the previous figure to check the syntax and results.

The SELECT statement shown in this figure illustrates how you can use the LEFT and RIGHT functions to format columns in a result set. In this case, the LEFT function is used to retrieve the first character of the VendorContactFName column in the Vendors table, which contains the first name of the vendor contact. In other words, this function retrieves the first initial of the vendor contact. Then, this initial is combined with the last name of the vendor contact and two literal values. You can see the result in the second column of the result set.

The third column in the result set lists the vendor's phone number without an area code. To accomplish that, this column specification uses the RIGHT function to extract the eight rightmost characters of the VendorPhone column. This assumes, of course, that all of the phone numbers are stored in the same format, which isn't necessarily the case since the VendorPhone column is defined as varchar(50).

This SELECT statement also shows how you can use a function in the search condition of a WHERE clause. This condition uses the SUBSTRING function to select only those rows with an area code of 559. To do that, it retrieves three characters from the VendorPhone column starting with the second character. Again, this assumes that the phone numbers are all in the same format and that the area code is enclosed in parentheses.

String function examples

Function	Result
LEN('SQL Server')	10
LEN(' SQL Server ')	12
LEFT('SQL Server', 3)	'SQL'
LTRIM(' SQL Server ')	'SQL Server '
RTRIM(' SQL Server ')	' SQL Server'
LTRIM(RTRIM(' SQL Server '))	'SQL Server'
LOWER('SQL Server')	'sql server'
UPPER('ca')	CA
PATINDEX('%v_r%', 'SQL Server')	8
CHARINDEX('SQL', ' SQL Server')	3
CHARINDEX('-', '(559) 555-1212')	10
SUBSTRING('(559) 555-1212', 7, 8)	555-1212
REPLACE(RIGHT('(559) 555-1212', 13), ') ', '-')	559-555-1212

A SELECT statement that uses the LEFT, RIGHT, and SUBSTRING functions

```
Select VendorName, VendorContactLName + ', ' + LEFT(VendorContactFName, 1)
       + '.' AS ContactName, RIGHT(VendorPhone, 8) AS Phone
FROM Vendors
WHERE SUBSTRING(VendorPhone, 2, 3) = 559
ORDER BY VendorName
```

	VendorName	ContactName	Phone
1	Abbey Office Furnishings	Francis, K.	555-8300
2	BFI Industries	Kaleigh, E.	555-1551
3	Bill Marvin Electric Inc	Hostlery, K.	555-5106
4	Cal State Termite	Hunter, D.	555-1534
5	California Business Machines	Rohansen, A.	555-5570

Figure 8-10   Examples that use string functions

How to solve common problems that occur with string data

Figure 8-11 presents solutions to two common problems that occur when you work with string data. The first problem occurs when you store numeric data in a character column and then want to sort the column in numeric sequence.

To illustrate, look at the first example in this figure. Here, the columns in the StringSample table are defined with character data types. The first SELECT statement shows the result of sorting the table by the first column, which contains a numeric ID. As you can see, the rows are not in numeric sequence. That's because SQL Server interprets the values as characters, not as numbers.

One way to solve this problem is to convert the values in the ID column to integers for sorting purposes. This is illustrated in the second SELECT statement in this example. As you can see, the rows are now sorted in numeric sequence.

Another way to solve this problem is to pad the numbers with leading zeroes or spaces so that the numbers are aligned on the right. This is illustrated by the AltID column in this table, which is padded with zeroes. If you sorted by this column instead of the first column, the rows would be returned in numeric sequence.

The second problem you'll encounter when working with string data occurs when two or more values are stored in the same string. For example, both a first and a last name are stored in the Name column of the StringSample table. If you want to work with the first and last names independently, you have to parse the string using the string functions. This is illustrated by the SELECT statement in the second example in this figure.

To extract the first name, this statement uses the LEFT and CHARINDEX functions. First, it uses the CHARINDEX function to locate the first space in the Name column. Then, it uses the LEFT function to extract all of the characters up to that space. Notice that one is subtracted from the value that's returned by the CHARINDEX function, so the space itself isn't included in the first name.

To extract the last name, this statement uses the RIGHT, LEN, and CHARINDEX functions. It uses the LEN function to get the number of characters in the Name column. Then, it uses the CHARINDEX function to locate the first space in the Name column, and it subtracts that value from the value returned by the LEN function. The result is the number of characters in the last name. That value is then used in the RIGHT function to extract the last name from the Name column.

As you review this example, you should keep in mind that I kept it simple so that you can focus on how the string functions are used. You should realize, however, that this code won't work for all names. If, for example, a first name contains a space, such as in the name Jean Paul, this code won't work properly. That illustrates the importance of designing a database so that this type of problem doesn't occur. You'll learn more about that in the next chapter. For now, just realize that if a database is designed correctly, you won't have to worry about this type of problem. Instead, this problem should occur only if you're importing data from another file or database system.

How to use the CAST function to sort by a string column that contains numbers

The StringSample table sorted by the ID column

```
SELECT * FROM StringSample
ORDER BY ID
```

	ID	Name	AltID
1	1	Lizbeth Darien	01
2	17	Lance Pinos-Potter	17
3	2	Darnell O'Sullivan	02
4	20	Jean Paul Renard	20
5	3	Alisha von Strump	03

The StringSample table sorted by the ID column cast to an integer

```
SELECT * FROM StringSample
ORDER BY CAST(ID AS int)
```

	ID	Name	AltID
1	1	Lizbeth Darien	01
2	2	Darnell O'Sullivan	02
3	3	Alisha von Strump	03
4	17	Lance Pinos-Potter	17
5	20	Jean Paul Renard	20

How to use the string functions to parse a string

```
SELECT Name,
    LEFT(Name, CHARINDEX(' ', Name) - 1) AS First,
    RIGHT(Name, LEN(Name) - CHARINDEX(' ', Name) ) AS Last
FROM StringSample
```

	Name	First	Last
1	Lizbeth Darien	Lizbeth	Darien
2	Darnell O'Sullivan	Darnell	O'Sullivan
3	Lance Pinos-Potter	Lance	Pinos-Potter
4	Jean Paul Renard	Jean	Paul Renard
5	Alisha von Strump	Alisha	von Strump

Description

- If you sort by a string column that contains numbers, you may receive unexpected results. To avoid that, you can convert the string column to a numeric value in the ORDER BY clause.

- If a string consists of two or more components, you can parse it into its individual components. To do that, you can use the CHARINDEX function to locate the characters that separate the components. Then, you can use the LEFT, RIGHT, SUBSTRING, and LEN functions to extract the individual components.

Figure 8-11   How to solve common problems that occur with string data

How to work with numeric data

In addition to the string functions, SQL Server provides several numeric functions. Although you'll probably use only a couple of these functions on a regular basis, you should be aware of all of them in case you ever need them. After you learn about these functions, I'll show you how you can use them and some of the other functions you've learned about in this chapter to solve common problems that occur when you work with numeric data.

How to use the numeric functions

Figure 8-12 summarizes eight of the numeric functions SQL Server provides. The function you'll probably use most often is ROUND. This function rounds a number to the precision specified by the length argument. Note that you can round the digits to the left of the decimal point by coding a negative value for this argument. However, you're more likely to code a positive number to round the digits to the right of the decimal point. You can also use the ROUND function to truncate a number to the specified length. To do that, you can code any integer value other than zero for the optional function argument.

The first set of examples in this figure shows how the ROUND function works. The first example rounds the number 12.5 to a precision of zero, which means that the result has no significant digits to the right of the decimal point. Note that this function does not change the precision of the value. The result still has one digit to the right of the decimal point. The number has just been rounded so that the digit is insignificant. To make that point clear, the second example rounds a number with four decimal places to a precision of zero. Notice that the result still has four digits to the right of the decimal point; they're just all zero.

The next three examples show variations of the first two examples. The third example rounds a number with four decimal places to a precision of 1, and the fourth example rounds the digits to the left of the decimal point to a precision of one. Finally, the last example truncates a number to a precision of zero.

The other function you're likely to use is ISNUMERIC. This function returns a Boolean value that indicates if an expression is numeric. This is illustrated by the next set of examples in this figure. This function can be useful for testing the validity of a value before saving it in a table.

You can use the next three functions, ABS, CEILING, and FLOOR, to get the absolute value of a number, the smallest integer greater than or equal to a number, or the largest integer less than or equal to a number. If you study the examples, you shouldn't have any trouble figuring out how these functions work.

The next two functions, SQUARE and SQRT, are used to calculate the square and square root of a number. And the last function, RAND, generates a floating-point number with a random value between 0 and 1. SQL Server provides a variety of functions like these for performing mathematical calculations, but you're not likely to use them. You can refer to Books Online to get a complete list of these functions.

Some of the numeric functions

Function	Description
ROUND(number,length[,function])	Returns the number rounded to the precision specified by length. If length is positive, the digits to the right of the decimal point are rounded. If it's negative, the digits to the left of the decimal point are rounded. To truncate the number rather than round it, code a non-zero value for function.
ISNUMERIC(expression)	Returns a value of 1 (true) if the expression is a numeric value; returns a value of 0 (false) otherwise.
ABS(number)	Returns the absolute value of the number.
CEILING(number)	Returns the smallest integer that is greater than or equal to the number.
FLOOR(number)	Returns the largest integer that is less than or equal to the number.
SQRT(float_number)	Returns the square root of a floating-point number.
SQUARE(float_number)	Returns the square of a floating-point number.
RAND([integer])	Returns a random floating-point number between 0 and 1. If integer is coded, it provides a starting value for the function. Otherwise, the function will return the same number each time it's invoked within the same query.

Examples that use the numeric functions

Function	Result
ROUND(12.5,0)	13.0
ROUND(12.4999,0)	12.0000
ROUND(12.4999,1)	12.5000
ROUND(12.4999,-1)	10.0000
ROUND(12.5,0,1)	12.0
ISNUMERIC(-1.25)	1
ISNUMERIC('SQL Server')	0
ISNUMERIC('2001-09-30')	0
ABS(-1.25)	1.25
CEILING(-1.25)	-1
FLOOR(-1.25)	-2
CEILING (1.25)	2
FLOOR(1.25)	1
SQUARE(5.2786)	27.863617959999999
SQRT(125.43)	11.199553562530964
RAND()	0.243729

Note

- To calculate the square or square root of a number with a data type other than float or real, you must cast it as a floating-point number.

Figure 8-12   How to use the numeric functions

How to solve common problems that occur with numeric data

Earlier in this chapter, you learned that numbers with the real data types don't contain exact values. The details of why that is are beyond the scope of this book. From a practical point of view, though, that means that you don't want to search for exact values when you're working with real numbers. If you do, you'll miss values that are in essence equal to the value you're looking for.

To illustrate, consider the RealSample table shown in figure 8-13. This table includes a column named R that's defined with the float(53) data type. Now, consider what would happen if you selected all the rows where the value of R is equal to 1. The result set would include only the second row, even though the table contains two other rows that have values approximately equal to 1.

When you perform a search on a column with a real data type, then, you usually want to search for an approximate value. This figure shows two ways to do that. First, you can search for a range of values. The first SELECT statement in this figure, for example, searches for values between .99 and 1.01. Second, you can search for values that round to an exact value. This is illustrated by the second SELECT statement. Both of these statements return the three rows in the RealSample table that are approximately equal to 1.

Although both of the SELECT statements shown here return the same results, you should realize that the first statement is more efficient than the second one. That's because SQL Server isn't able to optimize a query that uses a function in its search condition. Because of that, I recommend you use the range technique to search for a real value whenever possible.

Another problem you may face is formatting numeric values so that they're easy to read. One way to do that is to format them so they're aligned on the right, as shown in the third SELECT statement. To do this, the real numbers in the R column are first cast as decimal numbers to give them a consistent scale. Then, the decimal values are cast as character data and padded on the left with spaces to right-align the data as shown in the column named R_Formatted.

If you look at the expression for the last column, you'll see that it's quite complicated. If you break it down into its component parts, however, you shouldn't have much trouble understanding how it works. To help you break it down, the third, fourth, and fifth columns in the result set show the interim results returned by portions of the expression. The third column shows the result of casting the real values as decimal values, and the fourth column shows the result of casting the decimal values as string values. This is necessary so that the LEN function can be used to calculate the number of characters in each value. The result of this function is shown in the fifth column.

To align the values at the right, the last column specification assumes a column width of nine characters. Then, the length of the number to be formatted is subtracted from nine, and the SPACE function is used to create a string with the resulting number of spaces. Finally, the number is concatenated to the string of spaces after it's converted to a string value. The result is a string column with the numbers aligned at the right.

The RealSample table

	ID	R
1	1	1.0000000000000011
2	2	1.0
3	3	0.999999999999999
4	4	1234.5678901234501
5	5	999.04440209348002
6	6	24.048490000000001

How to search for approximate real values

A SELECT statement that searches for a range of values

```
SELECT * FROM RealSample
WHERE R BETWEEN 0.99 AND 1.01
```

A SELECT statement that searches for rounded values

```
SELECT * FROM RealSample
WHERE ROUND(R,2) = 1
```

The result set

	ID	R
1	1	1.0000000000000011
2	2	1.0
3	3	0.999999999999999

A SELECT statement that formats real numbers

```
SELECT ID, R, CAST(R AS decimal(9,3)) AS R_decimal,
    CAST(CAST(R AS decimal(9,3)) AS varchar(9)) AS R_varchar,
    LEN(CAST(CAST(R AS decimal(9,3)) AS varchar(9))) AS R_LEN,
    SPACE(9 - LEN(CAST(CAST(R AS decimal(9,3)) AS varchar(9)))) +
        CAST(CAST(R AS decimal(9,3)) AS varchar(9)) AS R_Formatted
FROM RealSample
```

	ID	R	R_decimal	R_varchar	R_LEN	R_Formatted
1	1	1.0000000000000011	1.000	1.000	5	1.000
2	2	1.0	1.000	1.000	5	1.000
3	3	0.999999999999999	1.000	1.000	5	1.000
4	4	1234.5678901234501	1234.568	1234.568	8	1234.568
5	5	999.04440209348002	999.044	999.044	7	999.044
6	6	24.048490000000001	24.048	24.048	6	24.048

Description

- Because real values are approximate, you'll want to search for approximate values when retrieving real data. To do that, you can specify a range of values, or you can use the ROUND function to search for rounded values.

- When you display real or decimal values, you may want to format them so they're aligned on the right.

Figure 8-13   How to solve common problems that occur with numeric data

How to work with date/time data

In the topics that follow, you'll learn how to use some of the functions SQL Server provides for working with dates and times. As you'll see, these include functions for extracting different parts of a date/time value and for performing operations on dates and times. In addition, you'll learn how to perform different types of searches on date/time values.

A summary of the date/time functions

Figure 8-14 presents a summary of the date/time functions and shows how some of them work. One of the functions you'll use frequently is GETDATE, which gets the current local date and time from your system. GETUTCDATE is similar, but it returns the *Universal Time Coordinate* (*UTC*) date, also known as *Greenwich Mean Time*. You can see the difference between these functions in the first two examples in this figure.

Although you probably won't use the GETUTCDATE function often, it's useful if your system will operate in different time zones. That way, the date/time values will always reflect Greenwich Mean Time, regardless of the time zone in which they're entered. For example, a date/time value entered at 11:00 a.m. Los Angeles time would be given the same value as a date/time value entered at 2:00 p.m. New York time. That makes it easy to compare and operate on these values.

The next five functions, DAY, MONTH, YEAR, DATENAME, and DATEPART, let you extract different parts of a date value. This is illustrated by the second set of examples, which all retrieve the month part of a date. You'll learn more about these functions in the next figure. For now, just realize that when you use the DATEPART and DATENAME functions, you can retrieve any of the date parts listed in this figure.

The DATEADD and DATEDIFF functions let you perform addition and subtraction operations on date/time values. As you can see, these functions let you specify the date part to be added. You'll see examples of these functions in a minute.

The last function, ISDATE, returns a Boolean value that indicates whether an expression can be cast as a valid date/time value. This function is useful for testing the validity of a date/time value before it's saved to a table. This is illustrated by the last set of examples. Here, you can see that the first and third expressions are valid dates, but the second and fourth expressions aren't. The second expression isn't valid because the month of September has only 30 days. And the fourth expression isn't valid because a time value can have a maximum of 59 minutes and 59 seconds. Note that this function checks for both a valid date format and a valid date value.

Some of the date/time functions

Function	Description
GETDATE()	Returns the current local date and time based on the system's clock.
GETUTCDATE()	Returns the current UTC date and time based on the system's clock and time zone setting. UTC (Universal Time Coordinate) is the same as Greenwich Mean Time.
DAY(date)	Returns the day of the month as an integer.
MONTH(date)	Returns the month as an integer.
YEAR(date)	Returns the 4-digit year as an integer.
DATENAME(datepart,date)	Returns the part of the date specified by datepart as a character string.
DATEPART(datepart,date)	Returns the part of the date specified by datepart as an integer.
DATEADD(datepart,number,date)	Returns the date that results from adding the specified number of datepart units to the date.
DATEDIFF(datepart,startdate,enddate)	Returns the number of datepart units between the specified start and end dates.
ISDATE(expression)	Returns a value of 1 (true) if the expression is a valid date/time value; returns a value of 0 (false) otherwise.

Date part values and abbreviations

Argument	Abbreviations	Argument	Abbreviations
year	yy, yyyy	weekday	dw
quarter	qq, q	hour	hh
month	mm, m	minute	mi, n
dayofyear	dy, y	second	ss, s
day	dd, d	millisecond	ms
week	wk, ww		

Examples that use some of the date/time functions

Function	Result
GETDATE()	2002-08-06 14:10:13.947
GETUTCDATE()	2002-08-06 21:10:13.947
MONTH('2002-09-30')	9
DATEPART(m,'2002-09-30')	9
DATENAME(month,'2002-09-30')	September
ISDATE('2002-09-30')	1
ISDATE('2002-09-31')	0
ISDATE('23:59:59')	1
ISDATE('23:99:99')	0

Figure 8-14   A summary of the date/time functions

How to parse dates and times

Figure 8-15 shows you how to use the DAY, MONTH, YEAR, DATEPART, and DATENAME functions to parse dates and times. If you just need to get an integer value for a day, month, or year, you should use the DAY, MONTH, and YEAR functions as shown in the examples at the top of this figure since these are ANSI-standard functions. If you need to extract another part of a date or time as an integer, however, you'll need to use the DATEPART function. And if you need to extract a date part as a string, you'll need to use the DATENAME function.

This figure shows the result of using each of the date part values with the DATEPART and DATENAME functions. As you can see, many of the values returned by the two functions appear to be the same. Keep in mind, however, that all of the values returned by DATEPART are integers. In contrast, all of the values returned by DATENAME are strings. That's why the month and week day are returned as names rather than numbers when you use DATENAME. The function you use, then, will depend on what you need to do with the date part. If you need to use it in an arithmetic operation, for example, you'll want to use the DATEPART function. But if you need to use it in a concatenation, you'll want to use the DATENAME function.

Examples that use the DAY, MONTH, and YEAR functions

Function	Result
`DAY('2002-09-30')`	30
`MONTH('2002-09-30')`	9
`YEAR('2002-09-30')`	2002

Examples that use the DATEPART function

Function	Result
`DATEPART(day, '2002-09-30 11:35:00')`	30
`DATEPART(month, '2002-09-30 11:35:00')`	9
`DATEPART(year, '2002-09-30 11:35:00')`	2002
`DATEPART(hour, '2002-09-30 11:35:00')`	11
`DATEPART(minute, '2002-09-30 11:35:00')`	35
`DATEPART(second, '2002-09-30 11:35:00')`	0
`DATEPART(quarter, '2002-09-30 11:35:00')`	3
`DATEPART(dayofyear, '2002-09-30 11:35:00')`	273
`DATEPART(week, '2002-09-30 11:35:00')`	40
`DATEPART(weekday, '2002-09-30 11:35:00')`	2

Examples that use the DATENAME function

Function	Result
`DATENAME(day, '2002-09-30 11:35:00')`	30
`DATENAME(month, '2002-09-30 11:35:00')`	September
`DATENAME(year, '2002-09-30 11:35:00')`	2002
`DATENAME(hour, '2002-09-30 11:35:00')`	11
`DATENAME(minute, '2002-09-30 11:35:00')`	35
`DATENAME(second, '2002-09-30 11:35:00')`	0
`DATENAME(quarter, '2002-09-30 11:35:00')`	3
`DATENAME(dayofyear, '2002-09-30 11:35:00')`	273
`DATENAME(week, '2002-09-30 11:35:00')`	40
`DATENAME(weekday, '2002-09-30 11:35:00')`	Monday

Notes

- When you use weekday with the DATEPART function, it returns an integer that indicates the day of the week where 1=Sunday, 2=Monday, etc.
- The DAY, MONTH, and YEAR functions are ANSI-standard functions. The DATEPART and DATENAME functions are more general-purpose functions provided by SQL Server.

Figure 8-15   How to parse dates and times

How to perform operations on dates and times

Figure 8-16 shows you how to use the DATEADD and DATEDIFF functions to perform operations on dates and times. You can use the DATEADD function to add a specified number of date parts to a date. The first eight DATEADD functions in this figure, for example, show how you can add one day, month, year, hour, minute, second, quarter, and week to a date/time value. If you want to subtract date parts from a date/time value, you can do that with the DATEADD function too. Just code the number argument as a negative value, as illustrated by the next to last DATEADD function. The last DATEADD function illustrates that you can't add a fractional number of date parts to a date/time value. If you try to, the fractional portion is ignored.

If you need to find the difference between two date/time values, you can use the DATEDIFF function as illustrated by the second set of examples in this figure. As you can see, the result is expressed in the date part units you specify. The first function, for example, returns the number of days between two dates, and the second example returns the number of months between the same two dates.

In most cases, the earlier date is specified as the second argument in the DATEDIFF function and the later date is specified as the third argument. That way, the result of the function is a positive value. However, you can also code the later date first. Then, the result is a negative value as you can see in the last DATEDIFF function in this figure.

If you use the DATEDIFF function, you should realize that it returns the number of date/time boundaries crossed, which is not necessarily the same as the number of intervals between two dates. To understand this, consider the third DATEDIFF function. This function returns the difference in years between the dates 2001-12-01 and 2002-09-30. Since the second date is less than one year after the first date, you might expect this function to return a value of zero. As you can see, however, it returns a value of 1 because it crossed the one-year boundary between the years 2001 and 2002. Because this is not intuitive, you'll want to use this function carefully.

The last three examples in this figure show how you can perform operations on dates and times without using the DATEADD and DATEDIFF functions. The first expression, for example, adds one day to a date/time value, and the second expression subtracts one day from the same value. When you use this technique, SQL Server assumes you're adding or subtracting days. So you can't add or subtract other date parts unless you express them as multiples or fractions of days.

The last expression shows how you can subtract two date/time values to calculate the number of days between them. Notice that after the dates are subtracted, the result is converted to an integer. That's necessary because the result of the subtraction operation is implicitly cast as a date/time value that represents the number of days after January 1, 1900. For this reason, the integer difference of 303 days is interpreted as the following date/time value: 1900-10-31 00:00:00:000.

Examples that use the DATEADD function

Function	Result
DATEADD(day, 1, '2002-09-30 11:35:00')	2002-10-01 11:35:00.000
DATEADD(month, 1, '2002-09-30 11:35:00')	2002-10-30 11:35:00.000
DATEADD(year, 1, '2002-09-30 11:35:00')	2003-09-30 11:35:00.000
DATEADD(hour, 1, '2002-09-30 11:35:00')	2002-09-30 12:35:00.000
DATEADD(minute, 1, '2002-09-30 11:35:00')	2002-09-30 11:36:00.000
DATEADD(second, 1, '2002-09-30 11:35:00')	2002-09-30 11:35:01.000
DATEADD(quarter, 1, '2002-09-30 11:35:00')	2002-12-30 11:35:00.000
DATEADD(week, 1, '2002-09-30 11:35:00')	2002-10-07 11:35:00.000
DATEADD(month, -1, '2002-09-30 11:35:00')	2002-08-30 11:35:00.000
DATEADD(year, 1.5, '2002-09-30 11:35:00')	2003-09-30 11:35:00.000

Examples that use the DATEDIFF function

Function	Result
DATEDIFF(day, '2001-12-01', '2002-09-30')	303
DATEDIFF(month, '2001-12-01', '2002-09-30')	9
DATEDIFF(year, '2001-12-01', '2002-09-30')	1
DATEDIFF(hour, '06:46:45', '11:35:00')	5
DATEDIFF(minute, '06:46:45', '11:35:00')	289
DATEDIFF(second, '06:46:45', '11:35:00')	17295
DATEDIFF(quarter, '2001-12-01', '2002-09-30')	3
DATEDIFF(week, '2001-12-01', '2002-09-30')	44
DATEDIFF(day, '2002-09-30', '2001-12-01')	-303

Examples that use the addition and subtraction operators

Operation	Result
CAST('2002-09-30 11:35:00' AS smalldatetime) + 1	2002-10-01 11:35:00
CAST('2002-09-30 11:35:00' AS smalldatetime) - 1	2002-09-29 11:35:00
CAST(CAST('2002-09-30' AS datetime) - CAST('2001-12-01' AS datetime) AS int)	303

Description

- You can use the DATEADD function to subtract a specified number of date parts from a date by coding the number of date parts as a negative value, as illustrated by the next to last DATEADD example above.

- If the number of date parts you specify in the DATEADD function isn't an integer, the fractional portion of the number is ignored as illustrated by the last DATEADD example above.

- If the end date you specify in a DATEDIFF function is before the start date, the function will return a negative value as illustrated by the last DATEDIFF example above.

- You can also use the addition and subtraction operators to add and subtract days from a date value. To add and subtract days from a date string, cast the string to a date/time value as shown in the last set of examples above.

- You can also calculate the number of days between two dates by subtracting the date/time values and converting the result to an integer as illustrated by the last example above.

Figure 8-16   How to perform operations on dates and times

How to perform a date search

Because date/time values always contain both a date and a time component, searching for specific dates and times can be difficult. In this topic, you'll learn a variety of ways to ignore the time component when you search for a date value. And in the next topic, you'll learn how to ignore date components when you search for time values.

Figure 8-17 illustrates the problem you can encounter when searching for dates. The examples in this figure use a table named DateSample. This table includes an ID column that contains an integer value and a StartDate column that contains a datetime value. Notice that the time components in the first three rows in this table have a zero value. In contrast, the time components in the next three rows have non-zero time components.

The problem occurs when you try to search for a date value. The first SELECT statement in this figure, for example, searches for rows in the DateSample table with the date 1992-02-28. Because a time component isn't specified, a zero time component is added when the date string is converted to a datetime value. However, because the row with this date has a non-zero time value, no rows are returned by this statement.

To solve this problem, you can use one of the four techniques shown in this figure. First, you can search for a range of dates that includes only the date you're looking for as illustrated by the second SELECT statement in this figure. The search condition in this statement searches for dates that are greater than or equal to the date you're looking for and less than the date that follows the date you're looking for. Because a time component of zero is implicitly added to both of the dates in the search condition, this statement returns the one row with the date you want.

Notice that this SELECT statement doesn't use any functions. In particular, it doesn't use any functions in the WHERE clause. Because of that, this is the most efficient technique for searching for dates. In contrast, the other three techniques all require the use of functions in the WHERE clause, as you can see in the last three SELECT statements in this figure.

The second technique uses the MONTH, DAY, and YEAR functions to search for just for those three components. The third technique is to use the CAST function to convert the value in the StartDate column to an 11-character string. That causes the time portion of the date to be truncated (if you look back at figure 8-6, you'll see that when a date/time data type is cast to a string data type, the date portion contains 11 characters in the format "Mon dd yyyy"). Then, the string is converted back to a datetime value, which adds a zero time component. The last technique is similar, but it uses the CONVERT function instead of the CAST function. The style code used in this function converts the datetime value to a 10-character string that doesn't include the time. Then, the string is converted back to a date with a zero time component.

The contents of the DateSample table

	ID	StartDate
1	1	1965-03-01 00:00:00.000
2	2	1985-02-28 00:00:00.000
3	3	1989-10-31 00:00:00.000
4	4	1991-02-28 10:00:00.000
5	5	1992-02-28 13:58:32.823
6	6	1992-02-29 09:02:25.383

A search condition that fails to return a row

```
SELECT * FROM DateSample
WHERE StartDate = '1992-02-28'
```

Search conditions that ignore time values

A SELECT statement that searches for a range of dates

```
SELECT * FROM DateSample
WHERE StartDate >= '1992-02-28' AND StartDate < '1992-02-29'
```

A SELECT statement that searches for month, day, and year components

```
SELECT * FROM DateSample
WHERE MONTH(StartDate) = 2 AND DAY(StartDate) = 28
    AND YEAR(StartDate) = 1992
```

	ID	StartDate
1	5	1992-02-28 13:58:32.823

A SELECT statement that uses the CAST function to remove time values

```
SELECT *, CAST(CAST(StartDate AS char(11)) AS datetime) AS DateOnly
FROM DateSample
WHERE CAST(CAST(StartDate AS char(11)) AS datetime) = '1992-02-28'
```

A SELECT statement that uses the CONVERT function to remove time values

```
SELECT *, CAST(CONVERT(char(10), StartDate, 110) AS datetime) AS DateOnly
FROM DateSample
WHERE CAST(CONVERT(char(10), StartDate, 110) AS datetime) = '1992-02-28'
```

	ID	StartDate	DateOnly
1	5	1992-02-28 13:58:32.823	1992-02-28 00:00:00.000

Description

- If you perform a search using a date string that doesn't include the time, the date string is converted implicitly to a date/time value with a zero time component. Then, if the date columns you're searching have non-zero time components, you have to accommodate the times in the search condition.

- You can accommodate non-zero time components by searching for a range of dates rather than specific dates, by using the MONTH, DAY, and YEAR functions to search only the month, day, and year components, or by using the CAST or CONVERT function to cast the date value to a string to remove the time component.

Figure 8-17   How to perform a date search

How to perform a time search

When you search for a time value without specifying a date component, SQL Server automatically uses the default date of January 1, 1900. That's why neither of the first two SELECT statements in figure 8-18 return any rows. Even though at least one row has the correct time value for each search condition, those rows don't have the correct date value.

The third SELECT statement in this figure shows how you can solve this problem. The search condition in this statement uses the CONVERT function to convert the datetime values in the StartDate column to string values without dates. To do that, it uses a style argument of 8. Then, it converts the string values back to datetime values, which causes the default date to be used. That way, the date will match the dates that are added to the date literals.

Before I go on, you should realize that many of the problems that can occur when searching for dates or times can be avoided by designing the database properly. For example, if you know that you will need to search for dates, you can design the database with a separate column that holds the date and a zero time component. Of course, if the time component isn't important, you could just set it to zero before the date/time value is saved. Similarly, if you know that you will need to search for times, you can design the database with a separate column that holds the time and the default date. That way, you can perform date and time searches without having to do any conversion or range checking.

The contents of the DateSample table

	ID	StartDate
1	1	1965-03-01 00:00:00.000
2	2	1985-02-28 00:00:00.000
3	3	1989-10-31 00:00:00.000
4	4	1991-02-28 10:00:00.000
5	5	1992-02-28 13:58:32.823
6	6	1992-02-29 09:02:25.383

Two search conditions that fail to return a row

```
SELECT * FROM DateSample
WHERE StartDate = CAST('10:00:00' AS datetime)

SELECT * FROM DateSample
WHERE StartDate >= '09:00:00' AND
    StartDate < '12:59:59:999'
```

A SELECT statement that ignores date values

```
SELECT *, CAST(CONVERT(char(12), StartDate, 8) AS datetime) AS TimeOnly
FROM DateSample
WHERE CAST(CONVERT(char(12), StartDate, 8) AS datetime) >= '09:00:00' AND
    CAST(CONVERT(char(12), StartDate, 8) AS datetime) < '12:59:59:999'
```

	ID	StartDate	TimeOnly
1	4	1991-02-28 10:00:00.000	1900-01-01 10:00:00.000
2	6	1992-02-29 09:02:25.383	1900-01-01 09:02:25.000

Description

- If you perform a search using a date string that includes only a time, the date is converted implicitly to a date/time value with a default date component of 1900-01-01. Then, if the date columns you're searching have other dates, you have to accommodate those dates in the search condition.

- You can accommodate non-default date components by converting the date/time values to values with default dates. To do that, you can use the CONVERT function with a style code of 8 as shown above.

Figure 8-18   How to perform a time search

Other functions you should know about

In addition to the conversion functions and the functions for working with specific types of data, SQL Server provides four other functions you should know about: CASE, COALESCE, ISNULL, and GROUPING.

How to use the CASE function

Figure 8-19 presents the two formats of the CASE function. This function returns a value that's determined by the conditions you specify. The easiest way to describe how this function works is to look at the two examples shown in this figure.

The first example uses a simple CASE function. When you use this function, SQL Server compares the input expression you code in the CASE clause with the expressions you code in the WHEN clauses. In this example, the input expression is a value in the TermsID column of the Invoices table, and the when expressions are the valid values for this column. When SQL Server finds a when expression that's equal to the input expression, it returns the expression specified in the matching THEN clause. If the value of the TermsID column is 3, for example, this function returns the value "Net due 30 days." Although it's not shown in this example, you can also code an ELSE clause at the end of the CASE function. Then, if none of the when expressions are equal to the input expression, the function returns the value specified in the ELSE clause.

The simple CASE function is typically used with columns that can contain a limited number of values, such as the TermsID column used in this example. In contrast, the searched CASE function can be used for a wide variety of purposes. For example, you can test for conditions other than equal with this function. In addition, each condition can be based on a different column or expression. The second example in this figure illustrates how this function works.

This example determines the status of the invoices in the Invoices table. To do that, the searched CASE function uses the DATEDIFF function to get the number of days between the current date and the invoice due date. If the difference is greater than 30, the CASE function returns the value "Over 30 days past due." Similarly, if the difference is greater than 0, the function returns the value "1 to 30 days past due." Notice that if an invoice is 45 days old, both of these conditions are true. In that case, the function returns the expression associated with the first condition since this condition is evaluated first. In other words, the sequence of the conditions is critical to getting logical results. If neither of the conditions is true, the function returns the value "Current."

Because the WHEN clauses in this example use greater than conditions, this CASE function couldn't be coded using the simple syntax. Of course, CASE functions can be more complicated than what's shown here, but this should give you an idea of what you can do with this function.

The syntax of the simple CASE function

```
CASE input_expression
    WHEN when_expression_1 THEN result_expression_1
    [WHEN when_expression_2 THEN result_expression_2]...
    [ELSE else_result_expression]
END
```

The syntax of the searched CASE function

```
CASE
    WHEN conditional_expression_1 THEN result_expression_1
    [WHEN conditional_expression_2 THEN result_expression_2]...
    [ELSE else_result_expression]
END
```

A SELECT statement that uses a simple CASE function

```
SELECT InvoiceNumber, TermsID,
    CASE TermsID
        WHEN 1 THEN 'Net due 10 days'
        WHEN 2 THEN 'Net due 20 days'
        WHEN 3 THEN 'Net due 30 days'
        WHEN 4 THEN 'Net due 60 days'
        WHEN 5 THEN 'Net due 90 days'
    END AS Terms
FROM Invoices
```

	InvoiceNumber	TermsID	Terms
1	QP58872	4	Net due 60 days
2	Q545443	4	Net due 60 days
3	P-0608	5	Net due 90 days

A SELECT statement that uses a searched CASE function

```
SELECT InvoiceNumber, InvoiceTotal, InvoiceDate, InvoiceDueDate,
    CASE
        WHEN DATEDIFF(day, InvoiceDueDate, GETDATE()) > 30
            THEN 'Over 30 days past due'
        WHEN DATEDIFF(day, InvoiceDueDate, GETDATE()) > 0
            THEN '1 to 30 days past due'
        ELSE 'Current'
    END AS Status
FROM Invoices
WHERE InvoiceTotal - PaymentTotal - CreditTotal > 0
```

	InvoiceNumber	InvoiceTotal	InvoiceDate	InvoiceDueDate	Status
39	40318	21842.0000	2002-07-18 00:00:00	2002-07-20 00:00:00	1 to 30 days past due
40	31361833	579.4200	2002-05-23 00:00:00	2002-06-09 00:00:00	Over 30 days past due
41	456789	8344.5000	2002-08-01 00:00:00	2002-08-31 00:00:00	Current

Description

- The simple CASE function tests the expression in the CASE clause against the expressions in the WHEN clauses. Then, the function returns the result expression associated with the first test that results in an equal condition.

- The searched CASE function tests the conditional expression in each WHEN clause in sequence and returns the result expression for the first condition that evaluates to true.

Figure 8-19   How to use the CASE function

How to use the COALESCE and ISNULL functions

Figure 8-20 presents two functions that you can use to work with null values: COALESCE and ISNULL. Both of these functions let you substitute non-null values for null values. Although these two functions are similar, COALESCE is more flexible because it lets you specify a list of values. Then, it returns the first non-null value in the list. In contrast, the ISNULL function uses only two expressions. It returns the first expression if that expression isn't null. Otherwise, it returns the second expression.

The examples in this figure illustrate how these functions work. The first example uses the COALESCE function to return the value of the PaymentDate column, if that column doesn't contain a null value. Otherwise, it returns the date 1900-01-01. The second example performs the operation using the ISNULL function. Note that when you use either of these functions, all of the expressions must have the same data type. So, for example, you couldn't substitute the string "Not Paid" for a null payment date.

The third example shows how you can work around this restriction. In this example, the value of the InvoiceTotal column is converted to a character value. That way, if the InvoiceTotal column contains a null value, the COALESCE function can substitute the string "No invoices" for this value. Notice that this example uses an outer join to combine all of the rows in the Vendors table with the rows for each vendor in the Invoices table. Because of that, a null value will be returned for the InvoiceTotal column for any vendor that doesn't have invoices. As you can see, then, this function is quite useful with outer joins.

The syntax of the COALESCE function

```
COALESCE(expression_1 [, expression_2]...)
```

The syntax of the ISNULL function

```
ISNULL(check_expression, replacement_value)
```

A SELECT statement that uses the COALESCE function

```
SELECT PaymentDate,
    COALESCE(PaymentDate, '1900-01-01') AS NewDate
FROM Invoices
```

The same SELECT statement using the ISNULL function

```
SELECT PaymentDate,
    ISNULL(PaymentDate, '1900-01-01') AS NewDate
FROM Invoices
```

The result set

	PaymentDate	NewDate
1	2002-04-11 00:00:00	2002-04-11 00:00:00
2	2002-05-14 00:00:00	2002-05-14 00:00:00
3	NULL	1900-01-01 00:00:00
4	2002-05-12 00:00:00	2002-05-12 00:00:00

A SELECT statement that substitutes a different data type

```
SELECT VendorName,
    COALESCE(CAST(InvoiceTotal AS varchar), 'No invoices') AS InvoiceTotal
FROM Vendors LEFT JOIN Invoices
    ON Vendors.VendorID = Invoices.VendorID
ORDER BY VendorName
```

	VendorName	InvoiceTotal
1	Abbey Office Furnishings	17.50
2	American Booksellers Assoc	No invoices
3	American Express	No invoices
4	ASC Signs	No invoices
5	Ascom Hasler Mailing Systems	No invoices

Description

- The COALESCE and ISNULL functions let you substitute non-null values for null values.

- The COALESCE function returns the first expression in a list of expressions that isn't null. All of the expressions in the list must have the same data type. If all of the expressions are null, this function returns a null value.

- The ISNULL function returns the expression if it isn't null. Otherwise, it returns the value you specify. The expression and the value must have the same data type.

- COALESCE is not an ANSI-standard function, but it's more widely supported than ISNULL, which is unique to SQL Server.

Figure 8-20   How to use the COALESCE and ISNULL functions

How to use the GROUPING function

In chapter 5, you learned how to use the ROLLUP and CUBE operators to add summary rows to a summary query. You may recall that when you do that, a null value is assigned to any column in a summary row that isn't being summarized. If you need to, you can refer back to figures 5-7 and 5-8 to refresh your memory on how this works.

If you want to assign a value other than null to these columns, you can do that using the GROUPING function as illustrated in figure 8-21. This function accepts the name of a column as its argument. The column you specify must be one of the columns named in a GROUP BY clause that includes the ROLLUP or CUBE operator.

The example in this figure shows how you can use the GROUPING function in a summary query that summarizes vendors by state and city. This is the same summary query you saw back in figure 5-7. Instead of simply retrieving the values of the VendorState and VendorCity columns from the base table, however, this query uses the GROUPING function within a CASE function to determine the values that are assigned to those columns. If a row is added to summarize the VendorState column, for example, the value of the GROUPING function for that column is 1. Then, the CASE function assigns the value "All" to that column. Otherwise, it retrieves the value of the column from the Vendors table. Similarly, if a row is added to summarize the VendorCity column, the value "All" is assigned to that column. As you can see in the result set shown here, this makes it more obvious what columns are being summarized.

This technique is particularly useful if the columns you're summarizing can contain null values. In that case, it would be difficult to determine which rows are summary rows and which rows simply contain null values. Then, you may not only want to use the GROUPING function to replace the null values in summary rows, but you may want to use the COALESCE or ISNULL function to replace null values retrieved from the base table.

The syntax of the GROUPING function

```
GROUPING(column_name)
```

A summary query that uses the GROUPING function

```
SELECT
    CASE
        WHEN GROUPING(VendorState) = 1 THEN 'All'
        ELSE VendorState
    END AS VendorState,
    CASE
        WHEN GROUPING(VendorCity) = 1 THEN 'All'
        ELSE VendorCity
    END AS VendorCity,
    COUNT(*) AS QtyVendors
FROM Vendors
WHERE VendorState IN ('IA', 'NJ')
GROUP BY VendorState, VendorCity WITH ROLLUP
ORDER BY VendorState DESC, VendorCity DESC
```

The result set

	VendorState	VendorCity	QtyVendors
1	NJ	Washington	1
2	NJ	Fairfield	1
3	NJ	East Brunswick	2
4	NJ	All	4
5	IA	Washington	1
6	IA	Fairfield	1
7	IA	All	2
8	All	All	6

Description

- You can use the GROUPING function to determine when a null value is assigned to a column as the result of the ROLLUP or CUBE operator. The column you name in this function must be one of the columns named in the GROUP BY clause.

- If a null value is assigned to the specified column as the result of the ROLLUP or CUBE operator, the GROUPING function returns a value of 1. Otherwise, it returns a value of 0.

- You typically use the GROUPING function with the CASE function. Then, if the GROUPING function returns a value of 1, you can assign a value other than null to the column.

Figure 8-21   How to use the GROUPING function

Perspective

In this chapter, you learned about the different SQL Server data types and many of the functions that you can use to operate on SQL Server data. At this point, you have all of the essential skills you need to develop SQL code at a professional level.

However, there's a lot more to learn about SQL Server. In the next section of this book, then, you'll learn the basic skills for designing a database. Even if you never need to design your own database, understanding this material will help you work more efficiently with databases that have been designed by others.

Terms

data type
string data type
numeric data type
temporal data type
date/time data type
date data type
BLOB (binary large object)
integer data type
decimal data type
scale
precision
real data type
fixed-point number
floating-point number
significant digits
single-precision number
double-precision number

scientific notation
exact numeric data types
approximate numeric data types
Unicode character
Unicode specification
national character
fixed-length string
variable-length string
bit
ASCII (American Standard Code
    for Information Interchange)
implicit conversion
explicit conversion
cast
Universal Time Cordinate (UTC)
Greenwich Mean Time

Section 3

Database design and implementation

In large programming shops, database administrators are usually responsible for designing the databases that are used by production applications, and they may also be responsible for the databases that are used for testing those applications. Often, though, programmers are asked to design, create, or maintain small databases that are used for testing. And in a small shop, programmers may also be responsible for the production databases.

So whether you're a database administrator or a SQL programmer, you need the skills and knowledge presented in this section. That's true even if you aren't ever called upon to design or maintain a database. By understanding what's going on behind the scenes, you'll be able to use SQL more effectively.

So in chapter 9, you'll learn how to design a SQL Server database. In chapter 10, you'll learn how to use the Data Definition Language (DDL) statements to create and maintain the SQL Server objects of a database. And in chapter 11, you'll learn how to use the Enterprise Manager to do the same tasks.

9

How to design a database

In this chapter, you'll learn how to design a new database. This is useful information for the SQL programmer whether or not you ever design a database on your own. To illustrate this process, I'll use the accounts payable (AP) system that you've seen throughout this book because that will make it easier for you to understand the design techniques.

How to design a data structure

Databases are often designed by database administrators (DBAs) or design specialists. This is especially true for large, multiuser databases. How well this is done can directly affect your job as a SQL programmer. In general, a well designed database is easy to understand and query, while a poorly designed database is difficult to work with. In fact, when you work with a poorly designed database, you will often need to figure out how it is designed before you can code your queries appropriately.

The topics that follow will teach you a basic approach for designing a *data structure*. We use that term to refer to a model of the database rather than the database itself. Once you design the data structure, you can use the techniques presented in the next two chapters to create a database with that design. By understanding the right way to design a database, you'll work more effectively as a SQL programmer.

The basic steps for designing a data structure

In many cases, you can design a data structure based on an existing real-world system. The illustration at the top of figure 9-1 presents a conceptual view of how this works. Here, you can see that all of the information about the people, documents, and facilities within a real-world system is mapped to the tables, columns, and rows of a database system.

As you design a data structure, each table represents one object, or *entity*, in the real-world system. Then, within each table, each column stores one item of information, or *attribute*, for the entity, and each row stores one occurrence, or *instance*, of the entity.

This figure also presents the six steps you can follow to design a data structure. You'll learn more about each of these steps in the topics that follow. In general, though, step 1 is to identify all the data elements that need to be stored in the database. Step 2 is to break complex elements down into smaller components whenever that makes sense. Step 3 is to identify the tables that will make up the system and to determine which data elements are assigned as columns in each table. Step 4 is to define the relationships between the tables by identifying the primary and foreign keys. Step 5 is to normalize the database to reduce data redundancy. And step 6 is to identify the indexes that are needed for each table.

To model a database system after a real-world system, you can use a technique called *entity-relationship* (*ER*) *modeling*. Because this is a complex subject of its own, I won't present it in this book. However, I have applied some of the basic elements of this technique to the design diagrams presented in this chapter. In effect, then, you'll be learning some of the basics of this modeling technique.

A database system is modeled after a real-world system

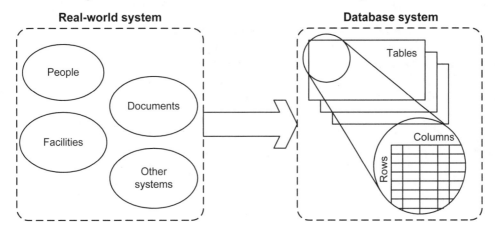

The six basic steps for designing a data structure

Step 1:   Identify the data elements

Step 2:   Subdivide each element into its smallest useful components

Step 3:   Identify the tables and assign columns

Step 4:   Identify the primary and foreign keys

Step 5:   Review whether the data structure is normalized

Step 6:   Identify the indexes

Description

- A relational database system should model the real-world environment where it's used. The job of the designer is to analyze the real-world system and then map it onto a relational database system.

- A table in a relational database typically represents an object, or *entity*, in the real world. Each column of a table is used to store an *attribute* associated with the entity, and each row represents one *instance* of the entity.

- To model a database and the relationships between its tables after a real-world system, you can use a technique called *entity-relationship* (*ER*) *modeling*. Some of the diagrams you'll see in this chapter apply the basic elements of ER modeling.

Figure 9-1   The basic steps for designing a data structure

How to identify the data elements

The first step for designing a data structure is to identify the data elements required by the system. You can use several techniques to do that, including analyzing the existing system if there is one, evaluating comparable systems, and interviewing anyone who will be using the system. One particularly good source of information are the documents used by an existing system.

In figure 9-2, for example, you can see an invoice that's used by an accounts payable system. We'll use this document as the main source of information for the database design presented in this chapter. Keep in mind, though, that you'll want to use all available resources when you design your own database.

If you study this document, you'll notice that it contains information about three different entities: vendors, invoices, and line items. First, the form itself has preprinted information about the vendor who issued the invoice, such as the vendor's name and address. If this vendor were to issue another invoice, this information wouldn't change.

This document also contains specific information about the invoice. Some of this information, such as the invoice number, invoice date, and invoice total, is general in nature. Although the actual information will vary from one invoice to the next, each invoice will include this information. In addition to this general information, each invoice includes information about the items that were purchased. Although each line item contains similar information, each invoice can contain a different number of line items.

One of the things you need to consider as you review a document like this is how much information your system needs to track. For an accounts payable system, for example, you may not need to store detailed data such as the information about each line item. Instead, you may just need to store summary data like the invoice total. As you think about what data elements to include in the database, then, you should have an idea of what information you'll need to get back out of the system.

An invoice that can be used to identify data elements

Acme Fabrication, Inc.				
Custom Contraptions, Contrivances and Confabulations			Invoice Number:	I01-1088
1234 West Industrial Way East Los Angeles California 90022			Invoice Date:	10/05/02
800.555.1212 fax 562.555.1213 www.acmefabrication.com			Terms:	Net 30

Part No.	Qty.	Description	Unit Price	Extension
CUST345	12	Design service, hr	100.00	1200.00
457332	7	Baling wire, 25x3ft roll	79.90	559.30
50173	4375	Duct tape, black, yd	1.09	4768.75
328771	2	Rubber tubing, 100ft roll	4.79	9.58
CUST281	7	Assembly, hr	75.00	525.00
CUST917	2	Testing, hr	125.00	250.00
		Sales Tax		245.20

Your salesperson:	Ruben Goldberg, ext 4512
Accounts receivable:	Inigo Jones, ext 4901

$7,557.83
PLEASE PAY THIS AMOUNT

Thanks for your business!

The data elements identified on the invoice document

Vendor name	Invoice date	Item extension
Vendor address	Invoice terms	Vendor sales contact name
Vendor phone number	Item part number	Vendor sales contact extension
Vendor fax number	Item quantity	Vendor AR contact name
Vendor web address	Item description	Vendor AR contact extension
Invoice number	Item unit price	Invoice total

Description

- Depending on the nature of the system, you can identify data elements in a variety of ways, including interviewing users, analyzing existing systems, and evaluating comparable systems.

- The documents used by a real-world system, such as the invoice shown above, can often help you identify the data elements of the system.

- As you identify the data elements of a system, you should begin thinking about the entities that those elements are associated with. That will help you identify the tables of the database later on.

Figure 9-2   How to identify the data elements

How to subdivide the data elements

Some of the data elements you identify in step 1 of the design procedure will consist of multiple components. The next step, then, is to divide these elements into their smallest useful values. Figure 9-3 shows how you can do that.

The first example in this figure shows how you can divide the name of the sales contact for a vendor. Here, the name is divided into two elements: a first name and a last name. When you divide a name like this, you can easily perform operations like sorting by last name and using the first name in a salutation, such as "Dear Ruben." In contrast, if the full name is stored in a single column, you have to use the string functions to extract the component you need. And, as you learned in the last chapter, that can lead to inefficient and complicated code. In general, then, you should separate a name like this whenever you'll need to use the name components separately. Later, when you need to use the full name, you can combine the first and last names using concatenation.

The second example shows how you typically divide an address. Notice in this example that the street number and street name are stored in a single column. Although you could store these components in separate columns, that usually doesn't make sense since these values are typically used together. That's what I mean when I say the data elements should be divided into their smallest *useful* values.

With that guideline in mind, you might even need to divide a single string into two or more components. A bulk mail system, for example, might require a separate column for the first three digits of the zip code. And a telephone number could require as many as four columns: one for the area code, one for the three-digit prefix, one for the four-digit number, and one for the extension.

As in the previous step, knowledge of the real-world system and of the information that will be extracted from the database is critical. In some circumstances, it may be okay to store data elements with multiple components in a single column. That can simplify your design and reduce the overall number of columns. In general, though, most designers divide data elements as much as possible. That way, it's easy to accommodate almost any query, and you don't have to change the database design later on when you realize that you need to use just part of a column value.

A name that's divided into first and last names

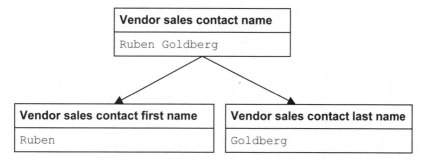

An address that's divided into street address, city, state, and zip code

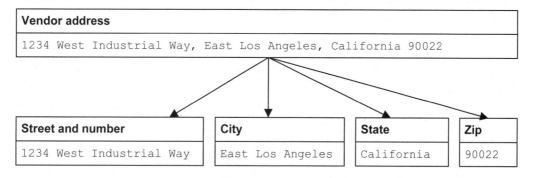

Description

- If a data element contains two or more components, you should consider subdividing the element into those components. That way, you won't need to parse the element each time you use it.

- The extent to which you subdivide a data element depends on how it will be used. Because it's difficult to predict all future uses for the data, most designers subdivide data elements as much as possible.

- When you subdivide a data element, you can easily rebuild it when necessary by concatenating the individual components.

Figure 9-3   How to subdivide the data elements

How to identify the tables and assign columns

Figure 9-4 presents the three main entities for the accounts payable system and lists the possible data elements that can be associated with each one. In most cases, you'll recognize the main entities that need to be included in a data structure as you identify the data elements. As I reviewed the data elements represented on the invoice document in figure 9-2, for example, I identified the three entities shown in this figure: vendors, invoices, and invoice line items. Although you may identify additional entities later on in the design process, it's sufficient to identity the main entities at this point. These entities will become the tables of the database.

After you identify the main entities, you need to determine which data elements are associated with each entity. These elements will become the columns of the tables. In many cases, the associations are obvious. For example, it's easy to determine that the vendor name and address are associated with the vendors entity and the invoice date and invoice total are associated with the invoices entity. Some associations, however, aren't so obvious. In that case, you may need to list a data element under two or more entities. In this figure, for example, you can see that the invoice number is included in both the invoices and invoice line items entities and the account number is included in all three entities. Later, when you normalize the data structure, you may be able to remove these repeated elements. For now, though, it's okay to include them.

Before I go on, I want to point out the notation I used in this figure. To start, any data elements I included that weren't identified in previous steps are shown in italics. Although you should be able to identify most of the data elements in the first two steps of the design process, you'll occasionally think of additional elements during the third step. In this case, since the initial list of data elements was based on a single document, I added several data elements to this list.

Similarly, you may decide during this step that you don't need some of the data elements you've identified. For example, I decided that I didn't need the fax number or web address of each vendor. So I used the strikethrough feature of my word processor to indicate that these data elements should not be included.

Finally, I identified the data elements that are included in two or more tables by coding an asterisk after them. Although you can use any notation you like for this step of the design process, you'll want to be sure that you document your design decisions. For a complicated design, you may even want to use a *CASE (computer-aided software engineering)* tool.

By the way, a couple of the new data elements I added may not be clear to you if you haven't worked with a corporate accounts payable system before. "Terms" refers to the payment terms that the vendor offers. For example, the terms might be net 30 (the invoice must be paid in 30 days) or might include a discount for early payment. "Account number" refers to the general ledger accounts that a company uses to track its expenses. For example, one account number might be assigned for advertising expenses, while another might be for office supplies. Each invoice that's paid is assigned to an account, and in some cases, different line items on an invoice are assigned to different accounts.

Possible tables and columns for an accounts payable system

Vendors	Invoices	Invoice line items
Vendor name	Invoice number*	Invoice number*
Vendor address	Invoice date	~~Item part number~~
Vendor city	Terms*	Item quantity
Vendor state	Invoice total	Item description
Vendor zip code	*Payment date*	Item unit price
Vendor phone number	*Payment total*	Item extension
~~Vendor fax number~~	*Invoice due date*	*Account number**
~~Vendor web address~~	*Credit total*	*Sequence number*
Vendor contact first name	*Account number**	
Vendor contact last name		
~~Vendor contact phone~~		
~~Vendor AR first name~~		
~~Vendor AR last name~~		
~~Vendor AR phone~~		
*Terms**		
*Account number**		

Description

- After you identify and subdivide all of the data elements for a database, you should group them by the entities with which they're associated. These entities will later become the tables of the database, and the elements will become the columns.
- If a data element relates to more than one entity, you can include it under all of the entities it relates to. Then, when you normalize the database, you may be able to remove the duplicate elements.
- As you assign the elements to entities, you should omit elements that aren't needed, and you should add any additional elements that are needed.

The notation used in this figure

- Data elements that were previously identified but aren't needed are crossed out.
- Data elements that were added are displayed in italics.
- Data elements that are related to two or more entities are followed by an asterisk.
- You can use a similar notation or develop one of your own. You can also use a *CASE* (*computer-aided software engineering*) tool if one is available to you.

Figure 9-4   How to identify the tables and assign columns

How to identify the primary and foreign keys

Once you identify the entities and data elements of a system, the next step is to identify the relationships between the tables. To do that, you need to identify the primary and foreign keys as shown in figure 9-5.

As you know, a primary key is used to uniquely identify each row in a table. In some cases, you can use an existing column as the primary key. For example, you might consider using the VendorName column as the primary key of the Vendors table. Because the values for this column can be long, however, and because it would be easy to enter a value incorrectly, that's not a good candidate. Instead, an identity column is used as the primary key.

Similarly, you might consider using the InvoiceNumber column as the primary key of the Invoices table. However, it's possible for different vendors to use the same invoice number, so this value isn't necessarily unique. Because of that, an identity column is used as the primary key of this table as well.

To uniquely identify the rows in the InvoiceLineItems table, a composite key is needed. This key includes the value of the InvoiceID column from the Invoices table, along with an invoice sequence. This is necessary because this table may contain more than one row (line item) for each invoice. And that means that the InvoiceID value by itself may not be unique.

After you identify the primary key of each table, you need to identify the relationships between the tables and add foreign key columns as necessary. In most cases, two tables will have a one-to-many relationship with each other. For example, each vendor can have many invoices, and each invoice can have many line items. To identify the vendor that each invoice is associated with, a VendorID column is included in the Invoices table. Because the InvoiceLineItems table already contains an InvoiceID column, it's not necessary to add another column to this table.

The diagram at the top of this figure illustrates the relationships I identified between the tables in the accounts payable system. As you can see, the primary keys are displayed in bold. Then, the lines between the tables indicate how the primary key in one table is related to the foreign key in another table. Here, a small, round connector indicates the one side of the relationship, and the connector with three lines indicates the many side of the relationship.

In addition to the one-to-many relationships shown in this diagram, you can also use many-to-many relationships and one-to-one relationships. The second diagram in this figure, for example, shows a many-to-many relationship between an Employees table and a Committees table. As you can see, this type of relationship can be implemented by creating a *linking table*, also called a *connecting table* or an *associate table*. This table contains the primary key columns from the two tables. Then, each table has a one-to-many relationship with the linking table. Notice that the linking table doesn't have its own primary key. Because this table doesn't correspond to an entity and because it's used only in conjunction with the Employees and Committees tables, a primary key isn't needed.

The relationships between the tables in the accounts payable system

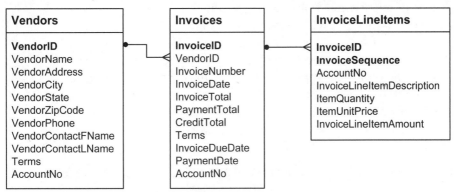

Two tables with a many-to-many relationship

Linking table

Two tables with a one-to-one relationship

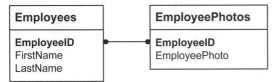

Description

- Each table should have a primary key that uniquely identifies each row. If possible, you should use an existing column for the primary key.

- The values of the primary keys should seldom, if ever, change. The values should also be short and easy to enter correctly.

- If a suitable column doesn't exist, you can create an identity column that can be used as the primary key.

- If two tables have a one-to-many relationship, you may need to add a foreign key column to the table on the "many" side. The foreign key column must have the same data type as the primary key column it's related to.

- If two tables have a many-to-many relationship, you'll need to define a *linking table* to relate them. Then, each of the tables in the many-to-many relationship will have a one-to-many relationship with the linking table. The linking table doesn't usually have a primary key.

- If two tables have a one-to-one relationship, they should be related by their primary keys. This type of relationship is typically used to improve performance. Then, columns with large amounts of data can be stored in a separate table.

Figure 9-5   How to identify the primary key and foreign keys

The third example illustrates two tables that have a one-to-one relationship. With this type of relationship, both tables have the same primary key, which means that the information could be stored in a single table. This type of relationship is often used when a table contains one or more columns with large amounts of data. In this case, the EmployeePhotos table contains a large binary column with a photo of each employee. Because this column is used infrequently, storing it in a separate table will make operations on the Employees table more efficient. Then, when this column is needed, it can be combined with the columns in the Employees table using a join.

How to enforce the relationships between tables

Although the primary keys and foreign keys indicate how the tables in a database are related, SQL Server doesn't enforce those relationships automatically. In that case, any of the operations shown in the table at the top of figure 9-6 would violate the *referential integrity* of the tables. If you deleted a row from a primary key table, for example, and the foreign key table included rows related to that primary key, the referential integrity of the two tables would be destroyed. In that case, the rows in the foreign key table that no longer have a related row in the primary key table would be *orphaned*. Similar problems can occur when you insert a row into the foreign key table or update a primary key or foreign value.

To enforce those relationships and maintain the referential integrity of the tables, you can use one of two features provided by SQL Server: declarative referential integrity or triggers. To use *declarative referential integrity*, you define *foreign key constraints* that indicate how the referential integrity between the tables is enforced. You'll learn more about defining foreign key constraints in the next two chapters. For now, just realize that these constraints can prevent all of the operations listed in this figure that violate referential integrity.

A *trigger* is a special type of procedure that can be executed automatically when an insert, update, or delete operation is executed on a table. Then, you can use the triggers to determine whether an operation violates referential integrity. If so, the trigger can cancel the operation. You'll learn more about coding triggers in chapter 14.

Operations that can violate referential integrity

This operation...	Violates referential integrity if...
Delete a row from the primary key table	The foreign key table contains one or more rows related to the deleted row
Insert a row in the foreign key table	The foreign key value doesn't have a matching primary key value in the related table
Update the value of a foreign key	The new foreign key value doesn't have a matching primary key value in the related table
Update the value of a primary key	The foreign key table contains one or more rows related to the row that's changed

Description

- *Referential integrity* means that the relationships between tables are maintained correctly. That means that a table with a foreign key doesn't have rows with foreign key values that don't have matching primary key values in the related table.

- In SQL Server, you can enforce referential integrity by using declarative referential integrity or by defining triggers.

- To use *declarative referential integrity (DRI)*, you define *foreign key constraints*. You'll learn how to do that in the next two chapters.

- When you define foreign key constraints, you can specify how referential integrity is enforced when a row is deleted from the primary key table. The options are to return an error or to delete the related rows in the foreign key table.

- You can also specify how referential integrity is enforced when the primary key of a row is changed and foreign key constraints are in effect. The options are to return an error or to change the foreign keys of all the related rows to the new value.

- To enforce referential integrity using *triggers*, you define the triggers that will be executed when an insert, update, or delete operation is performed on a table. If the operation violates referential integrity, the trigger prevents the change from occurring. You'll learn how to define triggers in chapter 14.

- If referential integrity isn't enforced and a row is deleted from the primary key table that has related rows in the foreign key table, the rows in the foreign key table are said to be *orphaned*.

- The three types of errors that can occur when referential integrity isn't enforced are called the *deletion anomaly*, the *insertion anomaly*, and the *update anomaly*.

Figure 9-6   How to enforce the relationships between tables

How normalization works

The next step in the design process is to review whether the data structure is *normalized*. To do that, you look at how the data is separated into related tables. If you follow the first four steps for designing a database that are presented in this chapter, your database will already be partially normalized when you get to this step. However, almost every design can be normalized further.

Figure 9-7 illustrates how *normalization* works. The first two tables in this figure show some of the problems caused by an *unnormalized* data structure. In the first table, you can see that each row represents an invoice. Because an invoice can have one or more line items, however, the ItemDescription column must be repeated to provide for the maximum number of line items. But since most invoices have fewer line items than the maximum, this can waste storage space.

In the second table, each line item is stored in a separate row. That eliminates the problem caused by repeating the ItemDescription column, but it introduces a new problem: the invoice number must be repeated in each row. This, too, can cause storage problems, particularly if the repeated column is large. In addition, it can cause maintenance problems if the column contains a value that's likely to change. Then, when the value changes, each row that contains the value must be updated. And if a repeated value must be reentered for each new row, it would be easy for the value to vary from one row to another.

To eliminate the problems caused by *data redundancy*, you can normalize the data structure. To do that, you apply the *normal forms* you'll learn about later in this chapter. As you'll see, there are a total of seven normal forms. However, it's common to apply only the first three. The diagram in this figure, for example, shows the accounts payable system in third normal form. Although it may not be obvious at this point how this reduces data redundancy, that will become clearer as you learn about the different normal forms.

A table that contains repeating columns

	InvoiceNumber	ItemDescription1	ItemDescription2	ItemDescription3
1	112897	VB ad	SQL ad	Library directory
2	97/522	Catalogs	SQL flyer	NULL
3	97/553B	Card revision	NULL	NULL

A table that contains redundant data

	InvoiceNumber	ItemDescription
1	112897	VB ad
2	112897	SQL ad
3	112897	Library directory
4	97/522	Catalogs
5	97/522	SQL flyer
6	97/553B	Card revision

The accounts payable system in third normal form

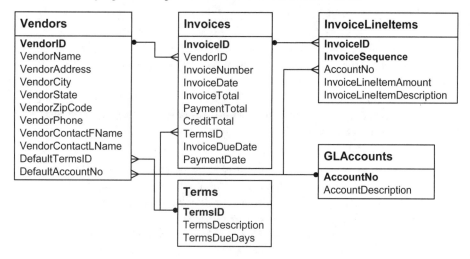

Description

- *Normalization* is a formal process you can use to separate the data in a data structure into related tables. Normalization reduces *data redundancy*, which can cause storage and maintenance problems.

- In an *unnormalized data structure*, a table can contain information about two or more entities. It can also contain repeating columns, columns that contain repeating values, and data that's repeated in two or more rows.

- In a *normalized data structure*, each table contains information about a single entity, and each piece of information is stored in exactly one place.

- To normalize a data structure, you apply the *normal forms* in sequence. Although there are a total of seven normal forms, a data structure is typically considered normalized if the first three normal forms are applied.

Figure 9-7   How normalization works

How to identify the columns to be indexed

The last step in the design process is to identify the columns that should be indexed. An *index* is a structure that provides for locating one or more rows directly. Without an index, SQL Server has to perform a *table scan*, which involves searching through the entire table. Just as the index of a book has page numbers that direct you to a specific subject, a database index has pointers that direct the system to a specific row. This can speed performance not only when you're searching for rows based on a search condition, but when you're joining data from tables as well. If a join is done based on a primary key to foreign key relationship, for example, and an index is defined for the foreign key column, SQL Server can use that index to locate the rows for each primary key value.

In general, a column should meet the guidelines listed at the top of figure 9-8 before you consider creating an index for it. To start, you should index a column if it will be used frequently in search conditions or joins. Since you use foreign keys in most joins, you should typically index each foreign key column. The column should also contain mostly distinct values, and the values in the column should be updated infrequently. If these conditions aren't met, the overhead of maintaining the index will probably outweigh the advantages of using it.

SQL Server provides for two types of indexes. A *clustered index* defines the sequence in which the rows of the table are stored. Because of that, each table can contain a single clustered index. Although SQL Server creates a clustered index automatically for the primary key, you can change that if you need to. The second list in this figure presents some guidelines you can use to determine when to change the clustered index from the primary key column to another column. If you review these guidelines, you'll see that the primary key is usually the best column to use for the clustered index.

The other type of index is a *nonclustered index*. You can define up to 249 nonclustered indexes for each table. You should be aware, however, that the indexes must be updated each time you add, update, or delete a row. Because of that, you don't want to define more indexes than you need.

As you identify the indexes for a table, keep in mind that, like a key, an index can consist of two or more columns. This type of index is called a *composite index*. A special type of composite index that includes all of the columns used by a query is called a *covering index*. Although a covering index speeds retrieval, the overhead to maintain this type of index is significant, particularly if the table is updated frequently. Because of that, you won't usually define covering indexes.

When to create an index

- When the column is a foreign key
- When the column is used frequently in search conditions or joins
- When the column contains a large number of distinct values
- When the column is updated infrequently

When to reassign the clustered index

- When the column is used in almost every search condition
- When the column contains mostly distinct values
- When the column is small
- When the column values seldom, if ever, change
- When most queries against the column will return large result sets

Description

- An *index* provides a way for SQL Server to locate information more quickly. When it uses an index, SQL Server can go directly to a row rather than having to search through all the rows until it finds the ones you want.
- An index can be either *clustered* or *nonclustered*. Each table can have one clustered index and up to 249 nonclustered indexes.
- The rows of a table are stored in the sequence of the clustered index. By default, SQL Server creates a clustered index for the primary key. If you don't identify a primary key, the rows of the table are stored in the order in which they're entered.
- Indexes speed performance when searching and joining tables. However, they can't be used in search conditions that use the LIKE operator with a pattern that starts with a wildcard. And they can't be used in search conditions that include functions or expressions.
- You can create *composite indexes* that include two or more columns. You should use this type of index when the columns in the index are updated infrequently or when the index will cover almost every search condition on the table.
- Because indexes must be updated each time you add, update, or delete a row, you shouldn't create more indexes than you need.

Figure 9-8   How to identify the columns to be indexed

How to normalize a data structure

The topics that follow describe the seven normal forms and teach you how to apply the first three. As I said earlier, you apply these three forms to some extent in the first four database design steps, but these topics will give you more insight into the process. Then, the last topic explains when and how to denormalize a data structure. When you finish these topics, you'll have the basic skills for designing databases that are efficient and easy to use.

The seven normal forms

Figure 9-9 summarizes the seven normal forms. Each normal form assumes that the previous forms have already been applied. Before you can apply the third normal form, for example, the design must already be in the second normal form.

Strictly speaking, a data structure isn't normalized until it's in the fifth or sixth normal form. However, the normal forms past the third normal form are applied infrequently. Because of that, I won't present those forms in detail here. Instead, I'll just describe them briefly so you'll have an idea of how to apply them if you need to.

The *Boyce-Codd normal form* can be used to eliminate *transitive dependencies*. With this type of dependency, one column depends on another column, which depends on a third column. To illustrate, consider the city, state, and zip code columns in the Vendors table. Here, a zip code identifies a city and state, which means that the city and state are dependent on the zip code. The zip code, in turn, is dependent on the VendorID column. To eliminate this dependency, you could store the city and state values in a separate table that uses zip code as its primary key.

The fourth normal form can be used to eliminate multiple *multivalued dependencies* from a table. A multivalued dependency is one where a primary key column has a one-to-many relationship with a non-key column. To illustrate, consider the vendor contact phone in the Vendors table. If you wanted to accommodate alternate phone numbers, such as a cellular or home phone, you could add extra columns for each type of number. However, this creates a multivalued dependency between the phone numbers and the VendorID. To be in fourth normal form, therefore, you'd need to store phone numbers in a separate table that uses VendorID as a foreign key.

To apply the fifth normal form, you continue to divide the tables of the data structure into smaller tables until all redundancy has been removed. When further splitting would result in tables that couldn't be used to reconstruct the original table, the data structure is in fifth normal form. In this form, most tables consist of little more than key columns with one or two data elements.

The *domain-key normal form*, sometimes called the sixth normal form, is only of academic interest since no database system has implemented a way to apply it. For this reason, even normalization purists might consider a database to be normalized in fifth normal form.

The seven normal forms

Normal form	Description
First (1NF)	The value stored at the intersection of each row and column must be a scalar value, and a table must not contain any repeating columns.
Second (2NF)	Every non-key column must depend on the entire primary key.
Third (3NF)	Every non-key column must depend only on the primary key.
Boyce-Codd (BCNF)	A non-key column can't be dependent on another non-key column. This prevents *transitive dependencies*, where column A depends on column C and column B depends on column C. Since both A and B depend on C, A and B should be moved into another table with C as the key.
Fourth (4NF)	A table must not have more than one *multivalued dependency*, where the primary key has a one-to-many relationship to non-key columns. This form gets rid of misleading many-to-many relationships.
Fifth (5NF)	The data structure is split into smaller and smaller tables until all redundancy has been eliminated. If further splitting would result in tables that couldn't be joined to recreate the original table, the structure is in fifth normal form.
Domain-key (DKNF) or Sixth (6NF)	Every constraint on the relationship is dependent only on key constraints and domain constraints, where a *domain* is the set of allowable values for a column. This form prevents the insertion of any unacceptable data by enforcing constraints at the level of a relationship, rather than at the table or column level. DKNF is less a design model than an abstract "ultimate" normal form. SQL Server has no way to implement the constraints required for DKNF.

The benefits of normalization

- Since a normalized database has more tables than an unnormalized database, and since each table can have a clustered index, the database has more clustered indexes. That makes data retrieval more efficient.

- Since each table contains information about a single entity, each index has fewer columns (usually one) and fewer rows. That makes data retrieval and insert, update, and delete operations more efficient.

- Each table has fewer indexes, which makes insert, update, and delete operations more efficient.

- Data redundancy is minimized, which simplifies maintenance and reduces storage.

Description

- Each normal form assumes that the design is already in the previous normal form.

- A database is typically considered to be normalized if it is in third normal form. The other four forms are not commonly used and are not covered in detail in this book.

Figure 9-9   The seven normal forms

Figure 9-9 also lists the benefits of normalizing a data structure. To summarize, normalization produces smaller, more efficient tables. In addition, it reduces data redundancy, which makes the data easier to maintain and reduces the amount of storage needed for the database. Because of these benefits, you should always consider normalizing your data structures.

You should also be aware that the subject of normalization is a contentious one in the database community. In the academic study of computer science, normalization is considered a form of design perfection that should always be strived for. In practice, though, database designers and DBAs tend to use normalization as a flexible design guideline.

How to apply the first normal form

Figure 9-10 illustrates how you apply the first normal form to an unnormalized invoice data structure consisting of the data elements that are shown in figure 9-2. The first two tables in this figure illustrate structures that aren't in first normal form. Both of these tables contain a single row for each invoice. Because each invoice can contain one or more line items, however, the first table allows for repeating values in the ItemDescription column. The second table is similar, except it includes a separate column for each line item description. Neither of these structures is acceptable in first normal form.

The third table in this figure has eliminated the repeating values and columns. To do that, it includes one row for each line item. Notice, however, that this has increased the data redundancy. Specifically, the vendor name and invoice number are now repeated for each line item. This problem can be solved by applying the second normal form.

Before I describe the second normal form, I want you to realize that I intentionally omitted many of the columns in the invoice data structure from the examples in this figure and the next figure. In addition to the columns shown here, for example, each of these tables would also contain the vendor address, invoice date, invoice total, etc. By eliminating these columns, it will be easier for you to focus on the columns that are affected by applying the normal forms.

The invoice data with a column that contains repeating values

	VendorName	InvoiceNumber	ItemDescription
1	Cahners Publishing	112897	VB ad, SQL ad, Library directory
2	Zylka Design	97/522	Catalogs, SQL flyer
3	Zylka Design	97/553B	Card revision

The invoice data with repeating columns

	VendorName	InvoiceNumber	ItemDescription1	ItemDescription2	ItemDescription3
1	Cahners Publishing	112897	VB ad	SQL ad	Library directory
2	Zylka Design	97/522	Catalogs	SQL flyer	NULL
3	Zylka Design	97/553B	Card revision	NULL	NULL

The invoice data in first normal form

	VendorName	InvoiceNumber	ItemDescription
1	Cahners Publishing	112897	VB ad
2	Cahners Publishing	112897	SQL ad
3	Cahners Publishing	112897	Library directory
4	Zylka Design	97/522	Catalogs
5	Zylka Design	97/522	SQL flyer
6	Zylka Design	97/553B	Card revision

Description

- For a table to be in first normal form, its columns must not contain repeating values. Instead, each column must contain a single, scalar value. In addition, the table must not contain repeating columns that represent a set of values.

- A table in first normal form often has repeating values in its rows. This can be resolved by applying the second normal form.

Figure 9-10   How to apply the first normal form

How to apply the second normal form

Figure 9-11 shows how to apply the second normal form. To be in second normal form, every column in a table that isn't a key column must be dependent on the entire primary key. This form only applies to tables that have composite primary keys, which is often the case when you start with data that is completely unnormalized. The table at the top of this figure, for example, shows the invoice data in first normal form after key columns have been added. In this case, the primary key consists of the InvoiceID and InvoiceSequence columns. The InvoiceSequence column is needed to uniquely identify each line item for an invoice.

Now, consider the three non-key columns shown in this table. Of these three, only one, ItemDescription, depends on the entire primary key. The other two, VendorName and InvoiceNumber, depend only on the InvoiceID column. Because of that, these columns should be moved to another table. The result is a data structure like the second one shown in this figure. Here, all of the information related to an invoice is stored in the Invoices table, and all of the information related to an individual line item is stored in the InvoiceLineItems table.

Notice that the relationship between these tables is based on the InvoiceID column. This column is the primary key of the Invoices table, and it's the foreign key in the InvoiceLineItems table that relates the rows in that table to the rows in the Invoices table. This column is also part of the primary key of the InvoiceLineItems table.

When you apply second normal form to a data structure, it eliminates some of the redundant row data in the tables. In this figure, for example, you can see that the invoice number and vendor name are now included only once for each invoice. In first normal form, this information was included for each line item.

The invoice data in first normal form with keys added

	InvoiceID	VendorName	InvoiceNumber	InvoiceSequence	ItemDescription
1	1	Cahners Publishing	112897	1	VB ad
2	1	Cahners Publishing	112897	2	SQL ad
3	1	Cahners Publishing	112897	3	Library directory
4	2	Zylka Design	97/522	1	Catalogs
5	2	Zylka Design	97/522	2	SQL flyer
6	3	Zylka Design	97/553B	1	Card revision

The invoice data in second normal form

Invoices

	InvoiceNumber	VendorName	InvoiceID
1	112897	Cahners Publishing	1
2	97/522	Zylka Design	2
3	97/553B	Zylka Design	3

InvoiceLineItems

	InvoiceID	InvoiceSequence	ItemDescription
1	1	1	VB ad
2	1	2	SQL ad
3	1	3	Library directory
4	2	1	Catalogs
5	2	2	SQL flyer
6	3	1	Card revision

Description

- For a table to be in second normal form, every non-key column must depend on the entire primary key. If a column doesn't depend on the entire key, it indicates that the table contains information for more than one entity. This is reflected by the table's composite key.

- To apply second normal form, you move columns that don't depend on the entire primary key to another table and then establish a relationship between the two tables.

- Second normal form helps remove redundant row data, which can save storage space, make maintenance easier, and reduce the chance of storing inconsistent data.

Figure 9-11   How to apply the second normal form

How to apply the third normal form

To apply the third normal form, you make sure that every non-key column depends *only* on the primary key. Figure 9-12 illustrates how you can apply this form to the data structure for the accounts payable system. At the top of this figure, you can see all of the columns in the Invoices and InvoiceLineItems tables in second normal form. Then, you can see a list of questions that you might ask about some of the columns in these tables when you apply third normal form.

First, does the vendor information depend only on the InvoiceID column? Another way to phrase this question is, "Will the information for the same vendor change from one invoice to another?" If the answer is no, the vendor information should be stored in a separate table. That way, can you be sure that the vendor information for each invoice for a vendor will be the same. In addition, you will reduce the redundancy of the data in the Invoices table. This is illustrated by the diagram in this figure that shows the accounts payable system in third normal form. Here, a Vendors table has been added to store the information for each vendor. This table is related to the Invoices table by the VendorID column, which has been added as a foreign key to the Invoices table.

Second, does the Terms column depend only on the InvoiceID column? The answer to that question depends on how this column is used. In this case, I'll assume that this column is used not only to specify the terms for each invoice, but also to specify the default terms for a vendor. Because of that, the terms information could be stored in both the Vendors and the Invoices tables. To avoid redundancy, however, the information related to different terms can be stored in a separate table, as illustrated by the Terms table in this figure. As you can see, the primary key of this table is an identity column named TermsID. Then, a foreign key column named DefaultTermsID has been added to the Vendors table, and a foreign key column named TermsID has been added to the Invoices table.

Third, does the AccountNo column depend only on the InvoiceID column? Again, that depends on how this column is used. In this case, it's used to specify the general ledger account number for each line item, so it depends on the InvoiceID and the InvoiceSequence columns. In other words, this column should be stored in the InvoiceLineItems table. In addition, each vendor has a default account number, which should be stored in the Vendors table. Because of that, another table named GLAccounts has been added to store the account numbers and account descriptions. Then, foreign key columns have been added to the Vendors and InvoiceLineItems tables to relate them to this table.

Fourth, can the InvoiceDueDate column in the Invoices table and the InvoiceLineItemAmount column in the InvoiceLineItems table be derived from other data in the database? If so, they depend on the columns that contain that data rather than on the primary key columns. In this case, the value of the InvoiceLineItemAmount column can always be calculated from the ItemQuantity and ItemUnitPrice columns. Because of that, this column could be omitted. Alternatively, you could omit the ItemQuantity and ItemUnitPrice columns and keep just the InvoiceLineItemAmount column. That's what I did in

The accounts payable system in second normal form

Invoices	
InvoiceID	
VendorName	InvoiceDate
VendorAddress	InvoiceTotal
VendorCity	PaymentTotal
VendorState	CreditTotal
VendorZipCode	Terms
VendorPhone	InvoiceDueDate
VendorContactFName	PaymentDate
VendorContactLName	AccountNo
InvoiceNumber	

InvoiceLineItems
InvoiceID
InvoiceSequence
AccountNo
InvoiceLineItemDescription
ItemQuantity
ItemUnitPrice
InvoiceLineItemAmount

Questions about the structure

1. Does the vendor information (VendorName, VendorAddress, etc.) depend only on the InvoiceID column?
2. Does the Terms column depend only on the InvoiceID column?
3. Does the AccountNo column depend only on the InvoiceID column?
4. Can the InvoiceDueDate and InvoiceLineItemAmount columns be derived from other data?

The accounts payable system in third normal form

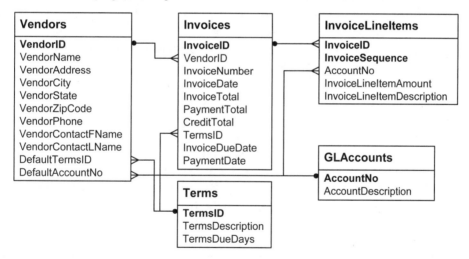

Description

- For a table to be in third normal form, every non-key column must depend *only* on the primary key.
- If a column doesn't depend only on the primary key, it implies that the column is assigned to the wrong table or that it can be computed from other columns in the table. A column that can be computed from other columns contains *derived data*.

Figure 9-12   How to apply the third normal form

the data structure shown in this figure. The solution you choose, however, depends on how the data will be used.

In contrast, although the InvoiceDueDate column could be calculated from the InvoiceDate column in the Invoices table and the TermsDueDays column in the related row of the Terms table, the system also allows this date to be overridden. Because of that, the InvoiceDueDate column should not be omitted. If the system didn't allow this value to be overridden, however, this column could be safely omitted.

When and how to denormalize a data structure

Denormalization is the deliberate deviation from the normal forms. Most denormalization occurs beyond the third normal form. In contrast, the first three normal forms are almost universally applied.

To illustrate when and how to denormalize a data structure, figure 9-13 presents the design of the accounts payable system in fifth normal form. Here, notice that the vendor zip codes are stored in a separate table that contains the city and state for each zip code. In addition, the area codes are stored in a separate table. Because of that, a query that retrieves vendor addresses and phone numbers would require two joins. In contrast, if you left the city, state, and area code information in the Vendors table, no joins would be required, but the Vendors table would be larger. In general, you should denormalize based on the way the data will be used. In this case, we'll seldom need to query phone numbers without the area code. Likewise, we'll seldom need to query city and state without the zip code. For these reasons, I've denormalized my design by eliminating the ZipCodes and AreaCodes tables.

You might also consider denormalizing a table if the data it contains is updated infrequently. In that case, redundant data isn't as likely to cause problems.

Finally, you should consider including derived data in a table if that data is used frequently in search conditions. For example, if you frequently query the Invoices table based on invoice balances, you might consider including a column that contains the balance due. That way, you won't have to calculate this value each time it's queried. Keep in mind, though, that if you store derived data, it's possible for it to deviate from the derived value. For this reason, you may need to protect the derived column so it can't be updated directly. Alternatively, you could update the table periodically to reset the value of the derived column.

Because normalization eliminates the possibility of data redundancy errors and optimizes the use of storage, you should carefully consider when and how to denormalize a data structure. In general, you should denormalize only when the increased efficiency outweighs the potential for redundancy errors and storage problems. Of course, your decision to denormalize should also be based on your knowledge of the real-world environment in which the system will be used. If you've carefully analyzed the real-world environment as outlined in this chapter, you'll have a good basis for making that decision.

The accounts payable system in fifth normal form

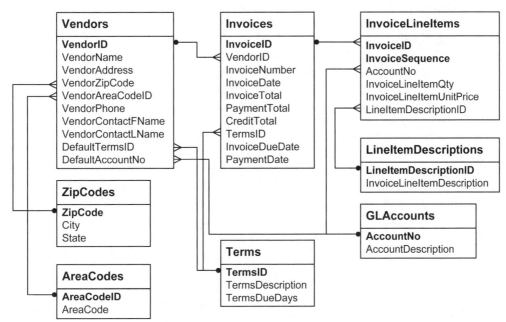

When to denormalize

- When a column from a joined table is used repeatedly in search criteria, you should consider moving that column to the primary key table if it will eliminate the need for a join.

- If a table is updated infrequently, you should consider denormalizing it to improve efficiency. Because the data remains relatively constant, you don't have to worry about data redundancy errors once the initial data is entered and verified.

- Include columns with derived values when those values are used frequently in search conditions. If you do that, you need to be sure that the column value is always synchronized with the value of the columns it's derived from.

Description

- Data structures that are normalized to the fourth normal form and beyond typically require more joins than tables normalized to the third normal form and can therefore be less efficient.

- SQL statements that work with tables that are normalized to the fourth normal form and beyond are typically more difficult to code and debug.

- Most designers *denormalize* data structures to some extent, usually to the third normal form.

- *Denormalization* can result in larger tables, redundant data, and reduced performance.

- Only denormalize when necessary. It is better to adhere to the normal forms unless it is clear that performance will be improved by denormalizing.

Figure 9-13   When and how to denormalize a data structure

Perspective

Database design is a complicated subject. Because of that, it's impossible to teach you everything you need to know in a single chapter. With the skills you've learned in this chapter, however, you should now be able to design simple databases of your own. More important, you should now be able to evaluate the design of any database that you work with. That way, you can be sure that the queries you code will be as efficient and as effective as possible.

Terms

data structure	normalization
entity	data redundancy
attribute	unnormalized data structure
instance	normalized data structure
entity-relationship (ER) modeling	normal forms
CASE (computer-aided software	index
engineering)	table scan
linking table	clustered index
connecting table	nonclustered index
associate table	composite index
referential integrity	covering index
declarative referential integrity	Boyce-Codd normal form
(DRI)	transitive dependency
foreign key constraints	multivalued dependency
triggers	domain-key normal form
orphaned row	derived data
update anomaly	denormalized data structure
insertion anomaly	denormalization
deletion anomaly	

10

How to create and maintain databases and tables

Now that you've learned how to design a database, you're ready to learn how to implement your design. To do that, you use the set of SQL statements that are known as the data definition language (DDL). As an application programmer, you can use the DDL statements to create and modify the database objects that you need for testing. Beyond that, knowing what these statements do will give you a better appreciation for how a database works.

An introduction to DDL

All of the SQL statements that you've seen so far have been part of the data manipulation language, or DML. But now, you'll learn how to use the SQL statements that are part of the data definition language. You use these statements to define the objects of a database.

The SQL statements for data definition

Figure 10-1 summarizes the *data definition language*, or *DDL*, statements that you use to create, delete, or change the *objects* of a database. In this chapter, you'll learn how to use the statements that work with databases, tables, and indexes. You'll learn how to use the statements that work with other objects in later chapters.

To work with the objects of a database, you normally use the Enterprise Manager that comes with SQL Server. This tool lets you create and change database objects using a graphical user interface. To do that, it generates and executes the DDL statements that implement the changes you've made. You'll learn how to use the Enterprise Manager to work with database objects in chapter 11.

But first, this chapter teaches you how to code the DDL statements yourself. This is useful for two reasons. First, you sometimes need to examine and verify the DDL that's generated by the Enterprise Manager. This is especially true for large database projects. Second, knowing the DDL statements helps you use the DML statements more effectively. Beyond that, if you ever use a DBMS that doesn't offer a graphical tool like the Enterprise Manager, you have to code the DDL yourself.

Because the syntax of each of the DDL statements is complex, this chapter doesn't present complete syntax diagrams for the statements. Instead, the diagrams present only the most commonly used clauses. If you're interested in the complete syntax of any statement, of course, you can find it in Books Online.

If you're working on a large database project, you probably won't have the option of coding DDL statements at all because that will be handled by a database administrator (DBA). This is a common practice because the DDL statements can destroy data if they're used incorrectly. In addition, many of the optional clauses for these statements are used for tuning the performance of the system, which is typically the role of a DBA.

For small projects, though, the SQL programmer may often have to serve as the DBA too. And even for large databases, the SQL programmer often uses the DDL to create and work with smaller databases that are needed for testing or for special projects.

DDL statements to create, modify, and delete objects

Statement	Description
CREATE DATABASE	Creates a new database.
CREATE TABLE	Creates a new table in the current database.
CREATE INDEX	Creates a new index for the specified table.
CREATE FUNCTION	Creates a new function in the current database.
CREATE PROCEDURE	Creates a new stored procedure in the current database.
CREATE TRIGGER	Creates a new trigger in the current database.
CREATE VIEW	Creates a new view in the current database.
ALTER TABLE	Modifies the structure of the specified table.
ALTER FUNCTION	Modifies the specified function.
ALTER PROCEDURE	Modifies the specified stored procedure.
ALTER TRIGGER	Modifies the specified trigger.
ALTER VIEW	Modifies the specified view.
DROP DATABASE	Deletes the specified database.
DROP TABLE	Deletes the specified table.
DROP INDEX	Deletes the specified index.
DROP FUNCTION	Deletes the specified function.
DROP PROCEDURE	Deletes the specified stored procedure.
DROP TRIGGER	Deletes the specified trigger.
DROP VIEW	Deletes the specified view.

Description

- You use the *data definition language* (*DDL*) statements to create, modify, and delete database objects such as the database itself, the tables contained in a database, and the indexes for those tables.

- Typically, a database administrator is responsible for using the DDL statements on production databases in a large database system. However, every SQL programmer should be comfortable using these statements so that they can create and work with small databases for testing.

- In most cases, you'll use the graphical user interface of the Enterprise Manager to create and maintain database objects as described in chapter 11. Although the Enterprise Manager generates DDL statements for you, you may need to verify or correct these statements. To do that, you need to understand their syntax and use.

- If you use a SQL database other than SQL Server, it may not have a graphical tool for managing database objects. In that case, you must use the DDL statements.

Figure 10-1 The SQL statements for data definition

Rules for coding object names

When you create most database objects, you give them names. In SQL Server, the name of an object is its *identifier*. Each identifier can be up to 128 characters in length. To code an identifier, you typically follow the formatting rules presented in figure 10-2.

As you can see, the formatting rules limit the characters you can use in an identifier. For example, the first character of an identifier can be a letter, an underscore, an at sign, or a number sign. The characters that can be used in the remainder of the identifier include all of the characters allowed as the first character, plus numbers and dollar signs. Note that a regular identifier can't include spaces and can't be a Transact-SQL reserved keyword, which is a word that's reserved for use by SQL Server.

The first set of examples in this figure presents some valid regular identifiers. Notice that the identifier in the second example starts with a number sign. This type of identifier is used for a temporary table or procedure. Similarly, an identifier that starts with an at sign as in the fifth example is used for a local variable or parameter. You'll learn about these special types of identifiers in chapters 13 and 14.

In most cases, you'll create objects with identifiers that follow the formatting rules shown here. If you're working with an existing database, however, the identifiers may not follow these rules. In that case, you have to delimit the identifiers to use them in SQL statements. You can code a delimited identifier by enclosing it in either brackets or double quotes. The second set of examples shows how this works. Here, two of the identifiers are enclosed in brackets and one is enclosed in double quotes. The identifier in the first example must be delimited because it starts with a percent sign. The identifier in the second example must be delimited because it includes spaces. The third example illustrates that even when a name follows the formatting rules, you can delimit it. In most cases, though, there's no reason to do that.

Formatting rules for identifiers

- The first character of an identifier must be a letter as defined by the Unicode Standard 2.0, an underscore (_), an at sign (@), or a number sign (#).
- All characters after the first must be a letter as defined by the Unicode Standard 2.0, a number, an at sign, a dollar sign ($), a number sign, or an underscore.
- An identifier can't be a Transact-SQL reserved keyword.
- An identifier can't contain spaces or special characters other than those already mentioned.

Valid regular identifiers

```
Employees
#PaidInvoices
ABC$123
Invoice_Line_Items
@TotalDue
```

Valid delimited identifiers

```
[%Increase]
"Invoice Line Items"
[@TotalDue]
```

Description

- The name of an object in SQL Server is called its *identifier*. Most objects are assigned an identifier when they're created. Then, the identifier can be used to refer to the object.
- SQL Server provides for two classes of identifiers. Regular identifiers follow the formatting rules for identifiers. Delimited identifiers are enclosed in brackets ([]) or double quotation marks ("") and may or may not follow the formatting rules. If an identifier doesn't follow the formatting rules, it must be delimited.
- An identifier can contain from 1 to 128 characters.
- An at sign at the beginning of an identifier indicates that the identifier is a local variable or parameter, a number sign indicates that the identifier is a temporary table or procedure, and two number signs indicates that the identifier is a global temporary object. See chapters 13 and 14 for details.

Figure 10-2   Rules for coding object names

How to create databases, tables, and indexes

The primary role of the DDL statements is to define database objects on the server. So to start, the three topics that follow will teach you how to code the DDL statements that you use to create databases, tables, and indexes.

How to create a database

Figure 10-3 presents the basic syntax of the CREATE DATABASE statement. This statement creates a new database on the current server. In many cases, you'll code this statement with just a database name to create the database with the default options. This is illustrated by the first example in this figure.

The CREATE DATABASE statement in this example creates a database named New_AP. Notice that this statement allocates space to two files. The first file, New_AP.mdf, will hold the data for the database. The second file, New_AP_log.ldf, will hold a record of any changes made to the database.

If you want to use a database that was created on another server, you can copy the mdf file to your server, but at that point, it's simply a data file. To be able to use the database, you have to *attach* it to your server. To do that, you use two of the optional clauses in the CREATE DATABASE statement, ON PRIMARY and FOR ATTACH. As you can see in the second example, you specify the name of the file that contains the database in the ON PRIMARY clause. Then, instead of creating a new database, SQL Server simply makes the existing database available from the current server. If you attached the AP database that's provided with this book as described in appendix A, you've already seen how this works.

Most of the clauses that aren't included in the syntax shown here are used to tune the database by changing the locations of the database files. For small databases, though, this tuning usually isn't necessary. If you want to learn about these options, you can refer to the description of this statement in Books Online.

The basic syntax of the CREATE DATABASE statement

```
CREATE DATABASE database_name
    [ON [PRIMARY] (FILENAME = 'file_name')]
    [FOR ATTACH]
```

A statement that creates a new database

```
CREATE DATABASE New_AP
```

The response from the system

```
The CREATE DATABASE process is allocating 0.63 MB on disk 'New_AP'.
The CREATE DATABASE process is allocating 0.49 MB on disk 'New_AP_log'.
```

A statement that attaches an existing database file

```
CREATE DATABASE Test_AP
    ON PRIMARY (FILENAME =
        'C:\Program Files\Microsoft SQL Server\MSSQL\Data\Test_AP_Data.mdf')
    FOR ATTACH
```

The response from the system

```
The command(s) completed successfully.
```

Description

- The CREATE DATABASE statement creates a new, empty database on the current server. Although the ANSI standards don't include this statement, it's supported by virtually all SQL database systems. The optional clauses shown here, however, are supported only by SQL Server.

- If you code this statement without any options, the new database is created using the default settings and the database files are stored in the default directory on the hard drive. For most small database projects, these settings are acceptable.

- One of the files SQL Server creates when it executes the CREATE DATABASE statement is a *transaction log file*. This file is used to record modifications to the database. SQL Server generates the name for this file by appending "_log" to the end of the database name. The database name is limited to 123 characters.

- If you have a copy of a database file that you'd like to work with on your server, you can use the FOR ATTACH clause in addition to the ON PRIMARY clause to *attach* the file as a database to the current server.

- Most of the optional clauses that have been omitted from this syntax are used to specify the underlying file structure of the database. These clauses are used by DBAs to tune the performance of the database. See Books Online for details.

Warning

- On some systems, the CREATE DATABASE statement can overwrite an existing database. Because of that, you'll want to check with the DBA before using this statement.

Figure 10-3   How to create a database

How to create a table

Figure 10-4 presents the basic syntax of the CREATE TABLE statement. This statement creates a new table in the current database. Because this statement has so many optional clauses and keywords, the complete syntax isn't shown here. However, all of the clauses and keywords can be divided into two categories: attributes that affect a single column and attributes that affect the entire table. This figure summarizes some of the common column attributes. You'll learn about the table attributes later in this chapter.

In its simplest form, the CREATE TABLE statement consists of the name of the new table followed by the names and data types of its columns. This is illustrated by the first example of this figure. Notice that the column definitions are enclosed in parentheses.

In most cases, you'll code one or more attributes for each column as illustrated by the second example in this figure. To identify whether a column can accept null values, you code either the NULL or NOT NULL keyword. If you omit both keywords, the default value is NULL unless the column is also defined as the primary key, in which case the default is NOT NULL. However, I recommend that you always code one of these keywords for two reasons. First, it makes it easier to understand the structure of the table. Second, it makes your code more portable. That's because the default values for some systems are different from the defaults for SQL Server.

The PRIMARY KEY keywords identify the primary key for the table. To create a primary key based on a single column, you code these keywords as an attribute of that column. To create a primary key based on two or more columns, however, you must code PRIMARY KEY as a table attribute. You'll see how to do that in a later figure.

When you identify a column as the primary key, two of the column's attributes are changed automatically. First, the column is forced to be NOT NULL. Even so, you typically code this attribute in the column definition for clarity. Second, the column is forced to contain a unique value for each row. In addition, a clustered index is automatically created based on the column.

In addition to a primary key, you can also define one or more unique keys using the UNIQUE keyword. Unlike a primary key column, a unique key column can contain null values. And instead of creating a clustered index for the key, SQL Server creates a nonclustered index. Like the PRIMARY keyword, you can code the UNIQUE keyword at either the column or the table level.

NOT NULL, PRIMARY KEY, and UNIQUE are examples of *constraints*. Constraints are special attributes that restrict the data that can be stored in the columns of a table. You'll learn how to code other constraints in a moment.

The IDENTITY keyword defines a column as an identity column. As you know, SQL Server assigns an identity column a unique integer value. This value is generated by incrementing the previous value for the column. SQL Server allows only one identity column per table, and that column is typically used as the primary key.

The basic syntax of the CREATE TABLE statement

```
CREATE TABLE table_name
(column_name_1 data_type [column_attributes]
[, column_name_2 data_type [column_attributes]]...
[, table_attributes])
```

Common column attributes

Attribute	Description
NULL|NOT NULL	Indicates whether or not the column can accept null values. If omitted, NULL is the default unless PRIMARY KEY is specified.
PRIMARY KEY|UNIQUE	Identifies the primary key or a unique key for the table. If PRIMARY is specified, the NULL attribute isn't allowed.
IDENTITY	Identifies an identity column. Only one identity column can be created per table.
DEFAULT default_value	Specifies a default value for the column.

A statement that creates a table without column attributes

```
CREATE TABLE Vendors
(VendorID        INT,
 VendorName      VARCHAR(50))
```

A statement that creates a table with column attributes

```
CREATE TABLE Invoices
(InvoiceID      INT    NOT NULL IDENTITY PRIMARY KEY,
 VendorID       INT    NOT NULL,
 InvoiceDate    SMALLDATETIME NULL,
 InvoiceTotal   MONEY NULL DEFAULT 0)
```

Description

- The CREATE TABLE statement creates a table based on the column definitions, column attributes, and table attributes you specify. A database can contain as many as two billion tables.

- A table can contain between one and 1,024 columns. Each column must have a unique name and must be assigned a data type. In addition, you can assign one or more of the column attributes shown above.

- You can also assign one or more constraints to a column or to the entire table. See figures 10-6, 10-7, and 10-8 for details.

- For the complete syntax of the CREATE TABLE statement, refer to Books Online.

How to test this code on your computer

- Before you run the examples in this figure and in the figures that follow on your computer, you'll want to create the New_AP database as shown in figure 10-3 and then make that the current database. To do that, just use the drop-down list in the Query Analyzer toolbar.

Figure 10-4   How to create a table

The last keyword shown here, DEFAULT, lets you specify a default value for a column. This value is used if another value isn't specified. The default value you specify must correspond to the data type for the column.

Before I go on, you should realize that if you test the code in this figure using the AP database, the statements will fail. That's because the AP database already contains tables named Vendors and Invoices. If you want to test these statements, then, you can create the New_AP database as shown in figure 10-3 and execute the statements on it.

How to create an index

Figure 10-5 presents the basic syntax of the CREATE INDEX statement, which creates an index based on one or more columns of a table. This syntax omits some of the optional clauses that you can use for tuning the indexes for better performance. This tuning is often done by DBAs working with large databases, but usually isn't necessary for small databases.

In the last chapter, you learned that a table can have one clustered index and up to 249 nonclustered indexes. By default, SQL Server creates a clustered index based on the primary key of a table, which is usually what you want. Because of that, you'll rarely create a clustered index. If you need to do that, though, you first have to drop the primary key constraint using the ALTER TABLE statement. You'll see how to use this statement later in this chapter. Then, you can use another ALTER TABLE statement to recreate the primary key with a nonclustered index, and you can create a new clustered index using a CREATE INDEX statement with the CLUSTERED keyword. If you omit the CLUSTERED keyword, a nonclustered index is created.

To create an index, you name the table and columns that the index will be based on in the ON clause. For each column, you can specify the ASC or DESC keyword to indicate whether you want the index sorted in ascending or descending sequence. If you don't specify a sort order, ASC is the default.

The first example in this figure creates an index based on the VendorID column in the Invoices table. Because none of the optional keywords are specified, a nonclustered index is created and the index is sorted in ascending sequence. The second example creates a nonclustered index based on two columns in the Invoices table: InvoiceDate and InvoiceTotal. Notice here that the InvoiceDate column is sorted in descending sequence. That way, the most recent invoices will occur first.

You should also notice the names that are assigned to the indexes in these examples. Although you can name an index anything you like, SQL Server's convention is to prefix index names with the characters *IX_*. So I recommend you do that too. Then, if the index is based on a single column, you should follow the prefix with the name of that column. The first index in this figure, for example, is assigned the name IX_VendorID because it's based on the VendorID column. If an index is based on two or more columns, however, I recommend you use the table name instead of the column names. The only time this will be a problem is if a table has two or more multi-column indexes, which is uncommon.

The basic syntax of the CREATE INDEX statement

```
CREATE [CLUSTERED|NONCLUSTERED] INDEX index_name
    ON table_name (column_name_1 [ASC|DESC] [, column_name_2 [ASC|DESC]]...)
```

A statement that creates a nonclustered index based on a single column

```
CREATE INDEX IX_VendorID
    ON Invoices (VendorID)
```

A statement that creates a nonclustered index based on two columns

```
CREATE INDEX IX_Invoices
    ON Invoices (InvoiceDate DESC, InvoiceTotal)
```

Description

- You use the CREATE INDEX statement to create an index for a table. An index can improve performance when SQL Server searches for rows in the table.

- SQL Server automatically creates a clustered index for a table's primary key. If that's not what you want, you can drop the primary key constraint using the ALTER TABLE statement shown in figure 10-10 and then recreate the primary key with a nonclustered index.

- Each table can have a single clustered index and up to 249 nonclustered indexes. SQL Server automatically creates a nonclustered index for each unique key other than the primary key.

- By default, an index is sorted in ascending sequence. If that's not what you want, you can code the DESC keyword. The sequence you use should be the sequence in which the rows are retrieved most often when using that index.

- You should use consistent names when creating indexes. SQL Server's convention is to name indexes using the name of the column it's based on prefixed with *IX_*. If an index is based on two or more columns, you can use the name of the table instead of a column name.

Figure 10-5   How to create an index

How to use constraints

As you've already learned, you can code constraints to restrict the values that can be stored in a table. These constraints are tested before a new row is added to a table or an existing row is updated. Then, if one or more of the constraints aren't satisfied, the operation isn't performed.

The constraints you've seen so far identify a primary key or unique key column or prevent null values in a column. Now you'll learn how to code other types of constraints. In particular, you'll learn how to code constraints to validate data and to enforce referential integrity.

An introduction to constraints

Figure 10-6 summarizes the five types of constraints provided by SQL Server. Except for NOT NULL, each of these constraints can be coded at either the column level or the table level. You've already seen how to code a primary key constraint at the column level, and you can code a unique key constraint in the same way. Now, the first example in this figure shows how to code a primary key constraint at the table level.

In this example, the primary key consists of two columns. Because of that, it can't be defined at the column level. Notice that when you code a constraint at the table level, you must code a comma at the end of the preceding column definition. If you don't, SQL Server will try to associate the constraint with the preceding column, and an error will result.

Two types of constraints you haven't seen yet are *check constraints* and *foreign key constraints*. You'll learn more about these types of constraints in the next two topics. To illustrate the difference between *column-level constraints* and *table-level constraints*, however, the second and third examples in this figure show two ways you can code the same two check constraints. The first example uses column-level constraints to limit the values in the InvoiceTotal and PaymentTotal columns to numbers greater than or equal to zero. The second example uses a compound condition to specify both constraints at the table level. Although the first technique is preferred, the second example illustrates that a table-level constraint can refer to any of the columns in a table. In contrast, a column-level constraint can refer only to the column that contains the constraint.

Column and table constraints

Constraint	Used as a column-level constraint	Used as a table-level constraint
NOT NULL	Prevents null values from being stored in the column.	n/a
PRIMARY KEY	Requires that each row in the table have a unique value in the column. Null values are not allowed.	Requires that each row in the table have a unique set of values over one or more columns. Null values are not allowed.
UNIQUE	Requires that each row in the table have a unique value in the column.	Requires that each row in the table have a unique set of values over one or more columns.
CHECK	Limits the values for a column.	Limits the values for one or more columns.
[FOREIGN KEY] REFERENCES	Enforces referential integrity between a column in the new table and a column in a related table.	Enforces referential integrity between one or more columns in the new table and one or more columns in the related table.

A statement that creates a table with a two-column primary key constraint

```
CREATE TABLE InvoiceLineItems1
(InvoiceID               INT         NOT NULL,
 InvoiceSequence         SMALLINT    NOT NULL,
 InvoiceLineItemAmount   MONEY       NOT NULL,
 PRIMARY KEY (InvoiceID, InvoiceSequence))
```

A statement that creates a table with two column-level check constraints

```
CREATE TABLE Invoices1
(InvoiceID      INT    NOT NULL IDENTITY PRIMARY KEY,
 InvoiceTotal   MONEY NOT NULL CHECK (InvoiceTotal >= 0),
 PaymentTotal   MONEY NOT NULL DEFAULT 0 CHECK (PaymentTotal >= 0))
```

The same statement with the check constraints coded at the table level

```
CREATE TABLE Invoices2
(InvoiceID      INT    NOT NULL IDENTITY PRIMARY KEY,
 InvoiceTotal   MONEY NOT NULL,
 PaymentTotal   MONEY NOT NULL DEFAULT 0,
 CHECK ((InvoiceTotal >= 0) AND (PaymentTotal >= 0)))
```

Description

- *Constraints* are used to enforce the integrity of the data in a table by defining rules about the values that can be stored in the columns of the table. Constraints can be used at the column level to restrict the value of a single column or at the table level to restrict the value of one or more columns.

- You code a *column-level constraint* as part of the definition of the column it constrains. You code a *table-level constraint* as if it were a separate column definition, and you name the columns it constrains within that definition.

- Constraints are tested before a new row is added to a table or an existing row is updated. If the new or modified row meets all of the constraints, the operation succeeds. Otherwise, an error occurs and the operation fails.

Figure 10-6   An introduction to constraints

How to use check constraints

To code a check constraint, you use the syntax presented in figure 10-7. As you can see, you code the CHECK keyword followed by the condition that the data must satisfy. This condition is evaluated as a Boolean expression. The insert or update operation that's being performed is allowed only if this expression evaluates to a True value.

The first example in this figure uses a column-level check constraint to limit the values in the InvoiceTotal column to numbers greater than zero. This is similar to the constraints you saw in the previous figure. Notice that if you try to store a negative value in this column as illustrated by the INSERT statement in this example, the system responds with an error and the insert operation is terminated.

The second example shows how you can use a check constraint to limit a column to values that have a specific format. Note that although this constraint limits the values in a single column, it's coded at the table level because it refers to a column other than the one being constrained. The first part of the condition in this check constraint uses a LIKE expression to restrict the VendorID column to six characters, consisting of two alphabetic characters followed by four numeric characters. Then, the second part of the condition restricts the first two characters of the VendorID column to the first two characters of the VendorName column.

In general, you should use check constraints to restrict the values in a column whenever possible. In some situations, however, check constraints can be too restrictive. As an example, consider a telephone number that's constrained to the typical "(000) 000-0000" format used for US phone numbers. The problem with this constraint is that it wouldn't let you store phone numbers with extensions (although you could store extensions in a separate column) or phone numbers with an international format.

For this reason, check constraints aren't used by all database designers. That way, the database can store values with formats that weren't predicted when the database was designed. However, this flexibility comes at the cost of allowing some invalid data. For some systems, this tradeoff is acceptable.

Keep in mind, too, that application programs that add and update data can also include data validation. In that case, check constraints may not be necessary. Because you can't always assume that an application program will check for valid data, though, you should include check constraints whenever that makes sense.

The syntax of a check constraint

```
CHECK (condition)
```

A column-level check constraint that limits invoices to positive amounts

A statement that defines the check constraint

```
CREATE TABLE Invoices3
(InvoiceID        INT    NOT NULL IDENTITY PRIMARY KEY,
InvoiceTotal      MONEY NOT NULL CHECK (InvoiceTotal > 0))
```

An INSERT statement that fails due to the check constraint

```
INSERT Invoices3
VALUES (-100)
```

The response from the system

```
INSERT statement conflicted with COLUMN CHECK constraint
'CK__Invoices3__Invoic__7F60ED59'. The conflict occurred in database
'New_AP', table 'Invoices3', column 'InvoiceTotal'.
The statement has been terminated.
```

A table-level check constraint that limits vendor IDs to a specific format

A statement that defines the check constraint

```
CREATE TABLE Vendors1
(VendorID         CHAR(6)     NOT NULL PRIMARY KEY,
VendorName        VARCHAR(50) NOT NULL,
CHECK        ((VendorID LIKE '[A-Z][A-Z][0-9][0-9][0-9][0-9]') AND
             (LEFT(VendorID,2) = LEFT(VendorName,2))))
```

An INSERT statement that fails due to the check constraint

```
INSERT Vendors1
VALUES ('Mc4559','Castle Printers, Inc.')
```

The response from the system

```
INSERT statement conflicted with TABLE CHECK constraint
'CK__Vendors1__023D5A04'. The conflict occurred in database 'New_AP', table
'Vendors1'.
The statement has been terminated.
```

Description

- *Check constraints* limit the values that can be stored in the columns of a table.
- The condition you specify for a check constraint is evaluated as a Boolean expression. If the expression is true, the insert or update operation proceeds. Otherwise, it fails.
- A check constraint that's coded at the column level can refer only to that column. A check constraint that's coded at the table level can refer to any column in the table.

Figure 10-7   How to use check constraints

How to use foreign key constraints

Figure 10-8 presents the syntax of a foreign key constraint, also known as a *reference constraint*. This type of constraint is used to define the relationships between tables and to enforce referential integrity.

To create a foreign key constraint at the column level, you code the REFER-ENCES keyword followed by the name of the related table and the name of the related column in parentheses. Although you can also code the FOREIGN KEY keywords, these keywords are optional and are usually omitted. After the REFERENCES clause, you can code the ON DELETE and ON UPDATE clauses. I'll have more to say about these clauses in a moment.

The first two statements in this figure show how to create two related tables. The first statement creates the primary key table, a table named Vendors9. Then, the second statement creates the foreign key table, named Invoices9. Notice that the VendorID column in this table includes a REFERENCES clause that identi-fies the VendorID column in the Vendors9 table as the related column.

The next statement in this figure is an INSERT statement that attempts to insert a row into the Invoices9 table. Because the Vendors9 table doesn't contain a row with the specified VendorID value, however, the insert operation fails.

Before I go on, you should realize that although the foreign key of one table is typically related to the primary key of another table, that doesn't have to be the case. Instead, a foreign key can be related to any unique key. For the pur-poses of this topic, though, I'll assume that the related column is a primary key column.

By default, you can't delete a row from the primary key table if related rows exist in a foreign key table. Instead, you have to delete the related rows from the foreign key table first. If that's not what you want, you can code the ON DELETE clause with the CASCADE option. Then, when you delete a row from the primary key table, the delete is *cascaded* to the related rows in the foreign key table. Because a *cascading delete* can destroy valuable data if it's used improperly, you should use it with caution.

The ON UPDATE clause is similar. If you code the CASCADE keyword in this clause, a change to the value of a primary key is automatically cascaded to the related rows in the foreign key table. Otherwise, the change isn't allowed. Since most tables are designed so their primary key values don't change, you won't usually code the ON UPDATE clause.

When you code a foreign key constraint at the column level, you relate a single column in the foreign key table to a single column in the primary key table. If the keys consist of two or more columns, however, you have to code the constraint at the table level. For example, suppose that a foreign key consists of two columns named CustomerID2 and CustomerID4 and that the foreign key is related to two columns with the same name in a table named Customers. Then, you would define the foreign key constraint like this:

```
FOREIGN KEY (CustomerID2, CustomerID4)
    REFERENCES Customers (CustomerID2, CustomerID4)
```

In this case, you must include the FOREIGN KEY keywords.

The syntax of a column-level foreign key constraint

```
[FOREIGN KEY] REFERENCES ref_table_name (ref_column_name)
    [ON DELETE {CASCADE|NO ACTION}]
    [ON UPDATE {CASCADE|NO ACTION}]
```

The syntax of a table-level foreign key constraint

```
FOREIGN KEY (column_name_1 [, column_name_2]...)
    REFERENCES ref_table_name (ref_column_name_1 [, ref_column_name_2]...)
    [ON DELETE {CASCADE|NO ACTION}]
    [ON UPDATE {CASCADE|NO ACTION}]
```

A foreign key constraint defined at the column level

A statement that creates the primary key table

```
CREATE TABLE Vendors9
(VendorID         INT NOT NULL PRIMARY KEY,
VendorName        VARCHAR(50) NOT NULL)
```

A statement that creates the foreign key table

```
CREATE TABLE Invoices9
(InvoiceID        INT NOT NULL PRIMARY KEY,
VendorID          INT NOT NULL REFERENCES Vendors9 (VendorID),
InvoiceTotal      MONEY NULL)
```

An INSERT statement that fails because a related row doesn't exist

```
INSERT Invoices9
VALUES (1, 99, 100)
```

The response from the system

```
INSERT statement conflicted with COLUMN FOREIGN KEY constraint
'FK__Invoices9__Vendor__0F975522'. The conflict occurred in database
'New_AP', table 'Vendors9', column 'VendorID'.
The statement has been terminated.
```

Description

- You use the FOREIGN KEY clause to define a *foreign key constraint*, also called a *reference constraint*. A foreign key constraint defines the relationship between two tables and enforces referential integrity.

- If you code a foreign key constraint at the column level, you can relate a single column in the new table to a single column in the related table. To define a relationship that consists of two or more columns, you must define the constraint at the table level.

- Typically, a foreign key constraint refers to the primary key of the related table. However, it can also refer to a unique key.

- The ON DELETE clause specifies what happens to rows in the table if the row in the related table with the same key value is deleted. The ON UPDATE clause specifies what happens to rows in the table if the key of the related row is updated.

- The CASCADE keyword causes the rows in this table to be deleted or updated to match the row in the related table. This is known as a *cascading delete* or a *cascading update*.

- The NO ACTION keyword prevents the row in the related table from being deleted or updated and causes an error to be raised. In most cases, this is the preferred option.

Figure 10-8   How to use foreign key constraints

How to change databases and tables

After you create a database, you may need to change it. For example, you may need to add a new table or index. To do that, you can use the CREATE statements that you've already learned. If you need to modify an existing table, however, or if you need to delete an existing index, table, or database, you'll need to use the statements that follow.

How to delete an index, table, or database

Figure 10-9 presents the syntax of the three DROP statements you use to delete an index, a table, or a database. Notice that you can use the DROP INDEX statement to delete one or more indexes from tables in the current database, and you can use the DROP DATABASE statement to drop one or more databases from the current server. In contrast, the DROP TABLE statement only lets you delete one table. However, that table doesn't need to be in the current database. Instead, you can qualify the table name so it names the database that contains the table you want to delete.

If other objects depend on the object you're trying to delete, SQL Server won't allow the deletion. For example, you can't delete a table if a foreign key constraint in another table refers to that table, and you can't delete an index if it's based on a primary key or a unique key. In addition, you can't drop a database that's currently in use.

You should also know that when you delete a table, many of the objects related to that table are deleted as well. That includes any indexes, triggers, or constraints defined for the table. In contrast, any views or stored procedures that are associated with a deleted table are not deleted. Instead, you have to delete these objects explicitly using the statements you'll learn in chapter 14.

Because the DROP statements delete objects permanently, you'll want to use them cautiously. In fact, you may want to create a backup copy of the database before using any of these statements. That way, you can restore the database if necessary.

The syntax of the DROP INDEX statement

```
DROP INDEX table_name_1.index_name_1 [, table_name_2.index_name_2]...
```

The syntax of the DROP TABLE statement

```
DROP TABLE table_name
```

The syntax of the DROP DATABASE statement

```
DROP DATABASE database_name_1 [, database_name_2]...
```

Statements that delete database objects

A statement that deletes an index from the Invoices table

```
DROP INDEX Invoices.IX_Invoices
```

A statement that deletes a table from the current database

```
DROP TABLE Vendors1
```

A statement that qualifies the table to be deleted

```
DROP TABLE New_AP.dbo.Vendors1
```

A statement that deletes a database

```
DROP DATABASE New_AP
```

Description

- You can use the DROP INDEX statement to delete one or more indexes from one or more tables in the current database.

- You can use the DROP DATABASE statement to delete one or more databases from the current server.

- You can use the DROP TABLE statement to delete a table from any database on the current server. To delete a table from a database other than the current database, you must qualify the table name with the database name.

- You can't delete a table if a foreign key constraint in another table refers to that table.

- When you delete a table, all of the data, indexes, triggers, and constraints are deleted. Any views or stored procedures associated with the table must be deleted explicitly.

- You can't delete an index that's based on a primary key or unique key constraint. To do that, you have to use the ALTER TABLE statement. See figure 10-10 for details.

Warnings

- You can't undo a delete operation. For this reason, you may want to back up the database before you use any of these statements so you can restore it if necessary.

- You should never use these statements on a production database without first consulting the DBA.

Figure 10-9   How to delete an index, table, or database

How to alter a table

Figure 10-10 presents the basic syntax of the ALTER TABLE statement. You can use this statement to modify an existing table in one of several ways. The clauses shown here are the ones you're most likely to use.

The first example in this figure shows how to add a new column to a table. As you can see, you code the column definition the same way you do when you create a new table: You specify the column name, followed by its data type and its attributes.

The second example shows how to drop an existing column. Note that SQL Server prevents you from dropping some columns. For example, you can't drop a column if it's the primary key column, if it's used in a check constraint or a foreign key constraint, or if an index is based on it.

The third and fourth examples show how to add constraints to a table. The third example adds a check constraint, and the fourth example adds a foreign key constraint. You can use the same technique to add a primary key or unique constraint. Note that you use this technique regardless of whether the constraint refers to a single column or to two or more columns. That's because the ALTER COLUMN clause only lets you change the data type or the NULL or NOT NULL attribute of an existing column. You can't use it to add column constraints.

When you add a table constraint, SQL Server automatically checks that existing data meets the constraint. If that's not what you want, you can include the WITH NOCHECK keywords in the ALTER statement. This is illustrated in the third example.

In addition to adding constraints, you can use the ALTER TABLE statement to delete constraints. To do that, you have to know the name of the constraint. Although you can name a constraint when you create it, you don't usually do that. That's why I didn't include that information in the syntax for creating constraints. Instead, you usually let SQL Server generate a constraint name for you. Then, if you need to delete the constraint, you can use the Enterprise Manager as described in the next chapter to find out what name SQL Server assigned to it.

The last example shows how to modify the data type of an existing column. In this case, a column that was defined as VARCHAR(100) is changed to VARCHAR(200). Because the new data type is wider than the old data type, you can be sure that the existing data will still fit. However, that's not always the case. Because of that, SQL Server checks to be sure that no data will be lost before it changes the data type. If the change will result in a loss of data, it's not allowed.

The basic syntax of the ALTER TABLE statement

```
ALTER TABLE table_name [WITH CHECK|WITH NOCHECK]
{ADD new_column_name data_type [column_attributes] |
 DROP COLUMN column_name |
 ALTER COLUMN column_name new_data_type [NULL|NOT NULL] |
 ADD [CONSTRAINT] new_constraint_definition |
 DROP [CONSTRAINT] constraint_name}
```

Examples of the ALTER TABLE statement

A statement that adds a new column

```
ALTER TABLE Vendors
ADD LastTranDate SMALLDATETIME NULL
```

A statement that drops a column

```
ALTER TABLE Vendors
DROP COLUMN LastTranDate
```

A statement that adds a new check constraint

```
ALTER TABLE Invoices WITH NOCHECK
ADD CHECK (InvoiceTotal >= 1)
```

A statement that adds a foreign key constraint

```
ALTER TABLE InvoiceLineItems WITH CHECK
ADD FOREIGN KEY (AccountNo) REFERENCES GLAccounts(AccountNo)
```

A statement that changes the data type of a column

```
ALTER TABLE InvoiceLineItems
ALTER COLUMN InvoiceLineItemDescription VARCHAR(200)
```

Description

- You use the ALTER TABLE statement to modify an existing table. You can use this statement to add columns or constraints, drop columns or constraints, or change the definition of an existing column, including changing the column's data type.

- Before SQL Server changes the data type of a column, it checks to be sure that no data will be lost. If it will, the operation isn't performed.

- You can modify a column to allow null values as long as the column isn't defined as the primary key. You can modify a column so that it doesn't allow null values as long as none of the existing rows contain null values in that column.

- You can add a column that doesn't allow null values only if you specify a default value for that column.

- To delete a constraint, you must know its name. Although you can name a constraint when you create it, you usually let SQL Server generate the name for you. Then, you can use the Enterprise Manager as shown in the next chapter to look up the name.

- By default, SQL Server verifies that existing data satisfies a new check or foreign key constraint. If that's not what you want, you can code the WITH NOCHECK keywords.

Warning

- You should never alter a table in a production database without first consulting the DBA.

Figure 10-10   How to alter a table

The script used to create the AP database

To complete this chapter, figure 10-11 presents the DDL statements that I used to create the AP database that's used in the examples throughout this book. By studying these DDL statements, you'll get a better idea of how a database is actually implemented. Note, however, that these statements are coded as part of a script. So before I describe the DDL statements, I'll introduce you to scripts.

How the script works

In this figure, all of the DDL statements are coded as part of a *script*, which consists of one or more SQL statements that are stored in a file. This is typically the way that all of the objects for a database are created. In chapter 13, you'll learn the details of coding scripts, but here are some basic concepts.

A script consists of one or more *batches*. The script shown in the two parts of this figure, for example, consists of two batches. Each batch consists of one or more SQL statements that are executed as a unit. To signal the end of a batch and execute the statements it contains, you use the GO command. As you can see, then, the first batch shown in this figure consists of a single CREATE DATABASE statement, and the second batch consists of several CREATE TABLE and CREATE INDEX statements. Notice that a GO command isn't required at the end of the second batch, which is the last batch in this script.

To create and execute a script, you can use the Query Analyzer. Although you may not be aware of it, you're creating a script each time you enter a SQL statement into the Query window. So far, though, the scripts you've created have consisted of a single batch.

The reason for breaking a script like the one shown here into batches is that some of the statements must be executed before others can execute successfully. Before any tables can be created in the AP database, for example, the database itself must be created.

The only other statement used in this script that you're not familiar with is the USE statement. You use this statement to change the current database. That way, after the script creates the AP database, the statements that follow will operate on that database rather than on the one that's selected in the Query Analyzer toolbar.

How the DDL statements work

Notice that each CREATE TABLE statement in this script lists the primary key column (or columns) first. Although this isn't required, it's a conventional coding practice. Also note that the order in which you declare the columns defines the default order for the columns. That means that when you use a SELECT * statement to retrieve all of the columns, they're returned in this order. For that reason, you'll want to define the columns in a logical sequence.

The SQL script that creates the AP database   **Page 1**

```
CREATE DATABASE AP
GO

USE AP
CREATE TABLE Terms
(TermsID                INT            NOT NULL PRIMARY KEY,
 TermsDescription       VARCHAR(50)    NOT NULL,
 TermsDueDays           SMALLINT       NOT NULL)

CREATE TABLE GLAccounts
(AccountNo              INT            NOT NULL PRIMARY KEY,
 AccountDescription     VARCHAR(50)    NOT NULL)

CREATE TABLE Vendors
(VendorID               INT            NOT NULL IDENTITY PRIMARY KEY,
 VendorName             VARCHAR(50)    NOT NULL,
 VendorAddress1         VARCHAR(50)    NULL,
 VendorAddress2         VARCHAR(50)    NULL,
 VendorCity             VARCHAR(50)    NOT NULL,
 VendorState            CHAR(2)        NOT NULL,
 VendorZipCode          VARCHAR(20)    NOT NULL,
 VendorPhone            VARCHAR(50)    NULL,
 VendorContactLName     VARCHAR(50)    NULL,
 VendorContactFName     VARCHAR(50)    NULL,
 DefaultTermsID         INT            NOT NULL
                                       REFERENCES Terms(TermsID),
 DefaultAccountNo       INT            NOT NULL
                                       REFERENCES GLAccounts(AccountNo))
```

Basic script concepts

- Instead of creating database objects one at a time, you can write a *script* that contains all of the statements needed to create the database and its tables and indexes.

- A script is a set of one or more *batches* that can be stored in a file. A batch is a sequence of SQL statements that are executed as a unit. You can use the Query Analyzer to create and execute script files.

- The GO command signals the end of the batch and causes all of the statements in the batch to be executed. You should issue a GO command when the execution of the next statement depends on the successful completion of the previous statements.

- SQL Server executes the last batch in a script automatically, so a final GO command isn't required.

- To change the current database within a script, you use the USE statement.

Note

- The Terms and GLAccounts tables are created first so the other tables can define foreign keys that refer to them. Similarly, the Vendors table is created before the Invoices table, and the Invoices table is created before the InvoiceLineItems table (see part 2).

Figure 10-11   The script used to create the AP database (part 1 of 2)

Also notice that most of the columns in this database are assigned the NOT NULL constraint. The exceptions are the VenderAddress1, VendorAddress2, VendorPhone, VendorContactLName, and VendorContactFName columns in the Vendors table and the PaymentDate column in the Invoices table. Because not all vendor addresses will require two lines and because some vendors won't provide a street address at all, a null value can be assigned to both address columns to indicate that they're not applicable. Similarly, you may not have a phone number and contact information for each vendor. For this reason, you could assign a null value to one of these columns to indicate an unknown value. Finally, an invoice wouldn't be assigned a payment date until it was paid. Until that time, you could assign a null value to the PaymentDate column to indicate that it hasn't been paid.

I could also have used a default date to indicate an unpaid invoice. To do that, I could have defined the PaymentDate column like this:

```
PaymentDate SMALLDATETIME NOT NULL DEFAULT '1900-01-01'
```

In this case, the date January 1, 1900 would be stored in the PaymentDate column unless another value was assigned to that column. Usually, a null value is a more intuitive representation of an unknown value than a default such as this, but either representation is acceptable. Keep in mind, though, that the technique you use will affect how you query the table.

Because each of the five tables in this database has a primary key, SQL Server creates a clustered index for each table based on that key. In addition, this script creates seven additional indexes to improve the performance of the database. The first five of these indexes are based on the foreign keys that each referring table uses to relate to another table. For example, since the VendorID column in the Invoices table references the VendorID column in the Vendors table, I created a nonclustered index on VendorID in the Invoices table. Similarly, I created indexes for TermsID in the Invoices table, DefaultTermsID and DefaultAccountNo in the Vendors table, and AccountNo in the InvoiceLineItems table. Finally, I created indexes for the VendorName column in the Vendors table and the InvoiceDate column in the Invoices table because these columns are frequently used to search for rows in these tables.

As you may have noticed, I created an index for each column that appears in a foreign key constraint except one: the InvoiceID column in the InvoiceLineItems table. Since this column is part of the composite primary key for this table, it's already included in the clustered index. For this reason, the addition of a nonclustered index on InvoiceID by itself won't improve performance.

The SQL script that creates the AP database

```
CREATE TABLE Invoices
(InvoiceID              INT             NOT NULL IDENTITY PRIMARY KEY,
VendorID               INT             NOT NULL
                       REFERENCES Vendors(VendorID),
InvoiceNumber          VARCHAR(50)     NOT NULL,
InvoiceDate            SMALLDATETIME   NOT NULL,
InvoiceTotal           MONEY           NOT NULL,
PaymentTotal           MONEY           NOT NULL DEFAULT 0,
CreditTotal            MONEY           NOT NULL DEFAULT 0,
TermsID                INT             NOT NULL
                       REFERENCES Terms(TermsID),
InvoiceDueDate         SMALLDATETIME   NOT NULL,
PaymentDate            SMALLDATETIME   NULL)

CREATE TABLE InvoiceLineItems
(InvoiceID              INT             NOT NULL
                       REFERENCES Invoices(InvoiceID),
InvoiceSequence        SMALLINT        NOT NULL,
AccountNo              INT             NOT NULL
                       REFERENCES GLAccounts(AccountNo),
InvoiceLineItemAmount  MONEY           NOT NULL,
InvoiceLineItemDescription VARCHAR(100) NOT NULL,
PRIMARY KEY (InvoiceID, InvoiceSequence))

CREATE INDEX IX_Invoices_VendorID
    ON Invoices (VendorID)
CREATE INDEX IX_Invoices_TermsID
    ON Invoices (TermsID)
CREATE INDEX IX_Vendors_TermsID
    ON Vendors (DefaultTermsID)
CREATE INDEX IX_Vendors_AccountNo
    ON Vendors (DefaultAccountNo)
CREATE INDEX IX_InvoiceLineItems_AccountNo
    ON InvoiceLineItems (AccountNo)
CREATE INDEX IX_VendorName
    ON Vendors (VendorName)
CREATE INDEX IX_InvoiceDate
    ON Invoices (InvoiceDate DESC)
```

Notes

- The InvoiceLineItems table has a composite primary key that consists of the InvoiceID and InvoiceSequence columns. For this reason, the PRIMARY KEY constraint must be defined as a table-level constraint.

- In addition to the five indexes that SQL Server automatically creates for the primary key of each table, this script creates seven additional indexes. The first five are indexes for the foreign keys that are used in the REFERENCES constraints. The last two create indexes on the VendorName column and the InvoiceDate column since these columns are used frequently in search conditions.

Figure 10-11   The script used to create the AP database (part 2 of 2)

Perspective

Now that you've completed this chapter, you should be able to create and modify databases, tables, and indexes by coding DDL statements. This provides a valuable background for working with any database. In practice, though, you usually use the Enterprise Manager to perform the functions that are done by DDL statements, so that's what you'll learn to do in the next chapter.

Terms

data definition language (DDL)
database objects
identifier
transaction log file
attach a database
constraint
column-level constraint
table-level constraint
check constraint
foreign key constraint
reference constraint
cascading delete
cascading update
script
batch

11

How to use the Enterprise Manager

Now that you've learned how to code all of the essential SQL statements for data manipulation and data definition, you're ready to learn how to use the Enterprise Manager to generate this code for you. The Enterprise Manager makes it easy to perform common tasks, and you'll use it frequently to work with the objects of a database. You may also use it to create and execute queries. Once you learn how to use the Enterprise Manager, you can decide when it make sense to use it to generate SQL code and when it makes sense to code the SQL yourself.

An introduction to the Enterprise Manager

The *Enterprise Manager* provides a graphical interface that you can use to generate SQL code. Since you were introduced to the Enterprise Manager in chapter 2, you should already have some idea of how it works. So the two topics that follow just review some of the basic information for using this tool.

The Enterprise Manager workspace

Figure 11-1 presents the Enterprise Manager workspace. This workspace consists of a window with two panes. The left pane contains the console tree, which displays a list of the database objects on the server grouped into *nodes*. You'll learn more about using the console tree in a moment.

The right pane of the window displays a list of the objects of the currently selected type. If you click on the Databases node, for example, all of the databases on the server are displayed in this pane. In this figure, the Tables node of the AP database is selected, so the right pane lists all of the tables in that database.

To work with the objects in either pane, you can use the menus or the toolbar. Note that the menu items and toolbar buttons that are available change depending on what node or item is currently selected. The Enterprise Manager also provides shortcut menus that you can use to work with the nodes and items. The shortcut menu in this figure, for example, shows the menu items that are available for the Tables node.

How to navigate through the SQL Server items

The console tree provides a hierarchical listing of the SQL Server items that are available to you. Each item is represented as a node. If a node can be expanded, a plus sign appears next to it. Then, you can click on this plus sign to display the contents of the node. After you expand a node, a minus sign appears next to it and you can click on the minus sign to collapse the node. The nodes at the lowest level can't be expanded or collapsed. To display the contents of one of these nodes, you simply click on it and a list is displayed in the right pane. If you've used other Windows programs like the Windows Explorer, you should already have a good idea of how this works.

Although you'll typically use the console tree for navigation, you don't have to do that. Instead, you can double-click on an item in the right pane to move down through the hierarchy, and you can use the Up one level toolbar button to move up through the hierarchy. If you're not using the console tree, you can close it by clicking on the Show/Hide Console Tree/Favorites toolbar button. Click on this button again to redisplay the console tree.

The Enterprise Manager workspace

Up one level button   Show/Hide Console Tree/Favorites button

How to start the Enterprise Manager

- To start the Enterprise Manager, click on the Start button and then select Programs→Microsoft SQL Server→Enterprise Manager.

How to navigate through the SQL Server items

- The console tree displays a hierarchical list of the database objects grouped into *nodes*. To display or hide the console tree, click the Show/Hide Console Tree/Favorites button.
- To expand a node, click the plus sign to the left of the node. To collapse a node, click the minus sign.
- To work with a node, right-click on it to display a shortcut menu or highlight it and then use the commands in the Action menu.
- When you highlight a node, the objects of that type are displayed in the right side of the Enterprise Manager window. Then, you can work with an object by using its shortcut menu or the Action menu.
- You can double-click on an item in the right pane to display the next level. If you double-click on a server or a database, its properties are displayed and the next level is displayed when you close the Properties dialog box. To redisplay the previous level, click on the Up one level toolbar button.

Description

- The Enterprise Manager provides a graphical user interface that you can use to work with a database. This tool makes it easy to create and manage database objects without having to write code. You can also use it to create and execute queries.

Figure 11-1   An introduction to the Enterprise Manager

How to create and edit queries

The Enterprise Manager provides a tool called the *Query Designer* that you can use to create queries. Because this tool lets you create a query using a graphical interface, it can sometimes be helpful for designing complex queries. And, as you'll see later, it lets you review the code it generates before it's executed. However, you'll often find that it's easier to just code the query yourself.

As you learn to use the Query Designer, you should keep in mind two differences between this program and the Query Analyzer. First, the Query Designer doesn't let you save a query so you can run it again later. Second, you can't use it to create scripts that contain two or more SQL statements. If you prefer to use the Enterprise Manager, however, you can always copy the code it generates to the Query Analyzer. Then, you can include it in a script that you can save and execute whenever you want.

An introduction to the Query Designer

Figure 11-2 presents the layout of the Query Designer window. In the next four figures, you'll learn the details for using the four panes of this window. In general, though, you use the *diagram pane* to select the tables and columns you want to include in the query. You use the *grid pane* to specify the search criteria and sort order and to create calculated columns and summary queries. You use the *SQL pane* to view and, if necessary, edit the generated SQL code. And you use the *results pane* to view and work with the results of the query.

When you first start the Query Designer, it creates a SELECT query that retrieves all of the columns and rows from the table you selected. You can see this statement in the SQL pane in this figure. If that's not what you want, you can use the diagram and grid panes as described next to modify this statement. In addition, you can change the query type from the default, SELECT, to an action query. To do that, you select the query type from the menu that's displayed when you click on the Change query type toolbar button.

The other toolbar buttons that are highlighted in this figure let you display and hide the window panes. By default, all of the panes are displayed, which is usually what you want. In some cases, though, you may want to hide one or more panes so you can focus on the others.

The Query Designer window

Show/Hide buttons   Change query type button

Diagram pane

Grid pane

SQL pane

Results pane

How to start the Query Designer

- Highlight the Tables node in the console tree to display the tables in the right pane. Then, highlight the table and select Action→Open Table→Query.

- By default, the Query Designer creates a SELECT query that retrieves all of the rows and columns from the table.

Description

- To select the tables and columns for the query, you use the *diagram pane*. You can also use this pane to join tables.

- To work with the selected columns, you use the *grid pane*. You can use this pane to specify the search criteria and sort order, create calculated columns and aliases, and specify grouping criteria for summary queries.

- To enter, edit, or examine the SQL code for a query, you use the *SQL pane*.

- To view and work with the results of a query, you use the *results pane*.

- You can also use the Query Designer to create action queries. To select the type of query you want to create, click on the Change query type toolbar button.

- The diagram, grid, and SQL panes are synchronized so that changes you make in one pane are reflected in the other panes.

- By default, all four panes of the Query Designer are displayed. To hide a pane, click on the appropriate button in the toolbar.

Figure 11-2   An introduction to the Query Designer

How to work in the diagram pane

Figure 11-3 presents the details for working in the diagram pane. You can use this pane to select the columns you want to include in the result set. To do that, you click on the check box to the left of the column. In this figure, for example, you can see that the VendorName column is selected from the Vendors table and the InvoiceNumber, InvoiceDate, and InvoiceTotal columns are selected from the Invoices table. I'll have more to say about including additional tables in a query in a moment.

You can also include all the columns in a table by selecting the * (All Columns) item at the top of the table's column list. Remember, though, that this is the default when you start a new query. If that's not what you want, you can remove this selection as described in the next figure. Unfortunately, you can't remove this default by unchecking the * item because it's not selected.

You can also use the diagram pane to specify the sort order for the result set. To do that, you highlight the column name and then click on the Sort ascending or Sort descending toolbar button. When you do, a sort icon appears to the right of the column. You can see this icon to the right of the VendorName column in this figure. If you want to sort by two or more columns, be sure to select the columns in the order you want them sorted.

If you've specified search criteria for a column, you can remove that criteria using the diagram pane. To do that, highlight the column and then click on the Remove filter toolbar button. Note that a filter icon appears to the right of any columns that are used to filter the result set. Also note that you can't use the diagram pane to add search criteria. To do that, you have to use the grid pane or the SQL pane.

If you want to create a query that includes columns from two or more tables, you can add tables by clicking on the Add table toolbar button. This displays a dialog box that lets you select the tables you want to add. Although that dialog box isn't shown here, you shouldn't have any trouble using it.

If you include two tables with an existing relationship, the Query Designer automatically joins them. The join is represented by a line whose endpoints identify the type of relationship. In this figure, for example, the join line indicates that the Vendors table has a one-to-many relationship with the Invoices table.

By default, the Query Designer creates an inner join between two related tables. If that's not what you want, you can use the shortcut menu shown in this figure to remove the join, create an outer join by selecting all the rows from one or both tables, or display the join properties. Note that when you remove a join, the underlying relationship isn't affected. If you display the Properties dialog box, you'll see that it also lets you create an outer join. In addition, it lets you change the join operator.

If you want to create an ad hoc relationship between two tables, you can do that too. Just drag a column from one table to the related column in the other table. Then, you can display the Properties dialog box to verify that the join was created correctly.

The diagram pane with two related tables

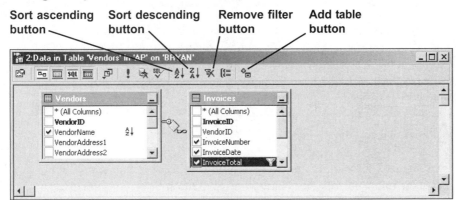

The shortcut menu that's displayed for a join

How to work with tables and columns

- To include a column in the result set, select the check box next to the column name. To remove a column from the result set, remove the check mark from this check box.

- To sort the result set by a column, highlight the column name and then click the Sort ascending or Sort descending toolbar button. A sort icon appears to the right of the column.

- If search criteria are specified for a column in another pane, a filter icon appears to the right of that column. To remove the filter, highlight the column and then click on the Remove filter toolbar button.

- To add another table to the diagram pane, click on the Add table toolbar button to display the Add Table dialog box. Then, highlight the table you want to add and click the Add button.

How to work with joins

- If a relationship exists between two tables in the diagram pane, an inner join is automatically created for them. This is illustrated by a join line with endpoints that indicate the type of relationship. A key indicates the "one" side of a relationship and the infinity symbol (∞) indicates the "many" side of a relationship.

- You can also create a join by dragging a column from one table to the related column in the other table. An inner join is created by default.

- You can use the shortcut menu that's displayed when you right-click on a join line to remove a join, create an outer join, or display the Properties dialog box for the join. The Properties dialog box lets you change the join operator and create an outer join.

Figure 11-3   How to work in the diagram pane

How to work in the grid pane

Figure 11-4 describes how you can work in the grid pane. To start, you'll want to know how to remove the default column specification that's added when you first start a query. To do that, right-click on the box to the left of the row that contains the * (all columns) specification and select Delete from the shortcut menu that's displayed. You'll want to delete this specification before you start selecting columns for the query. Otherwise, each column you select will be included twice.

Each row in the grid pane represents one column used in the query. The query in this figure, for example, uses two columns: the VendorName column in the Vendors table and a calculated column that's based on three columns from the Invoices table. Although the easiest way to include a column in the result set is to select it in the diagram pane, you can also select a column from the grid pane. To do that, select the table from the drop-down list in the Table column, and select the name of the column from the drop-down list in the Column column. To create a calculated column, you must use the grid pane. To do that, enter the expression that defines the column instead of a column name. In addition, you can enter an alias for the column in the Alias column.

By default, each column you add to the grid pane is included in the result set. Sometimes, though, you'll want to use a column in the query but not include it in the result set. To do that, you simply remove the check mark from the Output column for that column.

To specify the sort order for the result set, you use the Sort Type and Sort Order columns. To specify ascending or descending order for a column, select the appropriate option from the Sort Type column. In this figure, for example, you can see that the result set will be sorted in ascending sequence by the VendorName column. You can also see in the Sort Order column that this column is sorted first, which makes sense since it's the only column used for sorting. If you select two or more columns for sorting, however, you can use the Sort Order column to change the sequence in which the columns are sorted if you don't select them in the correct sequence.

To specify the search criteria for a query, you use the Criteria and Or... columns. For instance, the query in this figure specifies that only invoices with balances greater than 100 will be included in the result set. In this case, the search criteria consists of a single condition. However, you can code compound conditions by entering conditions in two or more cells in the grid. For example, if you code two conditions in the Criteria column of two rows, they'll be combined using the AND operator. On the other hand, if you code one condition in the Criteria column and a second in an Or... column, they'll be combined using the OR operator. You may need to experiment with this to fully understand how it works.

You can also use the grid pane to create a summary query. To do that, you start by clicking on the Use 'Group By' toolbar button. Then, a Group By column is added to the grid pane. By default, all of the columns are selected for grouping. Then, you can use the drop-down list in the Group By column to

The diagram, grid, and SQL panes for a summary query

How to work with columns

- To add a column to the query, select the table name from the Table column and select the column name from the Column column.

- To create a calculated column, enter the expression in the Column column.

- By default, each column you add will be included in the result set. If that's not what you want, remove the check mark from the Output column.

- To specify an alias for a column, enter it in the Alias column.

- To sort the result set by one or more columns, select the Ascending or Descending option from the Sort Type column for those columns in the sequence you want them sorted. You can also use the Sort Order column to set the sort sequence directly.

- To specify a search condition, enter the search criteria in the Criteria column. The conditions for two or more columns are automatically combined using the AND operator. To use the OR operator, enter the criteria in an Or… column.

- To delete a column from the query, right-click on the box to the left of the column and select Delete from the shortcut menu that's displayed.

How to create a summary query

- To create a summary query, click on the Use 'Group By' toolbar button to display the Group By column in the grid pane. By default, each column in the query is selected for grouping as indicated by the Group By option.

- To summarize a column in the query, select the aggregate function you want to use from the drop-down list in the Group By column.

- Search criteria for an aggregate column appear in the HAVING clause. To include the criteria in the WHERE clause, enter the column in the grid pane again, remove the check mark from the Output column, and select the Where option from the Group By column.

Figure 11-4   How to work in the grid pane

select the columns you want to summarize and the aggregate functions you want to use to summarize them. In this example, you can see that the result set will include the sum of the balance due for each vendor.

Notice that because the search criteria is included in an aggregate column, the search condition appears in the HAVING clause instead of the WHERE clause. If that's not what you want, you can include the column in the grid pane a second time and remove the check mark from the Output column so it's not included in the result set. Then, you can code the search criteria for that column and select the Where option from the Group By column.

How to work in the SQL pane

As you work in the diagram and grid panes, the Query Designer generates a SQL statement and displays it in the SQL pane. You can review this code before you execute it to be sure it's what you want. If not, you can make changes in the diagram or grid panes to modify it, or you can modify it directly in the SQL pane.

In most cases, you'll modify a statement in the SQL pane only if you need to create a query that can't be represented graphically. The query in figure 11-5, for example, includes a CASE function. Since you can't create this function using the diagram and grid panes, you have to enter it directly into the SQL pane. When you modify a statement this way, the Query Designer dims the diagram and grid panes to indicate that they're no longer synchronized with the SQL pane.

Before you execute a query that's been modified in the SQL pane, you may want to make sure that its syntax is correct. To do that, you can click on the Verify SQL toolbar button. Otherwise, you may get an error when you execute the statement.

You may also notice that the Query Designer reformats code that you enter directly into the SQL pane. When I entered the CASE function shown in this figure, for example, I entered each WHEN clause on a separate line. When I executed this statement, however, the Query Designer reformatted it as shown here.

The Query Designer after a CASE function is entered in the SQL pane

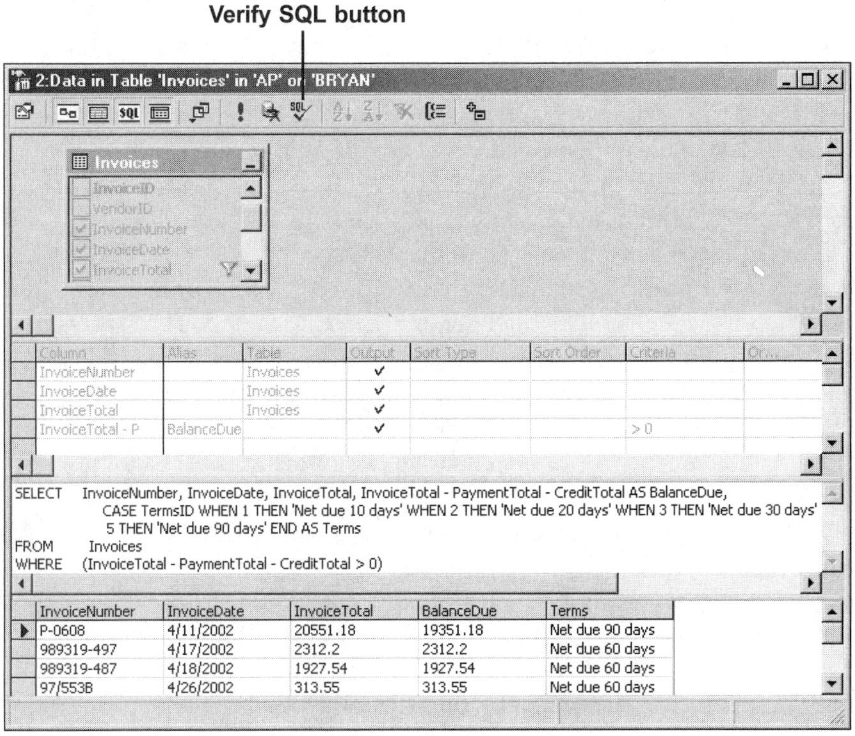

Verify SQL button

Description

- As you work in the diagram and grid panes, the Query Designer generates the SQL statement and displays it in the SQL pane. You can also edit the generated code or enter code directly into the SQL pane.

- If you enter code in the SQL pane, the diagram and grid panes are updated to reflect the changes if possible.

- If a statement can't be represented graphically, a dialog box is displayed when you click in the diagram or grid pane that asks if you want to undo the change or continue editing. If you continue editing, the diagram and grid panes are dimmed as shown above.

- Some of the queries that aren't supported by the graphical interface are queries that include the CASE function and queries that include a union. For a complete list of unsupported queries, see the "Query Designer considerations for SQL Server databases" topic in Books Online.

- If you make a change in the SQL pane and then run the query or continue working in the diagram or grid pane, the Query Designer may reformat the SQL statement.

- If you want to verify the syntax of the SQL statement before you execute it, click on the Verify SQL toolbar button.

Figure 11-5   How to work in the SQL pane

How to work in the results pane

To execute a query, you click on the Run toolbar button. Then, the results of the query are displayed in the results pane as shown in figure 11-6. You can use this pane to view and work with the result set.

Unlike the results of a query displayed in the Query Analyzer, you can edit the results of a query displayed in the Query Designer. To do that, simply move to the row and column you want to change and begin typing. As soon as you move to another row, the changes are saved in the database.

You can also use the result set to delete rows from the database or to insert new rows. To delete a row, select it by clicking on the box to its left. Then, press the Delete key on your keyboard. To insert a new row, navigate to the end of the result set and enter the data in the row that has an asterisk in the box to its left. In this figure, for example, you can see that I started to enter the data for a new row. When I did that, another row was added at the end of the result set for the next new row.

The results pane provides a quick and easy way to modify the data in a table without having to write INSERT, UPDATE, or DELETE statements. That can come in handy when you're testing a new database. You should realize, however, that to insert a row, the result set must include all of the columns for which data must be entered. The only columns that can be omitted are identity columns, columns with default values, and columns that allow nulls.

In addition, to update or delete an existing row, the Query Designer must be able to uniquely identify the corresponding row in the base table. In general, that means that the result set must include the table's primary key or another unique key. SQL Server places additional restrictions on update operations. For example, you can't update an aggregate query because each row in the result set is based on more than one row in the base table. For complete information on when a row can be updated, you can look up "updating results" in the Books Online index.

Because the results are editable, the Enterprise Manager is constantly checking them for changes. This requires a significant amount of system resources. For this reason, you should clear the results pane when you finish working with the result set. To do that, click on the Cancel Execution and Clear Results toolbar button. If the query is still executing, this also ends the execution.

The results pane with a new row being added

Run button

Cancel Execution and
Clear Results button

VendorID	VendorName	VendorAddress1	VendorAddress2	VendorCity	VendorState	VendorZipCode
118	Unocal	P.O. Box 860070	<NULL>	Pasadena	CA	91186
119	Yesmed, Inc	PO Box 2061	<NULL>	Fresno	CA	93718
120	Dataforms/West	1617 W. Shaw Avenue	Suite F	Fresno	CA	93711
121	Zylka Design	3467 W Shaw Ave #103	<NULL>	Fresno	CA	93711
122	United Parcel Service	P.O. Box 505820	<NULL>	Reno	NV	88905
123	Federal Express Corporation	P.O. Box 1140	Dept A	Memphis	TN	38101
	MidState					

Description

- To execute a query, click on the Run button. If the query is a SELECT query, the results are displayed in the results pane.

- To change the value of one or more columns in a row, click in the columns and enter the changes. A pencil appears in the box to the left of the row to indicate that it has been modified. To save the changes, move to another row.

- To add a new row, scroll to the bottom of the result set, click in the last row (the one with an asterisk in the box at the left), and enter the data for each required column.

- To delete a row, click on the box to the left of the row to select the row and then press the Delete key.

- To cancel a change to a column, move to that column and press the Esc key. To cancel all the changes to a row, move to a column that hasn't been modified and then press the Esc key.

- To change the width of a column, drag the line to the right of the column header to the desired width. You can also double-click on this line to change the column width so it accommodates the widest value in the column.

- If you modify the query after executing it, the results pane is dimmed. It's still active, however, and you can still use it to edit the data that's displayed.

- To cancel a query that's currently executing and clear the results pane, or to clear the results pane after a query completes execution, click on the Cancel Execution and Clear Results toolbar button.

Notes

- To update or delete a row in the results pane, the Query Designer must be able to uniquely identify which row in the base table is being modified. In most cases, including the primary key is sufficient.

- To insert a new row, the result set must include all of the required columns.

Figure 11-6   How to work in the results pane

How to create action queries

In addition to SELECT queries, you can use the Query Designer to create action queries. Figure 11-7 shows you how. Because you use the same basic techniques that you use for SELECT queries, this figure just summarizes what's different about creating the different types of action queries. You should be able to figure the rest out on your own.

The three examples in this figure show simple INSERT, UPDATE, and DELETE queries. To create an INSERT query, you select the Insert into option from the menu that's displayed when you click on the Change query type toolbar button. Then, you select the columns you want to enter values for and you enter those values in the New Value column of the grid pane. In this example, a new row is being added to the Invoices table. Notice that only the required columns are included in this query.

Although it's not illustrated here, you can also create an INSERT statement that uses a subquery to insert one or more rows. To do that, you select the Insert from option from the Create query type menu list. Then, the Query Designer lets you build the SELECT statement for the subquery.

To create an UPDATE query, you select the Update menu option. Then, you select the columns you want to modify and you specify the new values for those columns in the grid pane. You can also specify search criteria that will be used to determine which rows are updated.

Finally, to create a DELETE query, you select the Delete menu option. Then, you specify the search criteria you want to use to determine which rows are deleted. Be sure you specify a search condition for a DELETE statement. If you don't, all of the rows in the table will be deleted.

One additional query you can create using the Query Designer is a SELECT INTO query. To create this type of query, you select the Create Table menu option. Then, the Query Designer asks you for the name of the table you want to create and lets you specify the columns and rows you want to include in that table.

The grid and SQL panes for an INSERT query

Column	New Value
VendorID	12
InvoiceNumber	'3289175'
InvoiceDate	'9/19/2002'
InvoiceTotal	165.00
TermsID	3
InvoiceDueDate	'10/19/2002'

```
INSERT INTO Invoices
          (VendorID, InvoiceNumber, InvoiceDate, InvoiceTotal, TermsID, InvoiceDueDate)
VALUES    (12, '3289175', '9/19/2002', 165.00, 3, '10/19/2002')
```

The grid and SQL panes for an UPDATE query

Column	Table	New Value	Criteria	Or...	Or...	Or...
CreditTotal	Invoices	35.89				
InvoiceNumber	Invoices		= '367447'			

```
UPDATE   Invoices
SET       CreditTotal = 35.89
WHERE    (InvoiceNumber = '367447')
```

The grid and SQL panes for a DELETE query

Column	Table	Criteria	Or...	Or...
InvoiceTotal - PaymentTotal - CreditTotal		= 0		

```
DELETE FROM Invoices
WHERE    (InvoiceTotal - PaymentTotal - CreditTotal = 0)
```

Description

- To create a query other than a SELECT query, select the type of query you want to create from the drop-down menu that's displayed when you click on the Change query type toolbar button.

- To add a row to a table, select the Insert into menu option. Then, select the columns you want to specify values for and enter the values for those columns in the New Value column.

- To update rows in a table, select the Update menu option. Then, select the columns you want to update and enter the new values for those columns. You can also select the columns you want to use to filter the update operation and then enter the search criteria.

- To delete rows from a table, select the Delete menu option. Then, select the columns you want to use to filter the delete operation and enter the search criteria.

- You can also use the Insert from menu option to insert rows from another table, and you can use the Create Table option to create a table from columns and rows you select from another table.

- When you execute an action query, a dialog box is displayed that indicates the number of rows affected by the query.

Figure 11-7   How to create action queries

How to edit query properties

In addition to the code you generate by working in the diagram and grid panes, you can also generate code by setting some of the properties of a query. To do that, you work in the Properties dialog box shown in figure 11-8. Most of the properties shown here are available only for SELECT and SELECT INTO queries and INSERT queries that include a subquery. For all other queries, only the SQL Comment option is available.

Each of the options you select in this dialog box adds one of the keywords you learned about earlier in this book. For example, the DISTINCT values option includes the DISTINCT keyword in the SELECT clause, and the TOP option includes the TOP clause. If your query includes a GROUP BY clause, the GROUP BY extension option is also available. If you select this option, you can also select the WITH CUBE, WITH ROLLUP, and ALL option.

In this figure, I created a summary query that's similar to the query you saw in figure 11-4. In this case, though, the result set is sorted by the sum of the invoice balances in descending sequence. Then, the TOP clause is used to return only the top ten vendors. In addition, the ROLLUP operator is included in the GROUP BY clause so that the result set will include a row that shows the total balance due for all ten vendors.

The Properties window for a summary query

The generated SQL code

```
SELECT    TOP 10 Vendors.VendorName, SUM(Invoices.InvoiceTotal - Invoices.PaymentTotal - Invoices.CreditTotal) AS BalanceDue
FROM      Vendors INNER JOIN
              Invoices ON Vendors.VendorID = Invoices.VendorID
GROUP BY Vendors.VendorName WITH ROLLUP
HAVING    (SUM(Invoices.InvoiceTotal - Invoices.PaymentTotal - Invoices.CreditTotal) > 0)
ORDER BY SUM(Invoices.InvoiceTotal - Invoices.PaymentTotal - Invoices.CreditTotal) DESC
```

Description

- To view or set the properties for a query, use the Properties dialog box. To display this dialog box, click on the Properties toolbar button (it's the leftmost button).

- To include the all columns operator (*) in the SELECT clause, select the Output all columns option.

- To include the DISTINCT keyword in the SELECT clause, select the DISTINCT values option.

- To include a WITH CUBE or WITH ROLLUP phrase or the ALL keyword on a query that includes the GROUP BY clause, select the GROUP BY extension check box and then the appropriate option.

- To include the TOP keyword in the SELECT clause, select the TOP check box. Then, you can specify the number of rows to return, or you can select the PERCENT option and specify the percent of rows to return. You can also select the WITH TIES option to include the WITH TIES keyword.

- These options are available only for SELECT queries, SELECT INTO queries, and INSERT queries that include a subquery. The only option that's available for the other queries is the SQL Comment option, which you can use to enter notes about the query.

Figure 11-8   How to edit query properties

How to work with a database

Now that you've seen how to use the Enterprise Manager to work with queries, you'll learn how to use it to work with database objects. In most cases, you'll see that this is quicker and easier than coding the DDL statements yourself. In addition, the Enterprise Manager can perform some tasks that would be difficult or impossible to code yourself.

How to create a database

Figure 11-9 presents the Action menu that's displayed when a database node is selected in the console tree. You can use the commands on this menu to perform common database management tasks. In particular, you can use it to create a new database.

To create a new database, select the New Database command from the Action menu to display the Database Properties dialog box. Then, you can enter the name of the new database in the General tab, and you can specify other options in the Data Files and Transaction Log tabs. Since most of these options are used to tune the performance of large databases, you can generally accept the default values.

How to attach or detach a database

If you want to use a database that was created on another server, you can copy the database file to your system and then attach it to your server. To attach a database file, you highlight the Databases node and use the Attach Database command in the Action→All Tasks menu to display the Attach Database dialog box. Then, you use this dialog box to locate and identify the database file.

You can also detach a database from SQL Server. You may want to do that, for example, so you can copy the database to another system. To detach a database, you highlight it in the console tree and then select the Detach Database command from the Action→All Tasks menu. SQL Server displays the Detach Database dialog box to confirm that the database should be detached.

How to delete a database

You can also delete a database by using the Action→Delete command for the database. Keep in mind, however, that this command permanently removes the database from the server. Because of that, you may want to create a backup copy of the database before you delete it. That way, you can restore the database if you later realize that you still need it.

The Action menu for database objects

How to create a new database

- Highlight the Databases node and select Action➔New Database to display the General tab of the Database Properties dialog box. Enter a name for the database and click OK.

- You can also specify the names and directory locations of the database files using the Data Files and Transaction Log tabs of the Database Properties dialog box. In general, however, the defaults are fine.

How to attach an existing database file

- Highlight the Databases node and select Action➔All Tasks➔Attach Database to display the Attach Database dialog box. Click on the button with the ellipsis (…) on it to locate and select the database file.

- Verify that the correct database name is displayed in the Attach as text box. Change it if needed, and then click OK.

How to detach a database

- Highlight the database you want to detach and select Action➔All Tasks➔Detach Database to display the Detach Database dialog box. Click the OK button.

How to delete a database

- Highlight the database you want to delete, then select Action➔Delete and verify the deletion.

Warning

- You can't restore a deleted database unless you have a backup copy. Because of that, you should never delete a production database without first consulting the DBA.

Figure 11-9   How to manage databases using the Enterprise Manager

How to make a backup copy of a database

The Enterprise Manager provides an easy way to back up a database. To do that, you use the SQL Server Backup dialog box shown in figure 11-10. This dialog box lets you assign a name and description to the backup and lets you set options that determine the type of backup that's performed, the destination of the backup, whether or not existing backups at the specified location are over-written, and whether the backup should be scheduled to run periodically.

You typically need to back up a database for one of two reasons. First, if a database is already in production, you'll want to schedule routine backups to prevent the loss of critical data. Second, if you're using a database for testing, you'll want to back up the database before you test any design changes. That way, you can restore the original database if you need to. As you can see in this figure, the backup options you choose vary depending on the purpose for the backup.

Before you can back up a database, you need to specify the destination for the backup. If this is the first time you've backed up the database, you can specify the destination by clicking on the Add button and completing the dialog box that's displayed. Otherwise, you can just select the destination from the list that's displayed.

If you're backing up a test database, you'll typically specify a location on your hard drive. If you're backing up a production database, however, the location should be a device with removable media like a tape drive or a disk drive with removable disks. That way, once the backup is complete, you can store the tapes or disks in a safe location.

In most cases, you'll perform a complete backup that includes all of the objects and data in the database. For a production database, however, you may perform a complete backup followed by periodic differential backups. A *differential backup* includes only data that has changed since the last backup, so it can be done more quickly than a complete backup. A typical backup schedule for a production database, for example, is to perform a complete backup once a week and a differential backup once a day. That way, you never lose more than one day's work. For critical data, though, you may want to perform backups more frequently.

If you perform a complete backup, you'll usually select the Overwrite existing media option. That way, the previous backup on the media will be deleted before the new backup is created. If you use this technique for a production database, you'll want to be sure that you don't overwrite the most current backup. Instead, you'll want to use a set of backups. For example, you could use a separate tape or disk for each day of the week. That way, if one tape or disk goes bad, you can use the previous one if you need to.

The last option, Schedule, provides a convenient way to set up periodic backups. To use this option, another SQL Server program called the SQL Server Agent is required. This program actually executes the scheduled backups. To start this program, display the SQL Server Service Manager dialog box by double-clicking on the SQL Server Service Manager icon in the system tray.

The SQL Server Backup dialog box

How to use the SQL Server backup utility

- Highlight the database you want to back up, and then select Action→All Tasks→Backup Database to display the SQL Server Backup dialog box.

- SQL Server creates a default name for the backup, but you can modify this name and add a description for the backup if you wish.

- Select the destination for the backup, set the options as described below, and click the OK button to perform the backup.

Option settings for routine backups on production databases

- Make a complete backup once a week and a daily *differential backup*. A differential backup includes only data that has changed since the last backup. For critical systems, you can do complete backups daily and differential backups every hour or two.

- The destination for each backup should be a device, like a tape or removable disk, whose media can be stored in a safe location.

- In general, you should store one backup per disk or tape, so you can select the Overwrite existing media option. If you're doing a differential backup, however, you may want to append the backup to the media that contains the last complete backup.

- You can set a schedule for backups to run automatically. This requires that your server run the SQL Server Agent, which you can start by displaying the SQL Server Service Manager dialog box and then selecting this service from the Services drop-down list.

Option settings for backups on test databases

- Make a complete backup before making any design changes.

- The destination for the backup can be the same hard drive on which the database resides.

- Select the Overwrite existing media option.

Figure 11-10   How to make a backup copy of a database

Then, select the SQL Server Agent program from the Services drop-down list and click on the Start/Continue button. To start this program each time you start your system, select the Auto-start option.

How to restore a database from a backup

Figure 11-11 presents the Restore database dialog box you use to restore a database from a backup. From this dialog box, you select the backups you want to restore. If you use complete backups, you usually restore the most recent backup. If you use differential backups, however, you'll want to restore the most recent complete backup followed by each of the differential backups that have been done since that complete backup.

You can also use a restore operation to create a copy of the original database. To do that, just assign a different name to the restored database. Then, you can use the restored database for testing design changes without affecting the original database.

The SQL Server Restore dialog box

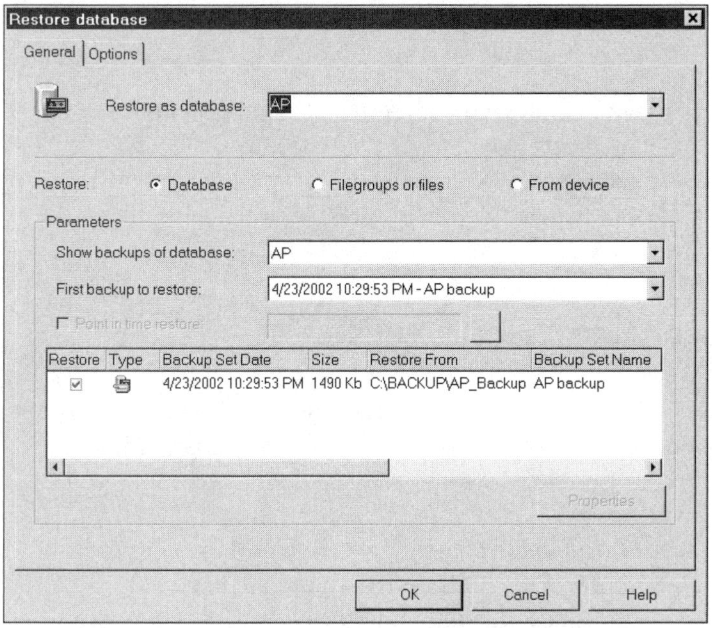

Description

- Highlight the database you want to restore and select Action→All Tasks→Restore Database to display the Restore database dialog box.

- Select the backup copy you want to restore by clicking in the check box to the left of the backup in the backup list.

- If you're using differential backups, you'll need to select the last complete backup followed by all the differential backups that were done after the complete backup.

- To restore the database with a different name, enter the name in the Restore as database text box. The default is the name of the original database.

Figure 11-11   How to restore a database from a backup

How to work with tables, indexes, and relationships

In the last chapter, you learned how to work with tables, indexes, and constraints by coding DDL statements. Now you'll learn how to work with these objects by using the Enterprise Manager. In addition, you'll learn how to use two features that let you summarize the relationships between tables in clear, understandable ways.

How to define the columns of a table

Figure 11-12 presents the Design Table window for the Vendors table. This window lets you edit the design of an existing table. You use a similar window, the New Table window, to design a new table. This figure summarizes how you use these windows.

Each column in a table is listed in the column grid. This grid includes the column name, the data type for the column, the length of the column, and whether the column allows null values. In addition to these properties, you can set the additional column properties that appear at the bottom of this window. For example, you can set the default value for a column or define it as an identity column. The properties that are available for each column change depending on the properties in the column grid.

You can also set the primary key from this window. To do that, click on the box to the left of the key column to select it and then click on the Set primary key toolbar button. If the key consists of two or more columns, you can drag over the boxes for those columns to select them. When you set the primary key, a key icon appears to the left of the key column(s) as shown in this figure.

If you want to look at the SQL code that the Enterprise Manager generates when you add or modify columns, you can click on the Save change script toolbar button. Then, you can open and view the script from the Query Analyzer. You can also copy statements from this script into your own scripts. Note, however, that the script the Enterprise Manager generates is likely to include statements that you're not familiar with.

The Design Table window

Save change script button   Set primary key button

Primary key
indicator

Column grid

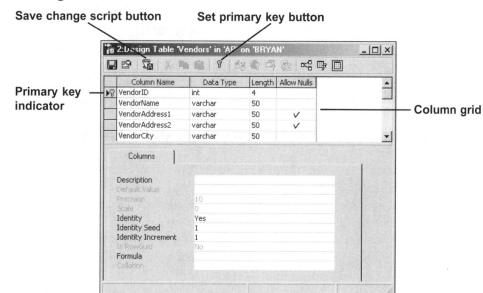

How to edit the design of an existing table

- Highlight the Tables node to display the tables in the database in the right side of the
  Enterprise Manager window. Then, highlight the table you want to modify and select
  Action→Design Table to display the Design Table window.

How to design a new table

- Highlight the node for the database and select Action→New→Table to display the New
  Table window, which is similar to the Design Table window shown above.

How to work in the Design Table/New Table window

- Use the column grid to set the basic attributes for each column, including column name,
  data type, length, and whether or not the column allows nulls.

- To set other column attributes, click in the column and then set the options that appear in
  the bottom of the window.

- To set the primary key, click on the box to the left of the key column or drag over the
  boxes for two or more key columns to select those columns. Then, click on the Set
  primary key toolbar button. A key icon appears in the key columns.

- To remove the primary key, select the column or columns and click on the Set primary
  key toolbar button.

- If you change the design of the table, you can click the Save change script toolbar button
  to examine or save the SQL script that the Enterprise Manager generates.

- When you close the Design Table window, SQL Server confirms that you want to save
  the changes or notifies you if the changes can't be applied. When you close the New
  Table window, SQL Server asks you to enter a name for the new table.

Figure 11-12   How to define the columns of a table

How to work with relationships

To work with the properties of a table, you use the Properties dialog box shown in figure 11-13. As you can see, this dialog box includes tabs that let you work with general table properties, properties related to relationships, properties related to indexes and keys, and properties related to check constraints. In this topic, you'll learn how to use the Relationships tab, and in the next two topics, you'll learn how to use the Indexes/Keys and Check Constraints tabs. The Tables tab isn't shown here because you usually don't need to change the properties it contains.

In this figure, you can see the relationship that's defined between the Invoices and Vendors tables. Notice that the Enforce relationship for INSERTs and UPDATEs option is selected so the referential integrity between these two tables will be maintained. In other words, this relationship defines a foreign key constraint. If this option wasn't selected, SQL Server would recognize but not enforce the relationship. In most cases, then, you'll want to be sure this option is selected.

Also notice that the Cascade Update and Cascade Delete options are not selected. That means that primary keys in the Vendors table can't be changed if related records exist in the Invoices table, and a row can't be deleted from the Vendors table if related rows exist in the Invoices table. In some cases, that's what you want. In other cases, though, you'll want to cascade update and delete operations to the foreign key table.

To create a new relationship, you click on the New button. Then, you select the primary key and foreign key tables and the columns in each table that are related. When you do, SQL Server will generate an appropriate relationship name for you, so you won't usually change this name. It will also select the first three options. I've already described the third option, which enforces the referential integrity between the tables. The first option causes the existing data to be checked to be sure that it satisfies the constraint.

Finally, the second option causes the relationship to be enforced when the database is replicated. *Replication* is a technique that's used to create multiple copies of the same database in different locations. By using replication, SQL Server can keep the various copies of a database synchronized. Because this feature is only used by DBAs for enterprise systems, a complete presentation is beyond the scope of this book.

The Relationships tab of the Properties dialog box

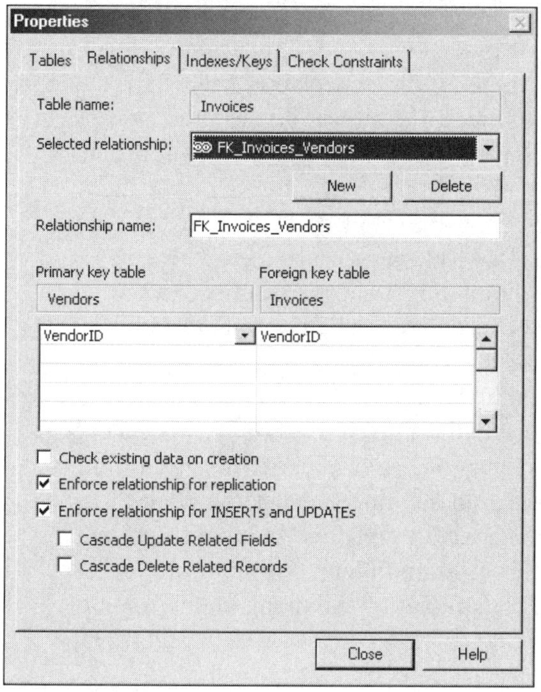

Description

- The Relationships tab of the Properties dialog box lets you work with the relationships between tables. To display this tab, click on the Manage Relationships toolbar button in the Design Table or New Table window.

- To view or edit an existing relationship, select the relationship from the Selected relationship drop-down list. The name and definition of the relationship are displayed in the dialog box.

- To add a new relationship, click on the New button. Then, select the primary key and foreign key table and the columns in each table that define the relationship.

- By default, SQL Server checks existing data when you add a new relationship to be sure it satisfies the foreign key constraint. If that's not what you want, you can remove the check mark from the Check existing data on creation option.

- To enforce the relationship for insert and update operations, select the Enforce relationship for INSERTs and UPDATEs option. This is the default.

- To cascade update and delete operations from the primary key table to the foreign key table, select the Cascade Update Related Fields and Cascade Delete Related Records options.

- To enforce the relationship when the database is *replicated*, select the Enforce the relationship for replication option. This is the default.

- To delete a relationship, select the relationship and then click on the Delete button.

Figure 11-13   How to work with relationships

How to work with check constraints

Figure 11-14 presents the Check Constraints tab of the Properties dialog box. You can use this tab to modify or delete existing check constraints for a table or to add new constraints. In this figure, for example, you can see a check constraint for the Invoices table. This constraint specifies that the InvoiceTotal column must be greater than or equal to zero.

As you know, when you create check constraints using DDL, you can define them at either the column level or the table level. In contrast, the check constraints you create using the Properties dialog box are always defined at the table level. Because of that, a constraint can refer to any column in the table where it's defined.

The options that are available from this tab are similar to the options you saw in the Relationships tab. The first one determines if existing data is checked when a new constraint is created. The second one determines if constraints are enforced when the database is replicated. And the third one determines if constraints are enforced when rows are inserted or updated. In most cases, you'll select all three of these options. If you want to temporarily disable a constraint during testing, however, you can do that by removing one or more of these check marks.

The Check Constraints tab of the Properties dialog box

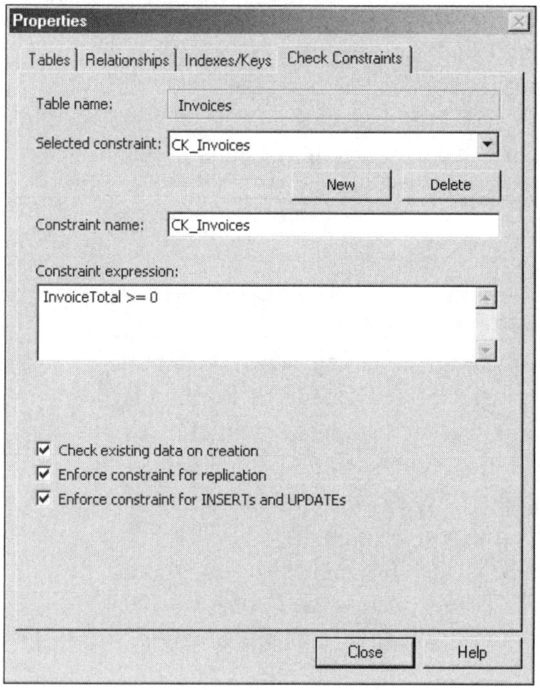

Description

- To display the Check Constraints tab of the Properties dialog box, click on the Manage Constraints toolbar button in the Design Table or New Table window.
- To view or edit an existing constraint, select the constraint from the Selected constraint drop-down list. The constraint name and expression are displayed in the dialog box.
- To define a new constraint, click the New button, enter the name you want to use for the constraint, and enter a conditional expression in the Constraint expression box. Because the Enterprise Manager automatically defines all check constraints as table-level constraints, you can use any column name defined for the table in the expression.
- By default, SQL Server checks existing data when you add a new check constraint to be sure it satisfies the constraint. If that's not what you want, you can remove the check mark from the Check existing data on creation option.
- To enforce the constraint for insert and update operations, select the Enforce constraint for INSERTs and UPDATEs option. This is the default.
- To enforce the constraint when the database is replicated, select the Enforce constraint for replication option. This is the default.
- To delete a constraint, select the constraint and then click on the Delete button.

Figure 11-14   How to work with check constraints

How to work with indexes and keys

Figure 11-15 presents the Indexes/Keys tab for the Vendors table. You can use this tab to modify and delete existing indexes and keys and add new indexes and keys. When you select an index, the Type box indicates whether the index is for a primary key, in which case it's a clustered index; a unique key, in which case it's a nonclustered index; or some other nonclustered index. This tab also lists the name of the index, the columns that make up the index, and other options related to the index.

To create a new index for a table, you click on the New button, enter a name for the index, and select the columns you want to include in the index and the sort order for each one. If you want to create a unique key, select the Create UNIQUE option. The Constraint option that's subordinate to that option is selected by default, which means that SQL Server will create a unique key constraint along with the index. By default, the index will be nonclustered. If the table doesn't have a primary key, however, you can select the Create as CLUSTERED option to create a clustered index.

You can also create an index that enforces the uniqueness of its values without using a unique key constraint. To do that, select the Create UNIQUE and Index options. In most cases, though, you'll want to enforce uniqueness by using a unique key constraint.

The Indexes/Keys tab of the Properties dialog box

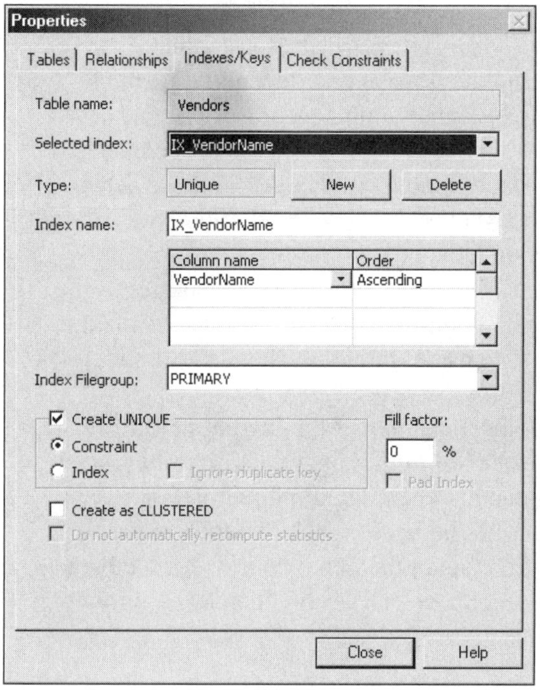

Description

- To display the Indexes/Keys tab of the Properties dialog box, click on the Manage Indexes/Keys toolbar button in the Design Table or New Table window.

- To view or edit an existing index, select the index from the Selected index drop-down list. The index name and definition appear in the dialog box.

- To define a new index, click the New button, enter the name you want to use for the index, and select the column name and sort order for each column in the index.

- To create a unique key and an index that's based on that key, select the Create UNIQUE check box and the Constraint option. To create a unique index without creating a unique key, select the Create UNIQUE check box and the Index option.

- To create a clustered index, select the Create as CLUSTERED option. Because a clustered index is created automatically for the primary key, you usually won't select this option.

- The other options in this dialog box are used for performance tuning. In most cases, the default values for these options are acceptable. For more information, see Books Online.

Figure 11-15   How to work with indexes and keys

How to examine table dependencies

Figure 11-16 shows how you can view the *dependencies* for a table. As you can see, the Dependencies dialog box lists the objects that depend on the table you select along with the objects that the selected table depends on. In this case, you can see that the InvoiceLineItems table depends on the Invoices table, and the Invoices table depends on the Terms and Vendors tables. All of these dependencies are based on the relationships between the tables. In addition, you can see that several views and stored procedures depend on the Invoices table. (These views and stored procedures aren't included in the AP database, but you'll learn how to add them in chapters 12 and 14.) Before you make a change to the Invoices table, then, you'll want to consider how that change will affect these objects.

In this example, only the *first-level dependencies* of the Invoices table are shown. In other words, all of the objects shown in this figure are directly related to the Invoices table. However, objects can also be related indirectly. For example, the GLAccounts table is related to the Vendors table, which means it's indirectly related to the Invoices table. To display the dependencies for a table at all levels, remove the check mark from the Show first level dependency only option.

The Dependencies dialog box

Dependencies for Invoices

General

Object: [Invoices (dbo)]

Objects that depend on Invoices:

Object (owner)	Sequence
OutstandingInvoices	1
VendorPayment (dbc	1
VendorPaymentChec	1
VendorsDue (dbo)	1
VendorShortList (dbc	1
InvoiceLineItems (db	1
sp_InvoiceReport (dl	1
testproc (dbo)	1

Objects that Invoices depends on:

Object (owner)	Sequence
Terms (dbo)	1
Vendors (dbo)	1

☑ Show first level dependency only

[Close]   [Help]

Description

- To display the *dependencies* for a table, highlight the table in the console tree and select Action→All Tasks→Display Dependencies. The Dependencies dialog box that's displayed lists the objects that depend on the selected table and the objects that the selected table depends on.

- By default, only first-level dependencies are shown. A *first-level dependency* is one where the objects are directly related. A table can also be related to an object through other objects. To display these dependencies, remove the check mark from the Show first level dependency only check box.

- You should check table dependencies before you delete a column or an entire table.

Figure 11-16   How to examine table dependencies

How to diagram a database

Another way to view and work with the relationships between the tables in a database is to use a *database diagram* like the one shown in figure 11-17. A diagram like this can be useful for designing a new database or for documenting an existing database. To create a diagram like this, you use the *Database Designer* that comes with the Enterprise Manager.

The Database Designer generates a diagram based on the relationships defined in your database. As this figure explains, you can use the Create Database Design wizard to select the tables you want to include in the diagram. You can also use the Add table on Diagram toolbar button to add a table to an existing diagram. The diagram in this figure includes all of the tables in the AP database. For a large database, though, you may want to create several diagrams that each contain a subset of the tables in the database.

If relationships exist between the tables in a diagram, those relationships are represented by lines, or links. These links have endpoints that indicate the kind of relationship that exists between the tables. In this figure, all of the relationships are one-to-many, so a key appears on the "one" side of the link and an infinity symbol (∞) appears on the "many" side.

You can also use the Database Designer to define new tables and relationships. This feature is powerful and intuitive to use. Keep in mind, however, that you can access only the basic table properties from the Designer. After you create a new table, then, you may need to use the Design Table window to set additional properties.

The Database Designer window

Add table on
Diagram button

Show button

New text annotation
button

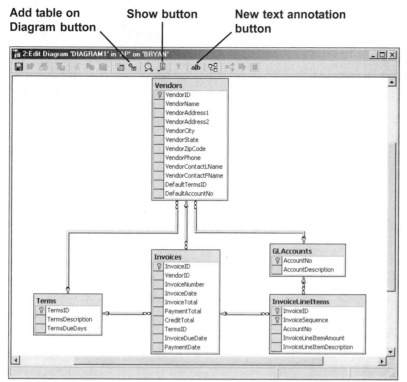

Description

- A *database diagram* illustrates the relationships between some or all of the tables in a database. To create and work with database diagrams, you use the Database Designer.

- To create a database diagram, highlight the Diagrams node and then select Action→New Database Diagram to display the Create Database Diagram wizard. This wizard lets you select the tables you want to include in the diagram.

- To modify an existing diagram, highlight the Diagrams node to display the list of diagrams for the database. Then, highlight the diagram and select Action→Design Diagram.

- To add a table to the diagram, click the Add table on Diagram toolbar button and select the table from the dialog box that's displayed.

- If relationships exist between two tables in the diagram, they appear as links where the endpoints of the links indicate the type of relationship. A key indicates the "one" side of a relationship, and the infinity symbol (∞) indicates the "many" side of a relationship.

- To change the information that's displayed for each table, click on the Show toolbar button and select the option you want.

- You can also use the Database Designer to create new tables and relationships. For more information, see Books Online.

- After you create a database diagram, you can save it and print it. You can also add annotations to it using the New text annotation toolbar button.

Figure 11-17   How to diagram a database

Perspective

In this chapter, you learned how to use the Enterprise Manager, a powerful database tool with an intuitive graphical interface. As you've seen, you can use this tool to create and work with database objects, such as tables, relationships, check constraints, and indexes as well as the database itself. You can also use the Query Designer that comes with the Enterprise Manager to create and execute queries.

Now that you know how to use both the Enterprise Manager and the Query Analyzer, you may be wondering when you should use each. Although it's often a matter of preference, many SQL programmers find it easier to use the Enterprise Manager to create and work with database objects. That way, they don't have to worry about the exact syntax of the DDL statements, which they may use infrequently. In contrast, once they learn the basic syntax of the DML statements, most programmers prefer to just enter the statements themselves using the Query Analyzer.

Terms

Enterprise Manager
node
Query Designer
diagram pane
grid pane
SQL pane
results pane
differential backup
replication
dependencies
first-level dependency
database diagram
Database Designer

Section 4

Advanced SQL skills

This section teaches SQL skills beyond the essentials. After reading all six chapters in this section, you'll have the skills of a professional SQL programmer. To make these chapters as easy to use as possible, they're designed as independent modules. That means that you can read them in any order you prefer.

In chapter 12, you can learn how to work with views, which let you simplify and restrict access to the data in a database. In chapter 13, you can learn how to use scripts to control the processing of SQL statements that you execute from a client tool like the Query Analyzer. Scripts are just one type of procedural program you can create in SQL Server. In chapter 14, you can learn about the other types of procedural programs: stored procedures, triggers, and functions.

In chapter 15, you can learn about cursors, which let you work with one row in a result set at a time. In chapter 16, you can learn how to use transactions and locking to prevent data errors in a multi-user environment. Finally, in chapter 17, you can learn how to secure a database to restrict who has access to it.

12

How to work with views

As you've seen throughout this book, SELECT queries can be complicated, particularly if they use multiple joins, subqueries, or complex functions. Because of that, you may want to save the queries you use regularly. One way to do that is to store the statement in a file using the Query Analyzer. Another way is to create a view.

Unlike a file you create with the Query Analyzer, a view is stored as part of the database. That's means it can be used not only by SQL programmers, but by users and application programs that have access to the database. This provides some distinct advantages over using tables directly, as you'll see in this chapter.

An introduction to views

In chapter 1, you learned the basics of how views work. In the next topic, then, I'll just review this information. Then, I'll present some of the benefits of views so you'll know when and why you should use them.

How views work

A *view* is a SELECT statement that's stored with the database. To create a view, you use a CREATE VIEW statement like the one shown in figure 12-1. This statement creates a view named VendorsMin that retrieves the VendorName, VendorState, and VendorPhone columns from the Vendors table.

You can think of a view as a virtual table that consists only of the rows and columns specified in its CREATE VIEW statement. The table or tables that are listed in the FROM clause are called the *base tables* for the view. Since the view refers back to the base tables, it doesn't store any data itself, and it always reflects the most current data in the base tables.

To use a view, you refer to it from another SQL statement. The SELECT statement in this figure, for example, uses the VendorsMin view in the FROM clause instead of a table. As a result, this SELECT statement extracts its result set from the virtual table that the view represents. In this case, all the rows for vendors in California are retrieved from the view.

Because a view is stored as an object in a database, it can be used by anyone who has access to the database. That includes users who have access to the database through end-user programs such as programs that provide for ad hoc queries and report generation, and application programs that are written specifically to work with the data in the database. In fact, views are often designed to be used with these types of programs. In the next topic, you'll learn why.

A CREATE VIEW statement for a view named VendorsMin

```
CREATE VIEW VendorsMin AS
    SELECT VendorName, VendorState, VendorPhone
    FROM Vendors
```

The virtual table that's represented by the view

	VendorName	VendorState	VendorPhone
1	US Postal Service	WI	(800) 555-1205
2	National Information Data Ctr	DC	(301) 555-8950
3	Register of Copyrights	DC	NULL
4	Jobtrak	CA	(800) 555-8725
5	Newbrige Book Clubs	NJ	(800) 555-9980
6	California Chamber Of Commerce	CA	(916) 555-6670
7	Towne Advertiser's Mailing Svcs	CA	NULL
8	BFI Industries	CA	(559) 555-1551
9	Pacific Gas & Electric	CA	(800) 555-6081

(122 rows)

A SELECT statement that uses the VendorsMin view

```
SELECT * FROM VendorsMin
WHERE VendorState = 'CA'
ORDER BY VendorName
```

The result set that's returned by the SELECT statement

	VendorName	VendorState	VendorPhone
1	Abbey Office Furnishings	CA	(559) 555-8300
2	American Express	CA	(800) 555-3344
3	ASC Signs	CA	NULL
4	Aztek Label	CA	(714) 555-9000
5	Bertelsmann Industry Svcs. Inc	CA	(805) 555-0584
6	BFI Industries	CA	(559) 555-1551
7	Bill Jones	CA	NULL
8	Bill Marvin Electric Inc	CA	(559) 555-5106
9	Blanchard & Johnson Associates	CA	(214) 555-3647

(75 rows)

Description

- A *view* consists of a SELECT statement that's stored as an object in the database. The tables referenced in the SELECT statement are called the *base tables* for the view.

- When you create a view, the query on which it's based is optimized by SQL Server before it's saved in the database. Then, you can refer to the view anywhere you would normally use a table in any of the data manipulation statements: SELECT, INSERT, UPDATE, and DELETE.

- Although a view behaves like a virtual table, it doesn't store any data. Since the view refers back to its base tables, it always returns current data.

- A view can also be referred to as a *viewed table* because it provides a view to the underlying base tables.

Figure 12-1   How views work

Benefits of using views

Figure 12-2 describes some of the advantages of using views. To start, the data that you access through a view isn't dependent on the structure of the database. To illustrate, suppose a view refers to a table that you've decided to divide into two tables. To accommodate this change, you simply modify the view; you don't have to modify any statements that refer to the view. That means that users who query the database using the view don't have to be aware of the change in the database structure, and application programs that use the view don't have to be modified.

You can also use views to restrict access to a database. To do that, you include just the columns and rows you want a user or application program to have access to in the view. Then, you let the user or program access the data only through the views. The view shown in this figure, for example, restricts access to a table that contains information on investors. In this case, the view provides access to name and address information that might be needed by the support staff that maintains the table. In contrast, another view that includes investment information could be used by the consultants who manage the investments.

Views are also flexible. Because views can be based on almost any SELECT statement, they can be used to provide just the data that's needed for specific situations. In addition, views can hide the complexity of a SELECT statement. That makes it easier for end users and application programs to retrieve the data they need. Finally, views can be used not only to retrieve data, but to update data as well. You'll see how that works later in this chapter.

Some of the benefits provided by views

Benefit	Description
Design independence	Data that's accessed through a view is independent of the underlying database structure. That means that you can change the design of a database and then modify the view as necessary so that the queries that use it don't need to be changed.
Data security	You can create views that provide access only to the data that specific users are allowed to see.
Flexibility	You can create custom views to accommodate different needs.
Simplified queries	You can create views that hide the complexity of retrieval operations. Then, the data can be retrieved using simple SELECT statements.
Updatability	With certain restrictions, a view can be used to update, insert, and delete data from a base table.

The data in a table of investors

	ID	Last name	First name	Address	City	State	Zip code	Phone	Investments	Net gain
1	1	Anders	Maria	345 Winchell Pl	Anderson	IN	46014	(765) 555-7878	15000.0000	1242.5700
2	2	Trujillo	Ana	1298 E Smathers St	Benton	AR	72018	(501) 555-7733	43500.0000	8497.4400
3	3	Moreno	Antonio	6925 N Parkland Ave	Puyallup	WA	98373	(253) 555-8332	22900.0000	2338.8700
4	4	Hardy	Thomas	83 d'Urberville Ln	Casterbridge	GA	31209	(478) 555-1139	5000.0000	-245.6900
5	5	Berglund	Christina	22717 E 73rd Ave	Dubuque	IA	52004	(319) 555-1139	11750.0000	865.7700

(10 rows)

A view that restricts access to certain columns

```
CREATE VIEW InvestorsGeneral
AS
SELECT InvestorID, InvestorLastName, InvestorFirstName, InvestorAddress,
    InvestorCity, InvestorState, InvestorZipCode, InvestorPhone
FROM Investors
```

The data retrieved by the view

	ID	Last name	First name	Address	City	State	Zip code	Phone
1	1	Anders	Maria	345 Winchell Pl	Anderson	IN	46014	(765) 555-7878
2	2	Trujillo	Ana	1298 E Smathers St	Benton	AR	72018	(501) 555-7733
3	3	Moreno	Antonio	6925 N Parkland Ave	Puyallup	WA	98373	(253) 555-8332
4	4	Hardy	Thomas	83 d'Urberville Ln	Casterbridge	GA	31209	(478) 555-1139
5	5	Berglund	Christina	22717 E 73rd Ave	Dubuque	IA	52004	(319) 555-1139

(10 rows)

Description

- You can create a view based on almost any SELECT statement. That means that you can code views that join tables, summarize data, and use subqueries and functions.

- You can restrict access to the data in a table by including selected columns in the SELECT clause for a view, or by including a WHERE clause in the SELECT statement so that only selected rows are retrieved by the view.

Figure 12-2   Benefits of using views

How to create and manage views

Now that you understand how views work and what benefits they provide, you're ready to learn how to create and manage them. That's what you'll learn in the topics that follow.

How to create a view

Figure 12-3 presents the CREATE VIEW statement you use to create a view. In its simplest form, you code the name of the view in the CREATE VIEW clause followed by the AS keyword and the SELECT statement that defines the view. The statement shown in this figure, for example, creates a view named VendorShortList. This view includes selected columns from the Vendors table for all vendors with invoices. When this statement is executed, the view is added to the current database and a message like the one shown in this figure is displayed to indicate that the statement was successful.

Because a SELECT statement can refer to a view, the SELECT statement you code within the definition of a view can also refer to another view. In other words, views can be *nested*. I recommend you avoid using nested views, however, because the dependencies between tables and views can become confusing, which can make problems difficult to locate.

The SELECT statement for a view can use any of the features of a normal SELECT statement with two exceptions. First, it can't include an ORDER BY clause unless it also uses the TOP keyword. That means that if you want to sort the result set that's extracted from a view, you have to include an ORDER BY clause in the SELECT statement that refers to the view. Second, it can't include the INTO keyword. That's because a view can't be used to create a permanent table.

By default, the columns in a view are given the same names as the columns in the base tables. If a view contains a calculated column, however, you'll want to name that column just as you do in other SELECT statements. In addition, you'll need to rename columns from different tables that have the same name. To do that, you can use the AS clause in the SELECT statement or you can code the column names in the CREATE VIEW clause. You'll see examples of both of these techniques in the next figure.

The CREATE VIEW statement also provides three optional clauses: WITH ENCRYPTION, WITH SCHEMABINDING, and WITH CHECK OPTION. The WITH ENCRYPTION clause prevents other users from examining the SELECT statement on which the view is based. In general, though, you don't need to use this option unless your system requires enhanced security.

The WITH SCHEMABINDING clause protects a view by binding it to the database structure, or *schema*. This prevents the underlying base tables from being deleted or modified in any way that affects the view. You'll typically use this option for production databases, but not for databases you're using for testing.

The syntax of the CREATE VIEW statement

```
CREATE VIEW view_name [(column_name_1 [, column_name_2]...)]
[WITH {ENCRYPTION|SCHEMABINDING|ENCRYPTION,SCHEMABINDING}]
AS
select_statement
[WITH CHECK OPTION]
```

A CREATE VIEW statement that creates a view of vendors that have invoices

```
CREATE VIEW VendorShortList
AS
SELECT VendorName, VendorContactLName, VendorContactFName, VendorPhone
FROM Vendors
WHERE VendorID IN (SELECT VendorID FROM Invoices)
```

The response from the system

```
The command(s) completed successfully.
```

Description

- You use the CREATE VIEW statement to create a view. The name you give the view must not be the same as the name of any existing table or view.

- The SELECT statement within the view can refer to as many as 256 tables and can use any valid combination of joins, unions, or subqueries.

- You can create a view that's based on another view rather than on a table, called a *nested view*. SQL Server views can be nested up to 32 levels deep.

- The SELECT statement for a view can't include an INTO clause, and it can include an ORDER BY clause only if the TOP keyword is used. To sort the rows in a view, you have to include the ORDER BY clause in the SELECT statement that uses it.

- You can name the columns in a view by coding a list of names in parentheses following the view name or by coding the new names in the SELECT clause. A column must be named if it's calculated from other columns or if a column with the same name already exists. Otherwise, the name from the base table can be used.

- You can use the WITH ENCRYPTION clause to keep users from examining the SQL code that defines the view. (See figure 12-10 for information on how to examine view definitions.)

- You can use the WITH SCHEMABINDING clause to bind a view to the database *schema*. Then, you can't drop the tables on which the view is based or modify the tables in a way that would affect the view.

- If you include the WITH SCHEMABINDING clause, you can't use the all columns operator (*) in the SELECT statement. In addition, you must qualify the names of tables and views in the FROM clause with the name of the database owner.

- You can use the WITH CHECK OPTION clause to prevent a row from being updated through a view if it would no longer be included in the view. See figure 12-7 for details.

Figure 12-3   How to create a view

The WITH CHECK OPTION clause prevents a row in a view from being updated if that would cause the row to be excluded from the view. I'll have more to say about this clause in the topic on updating rows using a view.

Examples that create views

To help you understand the flexibility that views provide, figure 12-4 presents several CREATE VIEW statements. The first statement creates a view that joins data from the Vendors and Invoices tables. The second statement creates a view that retrieves the top five percent of invoices in the Invoices table. Notice that this SELECT statement includes an ORDER BY clause that sorts the rows in descending sequence so that the invoices with the largest amounts are retrieved. This is the only case in which you can use the ORDER BY clause.

The third and fourth statements illustrate the two ways that you can name the columns in a view. In both cases, the SELECT statement retrieves a calculated column, so a name must be assigned to this column. The third statement shows how you would do this using the CREATE VIEW clause. Notice that even if you only want to name one column, you have to include the names for all the columns, even if they're the same as the names in the base tables. In contrast, if you name this column in the SELECT clause as shown in the fourth example, you can let the other column names default to the column names in the base table. Since this syntax is easier to use, you'll use it most of the time. Keep in mind, though, that the ANSI standards don't support this syntax for naming view columns. Because of that, you can use it only with SQL Server.

The fifth statement creates a view that summarizes the rows in the Invoices table by vendor. This illustrates the use of the aggregate functions and the GROUP BY clause in a view. In this case, the rows are grouped by vendor name, and a count of the invoices and the invoice total are calculated for each vendor.

Like the first statement, the last statement joins data from the Vendors and Invoices table. Unlike the first statement, though, this statement includes the WITH SCHEMABINDING clause. That means that neither the Vendors nor the Invoices table can be deleted without first deleting the view. In addition, no changes can be made to these tables that would affect the view. Notice that the table names in the FROM clause are qualified with the name of the table's owner, in this case, dbo. If you include the WITH SCHEMABINDING clause, you must qualify the table names in this way.

A CREATE VIEW statement that uses a join

```
CREATE VIEW VendorInvoices
AS
SELECT VendorName, InvoiceNumber, InvoiceDate, InvoiceTotal
FROM Vendors JOIN Invoices ON Vendors.VendorID = Invoices.VendorID
```

A CREATE VIEW statement that uses TOP and ORDER BY clauses

```
CREATE VIEW TopVendors
AS
SELECT TOP 5 PERCENT VendorID, InvoiceTotal
FROM Invoices
ORDER BY InvoiceTotal DESC
```

Two CREATE VIEW statements that name the columns in a view

A statement that names all the view columns in its CREATE VIEW clause

```
CREATE VIEW OutstandingInvoices
    (InvoiceNumber, InvoiceDate, InvoiceTotal, BalanceDue)
AS
SELECT InvoiceNumber, InvoiceDate, InvoiceTotal,
    InvoiceTotal - PaymentTotal - CreditTotal
FROM Invoices
WHERE InvoiceTotal - PaymentTotal - CreditTotal > 0
```

A statement that names just the calculated column in its SELECT clause

```
CREATE VIEW OutstandingInvoices
AS
SELECT InvoiceNumber, InvoiceDate, InvoiceTotal,
    InvoiceTotal - PaymentTotal - CreditTotal AS BalanceDue
FROM Invoices
WHERE InvoiceTotal - PaymentTotal - CreditTotal > 0
```

A CREATE VIEW statement that summarizes invoices by vendor

```
CREATE VIEW InvoiceSummary
AS
SELECT VendorName, COUNT(*) AS InvoiceQty, SUM(InvoiceTotal) AS InvoiceSum
FROM Vendors JOIN Invoices ON Vendors.VendorID = Invoices.VendorID
GROUP BY VendorName
```

A CREATE VIEW statement that uses the WITH SCHEMABINDING option

```
CREATE VIEW VendorsDue
WITH SCHEMABINDING
AS
SELECT InvoiceDate AS Date, VendorName AS Name,
    VendorContactFName + ' ' + VendorContactLName AS Contact,
    InvoiceNumber AS Invoice,
    InvoiceTotal - PaymentTotal - CreditTotal AS Balance
FROM dbo.Vendors JOIN dbo.Invoices
    ON Vendors.VendorID = Invoices.VendorID
WHERE InvoiceTotal - PaymentTotal - CreditTotal > 0
```

Note

- If you name the columns of a view in the CREATE VIEW clause, you have to name all of the columns, even if you want to use the names in the base table. In contrast, you can name just the columns you need to rename in the SELECT clause.

Figure 12-4   CREATE VIEW examples

How to create an updatable view

Once you create a view, you can refer to it in a SELECT statement as you saw in figure 12-1. In addition, you can refer to it in INSERT, UPDATE, and DELETE statements to modify an underlying table. To do that, the view must be updatable. Figure 12-5 lists the requirements for creating *updatable views*.

The first three requirements have to do with what you can code in the select list of the SELECT statement that defines the view. As you can see, the select list can't include the DISTINCT or TOP clause, it can't include aggregate functions, and it can't include calculated columns. In addition, the SELECT statement can't include a GROUP BY or HAVING clause, and two SELECT statements can't be joined by a union operation.

The first CREATE VIEW statement in this figure creates a view that's updatable. This view adheres to all of the requirements for updatable views. That means that you can refer to it in an INSERT, UPDATE, or DELETE statement. For example, you could use the UPDATE statement shown in this figure to update the CreditTotal column in the Invoices base table.

In contrast, the second CREATE TABLE statement in this figure creates a *read-only view*. This view is read-only because the select list contains a calculated value.

In general, using INSERT, UPDATE, and DELETE statements to update data through a view is inflexible and prone to errors. Because of that, you should avoid this technique whenever possible. Instead, you should consider using INSTEAD OF triggers to update data through a view. You'll learn about this type of trigger in chapter 14.

Requirements for creating updatable views

- The select list can't include a DISTINCT or TOP clause.
- The select list can't include an aggregate function.
- The select list can't include a calculated value.
- The SELECT statement can't include a GROUP BY or HAVING clause.
- The view can't include the UNION operator.

A CREATE VIEW statement that creates an updatable view

```
CREATE VIEW InvoiceCredit
AS
SELECT InvoiceNumber, InvoiceDate, InvoiceTotal, PaymentTotal, CreditTotal
FROM Invoices
WHERE InvoiceTotal - PaymentTotal - CreditTotal > 0
```

An UPDATE statement that updates the view

```
UPDATE InvoiceCredit
SET CreditTotal = CreditTotal + 200
WHERE InvoiceTotal - PaymentTotal - CreditTotal >= 200
```

A CREATE VIEW statement that creates a read-only view

```
CREATE VIEW OutstandingInvoices
AS
SELECT InvoiceNumber, InvoiceDate, InvoiceTotal,
    InvoiceTotal - PaymentTotal - CreditTotal AS BalanceDue
FROM Invoices
WHERE InvoiceTotal - PaymentTotal - CreditTotal > 0
```

Description

- An *updatable view* is one that can be used in an INSERT, UPDATE, or DELETE statement to modify the contents of a base table that the view refers to. If a view is not updatable, it's called a *read-only view*.
- The requirements for coding updatable views are more restrictive than for coding read-only views. That's because SQL Server must be able to unambiguously determine which base tables and which columns are affected.
- You can also insert, update, and delete data through a view using an INSTEAD OF trigger. See chapter 14 for details.

Figure 12-5   How to create an updatable view

How to delete or modify a view

Figure 12-6 presents the statements you use to delete or modify a view. To delete a view, you use the DROP VIEW statement. In this statement, you simply name the view you want to delete. Like the other statements for deleting database objects, this statement deletes the view permanently. So you may want to make a backup copy of the database first if there's any chance that you may want to restore the view later.

To modify a view, you can use the ALTER VIEW statement. Notice that the syntax of this statement is the same as the syntax of the CREATE VIEW statement. If you understand the CREATE VIEW statement, then, you won't have any trouble using the ALTER VIEW statement.

Instead of using the ALTER VIEW statement to modify a view, you can delete the view and then recreate it. If you've created stored procedures or triggers that depend on the view, however, or if you've defined permissions for the view, you should know that those stored procedures, triggers, and permissions are deleted when the view is deleted. If that's not what you want, you should use the ALTER VIEW statement instead.

The examples in this figure show how you can use the DROP VIEW and ALTER VIEW statements. The first example is a CREATE VIEW statement that creates a view named Vendors_SW. As you can see, this view retrieves rows from the Vendors table for vendors located in four states. Then, the second example is an ALTER VIEW statement that modifies this view so it includes vendors in two additional states. Finally, the third example is a DROP VIEW statement that deletes this view.

In the last chapter, you learned how to display the dependencies for a table. Before you delete a table, you should display its dependencies to determine if any views are dependent on the table. If so, you should delete the views along with the tables. If you don't, a query that refers to the view will cause an error. To prevent this problem, you can bind the view to the database schema by specifying the WITH SCHEMABINDING option in the CREATE VIEW or ALTER VIEW statement. Then, you won't be able to delete the base table without deleting the views that depend on it first.

The syntax of the DROP VIEW statement

```
DROP VIEW view_name
```

The syntax of the ALTER VIEW statement

```
ALTER VIEW view_name [(column_name_1 [, column_name_2]...)]
[WITH {ENCRYPTION|SCHEMABINDING|ENCRYPTION,SCHEMABINDING}]
AS
select_statement
[WITH CHECK OPTION]
```

A statement that creates a view

```
CREATE VIEW Vendors_SW
AS
SELECT *
FROM Vendors
WHERE VendorState IN ('CA','AZ','NV','NM')
```

A statement that modifies the view

```
ALTER VIEW Vendors_SW
AS
SELECT *
FROM Vendors
WHERE VendorState IN ('CA','AZ','NV','NM','UT','CO')
```

A statement that deletes the view

```
DROP VIEW Vendors_SW
```

Description

- To delete a view from the database, use the DROP VIEW statement.
- To modify the definition of a view, you can delete the view and then create it again, or you can use the ALTER VIEW statement to specify the new definition.
- When you delete a view, any procedures or triggers that are dependent on that view and any permissions that are assigned to the view are also deleted. In that case, you'll want to use the ALTER VIEW statement to modify the view.
- If you delete a table, you should also delete any views that are based on that table. Otherwise, an error will occur when you run a query that refers to one of those views. To find out what views are dependent on a table, display the table's dependencies as described in the last chapter.
- If you specify the WITH SCHEMABINDING option when you create or modify a view, you won't be able to delete the base tables without first deleting the view.

Note

- ALTER VIEW isn't an ANSI-standard statement. Although it's supported on other SQL-based systems, its behavior on each system is different.

Figure 12-6   How to delete or modify a view

How to use views

So far, you've seen how to use views in SELECT statements to retrieve data from one or more base tables. But you can also use views in INSERT, UPDATE, and DELETE statements to modify the data in a base table. You'll learn how to do that in the topics that follow. In addition, you'll learn how to use some views provided by SQL Server to get information about the database schema.

How to update rows through a view

Figure 12-7 shows how you can update rows in a table through a view. To do that, you simply name the view that refers to the table in the UPDATE statement. Note that for this to work, the view must be updatable as described in figure 12-5. In addition, the UPDATE statement can only update the data in a single base table, even if the view refers to two or more tables.

The examples in this figure illustrate how this works. First, the CREATE VIEW statement creates an updatable view named VendorPayment that joins data from the Vendors and Invoices tables. The data that's retrieved by this view is shown in this figure. Then, the UPDATE statement uses this view to modify the PaymentDate and PaymentTotal columns for a specific vendor and invoice. As you can see, the Invoices table reflects this update.

Notice, however, that the row that was updated is no longer included in the view. That's because the row no longer meets the criteria in the WHERE clause of the SELECT statement that defines the view. If that's not what you want, you can include the WITH CHECK OPTION clause in the CREATE VIEW statement. Then, an update through the view isn't allowed if it causes the row to be excluded from the view. If the WITH CHECK OPTION clause had been included in the definition of the VendorPayment view, for example, the UPDATE statement in this figure would have resulted in an error message like the one shown.

A statement that creates an updatable view

```
CREATE VIEW VendorPayment
AS
SELECT VendorName, InvoiceNumber, InvoiceDate, PaymentDate,
    InvoiceTotal, CreditTotal, PaymentTotal
FROM Invoices JOIN Vendors ON Invoices.VendorID = Vendors.VendorID
WHERE InvoiceTotal - PaymentTotal - CreditTotal > 0
```

The data retrieved by the view before the update

	VendorName	InvoiceNumber	InvoiceDate	PaymentDate	InvoiceTotal	CreditTotal	PaymentTotal
1	Malloy Lithographing Inc	P-0608	2002-04-11 00:00:00	NULL	20551.1800	1200.0000	.0000
2	United Parcel Service	989319-497	2002-04-17 00:00:00	NULL	2312.2000	.0000	.0000
3	United Parcel Service	989319-487	2002-04-18 00:00:00	NULL	1927.5400	.0000	.0000
4	Zylka Design	97/553B	2002-04-26 00:00:00	NULL	313.5500	.0000	.0000

A statement that updates the Invoices table through the view

```
UPDATE VendorPayment
SET PaymentTotal = 19351.18, PaymentDate = '2002-08-01'
WHERE VendorName = 'Malloy Lithographing Inc' AND InvoiceNumber = 'P-0608'
```

The updated Invoices table

	InvoiceID	VendorID	InvoiceNumber	InvoiceDate	InvoiceTotal	PaymentTotal	CreditTotal	PaymentDate
1	1	34	QP58872	2002-02-25 00:00:00	116.5400	116.5400	.0000	2002-04-11 00:00:00
2	2	34	Q545443	2002-03-14 00:00:00	1083.5800	1083.5800	.0000	2002-05-14 00:00:00
3	3	110	P-0608	2002-04-11 00:00:00	20551.1800	19351.1800	1200.0000	2002-08-01 00:00:00
4	4	110	P-0259	2002-04-16 00:00:00	26881.4000	26881.4000	.0000	2002-05-12 00:00:00

The data retrieved by the view after the update

	VendorName	InvoiceNumber	InvoiceDate	PaymentDate	InvoiceTotal	CreditTotal	PaymentTotal
1	United Parcel Service	989319-497	2002-04-17 00:00:00	NULL	2312.2000	.0000	.0000
2	United Parcel Service	989319-487	2002-04-18 00:00:00	NULL	1927.5400	.0000	.0000
3	Zylka Design	97/553B	2002-04-26 00:00:00	NULL	313.5500	.0000	.0000
4	Zylka Design	97/553	2002-04-27 00:00:00	NULL	904.1400	.0000	.0000

The response if the WITH CHECK OPTION is specified for the view

```
The attempted insert or update failed because the target view either specifies
WITH CHECK OPTION or spans a view that specifies WITH CHECK OPTION and one or
more rows resulting from the operation did not qualify under the CHECK OPTION
constraint.
The statement has been terminated.
```

Description

- You can use the UPDATE statement to update a table through a view. To do that, you name the view in the UPDATE clause.

- The view you name in the UPDATE statement must be updatable. In addition, the UPDATE statement can't update data in more than one base table.

- If you don't specify WITH CHECK OPTION when you create a view, a change you make through the view can cause the modified rows to no longer be included in the view.

- If you specify WITH CHECK OPTION when you create a view, an error will occur if you try to modify a row in such a way that it would no longer be included in the view.

Figure 12-7   How to update rows through a view

How to insert rows through a view

To insert rows through a view, you use the INSERT statement as shown in figure 12-8. At the top of this figure, you can see a CREATE VIEW statement for a view named IBM_Invoices. This view retrieves columns and rows from the Invoices table for the vendor named IBM. Then, the INSERT statement attempts to insert a row into the Invoices table through this view.

This insert operation fails, though, because the view and the INSERT statement don't include all of the required columns for the Invoices table. In this case, a value is required for the InvoiceNumber, InvoiceDate, InvoiceTotal, TermsID, and InvoiceDueDate columns. In contrast, the InvoiceID column can be omitted because it's an identity column; the PaymentTotal and CreditTotal columns can be omitted because they have default values; and the PaymentDate column can be omitted because it allows null values.

In addition to providing values for all the required columns in a table, you should know that the INSERT statement can insert rows into only one table. That's true even if the view is based on two or more tables and all of the required columns for those tables are included in the view. In that case, you could use a separate UPDATE statement to update each table through the view.

How to delete rows through a view

Figure 12-8 also shows how to delete rows through a view. To do that, you use a DELETE statement like the one shown here. This statement deletes an invoice from the Invoices table through the IBM_Invoices view. Note that for this to work, the view must be based on a single table. If it's based on two or more tables, the delete operation will fail.

A statement that creates an updatable view

```
CREATE VIEW IBM_Invoices
AS
SELECT InvoiceNumber, InvoiceDate, InvoiceTotal
FROM Invoices
WHERE VendorID = (SELECT VendorID FROM Vendors WHERE VendorName = 'IBM')
```

The contents of the view

	InvoiceNumber	InvoiceDate	InvoiceTotal
1	QP58872	2002-02-25 00:00:00	116.5400
2	Q545443	2002-03-14 00:00:00	1083.5800

An INSERT statement that fails due to columns with null values

```
INSERT INTO IBM_Invoices
     (InvoiceNumber, InvoiceDate, InvoiceTotal)
VALUES ('RA23988', '2002-07-31', 417.34)
```

The response from the system

```
Server: Msg 515, Level 16, State 2, Line 1
Cannot insert the value NULL into column 'InvoiceDueDate', table
'AP.dbo.Invoices'; column does not allow nulls. INSERT fails.
The statement has been terminated.
```

A DELETE statement that succeeds

```
DELETE FROM IBM_Invoices
WHERE InvoiceNumber = 'Q545443'
```

The response from the system

```
(1 row(s) affected)
```

Description

- You can use the INSERT statement to insert rows into a base table through a view. To do that, you name the view in the INSERT clause. Both the view and the INSERT statement must include all of the columns from the base table that require a value.

- If the view names more than one base table, an INSERT statement can insert data into only one of those tables.

- You can use the DELETE statement to delete rows from a base table through a view. To do that, you name the table in the DELETE clause. For this to work, the view must be based on a single table.

Figure 12-8   How to insert or delete rows through a view

How to use the information schema views

The ANSI standards specify that a SQL database must maintain an online *system catalog* that lists all of the objects in the database. Although SQL Server lets you query the system catalogs directly, I don't recommend you do that. That's because if you do, you have to code queries that are dependent on the structure of the system tables that make up the system catalog. So if the system tables change in a future release of SQL Server, you have to change your queries.

Instead of querying the system tables directly, you can use the *information schema views* provided by SQL Server. Because these views are independent of the structure of the system tables, you don't have to worry about changing the queries that refer to them if the structure changes. Figure 12-9 lists some of these views and shows you how to use them.

To display the data defined by an information schema view, you use a SELECT statement just as you would for any other view. The SELECT statement shown in this figure, for example, displays the data defined by the view named TABLES. This view contains information about each table in the current database, including the name of the database (TABLE_CATALOG), the owner of the table (TABLE_SCHEMA), the name of the table (TABLE_NAME), and whether the table is a view or a base table (TABLE_TYPE). Notice that when you refer to an information schema view, you must code the schema name "INFORMATION_SCHEMA" where you would normally code the owner name.

At this point, you may be wondering why you would want to use the information schema views. After all, you can get the same information using the Enterprise Manager. The answer is that you may occasionally need to get information about the objects in a database from a script. You'll learn how to do that in the next chapter.

Some of the SQL Server information schema views

View name	Contents
TABLES	One row for each table in the current database.
VIEWS	One row for each view in the current database.
COLUMNS	One row for each column in each table in the current database.
KEY_COLUMN_USAGE	One row for each key in each table in the current database, including primary keys, unique keys, and foreign keys.
TABLE_CONSTRAINTS	One row for each table constraint in each table in the current database.
CHECK_CONSTRAINTS	One row for each check constraint in each table in the current database.
CONSTRAINT_COLUMN_USAGE	One row for each column in each table in the current database with a constraint.
CONSTRAINT_TABLE_USAGE	One row for each table in the current database with a constraint.

A SELECT statement that queries the TABLES view

```
SELECT *
FROM INFORMATION_SCHEMA.TABLES
```

The result set

	TABLE_CATALOG	TABLE_SCHEMA	TABLE_NAME	TABLE_TYPE
3	AP	dbo	GLAccounts	BASE TABLE
4	AP	dbo	InvoiceLineItems	BASE TABLE
5	AP	dbo	Invoices	BASE TABLE
6	AP	dbo	NewInvoices	BASE TABLE
7	AP	dbo	OutstandingInvoices	VIEW
8	AP	dbo	sysconstraints	VIEW

Description

- You can use the *information schema views* to examine the *system catalog*, which lists all of the system objects that define a database, including tables, views, columns, keys, and constraints.

- To use one of the information schema views, you must qualify it with the schema name instead of the owner name. The schema name for all of the information schema views is INFORMATION_SCHEMA.

- For a complete listing of the information schema views, look up "Information Schema Views" in Books Online.

Note

- Although it's possible to query the system catalog directly, I don't recommend it.

Figure 12-9   How to use the information schema views

How to use the Enterprise Manager to work with views

As you might expect, you can also create and work with views using the Enterprise Manager. Because many of the skills you use are the same as those you learned in the last chapter for working with tables, I'll just present some new skills here. Then, you can experiment with the other skills on your own.

How to display the definition of a view

Figure 12-10 presents the Action menu for a view. As you can see, you can use this menu to perform a variety of functions, including creating a new view and modifying an existing view. You can also use the Properties command in this menu to display the general properties for a view. When you select this command, the View Properties window shown in this figure is displayed.

As you can see, the View Properties window displays the definition of the view. Although you can modify the definition directly in this window, you're not likely to do that. Instead, you can open the view in the Design View window as you'll see in the next figure. Or, you can copy the view definition to the Query Analyzer and work with it there. If you do modify the view in this window, however, you'll want to use the Check Syntax button to check the syntax of the view before you save it. You can also use this window to set the permissions for the view. You'll learn more about permissions in chapter 17.

The Enterprise Manager with the definition of a view displayed

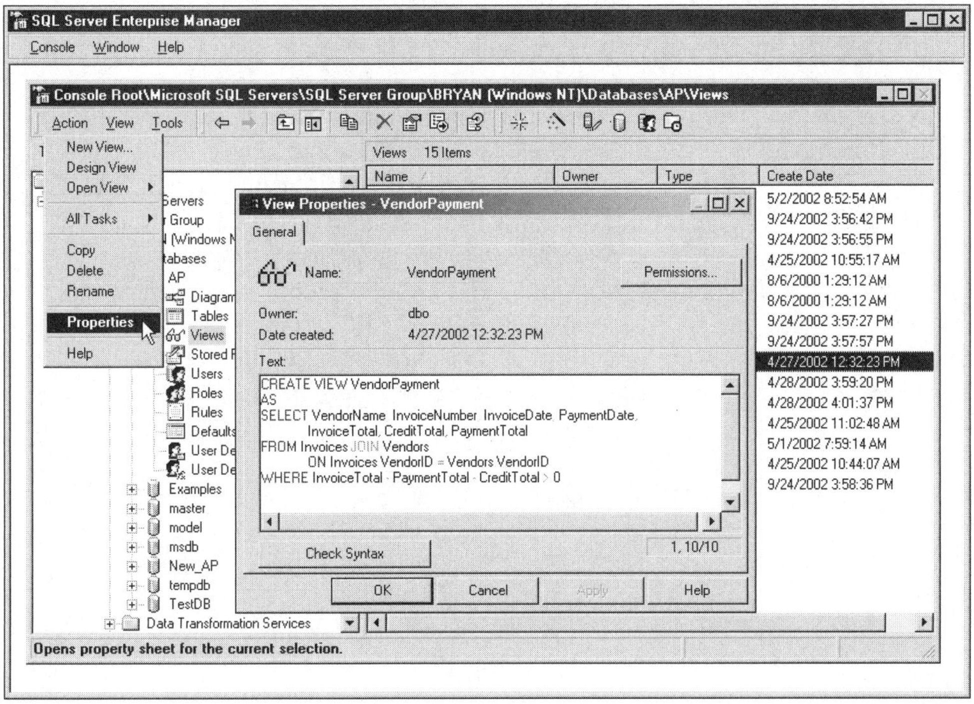

Description

- To display a list of views in a database, highlight the Views node in the console tree.

- To work with a view, highlight the view and then use the commands in the Action menu, or right-click on the view and use the commands in the shortcut menu that's displayed.

- To display the definition of a view, use the Action→Properties command to display the View Properties window shown above. You can use this window to modify the view, check its syntax, and set permissions for it.

- To modify a view, use the Action→Design View command. See figure 12-11 for details.

- To create a new view, use the Action→New View command.

- To display the dependencies for a view, use the Action→All Tasks→Display Dependencies command.

- To create a query that's based on a view, use the Action→Open View→Query command to display the Query Designer.

- Each database includes two views that are created automatically: sysconstraints and syssegments. Since these are system objects, you can't change or delete them.

Figure 12-10   How to work with views

How to create and modify views

If you select the Design View command from the Action menu for a view, a Design View window like the one in figure 12-11 is displayed. This window works just like the Query Designer you learned about in the last chapter. You can use it to modify the SELECT statement that defines the view.

If you select the New View command from the Action menu, the New View window is displayed. This window is similar to the Design View window, except that it's blank by default. Then, you can use the diagram and grid panes to define the SELECT statement for the new view, you can modify the code in the SQL pane if necessary, and you can execute the SELECT statement to be sure it retrieves the rows you want. When you're done, you can close the window and the Enterprise Manager will ask you to enter a new name for the view.

The Design View window for the VendorPayment view

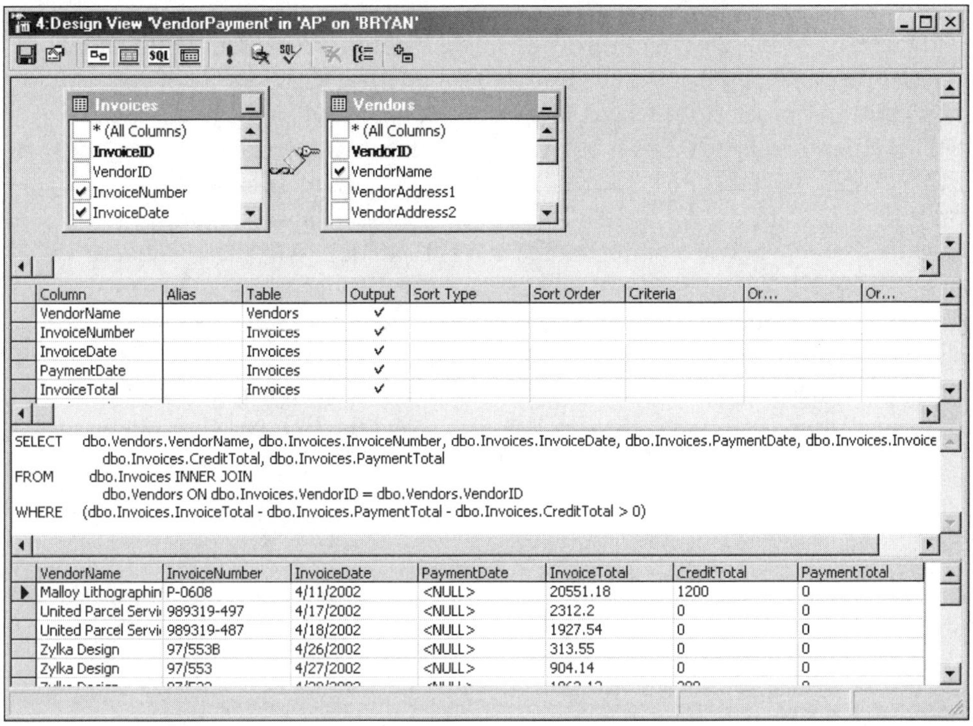

Description

- To work with the design of an existing view, you use the Design View window shown above. This window is similar to the Query Designer you learned about in chapter 11.

- To design a new view, you use the New View window. This window works just like the Design View window.

- To select the tables, views, and columns for a view, use the diagram pane. You can also create and work with joins in this pane.

- To specify the characteristics for the columns used by the view, use the grid pane.

- To view the code that's generated for the view or to modify the generated code, use the SQL pane.

- To display the results of the view in the results pane, click on the Run toolbar button.

- When you close the Design View or New View window, the Enterprise Manager will ask if you want to save the changes. In addition, when you close the New View window and indicate that you want to save the changes, the Enterprise Manager will ask you to enter the name of the new view.

Figure 12-11   How to create and modify views

How to edit view properties

Figure 12-12 presents the Properties dialog box for a view. This dialog box provides the same options that are available for queries, with four additions.

First, you can select the Check Option check box to add a WITH CHECK OPTION clause to the CREATE VIEW statement. Second, you can use the Owner drop-down list to select the owner of the view. In most cases, though, you'll leave it at the default, which is the owner of the database. Third, you can select the Bind To Schema option to add a WITH SCHEMABINDING clause to the CREATE VIEW statement. If you do that, you'll notice that the Owner drop-down list is dimmed. That's because to bind the view to the database schema, it must have the same owner as the database. Similarly, if you select an owner other than the database owner from the Owner drop-down list, the Bind To Schema option is dimmed. Finally, you can select the Encrypt view option to add the WITH ENCRYPTION clause to the CREATE VIEW statement.

The Properties dialog box for a view

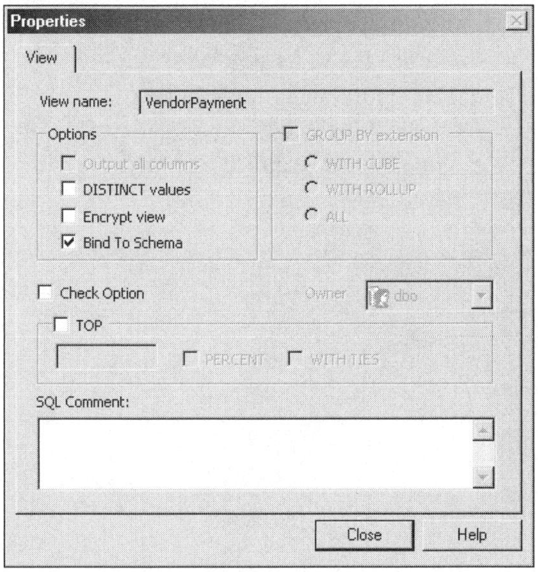

Description

- To examine or set the properties for a view, use the Properties dialog box. To display this dialog box, click on the Properties toolbar button in the Design View or New View window.

- To include the all columns operator (*) in the SELECT clause, select the Output all columns option. This option isn't available if you select the Bind To Schema option.

- To include the DISTINCT keyword in the SELECT clause, select the DISTINCT values option.

- To include the WITH ENCRYPTION clause in the CREATE VIEW statement, select the Encrypt view option.

- To include the WITH SCHEMABINDING clause in the CREATE VIEW statement, select the Bind To Schema option. This option isn't available if you select a different owner for the view.

- To change the owner of the view, select the owner from the Owner drop-down list. This list isn't available if you select the Bind To Schema option.

- To include a WITH CUBE or WITH ROLLUP operator or the ALL keyword in a query that includes the GROUP BY clause, select the GROUP BY extension check box and then the appropriate option.

- To include the WITH CHECK OPTION clause in the CREATE VIEW statement, select the Check Option check box.

- To include the TOP clause in the SELECT clause, select the TOP check box. Then, you can specify the other options for this clause.

- You can also enter a comment about the view in the SQL Comment box.

Figure 12-12   How to edit view properties

Perspective

In this chapter, you learned how to create and use views. As you've seen, views provide a powerful and flexible way to predefine the data that can be retrieved from a database. By using them, you can restrict the access to a database while providing a consistent and simplified way for end users and application programs to access that data.

Terms

view
viewed table
base table
nested view
database schema
updatable view
read-only view
information schema view
system catalog

13

How to code scripts

At the end of chapter 10, you saw a simple script that defines the AP database and the tables it contains. Now, this chapter teaches you how to code more complex scripts. With the skills you'll learn in this chapter, you'll be able to code scripts with functionality that's similar to the functionality provided by procedural programming languages like Visual Basic, Java, and C++.

If you have experience with another procedural programming language, you shouldn't have any trouble with the skills presented in this chapter. However, you should know that the programming power of Transact-SQL is limited when compared to other languages. That's because Transact-SQL is designed specifically to work with SQL Server databases rather than as a general-purpose programming language. For its intended use, Transact-SQL programming is powerful and flexible.

An introduction to scripts

To start, this chapter reviews and expands on the script concepts you learned in chapter 10. Then, it summarizes the Transact-SQL statements you can use within scripts. Most of these statements will be presented in detail later in this chapter.

How to work with scripts

Most of the *scripts* you've created so far in this book have consisted of a single SQL statement. However, a script can include any number of statements, and those statements can be divided into one or more *batches*. To indicate the end of a batch, you code a GO command. The script in figure 13-1, for example, consists of two batches. The first one creates a database, and the second one creates three tables in that database.

Because the new database must exist before you can add tables to it, the CREATE DATABASE statement must be coded in a separate batch that's executed before the CREATE TABLE statements. In contrast, the three CREATE TABLE statements don't have to be in separate batches. However, notice that these three statements are coded in a logical sequence within the second batch. In this case, the CommitteeAssignments table references the other two tables, so I created the other tables first. If I'd created the CommitteeAssignments table first, I couldn't have declared the foreign key constraints. In that case, I would have had to add these constraints in an ALTER TABLE statement after the other two tables were created.

There are four statements that you do have to code in separate batches, and they're listed in this figure. Each of these statements must be the first and only statement in the batch. You learned how to code the CREATE VIEW statement in the last chapter, and you'll learn how to code the CREATE PROCEDURE, CREATE FUNCTION, and CREATE TRIGGER statements in the next chapter.

Before I go on, you should realize that GO isn't a Transact-SQL statement. Instead, it's a command that's interpreted by three of the software tools that are included with SQL Server: the Query Analyzer, OSQL, and ISQL. When one of these tools encounters a GO command, it sends the preceding statements to the server to be executed. You already know how to use the Query Analyzer, and you'll learn the basics of working with OSQL later in this chapter. *ISQL* is an older version of OSQL that's included for backward compatibility. Since ISQL doesn't support several of the features of SQL Server 2000, it's not presented in this book.

A script with two batches

```
/*
Creates three tables in a database named ClubRoster.

Author:    Bryan Syverson
Created:   2002-08-12
Modified:  2002-09-26
*/


CREATE DATABASE ClubRoster
GO

USE ClubRoster

CREATE TABLE Members
(MemberID int NOT NULL IDENTITY PRIMARY KEY,
LastName varchar(75) NOT NULL,
FirstName varchar(50) NOT NULL,
MiddleName varchar(50) NULL)

CREATE TABLE Committees
(CommitteeID int NOT NULL IDENTITY PRIMARY KEY,
CommitteeName varchar(50) NOT NULL)

CREATE TABLE CommitteeAssignments
(MemberID int NOT NULL REFERENCES Members(MemberID),
CommitteeID int NOT NULL REFERENCES Committees(CommitteeID))
```

Statements that must be in their own batch

```
CREATE VIEW        CREATE PROCEDURE      CREATE FUNCTION       CREATE TRIGGER
```

Description

- A *script* is a series of SQL statements that you can store in a file. Each script can contain one or more *batches* that are executed as a unit.

- To signal the end of a batch, you use the GO command. A GO command isn't required after the last batch in a script or for a script that contains a single batch.

- If a statement must be executed before the statements that follow can succeed, you should include a GO command after it.

- The statements within a batch are executed in the order that they appear in the batch. Because of that, you need to code statements that depend on other statements after the statements they depend on.

- If you create a database within a script, you have to execute the batch that contains the CREATE DATABASE statement before you can execute other statements that refer to the database.

- The four statements listed above, CREATE VIEW, CREATE PROCEDURE, CREATE FUNCTION, and CREATE TRIGGER, can't be combined with other statements in a batch.

- If a script will be used with a production database, you should include documentation as shown above. Additional information should be included when appropriate.

Figure 13-1   How to work with scripts

The Transact-SQL statements for script processing

Figure 13-2 presents the Transact-SQL statements used to process scripts. These statements, which are sometimes referred to as *T-SQL statements*, are specific to SQL Server. You'll learn how to code many of these statements throughout this chapter.

Two statements I want to present right now are USE and PRINT. You can see both of these statements in the script presented in this figure. You use the USE statement to change the current database within a script. In this example, the USE statement makes the AP database the current database. That way, you don't have to worry about setting the current database using the drop-down list in the Query Analyzer. And when you create stored procedures, functions, and triggers as you'll learn in the next chapter, you have to use the USE statement.

You use the PRINT statement to return a message to the client. If the client is the Query Analyzer, for example, the message is displayed in the Query Analyzer window. The script in this figure includes two PRINT statements. Notice that the first statement uses concatenation to combine a literal string with the value of a variable. You'll learn how to work with variables as well as the other statements in this script in a moment.

Two statements I won't present in this chapter are GOTO and RETURN. I recommend that you don't use the GOTO statement because it can make your scripts difficult to follow. And the RETURN statement is used most often with stored procedures, so I'll present it in the next chapter.

Transact-SQL statements for controlling the flow of execution

Keyword	Description
IF...ELSE	Controls the flow of execution based on a condition.
BEGIN...END	Defines a statement block.
WHILE	Repeats statements while a specific condition is true.
BREAK	Exits the innermost WHILE loop.
CONTINUE	Returns to the beginning of a WHILE loop.
GOTO	Unconditionally changes the flow of execution.
RETURN	Exits unconditionally.

Other Transact-SQL statements for script processing

Keyword	Description
USE	Changes the database context to the specified database.
PRINT	Returns a message to the client.
DECLARE	Declares a local variable.
SET	Sets the value of a local variable or a session variable.
EXEC	Executes a dynamic SQL statement or stored procedure.

The syntax of the USE statement

```
USE database
```

The syntax of the PRINT statement

```
PRINT string_expression
```

A script that uses some of the statements shown above

```
USE AP
DECLARE @TotalDue money
SET @TotalDue = (SELECT SUM(InvoiceTotal - PaymentTotal - CreditTotal)
    FROM Invoices)
IF @TotalDue > 0
    PRINT 'Total invoices due = $' + CONVERT(varchar,@TotalDue,1)
ELSE
    PRINT 'Invoices paid in full'
```

Description

- These statements are used within SQL scripts to add functionality similar to that provided by procedural programming languages.
- These statements are part of the Transact-SQL, or *T-SQL*, language and aren't available on SQL-based systems other than SQL Server.

Figure 13-2   The Transact-SQL statements for script processing

How to work with variables and temporary tables

If you need to store values within a script, you can store them in scalar variables, table variables, or temporary tables. You'll learn how to use all three of these techniques in the topics that follow. In addition, you'll see a comparison of the different types of SQL Server objects that you can use to work with table data, so you'll know when to use each type.

How to work with scalar variables

Figure 13-3 presents the DECLARE and SET statements that you use to work with *variables*. Specifically you use these statements to work with *scalar variables*, which can contain a single value. You use the DECLARE statement to create a variable and specify the type of data it can contain, and you use the SET statement to assign a value to a variable.

The variables you create using the DECLARE statement are also known as *local variables*. That's because a variable's scope is limited to a single batch. In other words, you can't refer to a variable from outside the batch. Variables are also described as local to distinguish them from *global variables*, which is an obsolete term for system functions. You'll learn about some of the system functions later in this chapter.

You can also assign a value to a variable within the select list of a SELECT statement. To do that, you use the alternate syntax shown in this figure. Although you can accomplish the same thing by using a SET statement to assign the result of a SELECT query to the variable, the alternate syntax usually results in more readable code. In addition, you can use this syntax to assign values to two or more variables with a single SELECT statement.

The script shown in this figure uses five variables to calculate the percent difference between the minimum and maximum invoices for a particular vendor. This script starts by declaring all of these variables. Then, it assigns values to two of the variables using SET statements. Notice that the second SET statement assigns the result of a SELECT statement to the variable, and the value of the first variable is used in the WHERE clause of that SELECT statement. The SELECT statement that follows this SET statement uses the alternate syntax to assign values to two more variables. Then, the next SET statement assigns the result of an arithmetic expression to the final variable. Finally, PRINT statements are used to display the values of four of the variables.

Although you can use a variable in any expression, you can't use it in place of a keyword or an object name. For example, this use is invalid:

```
DECLARE @TableNameVar varchar(128)
SET @TableNameVar = 'Invoices'
SELECT * FROM @TableNameVar
```

Later in this chapter, however, you'll learn how to execute a SQL statement like this one using dynamic SQL.

The syntax of the DECLARE statement for scalar variables

```
DECLARE @variable_name_1 data_type [, @variable_name_2 data_type]...
```

The syntax of the SET statement for a scalar variable

```
SET @variable_name = expression
```

An alternate syntax for setting a variable's value in a select list

```
SELECT @variable_name = column_specification
```

A SQL script that uses variables

```
USE AP

DECLARE @MaxInvoice money, @MinInvoice money
DECLARE @PercentDifference decimal(8,2)
DECLARE @InvoiceCount int, @VendorIDVar int

SET @VendorIDVar = 95
SET @MaxInvoice = (SELECT MAX(InvoiceTotal) FROM Invoices
    WHERE VendorID = @VendorIDVar)
SELECT @MinInvoice = MIN(InvoiceTotal), @InvoiceCount = COUNT(*)
FROM Invoices
WHERE VendorID = @VendorIDVar
SET @PercentDifference = (@MaxInvoice - @MinInvoice) / @MinInvoice * 100

PRINT 'Maximum invoice is $' + CONVERT(varchar,@MaxInvoice,1) + '.'
PRINT 'Minimum invoice is $' + CONVERT(varchar,@MinInvoice,1) + '.'
PRINT 'Maximum is ' + CONVERT(varchar,@PercentDifference) +
    '% more than minimum.'
PRINT 'Number of invoices: ' + CONVERT(varchar,@InvoiceCount) + '.'
```

The response from the system

```
Maximum invoice is $46.21.
Minimum invoice is $16.33.
Maximum is 182.97% more than minimum.
Number of invoices: 6.
```

Description

- A *variable* is used to store data. To create a variable, you use the DECLARE statement. The initial value of a variable is always null.

- A variable that's defined with a standard data type contains a single value and is called a *scalar variable*. You can also create table variables to store an entire result set.

- Whenever possible, you should use long, descriptive names for variables. The name of a variable must always start with an at sign (@).

- The scope of a variable is the batch in which it's defined, which means that it can't be referred to from outside that batch. Because of that, variables are often called *local variables*.

- To assign a value to a variable, you can use the SET statement. Alternatively, you can use the SELECT statement to assign a value to one or more variables.

- You can use a variable in any expression, but you can't use it in place of an object name or a keyword.

Figure 13-3 How to work with scalar variables

How to work with table variables

Figure 13-4 presents the syntax of the DECLARE statement you use to create table variables. A *table variable* is a variable that can store the contents of an entire table. To create this type of variable, you specify the table data type in the DECLARE statement rather than one of the standard SQL data types. Then, you define the columns and constraints for the table using the same syntax that you use for the CREATE TABLE statement.

The script shown in this figure illustrates how you might use a table variable. Here, a DECLARE statement is used to create a table variable named @BigVendors that contains two columns: VendorID and VendorName. Then, an INSERT statement is used to insert all of the rows from the Vendors table for vendors that have invoices totaling over $5000 into this table variable. Finally, a SELECT statement is used to retrieve the contents of the table variable.

Notice that the table variable in this example is used in place of a table name in the INSERT and SELECT statements. You can also use a table variable in place of a table name in an UPDATE or DELETE statement. The only place you can't use a table variable instead of a table name is in the INTO clause of a SELECT INTO statement.

The syntax of the DECLARE statement for a table variable

```
DECLARE @table_name TABLE
(column_name_1 data_type [column_attributes]
[, column_name_2 data_type [column_attributes]]...
[, table_attributes])
```

A SQL Script that uses a table variable

```
USE AP

DECLARE @BigVendors table
(VendorID int,
VendorName varchar(50))

INSERT @BigVendors
SELECT VendorID, VendorName
FROM Vendors
WHERE VendorID IN (SELECT VendorID FROM Invoices WHERE InvoiceTotal > 5000)

SELECT * FROM @BigVendors
```

The result set

	VendorID	VendorName
1	72	Data Reproductions Corp
2	99	Bertelsmann Industry Svcs. Inc
3	104	Digital Dreamworks
4	110	Malloy Lithographing Inc

Description

- A *table variable* can store an entire result set rather than a single value. To create a table variable, use a DECLARE statement with the table data type.

- You use the same syntax for defining the columns of a table variable as you do for defining a new table with the CREATE TABLE statement. See figure 10-4 in chapter 10 for details.

- Like a scalar variable, a table variable has local scope, so it's available only within the batch where it's declared.

- You can use a table variable like a standard table within SELECT, INSERT, UPDATE, and DELETE statements. The exception is that you can't use it within the INTO clause of a SELECT INTO statement.

Figure 13-4   How to work with table variables

How to work with temporary tables

In addition to table variables, you can use *temporary tables* to store table data within a script. Temporary tables are useful for storing table data within a complex script. In addition, they provide a way for you to test queries against temporary data rather than permanent data.

Unlike a table variable, a temporary table exists for the duration of the database session in which it's created. If you create a temporary table in the Query Analyzer, for example, it exists as long as the Query window is open. Because of that, you can refer to the table from more than one script.

Figure 13-5 presents two scripts that use temporary tables. The first script creates a temporary table named #TopVendors using a SELECT INTO query. This temporary table contains the VendorID and average invoice total for the vendor in the Vendors table with the greatest average. Then, the second SELECT statement joins the temporary table with the Invoices table to get the date of the most recent invoice for that vendor. Note, however, that you could have created the same result set using a single SELECT statement like the second one in this figure with a derived table in place of the temporary table. Because derived tables are more efficient to use than temporary tables, you should use them whenever possible.

The second script in this figure shows another use of a temporary table. This script creates a temporary table that contains two columns: an identity column and a character column with a nine-digit default value that's generated using the RAND function. Then, the script inserts two rows into this table using the default values. Finally, the script uses a SELECT statement to retrieve the contents of the table. A script like this can be useful during testing.

In these examples, you can see that the name of a temporary table begins with a number sign (#). If the name begins with a single number sign, the table is defined as a *local temporary table*, which means that it's visible only to the database session in which it's created. However, you can also create temporary tables that are visible to all open database sessions, called *global temporary tables*. To create a global temporary table, code two number signs at the beginning of the table name.

When a database session ends, any temporary tables created during that session are deleted. If you want to delete a temporary table before the session ends, however, you can do that by issuing a DROP TABLE statement. Note that although temporary tables are stored in a separate database named tempdb, you don't need to specify the name of this database when you delete a temporary table. That's because its name identifies it as a temporary table, so SQL Server knows where to look for it.

A script that uses a local temporary table instead of a derived table

```
SELECT TOP 1 VendorID, AVG(InvoiceTotal) AS AvgInvoice
INTO #TopVendors
FROM Invoices
GROUP BY VendorID
ORDER BY AvgInvoice DESC

SELECT Invoices.VendorID, MAX(InvoiceDate) AS LatestInv
FROM Invoices JOIN #TopVendors
    ON Invoices.VendorID = #TopVendors.VendorID
GROUP BY Invoices.VendorID
```

The result set

	VendorID	LatestInv
1	110	2001-07-01 00:00:00

A script that creates a global temporary table of random numbers

```
CREATE TABLE ##RandomSSNs
(SSN_ID int IDENTITY,
SSN char(9) DEFAULT
    LEFT(CAST(CAST(CEILING(RAND()*10000000000)AS bigint)AS varchar),9))

INSERT ##RandomSSNs VALUES (DEFAULT)
INSERT ##RandomSSNs VALUES (DEFAULT)

SELECT * FROM ##RandomSSNs
```

The result set

	SSN_ID	SSN
1	1	269114356
2	2	143843053

Description

- A *temporary table* exists only during the current database session. In the Query Analyzer, that means that the table is available until you close the window where you created the table.

- Temporary tables are stored in the system database named tempdb.

- If you need to drop a temporary table before the end of the current session, you can do that using the DROP TABLE statement.

- Temporary tables are useful for testing queries or for storing data temporarily in a complex script.

- A *local temporary table* is visible only within the current session, but a *global temporary table* is visible to all sessions. To identify a local temporary table, you prefix the name with a number sign (#). To identify a global temporary table, you prefix the name with two number signs (##). Temporary table names are limited to 116 characters.

- Because derived tables result in faster performance than temporary tables, you should use derived tables whenever possible. See figure 13-6 for details.

Figure 13-5   How to work with temporary tables

A comparison of the five types of Transact-SQL table objects

Now that you've learned about table variables and temporary tables, you might want to consider when you'd use them within a script and when you'd create a new standard table or view or simply use a derived table instead. Figure 13-6 presents a comparison of these five types of table objects. Note that although a view isn't technically a table, I've included it in this figure because it can be used in place of a table.

One of the biggest differences between these objects is their *scope*, which determines where it can be used in a script. Because standard tables and views are stored permanently within a database, they have the broadest scope and can be used anywhere, including in other scripts on the current connection or other scripts on other connections. In contrast, a derived table exists only while the query that creates it is executing. Because of that, a derived table can't be referred to from outside the query. As you've just learned, temporary tables and table variables fall somewhere in between.

Another difference between the five table types is where they're stored. Like standard tables, temporary tables are stored on disk. In contrast, table variables and derived tables are stored in memory if they're relatively small. Because of that, table variables and derived tables usually take less time to create and access than standard or temporary tables.

Although a view is also stored on disk, it can be faster to use than any of the other table objects. That's because it's simply a precompiled query, so it takes less time to create and access than an actual table. However, with the other table objects, you can insert, update, or delete data without affecting any of the base tables in your database, which isn't true of a view. For this reason, you can't use a view in the same way as the other table objects. But if you find that you're creating a table object that doesn't need to be modified within your script, then you should be defining it as a view instead.

In most scripts, table variables and temporary tables can be used interchangeably. Since a script that uses a table variable will outperform the same script with a temporary table, you should use table variables whenever possible. However, table variables are dropped when the batch finishes execution. So if you need to use the table in other batches, you'll need to use a temporary table instead.

The five types of Transact-SQL table objects

Type	Scope
Standard table	Available within the system until explicitly deleted.
Temporary table	Available within the system while the current database session is open.
Table variable	Available within a script while the current batch is executing.
Derived table	Available within a statement while the current statement is executing.
View	Available within the system until explicitly deleted.

Description

- Within a Transact-SQL script, you often need to work with table objects other than the base tables in your database.

- The *scope* of a table object determines what code in the script has access to that table.

- Standard tables and views are stored permanently on disk until they are explicitly deleted, so they have the broadest scope and are therefore always available for use.

- Derived tables and table variables are generally stored in memory, so they can provide the best performance. In contrast, standard tables and temporary tables are always stored on disk and therefore provide slower performance.

- To improve the performance of your scripts, use a derived table instead of creating a table variable. However, if you need to use the table in other batches, create a temporary table. Finally, if the data needs to be available to other connections to the database, create a standard table or, if possible, a view.

- Although a view isn't a table, it can be used like one. Views provide fast performance since they're predefined, and high availability since they're permanent objects. For these reasons, you should try to use a view rather than create a table whenever that's possible. However, if you need to insert, delete, or update the data in the table object without affecting the base tables of your database, then you can't use a view.

Figure 13-6   A comparison of the five types of Transact-SQL tables

How to control the execution of a script

The ability to control the execution of a program is an essential feature of any procedural programming language. T-SQL provides two basic control structures that you can use within scripts. You use one to perform conditional processing, and you use the other to perform repetitive processing. You'll learn how to use the statements that implement these structures in the topics that follow.

How to perform conditional processing

To execute a statement or a block of statements based on a condition, you use the IF...ELSE statement. This statement is presented in figure 13-7. When an IF...ELSE statement is executed, SQL Server evaluates the conditional expression after the IF keyword. If this condition is true, the statement or block of statements after the IF keyword is executed. Otherwise, the statement or block of statements after the ELSE keyword is executed if this keyword is included.

The first script in this figure uses a simple IF statement to test the value of a variable that's assigned in a SELECT statement. This variable contains the oldest invoice due date in the Invoices table. If this value is less than the current date, the PRINT statement that follows the IF keyword is executed. Otherwise, no action is taken.

In the second script, the logic of the first script has been enhanced. Here, a block of statements is executed if the oldest due date is less than the current date. Notice that this block of statements begins with the BEGIN keyword and ends with the END keyword. In addition, an ELSE clause has been added. Then, if the oldest due date is greater than or equal to the current date, a PRINT statement is executed to indicate that none of the invoices are overdue.

Notice the comment that follows the ELSE keyword. This comment describes the expression that would result in this portion of code being executed. Although it isn't required, this programming practice makes it easier to find and debug logical errors, especially if you're *nesting* IF...ELSE statements within other IF...ELSE statements.

The syntax of the IF...ELSE statement

```
IF expression
    {statement|BEGIN...END}
[ELSE
    {statement|BEGIN...END}]
```

A script that tests for outstanding invoices with an IF statement

```
USE AP
DECLARE @EarliestInvoiceDue smalldatetime
SELECT @EarliestInvoiceDue = MIN(InvoiceDueDate) FROM Invoices
    WHERE InvoiceTotal - PaymentTotal - CreditTotal > 0
IF @EarliestInvoiceDue < GETDATE()
    PRINT 'Outstanding invoices overdue!'
```

The response from the system

```
Outstanding invoices overdue!
```

An enhanced version of the same script that uses an IF...ELSE statement

```
USE AP
DECLARE @MinInvoiceDue money, @MaxInvoiceDue money
DECLARE @EarliestInvoiceDue smalldatetime, @LatestInvoiceDue smalldatetime
SELECT @MinInvoiceDue = MIN(InvoiceTotal - PaymentTotal - CreditTotal),
    @MaxInvoiceDue = MAX(InvoiceTotal - PaymentTotal - CreditTotal),
    @EarliestInvoiceDue = MIN(InvoiceDueDate),
    @LatestInvoiceDue = MAX(InvoiceDueDate)
FROM Invoices
WHERE InvoiceTotal - PaymentTotal - CreditTotal > 0
IF @EarliestInvoiceDue < GETDATE()
    BEGIN
        PRINT 'Outstanding invoices overdue!'
        PRINT 'Dated ' + CONVERT(varchar,@EarliestInvoiceDue,1) +
            ' through ' + CONVERT(varchar,@LatestInvoiceDue,1) + '.'
        PRINT 'Amounting from $' + CONVERT(varchar,@MinInvoiceDue,1) +
            ' to $' + CONVERT(varchar,@MaxInvoiceDue,1) + '.'
    END
ELSE --@EarliestInvoiceDue >= GETDATE()
    PRINT 'No overdue invoices.'
```

The response from the system

```
Outstanding invoices overdue!
Dated 06/09/02 through 07/20/02.
Amounting from $6.00 to $21,842.00.
```

Description

- You use the IF...ELSE statement to test a conditional expression. If that expression is true, the statements that follow the IF keyword are executed. Otherwise, the statements that follow the ELSE keyword are executed if that keyword is included.

- If you need to execute two or more SQL statements within an IF or ELSE clause, enclose them within a BEGIN...END block.

- You can *nest* IF...ELSE statements within other IF...ELSE statements. Although SQL Server doesn't limit the number of nested levels, you should avoid nesting so deeply that your script becomes difficult to read.

Figure 13-7   How to perform conditional processing

How to test for the existence of a database object

Frequently, you'll need to write scripts that create and work with database objects. If you try to create an object that already exists, SQL Server will return an error. Similarly, SQL Server will return an error if you try to work with an object that doesn't exist. To avoid these types of errors, you should check for the existence of an object before you create or work with it.

Figure 13-8 presents two functions you can use to check for the existence of database objects. You can use the OBJECT_ID function to check for the existence of a table, view, stored procedure, user-defined function, or trigger. To check for the existence of a database, you use the DB_ID function. If the specified object exists, these functions return the unique identification number assigned to that object by SQL Server. Otherwise, they return a null value.

You can use these functions within an IF...ELSE statement to test for a null return value. The first script in this figure, for example, uses the DB_ID function to test for the existence of a database. If the database already exists, a DROP DATABASE statement is executed to delete it. Notice that a USE statement is coded before the IF statement to change the current database to something other than the database you're testing. That's because a database can't be deleted if it's currently in use.

The second script tests for the existence of a table name InvoiceCopy. Then, if the table exists, a DROP TABLE statement is executed to delete it. Note, however, that when you use the OBJECT_ID function, you may not know what type of object you're dealing with. For example, InvoiceCopy could also be the name of a view or a stored procedure. In that case, the DROP TABLE statement would cause an error.

To avoid this situation, you can use the technique shown in the third script. Instead of using a function, it uses information in the information schema view named TABLES to determine if a base table named InvoiceCopy exists. If it does, the table is deleted. Otherwise, no action is taken. You can use similar code to check for the existence of a view.

The last script tests for the existence of a temporary table. Notice that the table name is qualified with the name of the database that contains temporary tables, tempdb. You can omit the owner qualification, though, since this is a system database.

The syntax of the OBJECT_ID function

```
OBJECT_ID('object')
```

The syntax of the DB_ID function

```
DB_ID('database')
```

Examples that use the OBJECT_ID and DB_ID functions

Code that tests whether a database exists before it deletes it

```
USE master
IF DB_ID('TestDB') IS NOT NULL
    DROP DATABASE TestDB

CREATE DATABASE TestDB
```

Code that tests for the existence of a table

```
IF OBJECT_ID('InvoiceCopy') IS NOT NULL
    DROP TABLE InvoiceCopy
```

Another way to test for the existence of a table

```
IF EXISTS (SELECT * FROM INFORMATION_SCHEMA.TABLES
        WHERE (TABLE_NAME = 'InvoiceCopy' AND
        TABLE_TYPE = 'BASE TABLE'))
    DROP TABLE InvoiceCopy
```

Code that tests for the existence of a temporary table

```
IF OBJECT_ID('tempdb..#AllUserTables') IS NOT NULL
    DROP TABLE #AllUserTables
```

Description

- Before you work with an object in a database, you'll want to be sure that it exists. Similarly, before you create an object in a database, you'll want to be sure that it doesn't already exist. To do that, you can use the OBJECT_ID and DB_ID functions within IF statements.

- You can use the OBJECT_ID function to check for the existence of a table, view, stored procedure, user-defined function, or trigger. You use the DB_ID function to check for the existence of a database. Both functions return a null value if the object doesn't exist. Otherwise, they return the object's identification number.

- To test for the existence of a temporary table, you must qualify the table name with the database that contains it: tempdb. Since this is a system database, though, you can omit the owner name as shown above.

Figure 13-8   How to test for the existence of a database object

How to perform repetitive processing

In some cases, you'll need to repeat a statement or a block of statements while a condition is true. To do that, you use the WHILE statement that's presented in figure 13-9. This coding technique is referred to as a *loop*.

The script in this figure illustrates how the WHILE statement works. Here, a WHILE loop is used to adjust the credit amount of each invoice in the Invoices table that has a balance due until the total balance due is less than $50,000. Although this example is unrealistic, it will help you understand how the WHILE statement works. A more realistic example would be to use a WHILE statement to process cursors, which you'll learn about in chapter 15.

This script starts by creating a copy of the Invoices table named InvoiceCopy that contains just the invoices that have a balance due. Since the WHILE statement will change the data in the table, this prevents corruption of the data in the source table. Then, the expression in the WHILE statement uses a SELECT statement to retrieve the sum of the invoices in this table. If the sum is greater than or equal to 50,000, the block of statements that follows is executed. Otherwise, the loop ends.

The UPDATE statement within the WHILE loop adds one cent to the CreditTotal column of each invoice that has a balance due. (Although the table initially contains only invoices that have a balance due, that may change as credits are applied to the invoices within the loop.) Then, an IF statement tests the maximum credit amount in the table to see if it's more than 3000. If it is, a BREAK statement is used to terminate the loop. Because this statement can make your scripts difficult to read and debug, I recommend you use it only when necessary. In this case, it's used only for illustrative purposes.

If the maximum credit total is less than or equal to 3000, the CONTINUE statement is executed. This statement causes control to return to the beginning of the loop. Then, the condition for the loop is tested again, and if it's true, the statements within the loop are processed again.

Note that because the CONTINUE statement is the last statement in the loop, it's not required. That's because control will automatically return to the beginning of the loop after the last statement in the loop is executed. For example, this code would produce the same result:

```
BEGIN
    ...
    IF (SELECT MAX(CreditTotal) FROM #InvoiceCopy) > 3000
        BREAK
END
```

Sometimes, though, the CONTINUE statement can clarify the logic of an IF statement, as it does in the example in this figure. In addition, since this statement returns control to the beginning of the loop, it can be used in an IF clause to bypass the remaining statements in the loop. However, like the BREAK statement, this makes your code confusing to read, so I recommend you code your IF statements in such a way that you avoid using CONTINUE.

The syntax of the WHILE statement

```
WHILE expression
    {statement|BEGIN...END}
    [BREAK]
    [CONTINUE]
```

A script that tests and adjusts credit amounts with a WHILE loop

```
USE AP
IF OBJECT_ID('tempdb..#InvoiceCopy') IS NOT NULL
    DROP TABLE #InvoiceCopy
SELECT * INTO #InvoiceCopy FROM Invoices
WHERE (InvoiceTotal - CreditTotal - PaymentTotal) > 0

WHILE (SELECT SUM(InvoiceTotal - CreditTotal - PaymentTotal)
        FROM #InvoiceCopy) >= 50000
    BEGIN
        UPDATE #InvoiceCopy
        SET CreditTotal = CreditTotal + .01
        WHERE InvoiceTotal - CreditTotal - PaymentTotal > 0
        IF (SELECT MAX(CreditTotal) FROM #InvoiceCopy) > 3000
            BREAK
        ELSE --(SELECT MAX(CreditTotal) FROM #InvoiceCopy) <= 3000
            CONTINUE
    END

SELECT InvoiceDate, InvoiceTotal, CreditTotal
FROM #InvoiceCopy
```

The result set

	InvoiceDate	InvoiceTotal	CreditTotal
1	2002-04-11 00:00:00	20551.1800	2722.3900
2	2002-04-17 00:00:00	2312.2000	1522.3900
3	2002-04-18 00:00:00	1927.5400	1522.3900
4	2002-04-26 00:00:00	313.5500	313.5500

Description

- To execute a SQL statement repeatedly, you use the WHILE statement. This statement is executed as long as the conditional expression in the WHILE clause is true.

- If you need to execute two or more SQL statements within a WHILE *loop*, enclose the statements within BEGIN and END keywords.

- To exit from a WHILE loop immediately without testing the expression, use the BREAK statement. To return to the beginning of a WHILE loop without executing any additional statements in the loop, use the CONTINUE statement.

- WHILE loops are frequently used to manage cursors, which you'll learn about in chapter 15.

Warning

- This script takes a long time to execute.

Figure 13-9   How to perform repetitive processing

Advanced scripting techniques

The remaining topics of this chapter present some additional techniques you can use in the scripts you write. Here, you'll learn how to use some of the system functions that come with SQL Server, change some of the settings for the current session, use dynamic SQL, and use OSQL to execute SQL statements and scripts. In addition, you'll see a complete script that uses many of the techniques presented in this chapter.

How to use the system functions

Figure 13-10 presents some of the Transact-SQL *system functions*. These functions are particularly helpful for writing Transact-SQL scripts. For example, you can use the @@ERROR function to determine if an SQL statement executed successfully. You'll learn how to use this function in the next chapter.

The script shown in this figure illustrates how you might use the @@IDENTITY and @@ROWCOUNT functions. This script starts by inserting a row into the Vendors table. Because the VendorID column in that table is defined as an identity column, SQL Server generates the value of this column automatically. Then, the script uses the @@IDENTITY function to retrieve this value so it can then insert an invoice for the new vendor. Before it does that, though, it uses the @@ROWCOUNT function to determine if the vendor row was inserted successfully.

Notice that this script stores the values returned by the @@IDENTITY and @@ROWCOUNT functions in variables named @MyIdentity and @MyRowCount. Alternatively, the script could have used the system functions directly in the IF and VALUES clauses. However, the values returned by these functions can change each time a SQL statement is executed on the system, so it usually makes sense to store these values in variables immediately after you execute a SQL statement.

The other functions I want to point out right now are the @@SERVERNAME, HOST_NAME, and SYSTEM_USER functions. The values returned by these functions can vary depending on who enters them and where they're entered. Because of that, they're often used to identify who entered or modified a row. For example, you could define a table with a column that defaults to the SYSTEM_USER function like this:

```
CREATE TABLE #SysFunctionEx
(EntryDBUser varchar(128) DEFAULT SYSTEM_USER)
```

This would cause the user name to be inserted automatically when each new row was added to the table.

At this point, you may be wondering why the names of some of the system functions are preceded with two at signs (@@) and some aren't. Those with @@ in their names have been a part of the T-SQL dialect for a long time and used to be called *global variables*. As of version 7.0, however, that term is no longer used. The other system functions have been added to T-SQL more recently.

Some of the Transact-SQL system functions

Function name	Description
`@@IDENTITY`	Returns the last value generated for an identity column on the server. Returns NULL if no identity value was generated.
`IDENT_CURRENT('tablename')`	Similar to @@IDENTITY, but returns the last identity value that was generated for a specified table.
`@@ROWCOUNT`	Returns the number of rows affected by the most recent SQL statement.
`@@ERROR`	Returns the error number generated by the execution of the most recent SQL statement. Returns 0 if no error occurred.
`@@SERVERNAME`	Returns the name of the local server.
`HOST_NAME()`	Returns the name of the current workstation.
`SYSTEM_USER`	Returns the name of the current user.

A script that inserts a new vendor and a new invoice

```
USE AP
DECLARE @MyIdentity int, @MyRowCount int

INSERT Vendors (VendorName, VendorAddress1, VendorCity, VendorState,
    VendorZipCode, VendorPhone, DefaultTermsID, DefaultAccountNo)
VALUES ('Peerless Binding', '1112 S Windsor St', 'Hallowell', 'ME',
    '04347', '(207) 555-1555', 4, 400)

SET @MyIdentity = @@IDENTITY
SET @MyRowCount = @@ROWCOUNT

IF @MyRowCount = 1
    INSERT Invoices
    VALUES (@MyIdentity, 'BA-0199', '2001-08-01', 4598.23,
        0, 0, 4, '2001-09-06', NULL)
```

The response from the system

```
(1 row(s) affected)

(1 row(s) affected)
```

Description

- The *system functions* return information about SQL Server values, objects, and settings. They can be used anywhere an expression is allowed.

- System functions are useful in writing scripts. In addition, some of these functions can be used to provide a value for a DEFAULT constraint on a column.

- System functions used to be called *global variables*, but that name is no longer used.

- In general, it's better to store the value returned by a system function in a variable than to use the system function directly. That's because the value of a system function can change when subsequent statements are executed.

Figure 13-10   How to use the system functions

How to change the session settings

Each time you start a new session, SQL Server sets the settings for that session to the defaults. If that's not what you want, you can change the settings using the SET statements presented in figure 13-11. Although SQL Server provides a variety of other statements, these are the ones you're most likely to use. And you're likely to use these only under special circumstances.

For example, because the default format for entering dates is "mdy," 05/06/07 is interpreted as May 6, 2007. If this date is being inserted from another data source, however, that data source could have used a date format where the year is entered first, followed by the month and the day. In that case, you could use a SET statement like the one shown in this figure to change the date format of the current session to "ymd." Then, the date would be interpreted as June 7, 2005.

The ANSI_NULLS option determines how null values are compared. By default, this option is set to ON, in which case you can't compare a value to the NULL keyword using a comparison operator. In that case,

```
PaymentDate = NULL
```

is always Unknown rather than True or False, even if PaymentDate contains a null value. To determine if a column contains a null value, you must use the IS NULL or IS NOT NULL clause. If you set the ANSI_NULLS option to OFF, however, the expression shown above would return True if PaymentDate contains a null value, and it would return False otherwise. I recommend that you keep this option set to ON since that's the ANSI-standard approach to handling null values.

The SET ROWCOUNT statement limits the number of rows that are processed by subsequent queries. For a SELECT query, this works the same way as coding a TOP clause. However, since most other dialects of SQL don't support the TOP clause, you'll often see SET ROWCOUNT used in the code of other SQL programmers. Be aware, though, that this session setting affects all queries, including action queries and queries stored within views and stored procedures. Since this can cause unexpected results, I recommend that you avoid modifying this session setting and use the TOP clause instead.

Transact-SQL statements for changing session settings

Statement	Description
`SET DATEFORMAT format`	Sets the order of the parts of a date (month/day/year) for entering date/time data. The default is mdy, but any permutation of m, d, and y is valid.
`SET NOCOUNT {ON|OFF}`	Determines whether SQL Server returns a message indicating the number of rows that were affected by a statement. OFF is the default.
`SET ANSI_NULLS {ON|OFF}`	Determines how SQL Server handles equals (=) and not equals (<>) comparisons with null values. The default is ON, in which case "WHERE column = NULL" will always return an empty result set, even if there are null values in the column.
`SET ANSI_PADDING {ON|OFF}`	Determines how SQL Server stores char and varchar values that are smaller than the maximum size for a column or that contain trailing blanks. Only affects new column definitions. The default is ON, which causes char values to be padded with blanks. In addition, trailing blanks in varchar values are not trimmed. If this option is set to OFF, char values that don't allow nulls are padded with blanks, but blanks are trimmed from char values that allow nulls as well as from varchar values.
`SET ROWCOUNT number`	Limits the number of rows that are processed by a query. The default setting is 0, which causes all rows to be processed.

A statement that changes the date format

```
SET DATEFORMAT ymd
```

Description

- You use the SET statement to change configuration settings for the current session. These settings control the way queries and scripts execute.
- If the ANSI_NULLS option is set to ON, you can only test for null values in a column by using the IS NULL clause. See figure 3-15 in chapter 3 for details.
- Instead of using the SET ROWCOUNT statement to limit the numbers of rows that are processed by a query, you should use the TOP clause. See figure 3-9 in chapter 3 for details.
- For a complete list of the Transact-SQL statements for changing session settings, see the topic on the SET statement in Books Online.

Figure 13-11   How to change the session settings

How to use dynamic SQL

So far, the scripts you've seen in this chapter have contained predefined SQL statements. In other words, the statements don't change from one execution of the script to another other than for the values of variables used in the statements. However, you can also define an SQL statement as a script executes. Then, you use the EXEC statement shown in figure 13-12 to execute the *dynamic SQL*. Notice that EXEC is an abbreviation for EXECUTE.

The EXEC statement executes a string that contains an SQL statement. To illustrate, the first script in this figure executes a SELECT statement against a table that's specified at run time. To do that, it concatenates the literal string "SELECT * FROM " with the value of a variable named @TableNameVar. If you think about it, you'll realize that there's no other way to do this in SQL. Of course, it would have been easier to submit the simple query shown here directly rather than to use dynamic SQL. However, a more complex script might use an IF...ELSE statement to determine the table that's used in the query. In that case, dynamic SQL can make the script easier to code.

The second script in this figure is more complicated. It creates a table with columns that represent each vendor with outstanding invoices. That means that the number of columns in the new table will vary depending on the current values in the Invoices table.

This script starts by creating a variable named @DynamicSQL that will store the SQL string that's executed. Next, the new table to be created is deleted if it already exists. Then, a SET statement assigns the beginning of the SQL string to @DynamicSQL, which includes the CREATE TABLE statement, the name of the new table, and an opening parenthesis. The SELECT statement that follows concatenates the name of each column (the name of the current vendor) and data type to the SQL string. Finally, the second SET statement concatenates a closing parenthesis to the string, and the string is executed.

Notice that for each row retrieved by the SELECT statement, the variable @DynamicSQL is concatenated with its previous value. Although this syntax is valid for any query, it isn't useful except when generating dynamic SQL as shown here. Also notice that the name of each vendor is enclosed in brackets. That's because many of the vendors have spaces or other special characters in their names, which aren't allowed in column names unless they're delimited.

This figure also shows the SQL statement that's created by one execution of this script along with the contents of the table that's created. Although this table isn't useful the way it is, it could be used to cross-tabulate data based on the Vendors table. For example, each row of this table could represent a date and the Boolean value in each column could represent whether the vendor has an invoice that's due on that date. Since more than one vendor's invoice can be due on the same date, a cross-tabulation is a good representation of this data.

As you may have noticed, the SQL string that's generated by this script has an extra comma following the last column specification. Fortunately, the CREATE TABLE statement ignores this extra comma without generating an error. However, if you wanted to, you could eliminate this comma by using the LEFT function before concatenating the closing parenthesis.

The syntax of the EXEC statement

```
{EXEC|EXECUTE} ('SQL_string')
```

A script that uses an EXEC statement

```
USE AP
DECLARE @TableNameVar varchar(128)
SET @TableNameVar = 'Invoices'
EXEC ('SELECT * FROM ' + @TableNameVar)
```

The contents of the SQL string at execution

```
SELECT * FROM Invoices
```

A script that creates a table with one column for each vendor with a balance due

```
USE AP
DECLARE @DynamicSQL varchar(8000)

IF OBJECT_ID('XtabVendors') IS NOT NULL
    DROP TABLE XtabVendors

SET @DynamicSQL = 'CREATE TABLE XtabVendors ('
    SELECT @DynamicSQL = @DynamicSQL + '[' + VendorName + '] bit,'
    FROM Vendors
    WHERE VendorID IN
        (SELECT VendorID
        FROM Invoices
        WHERE InvoiceTotal - CreditTotal - PaymentTotal > 0)
    ORDER BY VendorName
SET @DynamicSQL = @DynamicSQL + ')'

EXEC (@DynamicSQL)

SELECT * FROM XtabVendors
```

The contents of the SQL string

```
CREATE TABLE XtabVendors ([Abbey Office Furnishings] bit,[Blue Cross]
bit,[Cardinal Business Media, Inc.] bit,[Coffee Break Service]
bit,[Compuserve] bit,[Computerworld] bit,[Data Reproductions Corp]
bit,[Federal Express Corporation] bit,[Ford Motor Credit Company]
bit,[Ingram] bit,[Malloy Lithographing Inc] bit,[Pacific Bell] bit,[Roadway
Package System, Inc] bit,[United Parcel Service] bit,[Wells Fargo Bank]
bit,[Zylka Design] bit,)
```

The result set

Abbey Office Furnishings	Blue Cross	Cardinal Business Media, Inc.	Coffee Break Service	Compuserve

Description

- The EXEC statement executes the SQL statement contained in a string. Because you define the SQL string within the script, you can create and execute SQL code that changes each time the script is run. This is called *dynamic SQL*.

- You can use dynamic SQL to perform operations that can't be accomplished using any other technique.

Figure 13-12   How to use dynamic SQL

A script that summarizes the structure of a database

Figure 13-13 presents a script that you can use to summarize the structure of a database. This script illustrates many of the techniques you learned in this chapter. It also shows how you might use some of the information schema views you learned about in the last chapter.

This script starts by dropping the temporary table named #TableSummary if it already exists. Then, it recreates this table using a SELECT INTO statement and data from the information schema view named COLUMNS. This view provides basic information about the columns in the current database, including the name of the table that contains the column, the name of the column, and the data type of the column. Notice that the WHERE clause only includes tables of type BASE TABLE in the information schema view named TABLES, which eliminates views from the list. In addition, it excludes three tables by name, including the two temporary tables created by this script and the system table named dtproperties.

Next, this script drops and recreates another temporary table named #AllUserTables. This table will be used to generate the row count for each table. It has two columns: an identity column and a column for the table name. The INSERT statement that follows populates this table with the same list of table names that was inserted into the #TableSummary table.

A script that creates a summary of the tables in a database   **Page 1**

```
/*
Creates and queries a table, #TableSummary, that lists
the columns for each user table in the database, plus
the number of rows in each table.

Author:    Bryan Syverson
Created:   2002-07-02
Modified:  2002-07-16
*/

USE AP

IF OBJECT_ID('tempdb..#TableSummary') IS NOT NULL
    DROP TABLE #TableSummary

SELECT TABLE_NAME AS TableName, COLUMN_NAME AS ColumnName,
    DATA_TYPE AS Type
INTO #TableSummary
FROM INFORMATION_SCHEMA.COLUMNS
WHERE TABLE_NAME IN
    (SELECT TABLE_NAME
    FROM INFORMATION_SCHEMA.TABLES
    WHERE (TABLE_TYPE = 'BASE TABLE' AND
      TABLE_NAME NOT IN ('dtproperties', 'TableSummary', 'AllUserTables')))

IF OBJECT_ID('tempdb..#AllUserTables') IS NOT NULL
    DROP TABLE #AllUserTables

CREATE TABLE #AllUserTables
(TableID int IDENTITY, TableName varchar(128))
GO

INSERT #AllUserTables (TableName)
SELECT TABLE_NAME
FROM INFORMATION_SCHEMA.TABLES
WHERE (TABLE_TYPE = 'BASE TABLE' AND
    TABLE_NAME NOT IN ('dtproperties', 'TableSummary', 'AllUserTables'))
```

Description

- A SELECT INTO statement is used to retrieve information from the information schema view named COLUMNS and store it in a temporary table named #TableSummary. This table has one row for each column in each table of the database that includes the table name, column name, and data type.

- A CREATE TABLE statement is used to create a temporary table named #AllUserTables. Then, an INSERT statement is used to insert rows into this table that contain the name of each table in the database. This information is retrieved from the information schema view named TABLES. Each row also contains a sequence number that's generated by SQL Server.

- Both tables include information only about base tables. In addition, the system table named dtproperties and the two temporary tables themselves are omitted.

Figure 13-13   A script that summarizes the structure of a database (part 1 of 2)

Part 2 of this script includes a WHILE loop that uses dynamic SQL to insert an additional row into #TableSummary for each table in #AllUserTables. Each of these rows indicates the total number of rows in one of the base tables. The @LoopMax variable used by this loop is set to the maximum value of the TableID column in #AllUserTables. The @LoopVar variable is set to 1, which is the minimum value of TableID. The WHILE loop uses @LoopVar to step through the rows of #AllUserTables.

Within the loop, the SELECT statement sets @TableNameVar to the value of the TableName column for the current table. Then, @ExecVar is built by concatenating each of the clauses of the final SQL string. This string consists of three statements. The DECLARE statement is used to create a variable named @CountVar that will store the number of rows in the current table. Note that because this variable is created within the dynamic SQL statement, its scope is limited to the EXEC statement. In other words, it isn't available to the portion of the script outside of the EXEC statement.

The SELECT statement within the dynamic SQL statement retrieves the row count from the current table and stores it in the @CountVar variable. Then, the INSERT statement inserts a row into the #TableSummary table that includes the table name, a literal value that indicates that the row contains the row count, and the number of rows in the table. You can see the contents of the SQL string that's created for one table, the ContactUpdates table, in this figure.

After the SQL string is created, it's executed using an EXEC statement. Then, @LoopVar is increased by 1 and the loop is executed again. When the loop completes, the script executes a SELECT statement that retrieves the data from the #TableSummary table. That result set is also shown in this figure.

A script that creates a summary of the tables in a database   Page 2

```
DECLARE @LoopMax int, @LoopVar int
DECLARE @TableNameVar varchar(128), @ExecVar varchar(1000)

SELECT @LoopMax = MAX(TableID) FROM #AllUserTables

SET @LoopVar = 1

WHILE @LoopVar <= @LoopMax
    BEGIN
        SELECT @TableNameVar = TableName
            FROM #AllUserTables
            WHERE TableID = @LoopVar
        SET @ExecVar = 'DECLARE @CountVar int '
        SET @ExecVar = @ExecVar + 'SELECT @CountVar = COUNT(*) '
        SET @ExecVar = @ExecVar + 'FROM ' + @TableNameVar + ' '
        SET @ExecVar = @ExecVar + 'INSERT #TableSummary '
        SET @ExecVar = @ExecVar + 'VALUES (''' + @TableNameVar + ''','
        SET @ExecVar = @ExecVar + '''*Row Count*'','
        SET @ExecVar = @ExecVar + ' @CountVar)'
        EXEC (@ExecVar)
        SET @LoopVar = @LoopVar + 1
    END

SELECT * FROM #TableSummary
ORDER BY TableName, ColumnName
```

The contents of the SQL string for one iteration of the loop

```
DECLARE @CountVar int SELECT @CountVar = COUNT(*) FROM ContactUpdates
INSERT #TableSummary VALUES ('ContactUpdates','*Row Count*', @CountVar)
```

The result set

	TableName	ColumnName	Type
19	InvoiceLineItems	*Row Count*	118
20	InvoiceLineItems	AccountNo	int
21	InvoiceLineItems	InvoiceID	int
22	InvoiceLineItems	InvoiceLineItemAmount	money
23	InvoiceLineItems	InvoiceLineItemDescription	varchar
24	InvoiceLineItems	InvoiceSequence	smallint
25	Invoices	*Row Count*	114
26	Invoices	CreditTotal	money

Description

- The WHILE statement loops through the tables in the #AllUserTables table. For each table, it creates a dynamic SQL string that contains a SELECT statement and an INSERT statement. The SELECT statement retrieves the number of rows in the table, and the INSERT statement inserts a new row into the #TableSummary table that indicates the number of rows.

- The final SELECT statement retrieves all of the rows and columns from the #TableSummary table sorted by column name within table name.

Figure 13-13   A script that summarizes the structure of a database (part 2 of 2)

How to use OSQL

Unlike the Query Analyzer you've used throughout this book, *OSQL* lets you enter and execute scripts from a command line. This utility is often used by system administrators to execute scripts that are run infrequently or those that take a long time to run. Unless you're already comfortable working with the command prompt, DOS batch files, or Windows script files, however, you probably won't use OSQL.

Figure 13-14 presents an example of a Command Prompt window running an OSQL session. To open a session, you enter OSQL at the command prompt, followed by the appropriate command line switches. If you connect to SQL Server using Windows authentication, the only command line switch you need is -E as shown in this figure. If you connect using SQL Server authentication, though, you'll need to enter switches for the user name and password like this:

```
OSQL -U sa -P topsecret
```

You can also omit the password switch and SQL Server will prompt you for your password so it's not displayed on the screen. If you connect to a server other than the default, you'll also need to include the -S switch along with the name of the server.

Once you're connected, you can type one SQL statement per line as shown. Then, to execute the statements you've entered, you enter a GO command. When you're done, you can close the OSQL session by entering the Exit command. Then, you're returned to the command prompt.

You can also execute a script that's stored in a file on disk. To do that, you use the -i switch. To save the response from the server to a file, you use the -o switch. For example, this command would execute the script contained in a file named sql_test.sql and save the result set in a file named sql_out.txt:

```
osql -E -i sql_test.sql -o sql_out.txt
```

Note that the response also includes any result sets that are created.

A Command Prompt window running OSQL

```
Command Prompt                                                    _ □ X
Microsoft Windows 2000 [Version 5.00.2195]
(C) Copyright 1985-2000 Microsoft Corp.

C:\>osql -E
1> use ap
2> go
1> select invoicedate, invoicetotal from invoices where vendorid = 122
2> go
 invoicedate          invoicetotal
 -------------------- --------------------
 2001-06-10 00:00:00           2312.2000
 2001-06-11 00:00:00           1927.5400
 2001-06-12 00:00:00           2184.1100
 2001-06-17 00:00:00           2318.0300
 2001-06-17 00:00:00           3813.3300
 2001-06-17 00:00:00           3689.9900
 2001-06-17 00:00:00           2765.3600
 2001-06-18 00:00:00           2115.8100
 2001-06-19 00:00:00           2051.5900

(9 rows affected)
1> exit

C:\>exit
```

Command line switches

Switch	Function
-?	Show a summary of all command line switches.
-E	Use a trusted connection (Windows authentication mode).
-L	List the names of the available servers.
-S server_name	Log in to a specific server.
-U user_name	Log in as a specific user (SQL Server authentication mode).
-P password	Specify the password in the command line (SQL Server authentication mode).
-Q "query"	Execute the specified query, then exit.
-i file_name	Specify the name of the script file to be executed.
-o file_name	Specify an output file in which to save responses from the system.

Description

- *OSQL* is a utility that runs T-SQL scripts from a command line. This is useful for users and administrators who prefer to use a command line interface.
- To open a command prompt window where you can start OSQL, select Start→Programs→Accessories→Command Prompt. When you're done, enter "exit".
- To start an OSQL session, enter the OSQL command at the C:\> prompt along with the appropriate command line switches. Then, enter the statements you want to execute followed by the GO command, or use one of the command line switches shown above. To exit from OSQL, enter the Exit command.

Figure 13-14   How to use OSQL

Perspective

In this chapter, you've learned how to code procedural scripts in T-SQL. By using the techniques you've learned here, you'll be able to code scripts that are more general, more useful, and less susceptible to failure. In particular, when you use dynamic SQL, you'll be able to solve problems that can't be solved using any other technique.

In the next chapter, you'll expand on what you've learned here by learning how to code stored procedures, functions, and triggers. These objects are basically one-batch scripts that are stored with the database. But they provide special functionality that gives you greater control over a database, who has access to it, and how they can modify it.

Terms

script	table variable	WHILE loop
batch	temporary table	system function
T-SQL statement	local temporary table	global variable
variable	global temporary table	dynamic SQL
scalar variable	scope	OSQL
local variable	nested IF...ELSE statements	ISQL

14

How to code stored procedures, functions, and triggers

Now that you've learned how to work with scripts, you know that procedural statements can help you manage a database and automate tasks. In this chapter, you'll learn how to extend this functionality by creating database objects that store program code within a database for execution by anyone using the database. The three types of programs discussed in this chapter provide a powerful and flexible way to control how a database is used.

Procedural programming options in Transact-SQL

Figure 14-1 presents the four types of procedural programs you can code using Transact-SQL. Each program type contains SQL statements. However, they differ by how they're stored and executed.

Scripts

Of the four types of procedural programs, only scripts can contain two or more batches. That's because only scripts can be executed by SQL Server tools such as the Query Analyzer and OSQL. In addition, only scripts are stored in files outside of the database. For these reasons, scripts tend to be used most often by SQL Server programmers and database administrators.

Stored procedures, user-defined functions, and triggers

The other three types of procedural programs—*stored procedures*, *user-defined functions*, and *triggers*—are executable database objects. This means that each is stored within the database. To create these objects, you use the DDL statements you'll learn about in this chapter. Then, these objects remain as a part of the database until they're explicitly dropped.

Stored procedures, user-defined functions, and triggers differ by how they're executed. Stored procedures and user-defined functions can be run from any database connection that can run a SQL statement. In contrast, triggers run automatically in response to the execution of an action query on a specific table.

Stored procedures are frequently written by SQL programmers for use by end users or application programmers. If you code stored procedures in this way, you can simplify the way these users interact with a database. In addition, you can provide access to a database exclusively through stored procedures. This gives you tight control over the security of the data.

Both user-defined functions and triggers are used more often by SQL programmers than by application programmers or end users. SQL programmers often use their own functions within the scripts, stored procedures, and triggers they write. Since triggers run in response to an action query, programmers use them to help prevent errors caused by inconsistent or invalid data.

Stored procedures, functions, and triggers also differ by whether or not they can use parameters. *Parameters* are values that can be passed to or returned from a procedure. Both stored procedures and user-defined functions can use parameters, but triggers can't.

A comparison of the different types of procedural SQL programs

Type	Batches	How it's stored	How it's executed	Accepts parameters
Script	Multiple	In a file on a disk	From within a client tool such as the Query Analyzer or OSQL	No
Stored procedure	One only	In an object in the database	By an application or within a SQL script	Yes
User-defined function	One only	In an object in the database	By an application or within a SQL script	Yes
Trigger	One only	In an object in the database	Automatically by the server when a specific action query occurs	No

Description

- You can write procedural programs with Transact-SQL using scripts, stored procedures, user-defined functions, and triggers.

- Scripts are useful for those users with access to the SQL Server client tools, such as the Query Analyzer. Typically, these tools are used by SQL programmers and DBAs, not by application programmers or end users.

- Stored procedures, user-defined functions, and triggers are all executable database objects that contain SQL statements. Although they differ in how they're executed and by the kinds of values they can return, they all provide greater control and better performance than a script.

- *Stored procedures* give the SQL programmer control over who accesses the database and how. Since application programmers and end users generally don't have the expertise to write their own SQL queries, stored procedures can simplify their use of the database.

- *User-defined functions* are most often used by SQL programmers within the stored procedures and triggers that they write, although they can also be used by application programmers and end users.

- *Triggers* are special procedures that execute when an action query, such as INSERT, UPDATE, or DELETE statement, is executed. Like constraints, you can use triggers to prevent database errors, but triggers give you greater control and flexibility.

- Since procedures, functions, and triggers are database objects, the SQL statements you use to create, delete, and modify them are considered part of the DDL.

Figure 14-1   Procedural programming options in Transact-SQL

How to code stored procedures

A *stored procedure* is a database object that contains one or more SQL statements. In the topics that follow, you'll learn how to create and use stored procedures. In addition, you'll learn how to use some of the stored procedures provided by SQL Server.

An introduction to stored procedures

Figure 14-2 presents a script that creates a stored procedure, also called an *sproc* or just a *procedure*. To do that, you use the CREATE PROC statement. You'll learn the details of coding this statement in a moment.

The first time a procedure is executed, each SQL statement it contains is compiled and executed to create an *execution plan*. Then, the procedure is stored in compiled form within the database. For each subsequent execution, the SQL statements are executed without compilation, because they're *precompiled*. This makes the execution of a stored procedure faster than the execution of an equivalent SQL script.

To execute, or *call*, a stored procedure, you use the EXEC statement. If the EXEC statement is the first line in a batch, you can omit the EXEC keyword and just code the procedure name. Since this can lead to code that's confusing to read, however, I recommend that you include the EXEC keyword.

The script in this figure creates a stored procedure named spInvoiceReport. This procedure consists of a single statement: a SELECT statement that retrieves data from the Vendors and Invoices tables. As you'll see in the topics that follow, however, a stored procedure can contain more than one statement, along with the same procedural code used in scripts.

When you execute the script in this figure, you create the stored procedure. The response from the system shows that the procedure was created successfully. Then, when you execute the stored procedure, the result set retrieved by the SELECT statement is returned.

As you can see, a user or program that calls this procedure doesn't need to know the structure of the database to use the stored procedure. This simplifies the use of the database by eliminating the need to know SQL and the need to understand the structure of the database.

As you'll learn in chapter 17, you can allow a user or program to call specific stored procedures but not to execute other SQL statements. By doing this, you can secure your database by restricting access to only those rows, columns, and tables that you provide access to through the stored procedures. For those systems where security is critical, this can be the best way to secure the data.

A script that creates a stored procedure

```
USE AP
GO
CREATE PROC spInvoiceReport
AS

SELECT VendorName, InvoiceNumber, InvoiceDate, InvoiceTotal
FROM Invoices JOIN Vendors
    ON Invoices.VendorID = Vendors.VendorID
WHERE InvoiceTotal - CreditTotal - PaymentTotal > 0
```

The response from the system

```
The command(s) completed successfully.
```

A statement that calls the procedure

```
EXEC spInvoiceReport
```

The result set created by the procedure

	VendorName	InvoiceNumber	InvoiceDate	InvoiceTotal
1	Abbey Office Furnishings	203339-13	2002-05-02 00:00:00	17.5000
2	Blue Cross	547479217	2002-05-17 00:00:00	116.0000
3	Blue Cross	547480102	2002-05-19 00:00:00	224.0000
4	Blue Cross	547481328	2002-05-20 00:00:00	224.0000
5	Cardinal Business Media, Inc.	134116	2002-06-01 00:00:00	90.3600

Description

- A stored procedure is an executable database object that contains SQL statements. A stored procedure is also called a *sproc* (pronounced either as one word or as "ess-proc") or, simply a *procedure*.

- Stored procedures are *precompiled*. That means that the *execution plan* for the SQL code is compiled the first time the procedure is executed and is then saved in its compiled form. For this reason, stored procedures execute faster than an equivalent SQL script.

- You use the EXEC statement to run, or *call*, a procedure. If this statement is the first line in a batch, you can omit the EXEC keyword and code just the procedure name. To make your code easier to read, however, you should always include the EXEC keyword.

- You can call a stored procedure from within another stored procedure. You can even call a stored procedure from within itself. This technique, called a *recursive call* or *recursion*, is seldom used in SQL programming.

- One of the advantages of using procedures is that application programmers and end users don't need to know the structure of the database or how to code SQL.

- Another advantage of using procedures is that they can restrict and control access to a database. If you use procedures in this way, you can prevent both accidental errors and malicious damage.

Figure 14-2   An introduction to stored procedures

How to create a stored procedure

Figure 14-3 presents the syntax of the CREATE PROC statement you use to create a stored procedure. You code the name of the procedure in the CREATE PROC clause. Note that stored procedure names can't be the same as the name of any other object in the database. To help distinguish a stored procedure from other database objects, it's a good practice to prefix its name with the letters *sp*.

When the CREATE PROC statement is executed, the syntax of the SQL statements within the procedure is checked. If you've made a coding error, the system responds with an appropriate message and the procedure isn't created.

Because the stored procedure is created in the current database, you need to change the database context by coding a USE statement before the CREATE PROC statement. In addition, CREATE PROC must be the first and only statement in the batch. Since the script in this figure creates the procedure after a USE and DROP PROC statement, for example, it has a GO command just before the CREATE PROC statement.

In addition to stored procedures that are stored in the current database, you can create *temporary stored procedures* that are stored in the tempdb database. These procedures exist only while the current database session is open, so they aren't used often. To identify a temporary stored procedure, prefix the name with one number sign (#) for a *local procedure* and two number signs (##) for a *global procedure*.

After the name of the procedure, you code declarations for any parameters it uses. You'll learn more about that in the figures that follow.

You can also code the optional WITH clause with either the RECOMPILE option, the ENCRYPTION option, or both options. The WITH RECOMPILE option prevents the system from precompiling the procedure. That means that the execution plan for the procedure must be compiled each time it's executed, which will slow down most procedures. For this reason, you should generally omit this option.

Some procedures, however, might make use of unusual or atypical values. If so, the first compilation may result in an execution plan that isn't efficient for subsequent executions. In that case, the additional overhead involved in recompiling the procedure may be offset by the reduced query execution time. If you find that a stored procedure you've written performs erratically, you may want to try this option.

WITH ENCRYPTION is a security option that prevents the user from being able to view the declaration of a stored procedure. Since the system stores the procedure as an object in the database, it also stores the code for the procedure. If this code contains information that you don't want the user to examine, you should use this option.

The syntax of the CREATE PROC statement

```
CREATE {PROC|PROCEDURE} procedure_name
[parameter_declarations]
[WITH {RECOMPILE|ENCRYPTION|RECOMPILE,ENCRYPTION}]
AS sql_statements
```

A script that creates a stored procedure that copies a table

```
USE AP
IF OBJECT_ID('spCopyInvoices') IS NOT NULL
    DROP PROC spCopyInvoices
GO

CREATE PROC spCopyInvoices
AS
    IF OBJECT_ID('InvoiceCopy') IS NOT NULL
        DROP TABLE InvoiceCopy
    SELECT *
    INTO InvoiceCopy
    FROM Invoices
```

Description

- You use the CREATE PROC statement to create a stored procedure in the current database. The name of a stored procedure can be up to 128 characters and is typically prefixed with the letters *sp*.

- The CREATE PROC statement must be the first and only statement in a batch. If you're creating the procedure within a script, then, you must code a GO command just before the CREATE PROC statement.

- To create a *temporary stored procedure*, prefix the procedure name with a number sign (#) for a *local procedure* or two number signs (##) for a *global procedure*. A temporary stored procedure only exists while the current database session is open.

- You can use *parameters* to pass one or more values from the calling program to the stored procedure or from the procedure to the calling program. See figures 14-4 and 14-5 for more information on working with parameters.

- The AS clause contains the SQL statements to be executed by the stored procedure. Since a stored procedure must consist of a single batch, a GO command is interpreted as the end of the CREATE PROC statement.

- The WITH RECOMPILE clause prevents the system from precompiling the procedure, which means that it has to be compiled each time it's run. Since that reduces system performance, you don't typically use this option.

- The WITH ENCRYPTION clause prevents users from viewing the code in a stored procedure. See figure 14-10 for more information on viewing stored procedures.

Figure 14-3   How to create a stored procedure

How to declare and work with parameters

Figure 14-4 presents the syntax for declaring parameters in a CREATE PROC statement. Like a local variable, the name of a parameter must begin with an at sign (@). The data type for a parameter can be any valid SQL Server data type except for the table data type.

Stored procedures provide for two different types of parameters: input parameters and output parameters. An *input parameter* is passed to the stored procedure from the calling program. An *output parameter* is returned to the calling program from the stored procedure. You identify an output parameter with the OUTPUT keyword. If this keyword is omitted, the parameter is assumed to be an input parameter.

You can declare an input parameter so that it requires a value or so that its value is optional. The value of a *required parameter* must be passed to the stored procedure from the calling program or an error occurs. The value of an *optional parameter* doesn't need to be passed from the calling program. You identify an optional parameter by assigning a default value to it. Then, if a value isn't passed from the calling program, the default value is used. Although you can also code a default value for an output parameter, there's usually no reason for doing that.

You can also use output parameters as input parameters. That is, you can pass a value from the calling program to the stored procedure through an output parameter. However, that's an unusual way to use output parameters. To avoid confusion, you should use output parameters strictly for output.

Within the procedure, you use parameters like variables. Although you can change the value of an input parameter within the procedure, that change isn't returned to the calling program and has no effect on it. Instead, when the procedure ends, the values of any output parameters are returned to the calling program.

The syntax for declaring parameters

```
@parameter_name_1 data_type [= default] [OUTPUT]
[, @parameter_name_2 data_type [= default] [OUTPUT]]...
```

Typical parameter declarations

```
@DateVar smalldatetime              -- Input parameter that accepts
                                    -- a date/time value

@VendorVar varchar(40) = NULL       -- Optional input parameter that accepts
                                    -- a character value

@InvTotal money OUTPUT              -- Output parameter that returns
                                    -- a monetary value
```

A CREATE PROC statement that uses an input and an output parameter

```
CREATE PROC spInvTotal1
        @DateVar smalldatetime,
        @InvTotal money OUTPUT
AS
SELECT @InvTotal = SUM(InvoiceTotal)
FROM Invoices
WHERE InvoiceDate >= @DateVar
```

A CREATE PROC statement that uses an optional parameter

```
CREATE PROC spInvTotal2
        @DateVar smalldatetime = NULL
AS
IF @DateVar IS NULL
    SELECT @DateVar = MIN(InvoiceDate) FROM Invoices
SELECT SUM(InvoiceTotal)
FROM Invoices
WHERE InvoiceDate >= @DateVar
```

Description

- To declare a parameter within a stored procedure, you code the name of the parameter followed by its data type. The parameter name must start with an at sign (@), and the data type can be any type except table. Parameters are always local to the procedure.

- *Input parameters* accept values passed from the calling program.

- *Output parameters* store values that are passed back to the calling program. You identify an output parameter by coding the OUTPUT keyword after the parameter name and data type.

- *Optional parameters* are parameters that do not require that a value be passed from the calling program. To declare an optional parameter, you assign it a default value. Then, that value is used if one isn't passed from the calling program.

- A stored procedure can declare up to 2100 parameters. If you declare two or more parameters, the declarations must be separated by commas.

- It's a good programming practice to code your CREATE PROC statements so that they list required parameters first, followed by optional parameters.

Figure 14-4   How to declare and work with parameters

How to call procedures with parameters

Figure 14-5 shows how you call procedures that use parameters. The stored procedure in this figure accepts two input parameters and one output parameter. As you can see, both of the input parameters are optional because each has a default value.

To pass parameter values to a stored procedure, you code the values in the EXEC statement after the procedure name. You can pass parameters to a stored procedure either by position or by name. The first EXEC statement in this figure passes the parameters *by position*. When you use this technique, you don't include the names of the parameters. Instead, the parameters are listed in the same order as they appear in the CREATE PROC statement. This is the most common way to call stored procedures that have a short list of parameters.

The second EXEC statement shows how you can pass the parameters *by name*. To do that, you include the names of the parameters as defined in the CREATE PROC statement. When you use this technique, you can list parameters in any order. If the procedure has many parameters, particularly if some of them are optional, passing parameters by name is usually easier than passing parameters by position.

The third EXEC statement in this figure shows how you can omit an optional parameter when you pass the parameters by name. To do that, you simply omit the optional parameter. In contrast, when you pass parameters by position, you can omit them only if they appear after the required parameters. This is illustrated by the last EXEC statement in this figure.

Notice that in all four of these examples, the EXEC statement is preceded by a DECLARE statement that creates a variable named @MyInvTotal. This variable is used to store the value of the output parameter that's returned from the stored procedure. As you can see, the name of this variable is included in each of the EXEC statements in this figure. In addition, the variable name is followed by the OUTPUT keyword, which identifies it as an output parameter.

A CREATE PROC statement that includes three parameters

```
CREATE PROC spInvTotal3
        @InvTotal money OUTPUT,
        @DateVar smalldatetime = NULL,
        @VendorVar varchar(40) = '%'
AS

IF @DateVar IS NULL
    SELECT @DateVar = MIN(InvoiceDate) FROM Invoices

SELECT @InvTotal = SUM(InvoiceTotal)
FROM Invoices JOIN Vendors
    ON Invoices.VendorID = Vendors.VendorID
WHERE (InvoiceDate >= @DateVar) AND
        (VendorName LIKE @VendorVar)
```

Code that passes the parameters by position

```
DECLARE @MyInvTotal money
EXEC spInvTotal3 @MyInvTotal OUTPUT, '2002-06-01', 'P%'
```

Code that passes the parameters by name

```
DECLARE @MyInvTotal money
EXEC spInvTotal3 @DateVar = '2002-06-01', @VendorVar = 'P%',
    @InvTotal = @MyInvTotal OUTPUT
```

Code that omits one optional parameter

```
DECLARE @MyInvTotal money
EXEC spInvTotal3 @VendorVar = 'M%', @InvTotal = @MyInvTotal OUTPUT
```

Code that omits both optional parameters

```
DECLARE @MyInvTotal money
EXEC spInvTotal3 @MyInvTotal OUTPUT
```

Description

- To call a procedure that accepts parameters, you pass values to the procedure by coding them following the procedure name. You can pass the parameters by position or by name.

- To pass parameters *by position*, list them in the same order as they appear in the CREATE PROC statement and separate them with commas. When you use this technique, you can omit optional parameters only if they're declared after any required parameters.

- To pass parameters *by name*, code the name of the parameter followed by an equal sign and the value. You can separate multiple parameters with commas. When you use this technique, you can list the parameters in any order and you can easily omit optional parameters.

- To use an output parameter in the calling program, you must declare a variable to store its value. Then, you use the name of that variable in the EXEC statement, and you code the OUTPUT keyword after it to identify it as an output parameter.

Figure 14-5   How to call procedures with parameters

How to handle runtime errors

In addition to passing output parameters back to the calling program, stored procedures also pass back a *return value*. By default, this value is zero. If an error occurs during the execution of a stored procedure, however, you may want to pass a value back to the calling program that indicates the error that occurred. To do that, you use the RETURN statement and the @@ERROR function presented in figure 14-6.

The @@ERROR system function returns the error number that's generated by the execution of the most recent SQL statement. If the value is zero, it means that no error occurred. The stored procedure in this figure uses this function to test whether an INSERT statement that inserts a row into the Invoices table is successful. If it isn't, it tests the error number for a value of 547, which indicates that the foreign key for the Vendors table doesn't exist. Then, it prints an appropriate error message and issues a RETURN statement to return the error number to the calling program and terminate the procedure.

The script that calls the procedure uses a variable to store the return value. To do that, the name of the variable is coded in the EXEC statement, followed by an equals sign and the name of the stored procedure. After the procedure returns control to the script, the script uses a PRINT statement to print the return value.

In this case, the script attempts to insert a row into the Invoices table with VendorID 799. Since this VendorID doesn't exist in the Vendors table, the insertion causes an error. Notice in the system response shown here that the error message generated by SQL Server is displayed first, followed by the error that's printed by the procedure, followed by the return code that's printed by the calling script.

Before I go on, you should realize that you can also use the RETURN statement to pass an output value back to the calling program. I recommend you don't do that, however, because it can lead to confusing code and inconsistent procedure calls. Instead, you should only use the RETURN statement to pass return values back to the calling program.

If you've worked with procedural programming languages like Visual Basic or C++, you're probably familiar with the concept of error handling. When you write your code, you include routines for trapping system errors so that the user doesn't see the system error code. Instead, your code handles the error and, if the user needs to be notified, it displays a customized error message.

Unfortunately, Transact-SQL doesn't have a mechanism for handling errors in this way. Since the value of @@ERROR isn't set until after the statement has caused the error, a stored procedure can't trap an error before it occurs. However, you can use two other techniques to handle errors. In the next figure, you'll learn how you can validate data from a stored procedure to prevent errors from occurring. And, later in this chapter, you'll learn how to do similar processing using triggers. For most other errors, however, SQL's error handling capabilities are insufficient. For this reason, error handling must be done by the application program.

The syntax of the RETURN statement for a stored procedure

```
RETURN [integer_expression]
```

A stored procedure that uses the @@ERROR system function

```
CREATE PROC spInsertInvoice
        @VendorID    int,              @InvoiceNumber  varchar(50),
        @InvoiceDate smalldatetime, @InvoiceTotal   money,
        @TermsID     int,              @InvoiceDueDate smalldatetime
AS
DECLARE @ErrorVar int
INSERT Invoices
VALUES (@VendorID,      @InvoiceNumber,
        @InvoiceDate, @InvoiceTotal, 0, 0,
        @TermsID,       @InvoiceDueDate, NULL)
SET @ErrorVar = @@ERROR
IF @ErrorVar <> 0
    BEGIN
        IF @ErrorVar = 547
            PRINT 'Not a valid VendorID!'
        ELSE
            PRINT 'An unknown error occurred.'
        RETURN @ErrorVar
    END
```

A script that calls the stored procedure

```
DECLARE @ReturnVar int
EXEC @ReturnVar = spInsertInvoice
     799,'ZXK-799','2002-07-01',299.95,1,'2001-08-01'
PRINT 'Return code was: ' + CONVERT(varchar,@ReturnVar)
```

The response from the system

```
Server: Msg 547, Level 16, State 1, Procedure spInsertInvoice, Line 7
INSERT statement conflicted with COLUMN FOREIGN KEY constraint
'FK_Invoices_Vendors'. The conflict occurred in database 'AP', table 'Vendors',
column 'VendorID'.
The statement has been terminated.
Not a valid VendorID!
Return code was: 547
```

Description

- The RETURN statement immediately exits the procedure and returns an optional integer value to the calling program. If you don't specify a value in this statement, the *return value* is zero. When an error occurs, you'll typically return a non-zero value that can be used by the calling program to respond to that error.

- You can use the @@ERROR system function to get the error number of the last T-SQL statement that was executed. A value of zero indicates that no error occurred.

- To use the return value in the calling program, you must declare a variable to store its value. Then, you code that variable name followed by an equals sign and the name of the procedure in the EXEC statement.

Figure 14-6   How to handle runtime errors

How to validate data within a stored procedure

Figure 14-7 presents the syntax of the RAISERROR statement. You use this statement to manually set an error condition. This statement lets you raise a system error by coding the system error number for the message_id argument or raise a custom error by coding the error message you want to display for the message_string argument.

In addition to the message_id or message_string argument, you must code the severity and state arguments. The state code is strictly informational and has no system meaning. You can use any value between 1 and 127 to represent the state that the system was in when the error was raised. In most cases, you'll just code 1 for this argument.

The severity argument indicates how severe the error is. If you code a severity level between 1 and 10, for example, SQL Server considers the error to be informational. Although each number in this range is meant to imply a different level of severity, the action taken by the server is the same for each: no response. If you raise a system error with a severity level between 11 and 19, the error number is stored in the @@ERROR system function. And, if you code a severity level between 20 and 25, SQL Server considers the error as fatal. In that case, the client connection is terminated immediately. Like the state argument, you'll usually just code 1 for this argument.

The stored procedure in this figure is similar to the one shown in figure 14-6. However, the version in this figure checks the VendorID that's passed from the calling program before it performs the insert operation. That way, the foreign key error you saw in the previous procedure will never occur. Instead, if the VendorID value is invalid, the RAISERROR and RETURN statements provide information that can be interpreted by the calling script.

The process of checking data before it's used in an insert, update, or delete operation can be referred to as *data validation*. Most application programs validate the data entered by users before it's ever sent to your database. However, the application programmer may not know the structure and validation rules for a database as well as you do. For this reason, you should validate the data passed to the stored procedures you create whenever possible.

The syntax of the RAISERROR statement

```
RAISERROR ({message_id|message_string}, severity, state [, argument]...)
```

A stored procedure that tests for a valid foreign key

```
CREATE PROC spInsertInvoice
        @VendorID    int,              @InvoiceNumber  varchar(50),
        @InvoiceDate smalldatetime, @InvoiceTotal    money,
        @TermsID     int,              @InvoiceDueDate smalldatetime
AS

IF EXISTS(SELECT * FROM Vendors WHERE VendorID = @VendorID)
    BEGIN
        INSERT Invoices
        VALUES (@VendorID,@InvoiceNumber,
                @InvoiceDate,@InvoiceTotal,0,0,
                @TermsID,@InvoiceDueDate,NULL)
    END
ELSE
    BEGIN
        RAISERROR('Not a valid VendorID!',1,1)
        RETURN -100
    END
```

A script that calls the procedure

```
DECLARE @ReturnVar int
EXEC @ReturnVar = spInsertInvoice
    799,'ZXK-799','2002-07-01',299.95,1,'2001-08-01'
PRINT 'Return code was: ' + CONVERT(varchar,@ReturnVar)
```

The response from the system

```
Msg 50000, Level 1, State 50000
Not a valid VendorID!
Return code was: -100
```

Description

- The RAISERROR statement manually sets an error condition. Although you can use it to raise a system error by coding the error number in the message_id argument, you'll typically code a custom error message in the message_string argument.

- You can use special formatting characters to include argument values in the message_string argument. Refer to Books Online for the complete syntax of this argument.

- You use the severity and state arguments to identify how serious an error is. For the usage shown here, you can always code 1 for each of these arguments. However, SQL Server specifies ranges of severity, the most severe of which will close the client connection. For more information, see Books Online.

- The process of checking the values in one or more columns is known as *data validation*. Although data validation is frequently performed by application programs that work with the database, it's a good practice to validate the data within a procedure as well.

Figure 14-7   How to validate data within a stored procedure

A stored procedure that manages insert operations

Figure 14-8 presents a stored procedure that might be used by an application program that inserts new invoices into the Invoices table. This should give you a better idea of how you can use stored procedures.

This procedure starts with a comment that documents the stored procedure. This documentation includes the author's name, the date the procedure was created, the date it was last modified, and a general description of the procedure's purpose. Since this procedure returns error codes for specific errors, these are listed in the comments too. Of course, you can include any other information that you feel is useful.

This procedure uses ten parameters that correspond to the ten columns in the Invoices table. The first nine parameters are optional input parameters. The tenth parameter is an output parameter that passes the InvoiceID for the newly inserted row back to the calling program.

Notice that each of the input parameters is assigned the same data type as the matching column in the Invoices table. This means that if the calling program passes a value that can't be cast into the proper data type, an error will be raised as the procedure is called. In other words, this type of error won't be trapped by the procedure.

If the calling program was to pass a value of 13-15-89 to the @InvoiceDate parameter, for example, an error would occur because this value can't be cast as a date. To handle this type of error within the procedure, you could define each parameter with the varchar data type. Then, the procedure could test for invalid data types and return appropriate error codes when necessary.

All of the input parameters are also assigned a default value of NULL. Since most of the columns in the Invoices table can't accept null values, this might seem like a problem. As you'll see in a minute, however, the procedure tests the value of each parameter before the insertion is attempted. Then, if the parameter contains a invalid value, an appropriate error is returned to the calling program and the insert operation is never performed. By coding the procedure this way, an application program that uses the procedure will need to respond to a small set of errors rather than to the wide variety of errors that would be returned by the system.

After the AS keyword, the procedure declares ten local variables. Nine of these are used to define constant values that will be returned for each error code. Since Transact-SQL doesn't have a way of declaring constants, you must use local variables as shown here. The SELECT statement that follows sets the values of these variables. The tenth variable, @ErrorVar, will be used to store the value of the @@ERROR system function.

In addition to setting the values of the variables that contain error codes, the SELECT statement also initializes the value of the @NewInvoiceID parameter to NULL. That way, the calling program will know that the procedure failed both by its non-zero return value and by the null value for the new InvoiceID.

A stored procedure that validates the data in a new invoice   **Page 1**

```
/*
Handles insertion of new invoices into AP database,
including data validation.
Author:        Bryan Syverson
Created:       2002-07-17
Modified:      2002-07-29
Return codes:   100 = invalid VendorID      (RI violation)
                 99 = InvoiceNumber is null  (required)
                 98 = invalid InvoiceDate    (30 days old < x < now)
                 97 = invalid InvoiceTotal   (positive value required)
                 96 = invalid PaymentTotal   (> InvoiceTotal)
                 95 = invalid CreditTotal    (> InvoiceTotal)
                 94 = invalid TermsID        (RI violation)
                 93 = invalid InvoiceDueDate (> 180 days from now)
                 92 = invalid PaymentDate    (> 14 days from now)
OUTPUT parameter: InvoiceID for the new row if successful,
(@NewInvoiceID)   NULL if unsuccessful
*/
CREATE PROC spInsertInvoice
        @NewInvoiceID   int OUTPUT,
        @VendorID       int = NULL,
        @InvoiceNumber  varchar(50) = NULL,
        @InvoiceDate    smalldatetime = NULL,
        @InvoiceTotal   money = NULL,
        @PaymentTotal   money = NULL,
        @CreditTotal    money = NULL,
        @TermsID        int = NULL,
        @InvoiceDueDate smalldatetime = NULL,
        @PaymentDate    smalldatetime = NULL
AS
DECLARE @InvalidVendorID      int, @InvalidInvoiceNumber  int,
        @InvalidInvoiceDate   int, @InvalidInvoiceTotal    int,
        @InvalidPaymentTotal  int, @InvalidCreditTotal     int,
        @InvalidTermsID       int, @InvalidInvoiceDueDate int,
        @InvalidPaymentDate   int, @ErrorVar               int
SELECT  @InvalidVendorID     = 100, @InvalidInvoiceNumber = 99,
        @InvalidInvoiceDate  =  98, @InvalidInvoiceTotal  = 97,
        @InvalidPaymentTotal =  96, @InvalidCreditTotal   = 95,
        @InvalidTermsID      =  94, @InvalidInvoiceDueDate = 93,
        @InvalidPaymentDate  =  92, @NewInvoiceID = NULL
```

Description

- The ten parameters used in this procedure correspond to the ten columns in the Invoices table. The output parameter returns the InvoiceID for the new row to the calling program.

- The first nine variables represent specific errors. The values of these variables are set in the SELECT statement that follows the DECLARE statement. The tenth variable will be used to hold the return value from the @@ERROR function.

- As for any other program, you should include appropriate comments in your stored procedures. This documentation is helpful to you and other programmers when you need to debug, use, or modify the procedure.

Figure 14-8   A stored procedure that manages insert operations (part 1 of 3)

On page 2 of this listing, you can see the IF statements that are used to test the values in each input parameter. The first IF statement, for example, tests the value of @VendorID to determine if that vendor already exists in the Vendors table. If not, a RETURN statement is used to exit from the procedure and return the value in the @InvalidVendorID variable. If you look back to page 1, you'll see that this variable contains a value of 100.

The next five IF statements check for null values. In addition, the IF statement for the @InvoiceDate parameter checks to be sure that it falls between the current date and 30 days prior to the current date, and the IF statement for the @InvoiceTotal parameter checks to be sure that it's greater than zero. If not, an error is returned to the calling program.

Instead of returning an error if the @CreditTotal or @PaymentTotal parameter contains a null value, this procedures sets the value of the parameter to zero. It also checks that the credit total isn't greater than the invoice total, and it checks that the payment total isn't greater than the invoice total minus the credit total.

The next IF statement checks the value of the @TermsID parameter to see if a row with this value exists in the Terms table. If not, this parameter is set to the value of the DefaultTermsId column for the vendor if the parameter contains a null value. If it contains any other value, though, an error code is returned.

This procedure also sets the @InvoiceDueDate parameter if a due date isn't passed to the procedure. To do that, it adds the value of the TermsDueDays column in the Terms table to the value in the @InvoiceDate parameter. If a due date is passed to the procedure, the procedure checks that the date is after the invoice date but isn't more than 180 days after the invoice date. Finally, the procedure checks the @PaymentDate parameter to be sure that it's not less than the invoice date or more than 14 days before the current date.

As you can see, some of the data validation performed by this procedure duplicates the constraints for the Invoices table. If you didn't check the VendorID to be sure that it existed in the Vendors table, for example, the foreign key constraint would cause an error to occur when the row was inserted. By testing for the error before the insertion, however, the stored procedure can return an error message that might be more easily handled by the calling program.

Some of the data validation performed by this procedure goes beyond the constraints for the columns in the table. For example, all three of the date values are tested to determine whether they fall within an appropriate range. This illustrates the flexibility provided by using stored procedures to validate data.

A stored procedure that validates the data in a new invoice   Page 2

```
IF NOT EXISTS (SELECT * FROM Vendors WHERE VendorID = @VendorID)
    RETURN @InvalidVendorID
IF @InvoiceNumber IS NULL
    RETURN @InvalidInvoiceNumber
IF @InvoiceDate IS NULL OR @InvoiceDate > GETDATE() OR
        DATEDIFF(dd,@InvoiceDate,GETDATE()) > 30
    RETURN @InvalidInvoiceDate
IF @InvoiceTotal IS NULL OR @InvoiceTotal <= 0
    RETURN @InvalidInvoiceTotal
IF @PaymentTotal IS NULL
    SET @PaymentTotal = 0
IF @CreditTotal IS NULL
    SET @CreditTotal = 0
IF @CreditTotal > @InvoiceTotal
    RETURN @InvalidCreditTotal
IF @PaymentTotal > @InvoiceTotal - @CreditTotal
    RETURN @InvalidPaymentTotal
IF NOT EXISTS (SELECT * FROM Terms WHERE TermsID = @TermsID)
    IF @TermsID IS NULL
        SELECT @TermsID = DefaultTermsID
        FROM Vendors
        WHERE VendorID = @VendorID
    ELSE  -- @TermsID IS NOT NULL
        RETURN @InvalidTermsID
IF @InvoiceDueDate IS NULL
    SET @InvoiceDueDate = @InvoiceDate +
        (SELECT TermsDueDays FROM Terms WHERE TermsID = @TermsID)
ELSE  -- @InvoiceDueDate IS NOT NULL
    IF @InvoiceDueDate < @InvoiceDate OR
        DATEDIFF(dd,@InvoiceDueDate,GETDATE()) > 180
    RETURN @InvalidInvoiceDueDate
IF @PaymentDate < @InvoiceDate OR DATEDIFF(dd,@PaymentDate,GETDATE()) > 14
    RETURN @InvalidPaymentDate
```

Description

- A series of IF statements is used to validate the data in each column of the new invoice row. If the value in a column is invalid, a RETURN statement is used to return the variable that represents the error to the calling program.

- Some of the conditions tested by this code could be accomplished using constraints. However, testing these conditions before the INSERT statement is executed prevents an error from occurring. Other conditions tested by this code can't be enforced using constraints.

Figure 14-8   A stored procedure that manages insert operations (part 2 of 3)

If the input parameters pass all of the validation tests, the INSERT statement on page 3 of this listing is executed. Then, the procedure checks the error code that's returned by this statement. In most cases, this code will be zero because the data has already been validated. However, it's still possible for an unexpected error to occur. In that case, a RETURN statement is used to pass the error code back to the calling program. Otherwise, the @@IDENTITY function is used to get the value assigned to the identity column in the Invoices table, and that value is assigned to the @NewInvoiceID parameter. Then, a value of 0 is returned to the calling program.

In most cases, a stored procedure like this would be called from an application program. Since the details of doing that are beyond the scope of this book, however, this figure presents a SQL script that calls the procedure. You'd include processing similar to what's shown here in an application program.

After it calls the stored procedure, this script tests its return value. If the value is zero, the new InvoiceID value is displayed. Otherwise, a series of IF statements is used to handle each error. In this case, an error message that describes the error is displayed. In an application program, however, additional processing may be required.

A stored procedure that validates the data in a new invoice   Page 3

```
INSERT Invoices
VALUES (@VendorID,@InvoiceNumber,@InvoiceDate,@InvoiceTotal,
        @PaymentTotal,@CreditTotal,@TermsID,@InvoiceDueDate,@PaymentDate)
SET @ErrorVar = @@ERROR
IF @ErrorVar = 0
    BEGIN
        SET @NewInvoiceID = @@IDENTITY
        RETURN 0
    END
ELSE -- @ErrorVar <> 0
    RETURN @ErrorVar
```

A SQL script that calls the procedure

```
DECLARE @InvoiceIDvar int, @ReturnVar int
EXEC @ReturnVar = spInsertInvoice
    @NewInvoiceID = @InvoiceIDvar OUTPUT,
    @VendorID = 34,
    @InvoiceNumber = 'RZ99381',
    @InvoiceDate = '2002-07-24',
    @InvoiceTotal = 1292.45
IF @ReturnVar = 0
    BEGIN
        PRINT 'Success!'
        PRINT 'New InvoiceID: ' + CONVERT(varchar,@InvoiceIDVar)
    END
ELSE -- @ReturnVar <> 0
    BEGIN
        IF @ReturnVar = 100
          PRINT 'Bad VendorID'
        .
        .
    END
```

Description

- If the data in all of the columns of the new row is valid, the procedure executes an INSERT statement to insert the row. Then, it checks if the insert succeeded. If so, it gets the new InvoiceID value and returns a value of zero to the calling program. Otherwise, it returns the error number to the calling program.

- After it executes the procedure, the script that calls the procedure examines the return value. If it's zero, a message with the new InvoiceID value is displayed. Otherwise, an error message is displayed depending on the value that's returned.

- If this procedure was called by an application program, the program would need to handle any errors that occur. That includes expected errors detected by the procedure and unexpected errors that occurred as a result of the INSERT statement being executed.

Figure 14-8   A stored procedure that manages insert operations (part 3 of 3)

How to delete or change a stored procedure

Figure 14-9 presents the syntax of the DROP PROC statement. You use this statement to delete one or more stored procedures from the database. As with the other statements you've learned that delete objects from the database, the deletion is permanent.

This figure also presents the syntax of the ALTER PROC statement. You use this statement to redefine an existing stored procedure. As you can see, the syntax is the same as the syntax of the CREATE PROC statement.

Like the ALTER VIEW statement, ALTER PROC completely replaces the previous definition for the stored procedure. Because of that, you'll usually change the definition of a stored procedure by deleting the procedure and then recreating it. If you've assigned security permissions to restrict the users who can call the procedure, however, those permissions are lost when you delete the procedure. If you want to retain the permissions, then, you should use the ALTER PROC statement instead.

The examples in this figure show how you might use the ALTER PROC and DROP PROC statements. The first example creates a stored procedure named spVendorState that selects vendors from the state specified by the @StateVar parameter. Because the SELECT statement will fail if a state isn't specified, this parameter is required. In the second example, however, an ALTER PROC statement is used to modify this procedure so that the state is optional. The last example deletes this procedure.

If you delete a table or view used by a stored procedure, you should be sure to delete the stored procedure as well. If you don't, the stored procedure can still be called by any user or program that has access to it. Then, an error will occur because the table or view has been deleted.

The syntax of the DROP PROC statement

```
DROP {PROC|PROCEDURE} procedure_name [, ...]
```

The syntax of the ALTER PROC statement

```
ALTER {PROC|PROCEDURE} procedure_name
[parameter declarations]
[WITH {RECOMPILE|ENCRYPTION|RECOMPILE,ENCRYPTION}]
AS sql_statements
```

A statement that creates a procedure

```
CREATE PROC spVendorState
     @StateVar varchar(20)
AS
SELECT VendorName
FROM Vendors
WHERE VendorState = @StateVar
```

A statement that changes the parameter defined by the procedure

```
ALTER PROC spVendorState
     @StateVar varchar(20) = NULL
AS
IF @StateVar IS NULL
   SELECT VendorName
   FROM Vendors
ELSE
   SELECT VendorName
   FROM Vendors
   WHERE VendorState = @StateVar
```

A statement that deletes the procedure

```
DROP PROC spVendorState
```

Description

* To delete a stored procedure from the database, use the DROP PROC statement.
* To modify the definition of a procedure, you can delete the procedure and then create it again, or you can use the ALTER PROC statement to specify the new definition.
* When you delete a procedure, any security permissions that are assigned to the procedure are also deleted. In that case, you'll want to use the ALTER PROC statement to modify the procedure and preserve the permissions.

Figure 14-9   How to delete or change a stored procedure

How to work with system stored procedures

SQL Server comes with hundreds of *system stored procedures* that you can use to manage and maintain your databases. These procedures are stored in the Master database, but you can call them from any database. Figure 14-10 presents a table of commonly used system stored procedures.

This figure also presents a script that calls the sp_HelpText system stored procedure. This procedure returns the SQL code that was specified in the AS clause of the CREATE statement for a view, stored procedure, user-defined function, or trigger. If the object was created with the WITH ENCRYPTION option, however, the SQL code can't be returned. Because the code for system stored procedures is never encrypted, you can examine the code in these procedures too.

You should consider using the system stored procedures to simplify your administrative tasks. However, you should avoid using these procedures in production programs. That's because each time a new version of SQL Server is released, some of these stored procedures change. Then, you may have to rewrite the programs that uses them.

In addition to the system stored procedures provided by SQL Server, you can also create your own system stored procedures. To do that, you create the procedure in the Master database, and give the procedure a name that starts with *sp_*.

Commonly used system stored procedures

Procedure	Description
sp_Help [name]	Returns information about the specified database object or data type. Without a parameter, returns a summary of all objects in the current database.
sp_HelpText name	Returns the text of an unencrypted stored procedure, user-defined function, trigger, or view.
sp_HelpDb [database_name]	Returns information about the specified database or, if no parameter is specified, all databases.
sp_Who [login_ID]	Returns information about who is currently logged in and what processes are running. If no parameter is specified, information on all active users is returned.
sp_Columns name	Returns information about the columns defined in the specified table or view.
sp_DropLogin 'login_ID'	Deletes a SQL Server login ID.

How to use the sp_HelpText system stored procedure

```
USE AP
EXEC sp_HelpText spInvoiceReport
```

The results returned by the procedure

	Text
1	CREATE PROC spInvoiceReport
2	AS
3	
4	SELECT VendorName, InvoiceNumber, InvoiceDate, InvoiceTotal
5	FROM Invoices JOIN Vendors
6	ON Invoices.VendorID = Vendors.VendorID
7	WHERE InvoiceTotal - CreditTotal - PaymentTotal > 0
8	

The results if WITH ENCRYPTION is included in the procedure definition

```
The object comments have been encrypted.
```

Description

- Microsoft SQL Server 2000 includes many *system stored procedures* that you can use to perform useful tasks on a database. These procedures are identified by the prefix *sp_*. You can use these procedures in the scripts and procedures you write.

- System stored procedures are stored in the Master database, but you can execute them on any database. These procedures operate within the current database context that you've set with the USE statement.

- SQL Server 2000 has hundreds of system stored procedures. To view the complete list, look up "system stored procedures, listed" in the Books Online index.

- You can also create your own system stored procedures. To do that, give the procedure a name that begins with *sp_* and create it in the Master database.

- Because Microsoft changes many of the system stored procedures with each new version of SQL Server, you should use them as little as possible in your production code.

Figure 14-10   How to work with system stored procedures

How to code user-defined functions

In addition to the SQL Server functions you've learned about throughout this book, you can also create your own functions, called user-defined functions. To do that, you use code that's similar to the code you use to create a stored procedure. There are some distinct differences between stored procedures and user-defined functions, however. You'll learn about those differences in the topics that follow.

An introduction to user-defined functions

Figure 14-11 summarizes the three types of user-defined functions, also called *UDFs*, or just *functions*, that you can create using Transact-SQL. *Scalar-valued functions* are like the functions you learned about in chapter 8 that return a single value. In addition to scalar-valued functions, however, you can also create *table-valued functions*. As its name implies, a table-valued function returns an entire table. A table-valued function that's based on a single SELECT statement is called a *simple table-valued function*. In contrast, a table-valued function that's based on multiple SQL statements is called a *multi-statement table-valued function*.

Like a stored procedure, a UDF can accept one or more input parameters. The function shown in this figure, for example, accepts a parameter named @VendorName. However, a UDF can't be defined with output parameters. Instead, the RETURN statement must be used to pass a value back to the calling program. The value that's returned must be compatible with the data type that's specified in the RETURNS clause. In this example, an integer that contains a VendorID value selected from the Vendors table is returned.

To call, or *invoke*, a scalar-valued function, you include it in an expression. Then, the value returned by the function is substituted for the function. The first SELECT statement in this figure, for example, uses the value returned by the fnVendorID function in its WHERE clause. Note that when you refer to a user-defined function, you must include the name of the database owner. In this case, the owner is dbo.

To invoke a table-valued function, you refer to it anywhere you would normally code a table or view name. The second SELECT statement in this figure, for example, uses a function named fnTopVendorsDue in the FROM clause. You'll see the definition of this function later in this chapter.

Unlike a stored procedure, a UDF can't have a permanent effect on a database. In other words, it can't issue INSERT, UPDATE, and DELETE statements against tables or views in the database. However, within the code for a function, you can create a table, a temporary table, or a table variable. Then, the function can perform insert, update, and delete operations on that table.

The three types of user-defined functions

Function type	Description
Scalar-valued function	Returns a single value of any T-SQL data type.
Simple table-valued function	Returns a table that's based on a single SELECT statement.
Multi-statement table-valued function	Returns a table that's based on multiple statements.

A statement that creates a scalar-valued function

```
CREATE FUNCTION fnVendorID
    (@VendorName varchar(50))
    RETURNS int
BEGIN
    RETURN (SELECT VendorID FROM Vendors WHERE VendorName = @VendorName)
END
```

A statement that invokes the scalar-valued function

```
SELECT InvoiceDate, InvoiceTotal
FROM Invoices
WHERE VendorID = dbo.fnVendorID('IBM')
```

A statement that invokes a table-valued function

```
SELECT * FROM dbo.fnTopVendorsDue(5000)
```

Description

- A user-defined function, also called a *UDF* or just a *function*, is an executable database object that contains SQL statements. The name of a function can be up to 128 characters and is typically prefixed with the letters *fn*.

- Functions always return a value. A *scalar-valued function* returns a single value of any T-SQL data type. A *table-valued function* returns an entire table.

- A table-valued function can be based on a single SELECT statement, in which case it's called a *simple table-valued function*, or it can be based on two or more statements, in which case it's called a *multi-statement table-valued function*.

- A function can't have a permanent effect on the database. In other words, it can't run an action query against the database.

- You can call, or *invoke*, a scalar-valued function from within any expression. You can invoke to a table-valued function anywhere you'd refer to a table or a view.

- Unlike other database objects, you must specify the name of the database owner or schema when invoking a UDF.

Figure 14-11   An introduction to user-defined functions

How to create a scalar-valued function

Figure 14-12 presents the syntax of the CREATE FUNCTION statement you use to create a scalar-valued function. The CREATE FUNCTION clause names the function and declares the input parameters. If you don't specify the database owner name as part of the name, the function is created for the current database owner.

The syntax you use to declare parameters for a function is similar to the syntax you use to declare parameters for stored procedures. For a function, however, the declarations must be enclosed in parentheses. In addition, because a function can't have output parameters, the OUTPUT keyword isn't allowed.

To invoke a function that has parameters, you must pass the parameters by position. You can't pass them by name as you can when you call a stored procedure. For this reason, you should code required parameters first, followed by optional parameters. Furthermore, you can't simply omit optional parameters when invoking a function as you could with a stored procedure. Instead, you must use the DEFAULT keyword as a placeholder for the optional parameter. You'll see an example of that in figure 14-13.

The RETURNS clause specifies the data type of the value that's returned by the function. Because the value must be scalar, you can't specify the table data type. In addition, you can't specify text, ntext, image, or timestamp.

You code the statements for the function within a BEGIN...END block. Within that block, the RETURN statement specifies the value that's passed back to the invoking program. Since this statement causes the function to terminate, it's usually coded at the end of the function. Notice that unlike a RETURN statement you code within a stored procedure, a RETURN statement you code within a function can return a value with any data type. Within a specific function, however, it must return a value with a data type that's compatible with the data type specified by the RETURNS clause.

The scalar-valued function that's shown in this figure doesn't accept any input parameters and returns a value with the money data type. In this case, the code for the function consists of a single SELECT statement coded within the RETURN statement. However, a function can include as many statements as are necessary to calculate the return value.

If you find yourself repeatedly coding the same expression, you may want to create a scalar-valued function for the expression. Then, you can use that function in place of the expression, which can save you coding time. Most SQL programmers create a set of useful UDFs each time they work on a new database.

The syntax for creating a scalar-valued function

```
CREATE FUNCTION [owner_name.]function_name
    ([@parameter_name data_type [= default]] [, ...])
RETURNS data_type
[WITH {ENCRYPTION|SCHEMABINDING|ENCRYPTION,SCHEMABINDING}]
[AS]
BEGIN
    [sql_statements]
    RETURN scalar_expression
END
```

A statement that creates a scalar-valued function that returns the total invoice amount due

```
CREATE FUNCTION fnBalanceDue()
    RETURNS money
BEGIN
    RETURN (SELECT SUM(InvoiceTotal - PaymentTotal - CreditTotal)
            FROM Invoices
            WHERE InvoiceTotal - PaymentTotal - CreditTotal > 0)
END
```

A script that invokes the function

```
PRINT 'Current outstanding balance is: $' +
      CONVERT(varchar,dbo.fnBalanceDue(),1)
```

The response from the system

```
Current outstanding balance is: $66,796.24
```

Description

- Functions can be defined with from zero to 1024 input parameters. You specify these parameters in parentheses after the name of the function in the CREATE FUNCTION statement. Each parameter can be assigned an optional default value.

- A function can't contain output parameters. Instead, you specify the data type of the data to be returned by the function in the RETURNS clause.

- You code the statements that define the function within a BEGIN...END block. This block includes a RETURN statement that specifies the value to be returned.

- When you invoke a function, you list the parameters within parentheses after the name of the function. To use the default value of a parameter, code the DEFAULT keyword in place of the parameter value. You can't pass function parameters by name.

- When you create a function, it's assigned the current database owner if you don't specify an owner name. When you invoke the function, however, you must specify the owner name.

- The WITH SCHEMABINDING clause binds the function to the database schema. This prevents you from dropping or altering tables or views that are used by the function. This option is more commonly used for table-valued functions.

- The WITH ENCRYPTION clause prevents users from viewing the code in the function.

Figure 14-12 How to create and use a scalar-valued function

How to create a simple table-valued function

Figure 14-13 presents the syntax for creating a simple table-valued function, also called an *inline table-valued function*. You use this syntax if the result set can be returned from a single SELECT statement. Otherwise, you'll need to use the syntax that's presented in the next figure.

To declare the function as table-valued, you code the table data type in the RETURNS clause. Then, you code the SELECT statement that defines the table in parentheses in the RETURN statement. Note that because a table can't have any unnamed columns, you must assign a name to every calculated column in the result set.

The function shown in this figure returns a table with the total amount due for each vendor. The one input parameter, @CutOff, is an optional parameter because it's assigned a default value of 0. This parameter is used in the HAV-ING clause to return only those vendors with invoice totals greater than or equal to the specified amount. The first SELECT statement shown in this figure, for example, returns vendors with invoice totals greater than or equal to $5,000.

The second SELECT statement shows how you can join the result of a table-valued function with another table. Notice that to avoid having to code the function in both the FROM and ON clauses, the function is assigned a correlation name. Also notice in this example that a value isn't specified for the optional parameter. Instead, the DEFAULT keyword is specified so that the default value of the parameter will be used.

A table-valued function like the one shown here acts like a dynamic view. Because a function can accept parameters, the result set it creates can be modified. This is a powerful extension to standard SQL functionality.

The syntax for creating a simple table-valued function

```
CREATE FUNCTION [owner_name.]function_name
    ([@parameter_name data_type [= default]] [, ...])
RETURNS TABLE
[WITH {ENCRYPTION|SCHEMABINDING|ENCRYPTION,SCHEMABINDING}]
[AS]
RETURN [(] select_statement [)]
```

A statement that creates a simple table-valued function

```
CREATE FUNCTION fnTopVendorsDue
    (@CutOff money = 0)
    RETURNS table
RETURN
(SELECT VendorName, SUM(InvoiceTotal) AS TotalDue
FROM Vendors JOIN Invoices ON Vendors.VendorID = Invoices.VendorID
WHERE InvoiceTotal - CreditTotal - PaymentTotal > 0
GROUP BY VendorName
HAVING SUM(InvoiceTotal) >= @CutOff)
```

A SELECT statement that invokes the function

```
SELECT * FROM dbo.fnTopVendorsDue(5000)
```

The result set

	VendorName	TotalDue
1	Data Reproductions Corp	21927.3100
2	Malloy Lithographing Inc	31527.2400

A SELECT statement that uses the function in a join operation

```
SELECT Vendors.VendorName, VendorCity, TotalDue
FROM Vendors JOIN dbo.fnTopVendorsDue(DEFAULT) AS TopVendors
    ON Vendors.VendorName = TopVendors.VendorName
```

The result set

	VendorName	VendorCity	TotalDue
1	Abbey Office Furnishings	Fresno	17.5000
2	Blue Cross	Oxnard	564.0000
3	Cardinal Business Media, Inc.	Philadelphia	90.3600
4	Coffee Break Service	Fresno	41.8000

Description

- You create a simple table-valued function, also called an *inline table-valued function*, by coding the table data type in the RETURNS clause of the CREATE FUNCTION statement. Then, you code a SELECT statement that defines the table in the RETURN statement.

- To use a simple table-valued function, code the function name in place of a table name or a view name. If you use a table-valued function in a join operation, you'll want to assign a correlation name to it as shown above.

Figure 14-13   How to create and use a simple table-valued function

How to create a multi-statement table-valued function

Figure 14-14 presents the syntax for creating a multi-statement table-valued function. Although you should know about this syntax, you'll probably never need to use it. That's because a single SELECT statement with joins and subqueries can fulfill almost every query need.

Since a multi-statement table-valued function creates a new table, you must define the structure of that table. To do that, you declare a table variable in the RETURNS clause and then define the columns for the new table. The syntax you use to define the columns is similar to the syntax you use to define the columns of a table variable.

You code the SQL statements that create the table within a BEGIN…END block. This blocks ends with a RETURN keyword with no argument. This terminates the function and returns the table variable to the invoking program.

The function shown in this figure returns a table with one row for each invoice with a balance due. This function calculates the credit adjustment that would be necessary to reduce the total balance due to the threshold amount that's passed to the function. This function is similar to the script you saw in figure 13-9 in chapter 13 that uses a temporary table.

This function starts by using an INSERT statement to copy all the rows in the Invoices table with a balance due to the @OutTable table variable. Then, a WHILE statement is used to increment the CreditTotal column of each row in this table by one cent until the total amount due for all invoices falls below the threshold. The SELECT statement that uses this function summarizes the CreditTotal column by vendor.

The syntax for creating a multi-statement table-valued function

```
CREATE FUNCTION [owner_name.]function_name
    ([@parameter_name data_type [= default]] [, ...])
RETURNS @return_variable TABLE
(column_name_1 data_type [column_attributes]
[, column_name_2 data_type [column_attributes]]...)
[WITH {ENCRYPTION|SCHEMABINDING|ENCRYPTION,SCHEMABINDING}]
[AS]
BEGIN
    sql_statements
    RETURN
END
```

A statement that creates a multi-statement table-valued function

```
CREATE FUNCTION fnCreditAdj (@HowMuch money)
    RETURNS @OutTable table
            (InvoiceID int, VendorID int, InvoiceNumber varchar(50),
             InvoiceDate smalldatetime, InvoiceTotal money,
             PaymentTotal money, CreditTotal money)
BEGIN
    INSERT @OutTable
        SELECT InvoiceID, VendorID, InvoiceNumber, InvoiceDate,
               InvoiceTotal, PaymentTotal, CreditTotal
        FROM Invoices
        WHERE InvoiceTotal - CreditTotal - PaymentTotal > 0
    WHILE (SELECT SUM(InvoiceTotal - CreditTotal  -PaymentTotal)
        FROM @OutTable) >= @HowMuch
        BEGIN
            UPDATE @OutTable
            SET CreditTotal = CreditTotal + .01
            WHERE InvoiceTotal - CreditTotal - PaymentTotal > 0
        END
        RETURN
END
```

A SELECT statement that uses the function

```
SELECT VendorName, SUM(CreditTotal) AS CreditRequest
FROM Vendors JOIN dbo.fnCreditAdj(50000) AS CreditTable
    ON Vendors.VendorID = CreditTable.VendorID
GROUP BY VendorName
```

The response from the system

	VendorName	CreditRequest	
1	Abbey Office Furnishings	17.5000	
2	Blue Cross	564.0000	

Description

- To create a multi-statement table-valued function, create a table variable in the RE-TURNS clause of the CREATE FUNCTION statement that defines the columns in the table. Then, code the statements that create the table within a BEGIN...END block. Code a RETURN statement within this block to return the table to the calling program.

Warning

- Because this code must loop through the Invoices table thousands of times, this function can take a long time to execute.

Figure 14-14   How to create and use a multi-statement table-valued function

How to delete or change a function

Figure 14-15 presents the syntax of the DROP FUNCTION and ALTER FUNCTION statements. The DROP FUNCTION statement permanently deletes one or more user-defined functions from the database. In addition, it drops any security permissions defined for the function along with any dependencies between the function and the tables and views it uses.

The ALTER FUNCTION statement modifies the definition of a user-defined function. You should use this statement if you need to preserve permissions and dependencies that would be lost if you dropped the function and then recreated it. Just like the CREATE FUNCTION statement, the ALTER FUNCTION statement has three syntax variations for the three types of functions you can create.

The syntax of the DROP FUNCTION statement

```
DROP FUNCTION [owner_name.]function_name [, ...]
```

The syntax of the ALTER FUNCTION statement for a scalar valued function

```
ALTER FUNCTION [owner_name.]function_name
    ([@parameter_name data_type [= default]] [, ...])
RETURNS data_type
[WITH {ENCRYPTION|SCHEMABINDING|ENCRYPTION,SCHEMABINDING}]
BEGIN
    [sql_statements]
    RETURN scalar_expression
END
```

The syntax for altering a simple table-valued function

```
ALTER FUNCTION [owner_name.]function_name
    ([@parameter_name data_type [= default]] [, ...])
RETURNS TABLE
[WITH {ENCRYPTION|SCHEMABINDING|ENCRYPTION,SCHEMABINDING}]
RETURN [() select_statement [)]
```

The syntax for altering a multi-statement table-valued function

```
ALTER FUNCTION [owner_name.]function_name
    ([@parameter_name data_type [= default]] [, ...])
RETURNS @return_variable TABLE
(column_name_1 data_type [column_attributes]
[, column_name_2 data_type [column_attributes]]...)
[WITH {ENCRYPTION|SCHEMABINDING|ENCRYPTION,SCHEMABINDING}]
BEGIN
    sql_statements
    RETURN
END
```

Description

- To delete a user-defined function from the database, use the DROP FUNCTION statement.

- To modify the definition of a function, you can delete the function and then create it again, or you can use the ALTER FUNCTION statement to specify the new definition.

- When you delete a function, any security permissions that are assigned to the function and any dependencies between the function and the tables and views it uses are also deleted. In that case, you'll want to use the ALTER FUNCTION statement to modify the function and preserve the permissions and dependencies.

Figure 14-15   How to delete or change a function

How to code triggers

Triggers are a special type of procedure that are invoked, or *fired*, automatically when an action query is executed on a table or view. Triggers provide a powerful way to control how action queries modify the data in your database. Since you can program virtually any logic within the code for a trigger, you can enforce design rules, implement business logic, and prevent data inconsistency with a flexibility that can't be duplicated any other way.

How to create a trigger

Figure 14-16 presents the syntax of the CREATE TRIGGER statement you use to create a trigger. Notice in this syntax that a trigger can't use parameters. In addition, a trigger can't return a value.

The CREATE TRIGGER statement provides for two types of triggers: AFTER triggers and INSTEAD OF triggers. Both types of triggers can be defined to fire for an insert, update, or delete operation, or any combination of these operations. If an action query has an AFTER trigger, the trigger fires after the action query. If an action query has an INSTEAD OF trigger, the trigger is fired instead of the action query. In other words, the action query is never executed.

In addition to AFTER and INSTEAD OF, you can code the FOR keyword in the CREATE TRIGGER statement. A FOR trigger is identical to an AFTER trigger. FOR is an ANSI-standard keyword, and it was the only keyword allowed in previous versions of SQL Server. For these reasons, FOR is more commonly used than AFTER. I recommend that you use AFTER, however, since it more clearly describes when the trigger fires.

Each trigger is associated with the table or view named in the ON clause. Although each trigger is associated with a single table or view, a single table can have any number of AFTER triggers. Since two or more triggers for the same table can be confusing to manage and debug, however, I recommend you have no more than one trigger for each action. Each table or view can also have one INSTEAD OF trigger for each action. A view can't have AFTER triggers.

The CREATE TRIGGER statement in this figure defines an AFTER trigger for the Vendors table. Notice that the name of this trigger reflects the table it's associated with and the operations that will cause it to fire. This is a common naming convention. In this case, the trigger fires after an insert or update operation is performed on the table. As you can see, the trigger updates the VendorState column so that state codes are in upper case letters.

Notice that the WHERE clause in the trigger uses a subquery that's based on a table named Inserted. This is a special table that's created by SQL Server during an insert operation. It contains the rows that are being inserted into the table. Since this table only exists while the trigger is executing, you can only refer to it in the trigger code.

The syntax of the CREATE TRIGGER statement

```
CREATE TRIGGER trigger_name
ON {table_name|view_name}
[WITH ENCRYPTION]
{FOR|AFTER|INSTEAD OF} [INSERT] [,] [UPDATE] [,] [DELETE]
AS sql_statements
```

A CREATE TRIGGER statement that corrects mixed-case state names

```
CREATE TRIGGER Vendors_INSERT_UPDATE
    ON Vendors
    AFTER INSERT,UPDATE
AS
    UPDATE Vendors
    SET VendorState = UPPER(VendorState)
    WHERE VendorID IN (SELECT VendorID FROM Inserted)
```

An INSERT statement that fires the trigger

```
INSERT Vendors
VALUES ('Peerless Uniforms, Inc.','785 S Pixley Rd',NULL,
        'Piqua','Oh','45356','(937) 555-8845',NULL,NULL,4,550)
```

The new row that's inserted into the Vendors table

	VendorID	VendorName	VendorAddress1	VendorAddress2	VendorCity	VendorState
1	124	Peerless Uniforms, Inc.	785 S Pixley Rd	NULL	Piqua	OH

Description

- A trigger is a special kind of procedure that executes, or *fires*, in response to an action query. Unlike a stored procedure, you can't invoke a trigger directly, you can't pass parameters to a trigger, and a trigger can't pass back a return value.

- A trigger is associated with a single table or view, which you identify in the ON clause. The trigger can be set to fire on INSERT, UPDATE, or DELETE statements or on a combination of these statements.

- A trigger can be set to fire after the action query (AFTER) or instead of the action query (INSTEAD OF). A FOR trigger is the same as an AFTER trigger.

- A table can have multiple AFTER triggers, even for the same action. A view can't have an AFTER trigger. A table or view can have only one INSTEAD OF trigger for each action.

- To hide the code for the trigger from the user, include the WITH ENCRYPTION option.

- It's a common programming practice to name triggers based on the table or view and the actions that will cause the trigger to fire.

- Within a trigger, you can refer to two tables that are created by the system: Inserted and Deleted. The Inserted table contains the new rows for insert and update operations. The Deleted table contains the original rows for update and delete operations.

Figure 14-16   How to create a trigger

Similarly, a table named Deleted is created by SQL Server during a delete operation that contains the rows that are being deleted. For an update operation, SQL Server creates both tables. In that case, the Inserted table contains the rows with the updated data, and the Deleted table contains the original data from the rows that are being updated.

How to use AFTER triggers

Figure 14-17 presents a script that creates two AFTER triggers. These triggers are used to maintain the referential integrity between two tables.

The script starts by deleting the VendorCopy and InvoiceCopy tables that the triggers will be associated with. Then, it recreates these tables using SELECT INTO statements that copy the data from the Vendors and Invoices tables. Because the foreign key constraint in the Invoices table isn't copied, however, referential integrity won't be enforced between the two tables. Although you could add a foreign key constraint to the InvoiceCopy table using an ALTER TABLE statement, you don't need to do that with the triggers shown here.

The first trigger prevents the deletion of a vendor if that vendor is associated with one or more invoices. It also prevents an update of a VendorID value if the vendor is associated with one or more invoices. When a row is deleted or updated, it's copied to the Deleted table. Then, the trigger tests to see if any rows in the InvoiceCopy table have that same VendorID value as those rows. If so, the trigger raises an error and reverses the delete or update operation.

To reverse an operation, the trigger uses a ROLLBACK TRAN statement. This statement reverses, or rolls back, the SQL statement that caused the trigger to fire. You'll learn more about using this statement in chapter 16.

The second trigger prevents the insertion of an invoice that doesn't have a valid VendorID. It also prevents the update of a VendorID value if that value doesn't exist in the VendorCopy table. When an INSERT or UPDATE statement is executed, a copy of the new or updated row is added to the Inserted table. Then, the trigger tests to see whether the VendorID exists in the VendorCopy table. If not, the trigger raises an error and rolls back the operation.

Because an AFTER trigger fires after the action query is executed, the trigger doesn't fire if the action query causes an error. For this reason, you wouldn't use these triggers if the referential integrity between two tables was enforced by a foreign key constraint. Instead, you could use an INSTEAD OF trigger to check for referential integrity before an error occurs.

A script that creates AFTER triggers to maintain referential integrity

```
USE AP
IF OBJECT_ID('VendorCopy') IS NOT NULL
    DROP TABLE VendorCopy
IF OBJECT_ID('InvoiceCopy') IS NOT NULL
    DROP TABLE InvoiceCopy
SELECT * INTO VendorCopy FROM Vendors
SELECT * INTO InvoiceCopy FROM Invoices
GO

CREATE TRIGGER VendorCopy_UPDATE_DELETE_RI
    ON VendorCopy
    AFTER DELETE,UPDATE
AS
    IF EXISTS (SELECT * FROM Deleted JOIN InvoiceCopy
                        ON Deleted.VendorID = InvoiceCopy.VendorID)
    BEGIN
        RAISERROR('VendorID in use.',1,1)
        ROLLBACK TRAN
    END
GO

CREATE TRIGGER InvoiceCopy_INSERT_UPDATE_RI
    ON InvoiceCopy
    AFTER INSERT,UPDATE
AS
    IF NOT EXISTS (SELECT * FROM VendorCopy
                    WHERE VendorID IN (SELECT VendorID FROM Inserted))
    BEGIN
        RAISERROR('Invalid VendorID.',1,1)
        ROLLBACK TRAN
    END
```

A DELETE statement that would violate referential integrity

```
DELETE VendorCopy
WHERE VendorID = 34
```

The response from the system

```
Msg 50000, Level 1, State 50000
VendorID in use.
```

Description

- An AFTER trigger fires after the action query is executed. If the action query causes an error, the AFTER trigger never fires.

- AFTER triggers can be used to enforce referential integrity. Then, a trigger can test if related rows exist in the foreign key table when updating or deleting a row from the primary key table. And another trigger can test if a related row exists in the primary key table when inserting or updating a row in the foreign key table.

- The ROLLBACK TRAN statement causes the current *transaction* to be reversed. For an AFTER trigger, the transaction is the action query that caused the trigger to fire. See chapter 16 for more information on transactions.

Figure 14-17   How to use AFTER triggers

How to use INSTEAD OF triggers

An INSTEAD OF trigger can be associated with either a table or a view. However, INSTEAD OF triggers are used most often to provide better control of updatable views. Unlike AFTER triggers, each action can have only one INSTEAD OF trigger.

Figure 14-18 presents an INSTEAD OF trigger that's used to control an insert operation through a view named IBM_Invoices. You first saw this view in figure 12-10. It selects invoices from the Invoices table for the vendor named "IBM." If you look back to that figure, you'll see that the insert operation failed because some of the required columns weren't included in the view.

This trigger accommodates the missing columns by calculating their values based on three logical assumptions. First, the VendorID can be assumed because this view is explicitly for invoices for vendor "IBM." Second, the terms for the invoice can be assumed to be the default terms for the vendor. Third, the due date for the invoice can be calculated based on the invoice date and the terms.

After it declares the variables it uses, the trigger queries the Inserted table to get a count of the number of rows that are being inserted. Since this trigger will work only if a single row is being inserted, an error is raised if the row count is greater than one. Otherwise, the trigger queries the Inserted table to get the values of the three columns that were specified in an INSERT statement like the one shown in this figure. The SELECT statement assigns these values to three of the variables. Then, if all three variables contain values other than null, the trigger calculates the values of the missing columns.

Since an INSTEAD OF trigger is executed instead of the action query that caused it to fire, the action will never occur unless you code it as part of the trigger. For this reason, the last statement in this trigger is an INSERT that inserts the new row into the Invoices table. Without this statement, the row would never be inserted.

An INSTEAD OF INSERT trigger for a view

```
CREATE TRIGGER IBM_Invoices_INSERT
    ON IBM_Invoices
    INSTEAD OF INSERT
AS
DECLARE @InvoiceDate smalldatetime, @InvoiceNumber varchar(50),
        @InvoiceTotal money, @VendorID int,
        @InvoiceDueDate smalldatetime, @TermsID int,
        @DefaultTerms smallint, @TestRowCount int
SELECT @TestRowCount = COUNT(*) FROM Inserted
IF @TestRowCount = 1
    BEGIN
        SELECT @InvoiceNumber = InvoiceNumber, @InvoiceDate = InvoiceDate,
            @InvoiceTotal = InvoiceTotal
        FROM Inserted
        IF (@InvoiceDate IS NOT NULL AND @InvoiceNumber IS NOT NULL AND
            @InvoiceTotal IS NOT NULL)
            BEGIN
                SELECT @VendorID = VendorID, @TermsID = DefaultTermsID
                FROM Vendors
                WHERE VendorName = 'IBM'
                SELECT @DefaultTerms = TermsDueDays
                FROM Terms
                WHERE TermsID = @TermsID
                SET @InvoiceDueDate = @InvoiceDate + @DefaultTerms
                INSERT Invoices
                    (VendorID, InvoiceNumber, InvoiceDate, InvoiceTotal,
                     TermsID, InvoiceDueDate, PaymentDate)
                VALUES (@VendorID, @InvoiceNumber, @InvoiceDate,
                    @InvoiceTotal, @TermsID, @InvoiceDueDate, NULL)
            END
    END
ELSE
    RAISERROR('Limit INSERT to a single row.',1,1)
```

An INSERT statement that succeeds due to the trigger

```
INSERT IBM_Invoices
VALUES ('RA23988','2002-07-25',417.34)
```

Description

- An INSTEAD OF trigger is executed instead of the action query that causes it to fire. Because the action query is never executed, the trigger typically contains code that performs the operation.

- INSTEAD OF triggers are typically used to provide for updatable views. They can also be used to prevent errors, such as constraint violations, before they occur.

- Each table or view can have only one INSTEAD OF trigger for each type of action. However, if a table is defined with a foreign key constraint that specifies the CASCADE UPDATE or CASCADE DELETE option, INSTEAD OF UPDATE and INSTEAD OF DELETE triggers can't be defined for the table.

Figure 14-18   How to use INSTEAD OF triggers

How to use triggers to enforce data consistency

Triggers can also be used to enforce data consistency. For example, the sum of line item amounts in the InvoiceLineItems table should always be equal to the invoice total for the invoice in the Invoices table. However, you can't enforce this constraint on either the Invoices table or the InvoiceLineItems table. To do that, you can use a trigger like the one in figure 14-19.

To understand why this trigger is necessary, consider how an invoice is entered into the database. First, you must insert the invoice into the Invoices table. If you tried to insert the line items first, you'd violate referential integrity since the InvoiceID doesn't exist yet. Once the invoice has been inserted, you can insert the first line item into the InvoiceLineItems table. However, you can't constrain the value for InvoiceLineItemAmount because the constraint would have to be based on the value in the Invoices table. In addition, even if you could implement such a constraint, you would only want to do so once the last line item was inserted. Then, you'd want to be sure that the sum of the line item amounts equaled the invoice total.

The trigger shown here enforces this rule by firing after an update operation on the Invoices table. Since you can assume that posting a payment is likely to be the last action taken on an invoice, firing a trigger on this action is a good way to verify that all of the data is valid. If an update operation changes the PaymentTotal column, then the rest of the trigger verifies that the sum of line items is equal to the invoice total. If the data isn't valid, the trigger raises an error and rolls back the update.

Notice the two IF statements shown in this figure. They use the EXISTS keyword to test for the existence of the data specified by the subqueries that follow. In chapter 6, you saw how to use the EXISTS keyword in the WHERE clause. Because this keyword returns a Boolean value, however, you can use it in an IF statement as well.

You can use triggers like the one shown here to enforce business rules or verify data consistency. Since you can program a trigger to accommodate virtually any situation, triggers are more flexible than constraints. In addition, prior to version 6.5, SQL Server didn't support foreign key constraints, so triggers were the only way to enforce referential integrity. For this reason, some programmers still prefer to use triggers rather than constraints to enforce referential integrity, data consistency, and even check constraints and defaults.

A trigger that validates line item amounts when posting a payment

```
CREATE TRIGGER Invoices_UPDATE
    ON Invoices
    AFTER UPDATE
AS
IF EXISTS               --Test whether PaymentTotal was changed
  (SELECT *
   FROM Deleted JOIN Invoices
     ON Deleted.InvoiceID = Invoices.InvoiceID
   WHERE Deleted.PaymentTotal <> Invoices.PaymentTotal)
   BEGIN
     IF EXISTS          --Test whether line items and invoice amount match
       (SELECT *
        FROM Invoices JOIN
           (SELECT InvoiceID, SUM(InvoiceLineItemAmount) AS SumOfInvoices
            FROM InvoiceLineItems
            GROUP BY InvoiceID) AS LineItems
          ON Invoices.InvoiceID = LineItems.InvoiceID
        WHERE (Invoices.InvoiceTotal <> LineItems.SumOfInvoices) AND
              (LineItems.InvoiceID IN (SELECT InvoiceID FROM Deleted)))
       BEGIN
         RAISERROR('Correct line item amounts before posting payment.',1,1)
         ROLLBACK TRAN
       END
   END
```

An UPDATE statement that fires the trigger

```
UPDATE Invoices
SET PaymentTotal = 662, PaymentDate = '2002-07-25'
WHERE InvoiceID = 100
```

The response from the system

```
Msg 50000, Level 1, State 50000
Correct line item amounts before posting payment.
```

Description

- Triggers can be used to enforce database rules for data consistency that can't be enforced by constraints.

- Triggers can also be used to enforce the same rules as constraints, but with more flexibility.

Figure 14-19   How to use triggers to enforce data consistency

How to delete or change a trigger

Figure 14-20 presents the syntax of the DROP TRIGGER and ALTER TRIGGER statements. DROP TRIGGER permanently deletes one or more or triggers along with any security permissions associated with the trigger.

If you want to change the definition of a trigger without affecting permissions, you can use the ALTER TRIGGER statement. The statement shown in this figure, for example, modifies the trigger you saw in figure 14-16. This trigger now removes spaces from the beginning and end of the address columns in addition to converting the state code to upper case.

The syntax of the DROP TRIGGER statement

```
DROP TRIGGER trigger_name [, ...]
```

The syntax of the ALTER TRIGGER statement

```
ALTER TRIGGER trigger_name
ON {table_name|view_name}
[WITH ENCRYPTION]
{FOR|AFTER|INSTEAD OF} [INSERT] [,] [UPDATE] [,] [DELETE]
AS sql_statements
```

A statement that modifies the trigger in figure 14-16

```
ALTER TRIGGER Vendors_INSERT_UPDATE
    ON Vendors
    AFTER INSERT,UPDATE
AS
    UPDATE Vendors
    SET VendorState = UPPER(VendorState),
        VendorAddress1 = LTRIM(RTRIM(VendorAddress1)),
        VendorAddress2 = LTRIM(RTRIM(VendorAddress2))
    WHERE VendorID IN (SELECT VendorID FROM Inserted)
```

A statement that deletes the trigger

```
DROP TRIGGER Vendors_INSERT_UPDATE
```

Description

- To delete a trigger from the database, use the DROP TRIGGER statement.

- To modify the definition of a trigger, you can delete the trigger and then create it again, or you can use the ALTER TRIGGER statement to specify the new definition.

- When you delete a trigger, any security permissions that are assigned to the trigger are also deleted. In that case, you'll want to use the ALTER TRIGGER statement to modify the trigger and preserve the permissions.

Figure 14-20   How to delete or change a trigger

Perspective

In this chapter, you've learned how to create the three types of executable database objects supported by SQL Server. Stored procedures are the most flexible of the three because you can use them in so many different ways. You can code procedures to simultaneously simplify and restrict a user's access to the database, to verify data integrity, and to ease your own administrative tasks.

Although they're generally less flexible than stored procedures, functions and triggers are powerful objects. You can use them to solve problems that otherwise would be difficult or impossible to solve. In particular, table-valued functions are one of the most useful extensions provided by Transact-SQL because they behave like views but can accept parameters that can change the result set.

Terms

stored procedure
user-defined function (UDF)
trigger
sproc
call a procedure
precompiled
execution plan
recursive call
recursion
temporary stored procedure
local procedure
global procedure
parameter
input parameter
output parameter
required parameter

optional parameter
passing parameters by position
passing parameters by name
return value
data validation
system stored procedure
scalar-valued function
table-valued function
simple table-valued function
multi-statement table-valued
    function
invoke a function
inline table-valued function
fire a trigger
transaction

15

How to work with cursors

By default, all of the SQL statements work with an entire result set rather than individual rows. However, there are times when you need to be able to work with the data in a result set one row at a time. In this chapter, you'll learn how to do that using cursors.

How to use cursors in SQL Server

A *cursor* lets you retrieve data from a result set one row at a time. In the topics that follow, you'll learn about the different types of cursors that you can use with a SQL Server database. You'll also learn about the Transact-SQL statements for working with cursors.

An introduction to cursors

A cursor is a database object that points to a result set. You use a cursor to identify the row you want to retrieve from the result set. This concept is presented in the illustration at the top of figure 15-1.

Cursors are most often used by application programs that work with the data in a database. In most cases, these programs use a standard database *API* (*application programming interface*) that provides access to SQL Server databases through cursors. Then, application programmers can work with the programming language and API they're most familiar with.

Since an *API cursor* is managed by the API on the client machine, you don't need to write any SQL code to support this type of cursor on the server. If you need to, however, you can create and use your own *Transact-SQL cursors* on the server. You'll use this type of cursor in one of two ways. First, you can use them within your own scripts or procedures. Second, you can sometimes use them to provide database access to an application program that doesn't use one of the standard database APIs.

This figure also describes two situations when you might code Transact-SQL cursors for your own use. The more likely use is for administrative scripts or procedures that you use to manage your own database. In particular, this is useful for scripts that make use of system stored procedures or system tables to generate dynamic SQL. You'll see an example of this kind of script later in this chapter. Transact-SQL cursors can also be useful if you need to perform different operations on different rows in a table and the selection criteria are more complex than you can code in a WHERE clause.

Before you use a Transact-SQL cursor to solve a particular problem, you should consider other solutions first. That's because standard, set-based database access is faster and uses fewer server resources than cursor-based access. In some cases, however, you'll find that a problem can be solved only with the use of a cursor.

Although you'll probably use Transact-SQL cursors much less often than API cursors, I can't show you how to use API cursors because each API implements them in a different way. However, I can show you how to code Transact-SQL cursors. Since both API cursors and Transact-SQL cursors work similarly, learning how to code Transact-SQL cursors should prepare you for learning how to use API cursors.

How a cursor works

A result set with a cursor that points to the first row

	VendorID	VendorName	
1	94	Abbey Office Furnishings	◄── Cursor
2	61	American Booksellers Assoc	
3	98	American Express	

The first row of the result set retrieved through the cursor

	VendorID	VendorName
1	94	Abbey Office Furnishings

The two implementations of SQL Server cursors

- Cursors implemented through standard database APIs
- Cursors implemented through Transact-SQL

Two common uses for Transact-SQL cursors

- For your own use in scripts and procedures
- For use in procedures that provide database access to application programs that can't use standard database APIs

When to code Transact-SQL cursors for your own use

- For administrative scripts and procedures that manipulate database objects using dynamic SQL or system stored procedures
- For scripts or procedures that need to do something different to each row in a dataset based on criteria that are more complex than can be stated in a WHERE clause

Description

- By default, SQL statements work with all the rows in a result set. If you need to work with data one row at a time, you can use a *cursor*.
- The common database *APIs (application programming interfaces)*, such as ADO and ODBC, use cursors to provide application programs access to SQL Server data. Since the API manages the cursor on the client, you don't need to write any Transact-SQL code on the server.
- Although there are some programming problems that require the use of Transact-SQL cursors, you won't use them often. Since cursors are slower and take up more system resources than other database access techniques, you should avoid using them whenever possible.
- Transact-SQL cursors are similar to API cursors. If you understand how Transact-SQL cursors work, then, you'll have a general understanding of how you might work with API cursors.

Figure 15-1   An introduction to cursors

The seven types of SQL Server cursors

SQL Server supports seven different types of cursors. Of these seven types, four correspond to standard API cursors and the other three are only available as Transact-SQL cursors. Figure 15-2 presents the key characteristics of each type of cursor.

One of the characteristics of a cursor is its *scrollability*. A *forward-only cursor*, for example, can only retrieve the next row in the cursor result set. In contrast, a *scrollable* cursor can retrieve a row that's either before or after the current row.

The other key characteristic of a cursor is its *sensitivity*, which indicates whether the cursor is sensitive to changes in the database. If a cursor is sensitive to changes, that means it's aware of changes that occur after the cursor is created. Then, you'll see those changes when you retrieve the changed row.

For example, suppose another user changes row 5 while your cursor is positioned at row 4. When you retrieve the next row, a sensitive cursor will return the changed row, but an insensitive cursor will return the original, unchanged row.

Notice that there are three different levels of cursor sensitivity. A *static* cursor is insensitive to all changes. When you open a static cursor, the system makes a copy of the result set in the tempdb database. Then, when you fetch a row, it's returned from this copy, not from the base tables. Since changes to the base tables don't affect this static copy, the cursor isn't aware of them.

In contrast, a *dynamic* cursor is sensitive to all changes. To accomplish that, a dynamic cursor essentially reruns the SELECT query for the cursor each time you fetch a row. For this reason, any data that has changed since the previous row was fetched is included in the result set.

Finally, a *keyset-driven* cursor is sensitive to some, but not all, database changes. Specifically, a keyset-driven cursor will reflect updates and deletes to any row included in the result set, but it won't reflect new rows that have been inserted into the database. When you open a keyset-driven cursor, the system stores a copy of the unique key values (the *keyset*) for the result set in the tempdb database. Then, when you fetch a row, the cursor uses this keyset to query the base tables. Since the fetch goes back to the base table for the non-key columns, the cursor is sensitive to updates or deletions. Since membership in the keyset is set once the cursor is opened, however, the cursor can't detect insertions.

Notice that the names of the API cursor types are similar to the keywords you use to create them in SQL. Unfortunately, these naming schemes don't correspond exactly. Specifically, a forward-only cursor is a unique type of API cursor, but Transact-SQL has four different types of forward-only cursors. This should be clearer once you learn the syntax for declaring a cursor.

For now, you should try to understand the relative performance of the various cursor types. As you might expect, dynamic cursors require the most system resources and perform the slowest, static cursors are the fastest, and keyset-driven cursors are in between the other two. Furthermore, a scrollable

The seven types of SQL Server cursors

Standard API cursor type	Transact-SQL cursor keyword	Scrollable	Sensitive to database changes
Dynamic	DYNAMIC	Yes	Yes
Keyset-driven	KEYSET	Yes	Yes, for updates and deletes, but not for insertions
Static	STATIC	Yes	No
Forward-only	FORWARD_ONLY	No	Yes
(none)	FORWARD_ONLY KEYSET	No	Yes, for updates and deletes, but not for insertions
(none)	FORWARD_ONLY STATIC	No	No
(none)	FAST_FORWARD	No	No

Description

- Most database APIs support four basic types of cursors. SQL Server provides for these four types and three additional types. These types differ based on their *scrollability* and their *sensitivity*.

- If a cursor is *scrollable*, you can use it to retrieve a row before or after the current row. If a cursor isn't scrollable, you can use it only to retrieve the row after the current row. This type of cursor is called a *forward-only cursor*.

- If a cursor is *sensitive* to database changes, then it's aware of changes to the database that occur after the cursor is created.

- A *dynamic cursor* is sensitive to all changes to the source data. Since dynamic cursors basically rerun the cursor query every time you fetch a new row, they require the most system resources and result in the slowest system performance. By default, dynamic cursors are scrollable.

- A *keyset-driven cursor* is sensitive to updates and deletes to the source data, but it's insensitive to insertions. By default, keyset-driven cursors are scrollable.

- A *static cursor* is insensitive to any changes to the source data. By default, static cursors are scrollable.

- By default, a forward-only cursor is sensitive to database changes but isn't scrollable. Since forward-only cursors take up fewer system resources than scrollable cursors, they are faster.

- Transact-SQL supports three additional forward-only cursor types: KEYSET, STATIC, and FAST_FORWARD. A FAST_FORWARD cursor is optimized for performance, so it's the fastest of the Transact-SQL cursor types.

Figure 15-2   The seven types of SQL Server cursors

cursor uses more resources and performs slower than a forward-only cursor. Taking both of these characteristics into account, the table in figure 15-2 lists the cursor types by order of relative performance, from slowest to fastest.

SQL statements for cursor processing

Figure 15-3 presents the five SQL statements for working with Transact-SQL cursors. The first is the DECLARE statement, which you use to create a cursor and define its type. You'll learn how to code this statement in the next figure.

Once you've declared the cursor, you use the OPEN statement to populate it based on the SELECT query in the DECLARE CURSOR statement. Then you can use the FETCH statement to retrieve one row at a time from the result set through the cursor.

When you're finished using the cursor, you use the CLOSE statement to close the cursor. This releases the system resources that the cursor requires for storing and navigating through the result set. Note, however, that the definition of the cursor still exists after you close it. Because of that, you could open it and populate the result set again. However, it's unlikely that you'll ever need to do that. Instead, you'll use the DEALLOCATE statement to delete the cursor definition and release the remaining system resources associated with the cursor.

The script in this figure illustrates how these five statements are used together to work with a cursor. The first statement declares a static cursor named Vendors_Cursor. Notice that the SELECT statement in the FOR clause of the DECLARE statement defines the result set that will be used by the cursor. Then, the OPEN statement creates the cursor.

The FETCH NEXT statement that follows retrieves the next row from the cursor. Since this is the first fetch from a newly opened cursor, the first row is fetched. Then, within the WHILE loop, the script continues to fetch the next row until the last row in the result set is reached. The system function @@FETCH_STATUS used in the WHILE loop tests whether the latest FETCH statement succeeded. You'll learn more about using this function later in this chapter. Finally, the CLOSE and DEALLOCATE statements release all of the system resources used by the cursor.

The SQL statements for cursor processing

Statement	Description
DECLARE	Defines a new cursor.
OPEN	Opens and populates the cursor by executing the SELECT statement defined by the cursor.
FETCH	Retrieves a row from the cursor.
CLOSE	Closes the cursor.
DEALLOCATE	Deletes the cursor definition and releases all system resources associated with the cursor.

A SQL script that declares and uses a cursor

```
DECLARE Vendors_Cursor CURSOR
STATIC
FOR
    SELECT VendorID, VendorName
    FROM Vendors
    ORDER BY VendorName
OPEN Vendors_Cursor
FETCH NEXT FROM Vendors_Cursor
WHILE @@FETCH_STATUS = 0
    FETCH NEXT FROM Vendors_Cursor
CLOSE Vendors_Cursor
DEALLOCATE Vendors_Cursor
```

The response from the system

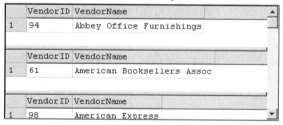

Description

- You typically code the cursor statements in the order shown above. The only argument you code in the OPEN, CLOSE, and DEALLOCATE statements is the name of the cursor.

- The DECLARE statement specifies the cursor options and defines the SELECT statement that will be used to populate the cursor. See figure 15-4 for the complete syntax of this statement.

- The FETCH statement provides a number of variations for retrieving a row from a cursor. See figure 15-5 for details.

- The @@FETCH_STATUS system function tests whether the last FETCH statement was successful. See figure 15-6 for details.

Figure 15-3   SQL statements for cursor processing

How to use cursors to retrieve data

Now that you've learned what cursors are and why you might use them, you're ready to begin working with them yourself. In the topics that follow, you'll learn the syntax of the DECLARE and FETCH statements. Then you'll learn how to use two system functions that help you manage cursors in your scripts and procedures.

How to declare a cursor

Figure 15-4 presents the syntax of the DECLARE statement for cursors. As you can see, you code the name of the new cursor between the DECLARE and CURSOR keywords. After that, you code one or more optional keywords that determine the cursor type. The second and third set of optional keywords define the scrollability and sensitivity of the cursor. I'll explain more about the other optional keywords shortly.

In the FOR clause, you code the SELECT statement that defines the result set for the cursor. You can code any SELECT query here, including one with joins, subqueries, or summary queries. However, you can't code a SELECT statement with the INTO clause.

You should be aware that if the type of cursor you request is incompatible with the type of SELECT statement you code, SQL Server will implicitly change the cursor type to match the SELECT statement. If you code a GROUP BY clause in the SELECT statement, for example, the cursor can't be dynamic so it's implicitly changed to a static cursor. For more information, refer to the index entry "implicit cursors" in Books Online.

The first set of optional keywords, LOCAL and GLOBAL, identifies the *scope* of the cursor. If you declare a local cursor, you can only use it within the current batch or procedure. If you declare a global cursor, you can use it from any script or procedure on the current connection. However, it can't be used from two or more connections. The default value is GLOBAL for most systems, but this default can be changed. Because of that, you should always include this keyword if you're unsure about your system's default setting.

The fourth set of optional keywords, READ_ONLY, SCROLL_LOCKS, and OPTIMISTIC, identifies the concurrency option for the cursor. As you'll learn later in this chapter, this setting identifies the kind of lock that's placed on a row when data is updated through the cursor.

The last clause for this statement, FOR UPDATE OF, is also used when updating data through a cursor. This clause is used to restrict the columns that can be updated. If you omit this clause, any column in the result set can be updated. If you include this clause, a column can be updated only if it's included in this list. Since views provide a more flexible technique for identifying specific columns, you'll typically base the cursor on a view that retrieves just the columns that can be updated instead of using the FOR UPDATE OF clause.

The syntax of the DECLARE CURSOR statement

```
DECLARE cursor_name CURSOR
    [LOCAL|GLOBAL]
    [FORWARD_ONLY|SCROLL]
    [FAST_FORWARD|STATIC|KEYSET|DYNAMIC]
    [READ_ONLY|SCROLL_LOCKS|OPTIMISTIC]
FOR select_statement
    [FOR UPDATE [OF column_name [, ...]]]
```

A DECLARE CURSOR statement that uses the default options

```
DECLARE Invoices_Cursor CURSOR
FOR
    SELECT * FROM Invoices
```

A DECLARE CURSOR statement that declares a dynamic local cursor

```
DECLARE VendorInvoice_Cursor CURSOR
LOCAL DYNAMIC
FOR
    SELECT VendorName, InvoiceDate, InvoiceTotal
    FROM Vendors JOIN Invoices ON Vendors.VendorID = Invoices.VendorID
```

A DECLARE CURSOR statement that declares a cursor for updating specific columns of the Vendors table

```
DECLARE VendorUpdate_Cursor CURSOR
GLOBAL SCROLL DYNAMIC SCROLL_LOCKS
FOR
    SELECT * FROM Vendors
    FOR UPDATE OF VendorName, VendorAddress1, VendorAddress2, VendorCity,
                  VendorState, VendorZipCode, VendorPhone
```

Description

- You code LOCAL or GLOBAL to identify the *scope* of the cursor. A local cursor can only be used within the batch or procedure in which it's declared, but a global cursor can be used by any script or procedure on the current connection.
- If you omit the scope, the default depends on the setting of the CURSOR_DEFAULT option for the database. The default for this setting is GLOBAL. See Books Online for more information on this option.
- You code FAST_FORWARD, STATIC, KEYSET, or DYNAMIC to identify the basic type of cursor. In addition, you can code FORWARD_ONLY and SCROLL to determine whether or not the cursor is scrollable.
- READ_ONLY, SCROLL_LOCKS, and OPTIMISTIC are concurrency options that determine how the cursor handles locking for update and delete operations. If you want to update or delete data through the cursor, you must use either OPTIMISTIC or SCROLL_LOCKS. See figure 15-8 for details.
- If you only want to allow updates to specific columns, you can code the FOR UPDATE OF clause with a list of the updatable column names.

Figure 15-4   How to declare a cursor

Figure 15-4 also presents three examples of the DECLARE CURSOR statement. The first example creates a cursor named Invoices_Cursor. Since none of the optional keywords are included, this cursor is created using the default settings: GLOBAL, FORWARD_ONLY, DYNAMIC, and OPTIMISTIC. Note, however, that the default settings change when one or more optional keywords are included. For example, the second DECLARE statement creates a dynamic cursor with local scope. Since the other two options aren't specified, they default to SCROLL and OPTIMISTIC.

The third example in this figure shows how you code the FOR UPDATE OF clause. In this case, all of the columns in the Vendors table are included in the result set, but only seven of those columns can be updated through the cursor.

How to retrieve a row using a cursor

Figure 15-5 presents the syntax of the FETCH statement, which retrieves a row from a Transact-SQL cursor. The keyword that follows specifies the direction of the fetch. If you don't specify a direction, FETCH NEXT is the default.

In the FROM clause, you code the name of the open cursor through which the row will be retrieved. Note that if both a global and a local cursor exist with the same name, a row will be fetched from the local cursor by default. In that case, you need to include the GLOBAL keyword to retrieve a row from the global cursor.

Generally, you'll want to assign the values retrieved by the FETCH statement into local variables. To do that, you code the INTO clause with a list of variable names. Note that you must list the variables in the proper order; the data type of each variable must match the data type of the corresponding column; and the number of variables you list must equal the number of columns in the result set. If you omit the INTO clause, the row is returned directly to the client. In the Query Analyzer, for example, the row is displayed in the Grids tab.

FETCH RELATIVE fetches the row *n* rows from the current row. If n is positive, it moves forward n rows. If n is negative, it moves backward n rows. And if n is zero, it fetches the same row again.

FETCH ABSOLUTE fetches the row *n* rows from the beginning of the result set. For this reason, FETCH FIRST and FETCH ABSOLUTE 1 are equivalent operations.

If the cursor is a forward-only cursor, FETCH NEXT is the only type of fetch that's allowed. For a scrollable cursor, you can fetch in any direction. You can't use FETCH ABSOLUTE with a dynamic cursor, however, because the number of rows in the result set can vary due to changes in the base table.

The syntax of the FETCH statement

```
FETCH [NEXT|PRIOR|FIRST|LAST|ABSOLUTE n|RELATIVE n]
FROM [GLOBAL] cursor_name
[INTO @variable_name [, ...]]
```

A DECLARE CURSOR statement

```
DECLARE Vendor_Cursor CURSOR
STATIC
FOR SELECT VendorID, VendorName FROM Vendors
```

FETCH statements for retrieving rows from the cursor

```
FETCH FROM Vendor_Cursor                 -- Retrieves the next row
FETCH NEXT FROM Vendor_Cursor            -- Retrieves the next row
FETCH PRIOR FROM Vendor_Cursor           -- Retrieves the previous row
FETCH FIRST FROM Vendor_Cursor           -- Retrieves the first row
FETCH LAST FROM Vendor_Cursor            -- Retrieves the last row
FETCH ABSOLUTE 3 FROM Vendor_Cursor      -- Retrieves the third row
FETCH RELATIVE 10 FROM Vendor_Cursor     -- Retrieves the tenth row after
                                         -- the current row

FETCH RELATIVE -2 FROM Vendor_Cursor     -- Retrieves the row two rows before
                                         -- the current row

FETCH RELATIVE 0 FROM Vendor_Cursor      -- Retrieves the current row again
FETCH FROM Vendor_Cursor                 -- Retrieves the next row and assigns
INTO @VendorIDVar,@VendorNameVar         -- the values to two local variables
```

Description

- The FETCH statement retrieves the specified row from the cursor. If you don't specify a direction for the fetch operation, NEXT is the default. If the cursor is forward-only, NEXT is the only valid direction.

- FETCH ABSOLUTE fetches the row *n* rows from the beginning of the result set, where the rows are numbered from 1 through the total number of rows. You can't use ABSOLUTE for dynamic cursors since the number of rows can change.

- FETCH RELATIVE fetches the row *n* rows after the last row fetched. If n is negative, the statement fetches backwards. If n is zero, it retrieves the same row again.

- The FROM clause names the cursor that contains the row to be fetched. If both a local and a global cursor exist with the same name, the local cursor is used by default. If that's not what you want, you can code the GLOBAL keyword.

- The INTO clause lets you assign the values in the retrieved row to local variables. If you omit this clause, the row is returned directly to the client. If you're using the Query Analyzer, that means that the row is displayed in the Grids tab.

Figure 15-5   How to retrieve a row using a cursor

How to use the @@FETCH_STATUS system function

You can use the @@FETCH_STATUS system function to determine the status of the most recently executed FETCH statement. As you can see in figure 15-6, if the function returns a zero value, the fetch was successful. If the fetch reached the end of the result set, @@FETCH_STATUS is -1. These are the only two possible values for dynamic or static cursors.

If you're fetching through a keyset-driven cursor, @@FETCH_STATUS can also return a value of -2. This means that you attempted to fetch a row that has been deleted. In other words, another user or process deleted a row that was a member of the keyset. Since a static cursor is insensitive to deletions, this error can't occur when you use those cursors. Similarly, a dynamic cursor is sensitive to deletions, so a fetch won't even try to retrieve a deleted row.

You typically test the value of the @@FETCH_STATUS system function in the conditional expression of a WHILE loop that repeatedly fetches rows from a cursor. For example, this WHILE statement

```
WHILE @@FETCH_STATUS <> -1
```

will work for any type of cursor. If you use this statement with a keyset-driven cursor, you'll also want to check the @@FETCH_STATUS function for a value of -2 within the loop. This is illustrated by the third example in this figure.

If the cursor isn't a keyset-driven cursor, you could also code the WHILE statement like this

```
WHILE @@FETCH_STATUS = 0
```

since you don't have to worry about it returning a value of -2. This is illustrated by the first two examples in this figure. Since keyset-driven cursors are used less frequently than dynamic or static cursors, you'll probably use this test more often.

The @@FETCH_STATUS system function reflects the status of the most recently executed FETCH statement on the current connection. Since you could have more than one cursor open on the same connection, you could accidentally check the status of the wrong cursor. To avoid this mistake, be sure to test the status immediately after the FETCH statement.

The values returned by the @@FETCH_STATUS system function

Value	Description
0	The FETCH was successful.
-1	The FETCH was unsuccessful because it reached the end of the result set.
-2	The FETCH was unsuccessful because the row was deleted.

A WHILE loop that steps forward through a result set

```
FETCH FIRST FROM Vendor_Cursor
WHILE @@FETCH_STATUS = 0
    BEGIN
        ...
        FETCH NEXT FROM Vendor_Cursor
    END
```

A WHILE loop that steps backward through a result set

```
FETCH LAST FROM Vendor_Cursor
WHILE @@FETCH_STATUS = 0
    BEGIN
        ...
        FETCH PRIOR FROM Vendor_Cursor
    END
```

A WHILE loop that fetches data through a keyset-driven cursor

```
FETCH FIRST FROM Vendor_Keyset_Cursor
WHILE @@FETCH_STATUS <> -1
    BEGIN
        IF @@FETCH_STATUS = -2
            PRINT 'Missing row. Value was deleted.'
        ...
        FETCH NEXT FROM Vendor_Keyset_Cursor
    END
```

Description

- The @@FETCH_STATUS system function returns the status of the most recent FETCH statement. You'll typically use this function in a WHILE loop after the first fetch to fetch the remaining rows in the result set.

- Unless you're using a keyset-driven cursor, @@FETCH_STATUS returns either 0 or -1. In that case, the WHILE loop can either test that the value of this function is equal to zero or not equal to -1.

- For a keyset-driven cursor, @@FETCH_STATUS can also return -2, which means that the row you're trying to fetch has been deleted. In that case, the WHILE loop should test that the value of this function is not equal to -1. In addition, you should test that this function isn't equal to -2 within the loop.

Warning

- @@FETCH_STATUS is global to all of the cursors open on the current connection. So if you're using multiple cursors, don't code other statements between the fetch and the test of @@FETCH_STATUS.

Figure 15-6   How to use the @@FETCH_STATUS system function

How to use the @@CURSOR_ROWS system function

You can use the value returned by the @@CURSOR_ROWS system function to get the number of rows in the result set of the most recently opened cursor. The values this function can return are listed in figure 15-7. If the value isn't negative, it represents the number of rows in the result set. If it's zero, it indicates that the result set is empty. And if it's -1, it indicates that the most recently opened cursor is a dynamic cursor. In that case, since the number of rows in a dynamic cursor can change with deletions and insertions by other users, the total number of rows is unknown.

The script in this figure shows how you might use the @@CURSOR_ROWS function. This script uses a cursor to retrieve and print 5% of the rows in the Vendors table. To do that, it divides the result of the @@CURSOR_ROWS function by 5 and stores it in a variable named @CursorIncrement. Then, after it retrieves and prints the first row in the result set, is uses the @CursorIncrement variable in a FETCH RELATIVE statement within a WHILE loop. The six rows that are printed by this script are shown in this figure.

The values returned by the @@CURSOR_ROWS system function

Value	Description
n	The number of eligible rows for the most recently opened cursor.
0	No cursor is open or no rows qualified for the cursor.
-1	The number of rows can change because this is a dynamic cursor.

A script that prints 5% of the rows in a result set

```
DECLARE Vendor_Cursor CURSOR
STATIC
FOR
    SELECT VendorID, VendorName FROM Vendors ORDER BY VendorName

DECLARE @CursorIncrement int, @VendorIDVar int, @VendorNameVar varchar(50)

OPEN Vendor_Cursor
IF @@CURSOR_ROWS > 0
    BEGIN
        SET @CursorIncrement = @@CURSOR_ROWS / 5
        FETCH NEXT FROM Vendor_Cursor INTO @VendorIDVar, @VendorNameVar
        WHILE @@FETCH_STATUS = 0
            BEGIN
                PRINT CONVERT(varchar,@VendorIDVar) + ', ' + @VendorNameVar
                FETCH RELATIVE @CursorIncrement FROM Vendor_Cursor
                INTO @VendorIDVar, @VendorNameVar
            END
    END
CLOSE Vendor_Cursor
DEALLOCATE Vendor_Cursor
```

The response from the system

```
94, Abbey Office Furnishings
12, City Of Fresno
107, Franchise Tax Board
111, Net Asset, Llc
56, Springhouse Corp
92, Zip Print & Copy Center
```

Description

- The @@CURSOR_ROWS system function returns the number of rows in the result set. If the number is zero, no rows qualified for the result set.

- The number of rows in a static or keyset-driven cursor is fixed when you open the cursor.

- Since the number of rows in a dynamic cursor can change, this function can't return a row count. Instead, it returns a value of -1.

Figure 15-7   How to use the @@CURSOR_ROWS system function

How to modify data through a cursor

Application programs commonly need to modify data through an API, and the various APIs provide the ability to do this using API cursors. As you've already learned, however, you don't need to write any Transact-SQL code for this to happen.

On the other hand, you'll seldom need to modify data through a Transact-SQL cursor. Instead, you'll use these cursors only to retrieve data. For completeness, though, I'm now going to show you how to use Transact-SQL cursors to modify data. But first, you need to understand how concurrency works.

How to use the cursor concurrency options

Database errors can occur when two or more users or processes try to modify the same data simultaneously. This problem is known as *concurrency*, and it will be presented in detail in the next chapter. At this point, you just need to understand that the likelihood of concurrency increases as the number of simultaneous users goes up. So, for small systems, concurrency may never be an issue.

One way that SQL Server can manage concurrency is to place a *lock* on a row while a user is working with it. Then, other users can't work with that row until the first user is done with it. You can use two different types of locks when you work with data through a cursor: optimistic and pessimistic. These two types of locks are summarized in figure 15-8.

If you use *pessimistic locking*, the system places a lock on a row when you fetch it. The lock remains until you fetch another row or close the cursor. This guarantees that no other user or process can modify or delete that row while you have it locked.

If you use *optimistic locking*, the system doesn't place a lock on the row. Then, if you subsequently update or delete the row through the cursor, the system checks if the row still exists and, if so, if the current version of the row is the same as the version of the row you fetched. If another user or process modified or deleted the row between the time you fetched it and updated it, you'll get an error message. Then, you can include code to handle the error. If the row was modified, for example, you could fetch it again and resubmit the update. If the row was deleted, however, you'd get an error when you tried to fetch it and you wouldn't be able to resubmit the original operation.

To use pessimistic locking, you specify the SCROLL_LOCKS keyword in the DECLARE CURSOR statement. To use optimistic locking, you specify the OPTIMISTIC keyword. The third keyword, READ_ONLY, prevents updates through the cursor, so no locking is necessary. If you omit all three keywords, the default concurrency option is OPTIMISTIC for dynamic and keyset-driven cursors and READ_ONLY for static cursors.

For most systems, optimistic concurrency is fine. However, if your system has many users and you need to routinely update through a cursor, you may

The three Transact-SQL cursor concurrency options

Option	Description
OPTIMISTIC	No lock is placed on the row. This means that a row can be modified by another process in the time between when you fetch and update the data.
SCROLL_LOCKS	Each row is locked when it's fetched. This means that no other process can modify the row until you release the lock by fetching a different row or closing the cursor.
READ_ONLY	You can't update data through the cursor, so rows are never locked.

Description

- In a multi-user database, two or more users can work with the same data at the same time. This is known as *concurrency*.

- The concurrency option you include in the DECLARE CURSOR statement specifies how the cursor handles concurrency.

- One way for a database to handle concurrency is to place a *lock* on a row when it's fetched. When the row is locked, the system prevents any other user or process from modifying or deleting that row.

- The OPTIMISTIC option implements *optimistic locking* for the cursor. This type of locking assumes that no other process is likely to modify the same row at the same time. For systems with a limited number of users, this assumption is usually true.

- If you use optimistic locking, the system tests to see if the row has been modified since you fetched it. If you try to update the row but it was changed or deleted by another user, the update raises error number 16934. Then, you can test for this error in your code and handle it accordingly.

- The SCROLL_LOCKS option implements *pessimistic locking*. This type of locking assumes that two or more processes will try to modify the same row at the same time. If you use this option, the cursor locks the row at the current position in the source table.

- A row that you fetch using pessimistic locking can't be modified or deleted by any other process. However, the other process doesn't get an error message stating that the row is locked. Instead, the update or delete is suspended until your lock is released. Since the lock remains in place until you fetch another row or until the cursor is closed, you shouldn't keep the cursor at the same position for long.

- By default, static cursors, including FAST_FORWARD cursors, are set to READ_ONLY and keyset-driven and dynamic cursors are set to OPTIMISTIC. These settings are acceptable for most small to medium-sized systems.

Figure 15-8   How to use the cursor concurrency options

want to use pessimistic locking. In particular, if the updates affect critical data that can't be corrected by simply resubmitting the update, then pessimistic locking may be called for. Since pessimistic locking uses more system resources and delays access to your data, however, you should only use it when absolutely necessary.

How to update or delete data through a cursor

Figure 15-9 presents the syntax of the WHERE CURRENT OF clause. You can use this clause in an UPDATE or DELETE statement to update or delete the last row fetched through a cursor. The examples in this figure illustrate how this works.

The script shown here declares a dynamic cursor that retrieves data from the Vendors table. Then, it opens the cursor and fetches the first row. Because the SCROLL_LOCKS option was specified in the DECLARE CURSOR statement, this row is locked so that it can't be modified except through the cursor.

The UPDATE statement shown in this figure could be used to modify the row that's retrieved by the script. To do that, it uses the CURRENT OF phrase in the WHERE clause. This phrase names the cursor that contains the row to be updated. In contrast, the UPDATE clause names the base table that contains the row to be updated. That makes sense because the data to be updated resides in the base table, not in the result set defined by the cursor. In this case, you're using the cursor to identify the row you want to update.

The third example in this figure shows how you can use the WHERE CURRENT OF clause in a DELETE statement. Note that in this case, the statement would result in an error. That's because the Invoices table contains invoices with the current VendorID, so deleting this vendor would violate referential integrity.

The syntax of the WHERE CURRENT OF clause

```
WHERE CURRENT OF cursor_name
```

A script that declares a cursor and fetches the first row

```
DECLARE Dynamic_Vendor_Cursor CURSOR
DYNAMIC SCROLL_LOCKS
FOR
    SELECT * FROM Vendors ORDER BY VendorName

OPEN Dynamic_Vendor_Cursor
FETCH Dynamic_Vendor_Cursor
```

The response from the system

	VendorID	VendorName	VendorAddress1	VendorAddress2	VendorC
1	94	Abbey Office Furnishings	4150 W Shaw Ave	NULL	Fresno

An UPDATE statement that modifies the row at the current cursor position

```
UPDATE Vendors
    SET VendorName = 'Peerless Networking'
    WHERE CURRENT OF Dynamic_Vendor_Cursor
```

A DELETE statement that deletes the row at the current cursor position

```
DELETE Vendors
    WHERE CURRENT OF Dynamic_Vendor_Cursor
```

Description

- You can update or delete the last row fetched through a cursor by using the WHERE CURRENT OF clause instead of a search condition in an UPDATE or DELETE statement. This clause names the cursor that was used to fetch the row.

- To use a cursor in a WHERE CURRENT OF clause, the cursor must be set for OPTIMISTIC or SCROLL_LOCKS concurrency.

Figure 15-9   How to update or delete data through a cursor

Additional cursor processing techniques

At the beginning of this chapter, I listed the two common uses for Transact-SQL cursors. In the two topics that follow, I'll present scripts that demonstrate these uses. If you understand how these examples work, you'll be able to code Transact-SQL cursors of your own.

How to use cursors with dynamic SQL

Figure 15-10 presents a script that uses a cursor to fetch data that's used to generate a dynamic SQL statement. This script creates a temporary table that summarizes the column names, data types, and row count for each table in a database. This is the same table that was created by the script in figure 13-13. Now, you can compare this cursor-based solution with the previous one.

This script starts by creating the temporary table named #TableSummary that's based on the information schema view named COLUMNS. Then, it declares two variables. The first one, @TableNameVar, will be used to hold the name of each table that's processed, and the second one, @ExecVar, will be used to hold the SQL string to be executed.

The second DECLARE statement declares the cursor that will be used to navigate through the temporary table. Since this cursor is used only to step through the distinct values of the TableName column in the temporary table in sequence, it's declared as a forward-only cursor. Specifically, it's defined with the FAST_FORWARD keyword since the result set that's retrieved by this cursor won't change. Note that by declaring a cursor over the temporary table, this script doesn't need to create the second temporary table used by the solution in chapter 13.

If you compare the WHILE loop in this example with the one in figure 13-13, you'll see that they both build a SQL string that consists of three SQL statements. The first one declares a variable named @CountVar that will be used to store the row count for each table. The second one is a SELECT statement that retrieves the row count for the current table. And the third one is an INSERT statement that inserts the row count into the temporary table.

You'll notice two key differences between the code in this loop and the one in figure 13-13. First, since the FETCH statement retrieves a single row into @TableNameVar, I didn't need to code a SELECT statement to do that. Second, the execution of the WHILE loop is controlled by the @@FETCH_STATUS system function rather than a variable that loops through all the tables.

As I mentioned earlier in this chapter, a set-based query will typically outperform an equivalent cursor-based query. In this case, however, the cursor-based query is faster despite the overhead required to support the cursor. That's because the set-based solution executes more operations within each iteration of the WHILE loop.

A script that creates a summary of the tables in a database

```
USE AP
IF OBJECT_ID('tempdb..#TableSummary') IS NOT NULL
    DROP TABLE #TableSummary
SELECT TABLE_NAME AS TableName, COLUMN_NAME AS ColumnName, DATA_TYPE AS Type
INTO #TableSummary
FROM INFORMATION_SCHEMA.COLUMNS
WHERE TABLE_NAME IN
      (SELECT TABLE_NAME FROM INFORMATION_SCHEMA.TABLES
       WHERE (TABLE_TYPE = 'BASE TABLE' AND
              TABLE_NAME NOT IN ('dtproperties', 'TableSummary')))

DECLARE @TableNameVar varchar(128), @ExecVar varchar(1000)
DECLARE TableSummary_Cursor CURSOR
FAST_FORWARD
FOR
    SELECT DISTINCT TableName
    FROM #TableSummary

OPEN TableSummary_Cursor
FETCH NEXT FROM TableSummary_Cursor INTO @TableNameVar
WHILE @@FETCH_STATUS = 0
BEGIN
    SET @ExecVar = 'DECLARE @CountVar int ' + 'SELECT @CountVar = COUNT(*) '
    SET @ExecVar = @ExecVar + 'FROM ' + @TableNameVar + ' '
    SET @ExecVar = @ExecVar + 'INSERT #TableSummary '
    SET @ExecVar = @ExecVar + 'VALUES (''' + @TableNameVar + ''','
    SET @ExecVar = @ExecVar + '''*Row Count*'',' + ' @CountVar)'
    EXEC (@ExecVar)
    FETCH NEXT FROM TableSummary_Cursor INTO @TableNameVar
END
CLOSE TableSummary_Cursor
DEALLOCATE TableSummary_Cursor

SELECT * FROM #TableSummary
ORDER BY TableName, ColumnName
```

The result set returned by the script

	TableName	ColumnName	Type
19	InvoiceLineItems	*Row Count*	118
20	InvoiceLineItems	AccountNo	int
21	InvoiceLineItems	InvoiceID	int
22	InvoiceLineItems	InvoiceLineItemAmount	money
23	InvoiceLineItems	InvoiceLineItemDescription	varchar

Description

- This script creates a temporary table named #TableSummary that has one row for each column in the database, including the table name and the data type. In addition, it adds a row that shows the row count for each table.

- This script runs faster than the one shown in figure 13-13 because it doesn't have to rerun the query each time through the loop. For this reason, it's more efficient despite the overhead required by the cursor.

Figure 15-10   How to use cursors with dynamic SQL

How to code Transact-SQL cursors for use by an application program

Figure 15-11 illustrates how you might use Transact-SQL cursors to provide an application program access to a database. Since the database APIs provide built-in support for this kind of access, application programmers should use them whenever possible. However, there are rare situations where a programmer can't use an API or prefers not to. In those situations, you may be able to provide access as shown here.

The code in the first part of this figure creates three stored procedures. The first procedure, spOpenInvoices, declares and opens a cursor over selected rows in the Invoices table. The second procedure, spGetInvoice, fetches a row from the cursor result set and returns it through a set of output parameters. Notice that the return value of this procedure is the value of @@FETCH_STATUS. The third procedure, spCloseInvoices, closes and deallocates the cursor.

The second part of this figure presents pseudocode that illustrates how an application program might use these stored procedures to read data from the Invoices table. I've used pseudocode here to reflect the fact that this code doesn't have to be written in a particular language. Instead, this code represents functionality that should be available in any language.

The pseudocode starts by declaring two variables. The first one is an integer that will be used to store the return code from the spGetInvoice procedure. The second is a record that will be used to hold the invoice row returned by the spGetInvoice procedure.

The next statement opens the connection to SQL Server. Since this program isn't using an API, the programmer would have to code this function himself or get it from a library of procedures or methods other than a standard database API. Since this code is quite complicated, omitting it from this example makes this technique appear simpler than it really is. Luckily, you don't need to understand how to manage a database connection to understand this example. You should keep in mind, however, that the complexity of this kind of code is one of the reasons programmers prefer to use standard APIs.

Once the connection is established, the program can issue SQL commands. In this pseudocode, the Execute statement is used to execute a stored procedure on the server. So the first Execute statement declares and opens the cursor, and the second Execute statement fetches the first row. Notice that when a row is fetched, the parameters defined by the stored procedure are stored in invoice_record. In addition, the return value from the stored procedure is stored in return_code. This value is used to control the WHILE loop that follows.

Within the WHILE loop, the program can work with the values returned by spGetInvoice. In this example, the program simply displays invoice_record. Then, it fetches the next row.

The last two statements execute the spCloseInvoices stored procedure and disconnect from the database. That's important because if the cursor remains open on the server, it will take up server resources and affect performance. An open database connection will similarly affect the server.

Three stored procedures that manage a global cursor

```
CREATE PROC spOpenInvoices
AS
    DECLARE Invoices_Cursor CURSOR
    GLOBAL SCROLL DYNAMIC
    FOR
        SELECT *
        FROM Invoices WHERE InvoiceTotal - CreditTotal - PaymentTotal > 0
    OPEN Invoices_Cursor
GO

CREATE PROC spGetInvoice
    @InvoiceID      int             OUTPUT, @VendorID      int           OUTPUT,
    @InvoiceNumber  varchar(50)     OUTPUT, @InvoiceDate   smalldatetime OUTPUT,
    @InvoiceTotal   money           OUTPUT, @PaymentTotal  money         OUTPUT,
    @CreditTotal    money           OUTPUT, @TermsID       int           OUTPUT,
    @InvoiceDueDate smalldatetime OUTPUT, @PaymentDate   smalldatetime OUTPUT
AS
    FETCH NEXT FROM Invoices_Cursor INTO
        @InvoiceID, @VendorID, @InvoiceNumber, @InvoiceDate, @InvoiceTotal,
        @PaymentTotal, @CreditTotal, @TermsID, @InvoiceDueDate, @PaymentDate
    RETURN @@FETCH_STATUS
GO

CREATE PROC spCloseInvoices
AS
    CLOSE Invoices_Cursor
    DEALLOCATE Invoices_Cursor
```

Pseudocode that displays rows using the stored procedures

```
Declare return_code, invoice_record

Open database_connection
Execute('spOpenInvoices')

return_code = Execute('spGetInvoice' stored into invoice_record)

While return_code = 0
    Display(invoice_record)
    return_code = Execute('spGetInvoice' stored into invoice_record)
Loop

Execute('spCloseInvoices')
Close database_connection
```

Description

- If an application doesn't use one of the database APIs, you can sometimes provide database access through Transact-SQL cursors.

Warning

- Until they're closed and deallocated, global cursors continue to use server resources until the connection is closed. Since this can slow server performance, you should always verify that the application closes and deallocates any open cursors.

Figure 15-11   How to code Transact-SQL cursors for use by an application program

Perspective

In this chapter, you learned about the two ways that cursors are implemented in SQL Server. Despite the fact that you'll probably use cursors infrequently, knowing how to use them gives you an additional problem-solving tool. In addition, knowing how Transact-SQL cursors work can help you better understand how the standard database API cursors work.

In the next chapter, you'll learn more about the concepts of concurrency and locking that were introduced in this chapter. But first, you'll learn how to work with transactions, which give you a powerful tool for effectively managing database changes.

Terms

cursor
API (application programming interface)
API cursor
Transact-SQL cursor
cursor scrollability
cursor sensitivity
forward-only cursor
dynamic cursor

keyset-driven cursor
keyset
static cursor
scope
concurrency
lock
optimistic locking
pessimistic locking

16

How to manage transactions and locking

If you've been working with a stand-alone copy of SQL Server, you've been the only user of your database. In the real world, though, a database is typically used by many users working simultaneously. Then, what happens when two users try to update the same data at the same time?

In this chapter, you'll learn how SQL Server manages concurrent changes. But first, you'll learn how to combine related SQL statements into a single unit, called a transaction. By learning these skills, you'll be able to write code that anticipates these conflicts.

How to work with transactions

A *transaction* is a group of database operations that you combine into a single logical unit. By combining operations in this way, you can prevent certain kinds of database errors. In the topics that follow, you'll learn the SQL statements for managing transactions.

How transactions maintain data integrity

Figure 16-1 presents an example of three INSERT statements that are good candidates for a transaction. As you can see, the first INSERT statement adds a new invoice to the Invoices table. Next, a SET statement assigns the identity value for the newly inserted invoices to the @InvoiceID variable. Then, the last two INSERT statements insert rows into the InvoiceLineItems table that represent the two line items associated with the invoice.

What would happen if one or more of these INSERT statements failed? If the first statement failed, @NewInvoiceID wouldn't be assigned a valid value, so the last two insertions would also fail. However, if the first statement succeeded and one or both of the other INSERT statements failed, the Invoices and InvoiceLineItems tables wouldn't match. Specifically, the total of the InvoieLineItemAmount columns in the InvoiceLineItems table wouldn't equal the InvoiceTotal column in the Invoices table, so the data would be invalid.

Now, suppose that these three INSERT statements were executed as part of the same transaction as illustrated in the second example in this figure. Here, you can see that a BEGIN TRAN statement is executed before the first INSERT statement. Then, after the INSERT statement, an @@ERROR function tests if the statement completed successfully. If so, the @InvoiceID variable is set and the second INSERT statement is executed. The @@ERROR function is used again after this INSERT statement to be sure that it completed successfully. If it did, the third INSERT statement is executed. If this statement completes successfully, a COMMIT TRAN statement *commits* the changes to the database making them permanent. Otherwise, if an error occurs for any of the three INSERT statements, a ROLLBACK TRAN statement is executed to undo, or *rollback*, all of the changes made since the beginning of the transaction.

By grouping these SQL statements together in a single transaction, you can control whether and how changes are made to the database. Since all three INSERT statements must succeed for the transaction to be committed, a failure of any of the statements will cause the entire transaction to be rolled back. Note, however, that once you commit the transaction, you can't roll it back. Likewise, once you roll a transaction back, you can't commit it.

In this particular example, an error in one of the INSERT statements wouldn't be catastrophic. If a statement failed because you coded it incorrectly, you could easily correct the error by resubmitting the failed INSERT statement. If the failure was due to a system error such as a server crash, however, you wouldn't discover the error unless you looked for it after the server was restored.

Three INSERT statements that work with related data

```
DECLARE @InvoiceID int
INSERT Invoices
    VALUES (34,'ZXA-080','2002-08-30',14092.59,0,0,3,'2002-09-30',NULL)
SET @InvoiceID = @@IDENTITY
INSERT InvoiceLineItems VALUES (@InvoiceID,1,160,4447.23,'HW upgrade')
INSERT InvoiceLineItems VALUES (@InvoiceID,2,167,9645.36,'OS upgrade')
```

The same statements coded as a transaction

```
DECLARE @InvoiceID int
BEGIN TRAN
INSERT Invoices
  VALUES (34,'ZXA-080','2002-08-30',14092.59,0,0,3,'2002-09-30',NULL)
IF @@ERROR = 0
  BEGIN
    SET @InvoiceID = @@IDENTITY
    INSERT InvoiceLineItems VALUES (@InvoiceID,1,160,4447.23,'HW upgrade')
    IF @@ERROR = 0
      BEGIN
        INSERT InvoiceLineItems
            VALUES (@InvoiceID,2,167,9645.36,'OS upgrade')
        IF @@ERROR = 0
          COMMIT TRAN
        ELSE
          ROLLBACK TRAN
      END
    ELSE
      ROLLBACK TRAN
  END
ELSE
  ROLLBACK TRAN
```

When to use explicit transactions

- When you code two or more action queries that affect related data
- When you update foreign key references
- When you move rows from one table to another table
- When you code a SELECT query followed by an action query and the values inserted in the action query are based on the results of the SELECT query
- When a failure of any set of SQL statements would violate data integrity

Description

- A *transaction* is a group of database operations that are combined into a logical unit. By default, each SQL statement is treated as a separate transaction. However, you can combine any number of SQL statements into a single transaction as shown above.
- When you *commit* a transaction, the operations performed by the SQL statements become a permanent part of the database. Until it's committed, you can undo all of the changes made to the database since the beginning of the transaction by *rolling back* the transaction.
- A transaction is either committed or rolled back in its entirety. Once you commit a transaction, it can't be rolled back.

Figure 16-1   How transactions maintain data integrity

For some systems, however, a violation of data integrity such as this one is critical. For instance, consider the classic example of a transfer between two accounts in a banking system. In that case, one update reduces the balance in the first account and another update increases the balance in the second account. If one of these updates fails, either the bank or the customer gets an unexpected windfall. Because an error like this could cause problems even during the short period of time it may take to fix it, these two updates should be coded as a transaction.

SQL statements for handling transactions

Figure 16-2 summarizes the SQL statements used to process transactions. As you can see, you can code either the TRAN or the TRANSACTION keyword in each of these statements, although TRAN is used more commonly. You can also omit this keyword entirely from the COMMIT and ROLLBACK statements. However, it's customary to include this keyword since it makes your code easier to read.

The BEGIN TRAN statement explicitly marks the starting point of a transaction. If you don't code this statement, SQL Server implicitly starts a new transaction for each SQL statement you code. If the statement succeeds, the implicit transaction is committed automatically. For this reason, this mode is called *autocommit* mode. Note that you can't use the COMMIT TRAN statement to commit an implicit transaction.

However, you can code a ROLLBACK TRAN statement to roll back an implicit transaction. You saw examples of that in some of the triggers presented in chapter 14. The triggers in figure 14-17 rolled back an action query if it violated referential integrity between the Vendors and Invoices tables. And the trigger in figure 14-19 rolled back an UPDATE statement if it caused the data in the Invoices and InvoiceLineItems tables to be inconsistent.

You can also use the SAVE TRAN statement to declare one or more *save points* within a transaction. Then, you can roll back part of a transaction by coding the save point name in the ROLLBACK TRAN statement. You'll learn more about how that works in a moment.

This figure presents another script that uses a transaction. This script deletes the invoices for a particular vendor and then deletes the vendor. Notice that the script tests the value of the @@ROWCOUNT system function after rows are deleted from the Invoices table to see if more than one invoice was deleted. If so, the transaction is rolled back, so the deletion from the Invoices table is undone. If only one invoice was deleted, however, the code proceeds to delete the vendor from the Vendors table and then commit the transaction.

Before I go on, you should realize that you can also name a transaction in the BEGIN TRAN statement, and you can refer to that name in the COMMIT TRAN and ROLLBACK TRAN statements. Since there's usually no reason to do that, however, I've omitted that option from the syntax shown in this figure and from the examples shown in this chapter.

Summary of the SQL statements for processing transactions

Statement	Description
BEGIN {TRAN|TRANSACTION}	Marks the starting point of a transaction.
SAVE {TRAN|TRANSACTION} save_point	Sets a new save point within a transaction.
COMMIT [TRAN|TRANSACTION]	Marks the end of a transaction and makes the changes within the transaction a permanent part of the database.
ROLLBACK [[TRAN|TRANSACTION] [save_point]]	Rolls back a transaction to the starting point or to the specified save point.

A script that performs a test before committing the transaction

```
BEGIN TRAN
DELETE Invoices
WHERE VendorID = 34
IF @@ROWCOUNT > 1
    BEGIN
        ROLLBACK TRAN
        PRINT 'More invoices than expected. Deletions rolled back.'
    END
ELSE
    BEGIN
        DELETE Vendors
        WHERE VendorID = 34
        COMMIT TRAN
        PRINT 'Deletions committed to the database.'
    END
```

The response from the system

```
(3 row(s) affected)
More invoices than expected. Deletions rolled back.
```

Description

- Although you can omit the TRAN keyword from the COMMIT and ROLLBACK statements, it's generally included for readability.

- By default, SQL Server is in *autocommit mode*. Then, unless you explicitly start a transaction using the BEGIN TRAN statement, each statement is automatically treated as a separate transaction. If the statement causes an error, it's automatically rolled back. Otherwise, it's automatically committed.

- Even if you don't explicitly start a transaction, you can roll it back using the ROLLBACK TRAN statement. However, you can't explicitly commit an implicit transaction.

- When you use *save points*, you can roll a transaction all the way back to the beginning or to a particular save point. See figure 16-4 for details on using save points.

- Although you can name a transaction in the BEGIN TRAN statement and you can refer to that name in the COMMIT TRAN and ROLLBACK TRAN statements, you're not likely to do that.

Figure 16-2   SQL statements for handling transactions

How to work with nested transactions

A *nested transaction* is a transaction that's coded within another transaction. In other words, a BEGIN TRAN statement is coded after another BEGIN TRAN statement but before the COMMIT TRAN or ROLLBACK TRAN statement that ends the first transaction. Since there are few problems that can only be solved using nested transactions, it's unlikely that you'll ever need to code them. However, you should understand how the COMMIT TRAN statement behaves when you code it within a nested transaction. Figure 16-3 presents a script that illustrates how this works.

This example uses the @@TRANCOUNT system function, which returns the number of explicit transactions that are active on the current connection. If you haven't coded a BEGIN TRAN statement, @@TRANCOUNT returns zero. Then, each BEGIN TRAN statement increments @@TRANCOUNT by one, so its value indicates how deeply you've nested the transactions.

If the current value of @@TRANCOUNT is one, the COMMIT TRAN statement closes the current transaction and commits the changes to the database as you've seen in the last two figures. But if @@TRANCOUNT is greater than one, COMMIT TRAN simply decrements @@TRANCOUNT by 1. In other words, within a nested transaction, the COMMIT TRAN statement doesn't commit a transaction.

This counterintuitive behavior is illustrated by the script in this figure. Here, the COMMIT TRAN statement that follows the DELETE statement that deletes the Vendors table decrements @@TRANCOUNT, but doesn't commit the deletion. That's because this COMMIT TRAN statement is coded within a nested transaction.

On the other hand, the ROLLBACK TRAN statement always rolls back all of the uncommitted statements, whether or not they're coded within a nested transaction. In this script, for example, the ROLLBACK TRAN statement rolls back both DELETE statements. As you can see from the results of the last two statements in this script, neither DELETE statement was committed.

A script with nested transactions

```
BEGIN TRAN
PRINT 'First Tran  @@TRANCOUNT: ' + CONVERT(varchar,@@TRANCOUNT)
DELETE Invoices
  BEGIN TRAN
    PRINT 'Second Tran @@TRANCOUNT: ' + CONVERT(varchar,@@TRANCOUNT)
    DELETE Vendors
  COMMIT TRAN              -- This COMMIT decrements @@TRANCOUNT.
                          -- It doesn't commit 'DELETE Vendors'.
  PRINT 'COMMIT     @@TRANCOUNT: ' + CONVERT(varchar,@@TRANCOUNT)
ROLLBACK TRAN
PRINT 'ROLLBACK   @@TRANCOUNT: ' + CONVERT(varchar,@@TRANCOUNT)
SELECT 'Vendors count:  ' + CONVERT(varchar,COUNT(*)) FROM Vendors
SELECT 'Invoices count: ' + CONVERT(varchar,COUNT(*)) FROM Invoices
```

The response from the system

```
First Tran  @@TRANCOUNT: 1
(114 row(s) affected)
Second Tran @@TRANCOUNT: 2
(122 row(s) affected)
COMMIT      @@TRANCOUNT: 1
ROLLBACK    @@TRANCOUNT: 0
Vendors count:  122
Invoices count: 114
```

Description

- You can *nest* transactions by coding nested BEGIN TRAN statements. Each time this statement is executed, it increments the @@TRANCOUNT system function by 1. Then, you can query this function to determine how many levels deep the transactions are nested.

- If you execute a COMMIT TRAN statement when @@TRANCOUNT is equal to 1, all of the changes made to the database during the transaction are committed and @@TRANCOUNT is set to zero. If @@TRANCOUNT is greater than 1, however, the changes aren't committed. Instead, @@TRANCOUNT is simply decremented by 1.

- The ROLLBACK TRAN statement rolls back all active transactions regardless of the nesting level where it's coded. It also sets the value of @@TRANCOUNT back to 0.

- Since there are few programming problems that you can solve using nested transactions, you probably won't use them often.

Figure 16-3   How to work with nested transactions

How to work with save points

You can create save points within a transaction by coding the SAVE TRAN statement. In that case, you can roll back the transaction to that particular point by coding the save point name in the ROLLBACK TRAN statement. Figure 16-4 presents a script that shows how this works.

First, this script creates a temporary table named #VendorCopy that contains a copy of the VendorIDs and names and for the first four vendors in the Vendors table. After beginning a transaction, the script deletes a row and then sets a save point named Vendor1. Then the script deletes a second row, sets another save point named Vendor2, and deletes a third row. The result of the first SELECT statement that follows illustrates that only one row is left in the #VendorCopy table.

Next, a ROLLBACK TRAN statement rolls back the transaction to the Vendor2 save point. This rolls back the third delete, as illustrated by the second SELECT statement in this figure. The next ROLLBACK TRAN statement rolls the transaction back to the Vendor1 save point, which rolls back the second delete. At that point, the #VendorCopy table contains three rows, as illustrated by the third SELECT statement. Finally, a COMMIT TRAN statement commits the transaction. Since the only statement that hasn't already been rolled back is the statement that deleted the first row, this row is deleted permanently. The last SELECT statement illustrates the final result of this code.

You should note that if you don't code a save point name in the ROLLBACK TRAN statement, it ignores any save points and rolls back the entire transaction. In addition, you should notice that you can't code a save point name in a COMMIT TRAN statement. This means that you can't partially commit a transaction. Instead, a COMMIT TRAN statement ignores save points completely and commits the entire transaction.

As with nested transactions, you'll probably never need to use save points since there are few problems that can be solved by using them. Unlike the way nested transactions work, however, save points work in an intuitive way, so coding them is less confusing.

A transaction with two save points

```
SELECT VendorID, VendorName
INTO #VendorCopy
FROM Vendors
WHERE VendorID < 5
BEGIN TRAN
  DELETE #VendorCopy WHERE VendorID = 1
  SAVE TRAN Vendor1
    DELETE #VendorCopy WHERE VendorID = 2
    SAVE TRAN Vendor2
      DELETE #VendorCopy WHERE VendorID = 3
      SELECT * FROM #VendorCopy
    ROLLBACK TRAN Vendor2
    SELECT * FROM #VendorCopy
  ROLLBACK TRAN Vendor1
  SELECT * FROM #VendorCopy
COMMIT TRAN
SELECT * FROM #VendorCopy
```

The response from the system

```
VendorID     VendorName
-----------  -------------------------------------------------
4            Jobtrak

3            Register of Copyrights
4            Jobtrak

2            National Information Data Ctr
3            Register of Copyrights
4            Jobtrak

2            National Information Data Ctr
3            Register of Copyrights
4            Jobtrak
```

Description

- You can partially roll back a transaction if you use save points. If you code a save point name in the ROLLBACK TRAN statement, the system rolls back all of the statements to that save point.

- If you don't code a save point name, the ROLLBACK TRAN statement rolls back the entire transaction.

- Since you can't code a save point name in a COMMIT TRAN statement, the system always commits the entire transaction.

- As with nested transactions, there are few practical programming problems that you can solve using save points.

Figure 16-4   How to work with save points

An introduction to concurrency and locking

When two or more users have access to the same database, it's possible for them to be working with the same data at the same time. This is called *concurrency*. Concurrency isn't a problem when two users retrieve the same data at the same time. If they then try to update that data, however, that can be a problem. In the topics that follow, you'll learn more about concurrency and how SQL Server uses locking to prevent concurrency problems. You'll also learn how you can control the types of problems that are allowed.

How concurrency and locking are related

Figure 16-5 presents two transactions that select and then update data from the same row in the same table. If these two transactions are submitted at the same time, the one that executes first will be overwritten by the one that executes second. Since this means that one of the two updates is lost, this is known as a *lost update*.

This figure shows the result if the update operation in transaction A is executed first, in which case its update is lost when the update in transaction B is executed. Because transaction A is unaware that its update has been lost, however, this can leave the data in an unpredictable state that affects the integrity of the data. For the AP database, it's unlikely that a lost update will adversely affect the system. For some database systems, however, this sort of unpredictability can be disastrous.

If your database has a relatively small number of users, the likelihood of concurrency problems is low. However, the larger the system, the greater the number of users and transactions. For a large system, then, you should expect concurrency, and therefore concurrency problems, to occur more frequently.

One way to avoid concurrency problems is to use *locking*. By holding a lock on the data, the transaction prevents others from using that data. Then, after the transaction releases the lock, the next transaction can work with that data.

Since SQL Server automatically enables and manages locking, it may prevent most of the concurrency problems on your system. If the number of users of your system grows, however, you may find that the default locking mechanism is insufficient. In that case, you may need to override the default locking behavior. You'll learn how to do that in a moment. But first, you need to understand the four concurrency problems that locks can prevent.

Two transactions that retrieve and then modify the data in the same row

Transaction A

```
BEGIN TRAN
DECLARE @InvoiceTotal money, @PaymentTotal money, @CreditTotal money
SELECT @InvoiceTotal = InvoiceTotal, @CreditTotal = CreditTotal,
      @PaymentTotal = PaymentTotal FROM Invoices WHERE InvoiceID = 6
UPDATE Invoices
  SET InvoiceTotal = @InvoiceTotal, CreditTotal = @CreditTotal + 317.40,
      PaymentTotal = @PaymentTotal WHERE InvoiceID = 6
COMMIT TRAN
```

Transaction B

```
BEGIN TRAN
DECLARE @InvoiceTotal money, @PaymentTotal money, @CreditTotal money
SELECT @InvoiceTotal = InvoiceTotal, @CreditTotal = CreditTotal,
      @PaymentTotal = PaymentTotal FROM Invoices WHERE InvoiceID = 6
UPDATE Invoices
  SET InvoiceTotal = @InvoiceTotal, CreditTotal = @CreditTotal,
      PaymentTotal = @InvoiceTotal - @CreditTotal,
      PaymentDate = GetDate() WHERE InvoiceID = 6
COMMIT TRAN
```

The initial values for the row

	InvoiceTotal	PaymentTotal	CreditTotal	PaymentDate
1	2312.2000	.0000	.0000	NULL

The values after transaction A executes

	InvoiceTotal	PaymentTotal	CreditTotal	PaymentDate
1	2312.2000	.0000	317.4000	NULL

The values after transaction B executes, losing transaction A's updates

	InvoiceTotal	PaymentTotal	CreditTotal	PaymentDate
1	2312.2000	2312.2000	.0000	2002-10-07 16:16:00

Description

- *Concurrency* is the ability of a system to support two or more transactions working with the same data at the same time.

- Because small systems have few users, concurrency isn't generally a problem on these systems. On large systems with many users and many transactions, however, you may need to account for concurrency in your SQL code.

- Concurrency is a problem only when the data is being modified. When two or more transactions simply read the same data, the transactions don't affect each other.

- You can avoid some database concurrency problems by using *locks*, which delay the execution of a transaction if it conflicts with a transaction that's already running. Then, the second transaction can't use the data until the first transaction releases the lock.

- Although SQL Server automatically enforces locking, you can write more efficient code by understanding and customizing locking in your programs.

Figure 16-5   An introduction to concurrency and locking

The four concurrency problems that locks can prevent

Figure 16-6 describes the four types of concurrency problems. You've already learned about the first problem: lost updates. In a moment, you'll see how locking can be used to prevent all four of these problems.

Like lost updates, the other three problems may not adversely affect a database. That depends on the nature of the data. In fact, for many systems, these problems happen infrequently. Then, when they do occur, they can be corrected by simply resubmitting the query that caused the problem. On some database systems, however, these problems can affect data integrity in a serious way.

Although locks can prevent the problems listed in this figure, SQL Server's default locking behavior won't. If your transaction could adversely affect data integrity on your system, then, you should consider changing the default locking behavior by setting the transaction isolation level.

The four types of concurrency problems

Problem	Description
Lost updates	Occur when two transactions select the same row and then update the row based on the values originally selected. Since each transaction is unaware of the other, the later update overwrites the earlier update.
Dirty reads (uncommitted dependencies)	Occur when a transaction selects data that aren't committed by another transaction. For example, transaction A changes a row. Transaction B then selects the changed row before transaction A commits the change. If transaction A then rolls back the change, transaction B has selected a row that doesn't exist in the database.
Nonrepeatable reads (inconsistent analysis)	Occur when two SELECT statements of the same data result in different values because another transaction has updated the data in the time between the two statements. For example, transaction A selects a row. Transaction B then updates the row. When transaction A selects the same row again, the data is different.
Phantom reads	Occur when you perform an update or delete on a set of rows when another transaction is performing an insert or delete that affects one or more rows in that same set of rows. For example, transaction A updates the payment total for each invoice that has a balance due. Transaction B inserts a new, unpaid, invoice while transaction A is still running. After transaction A finishes, there is still an invoice with a balance due.

Description

- In a large system with many users, you should expect for these kinds of problems to occur. In general, you don't need to take any action except to anticipate the problem. In many cases, if the query is resubmitted, the problem goes away.

- On some systems, if two transactions overwrite each other, the validity of the database is compromised and resubmitting one of the transactions will not eliminate the problem. If you're working on such a system, you must anticipate these concurrency problems and account for them in your code.

- You should consider these locking problems as you write your code. If one of these problems would affect data integrity, you can change the default locking behavior by setting the transaction isolation level as shown in the next figure.

Figure 16-6   The four concurrency problems that locks can prevent

How to set the transaction isolation level

The simplest way to prevent concurrency problems is to reduce concurrency. To do that, you need to change SQL Server's default locking behavior. Figure 16-7 shows you how.

To change the default locking behavior, you use the SET TRANSACTION ISOLATION LEVEL statement to set the *transaction isolation level* for the current session. As you can see, this statement accepts one of four options. The table in this figure lists which of the four concurrency problems each option will prevent or allow. For example, if you code the SERIALIZABLE option, all four concurrency problems will be prevented.

When you set the isolation level to SERIALIZABLE, each transaction is completely isolated from every other transaction and concurrency is severely restricted. The server does this by locking each resource, preventing other transactions from concurrent access. Since each transaction must wait for the previous transaction to commit, the transactions are executed serially, one after another.

Since the SERIALIZABLE isolation level eliminates all possible concurrency problems, you may think that this is the best option. However, this option requires more server overhead to manage all of the locks. In addition, access time for each transaction is increased, since only one transaction can work with the data at a time. For most systems, this isolation level will actually eliminate few concurrency problems but will cause severe performance problems.

The lowest isolation level is READ UNCOMMITTED, which allows all four of the concurrency problems to occur. It does this by performing SELECT queries without setting any locks and without honoring any existing locks. Since this means that your SELECT statements will always execute immediately, this setting provides the best performance. Since other transactions can retrieve and modify the same data, however, this setting can't prevent concurrency problems.

The default isolation level, READ COMMITTED, is acceptable for most applications. However, the only concurrency problem it prevents is dirty reads. Although it can prevent some lost updates, it doesn't prevent them all.

The REPEATABLE READ level allows more concurrency than the SERIALIZABLE level but less than the READ COMMITTED level. As you might expect, then, it results in faster performance than SERIALIZABLE but permits more concurrency problems than READ COMMITTED.

The syntax of the SET TRANSACTION ISOLATION LEVEL statement

```
SET TRANSACTION ISOLATION LEVEL
    {READ UNCOMMITTED|READ COMMITTED|REPEATABLE READ|SERIALIZABLE}
```

The concurrency problems prevented by each transaction isolation level

Isolation level	Dirty reads	Lost updates	Nonrepeatable reads	Phantom reads
READ UNCOMMITTED	Allows	Allows	Allows	Allows
READ COMMITTED	Prevents	Allows	Allows	Allows
REPEATABLE READ	Prevents	Prevents	Prevents	Allows
SERIALIZABLE	Prevents	Prevents	Prevents	Prevents

Description

- Since SQL Server manages locking automatically, you can't control every aspect of locking for your transactions. However, you can set the isolation level in your code.

- The *transaction isolation level* controls the degree to which transactions are isolated from one another. The server isolates transactions by using more restrictive locking behavior. If you isolate your transactions from other transactions, concurrency problems are reduced or eliminated.

- You specify the transaction isolation level by changing the ISOLATION LEVEL session setting. The default transaction isolation level is READ COMMITTED. At this level, some lost updates can occur, but this is acceptable for most transactions.

- The READ UNCOMMITTED isolation level doesn't set any locks and ignores locks that are already held. Setting this level results in the highest possible performance for your query, but at the risk of every kind of concurrency problem. For this reason, you should only use this level for data that is rarely updated.

- The REPEATABLE READ level places locks on all data that's used in a transaction, preventing other users from updating that data. However, this isolation level still allows inserts, so phantom reads can occur.

- The SERIALIZABLE level places a lock on all data that's used in a transaction. Since each transaction must wait for the previous transaction to commit, the transactions are handled in sequence. This is the most restrictive of the four isolation levels.

- Both REPEATABLE READ and SERIALIZABLE prevent more concurrency problems than the default level, but at the cost of additional overhead and reduced system performance. For this reason, you should only use these levels for transactions that are likely to suffer from concurrency problems.

Figure 16-7   How to set the transaction isolation level

How SQL Server manages locking

SQL Server automatically manages locking by setting a lock on the data used by each transaction. By understanding how this process works, you'll be able to write better SQL code.

Lockable resources and lock escalation

A transaction like the one shown in figure 16-5 affects only one row in one table. In contrast, a transaction that uses DDL statements to change the design of a database can affect every object in the database. To accommodate these differences, SQL Server can lock data resources at six different levels. These levels are presented in figure 16-8.

A resource's *granularity* refers to the relative amount of data it includes. For example, a row is a *fine-grain resource* and has higher granularity than a database, which is a *coarse-grain resource*. As you can see, the resources listed in this figure are listed in order of increasing granularity.

The SQL Server *lock manager* automatically assigns locks for each transaction. Since a coarse-grain lock will lock out more transactions than a fine-grain lock, the lock manager always tries to lock resources at the highest possible granularity. However, it takes greater server resources to maintain several fine-grain locks compared to one coarse-grain lock. For this reason, the lock manager detects when several fine-grain locks apply to a single coarse-grain resource. Then it converts, or *escalates*, the finer-grained locks to a single coarse-grain lock.

The six levels of lockable resources

Granularity	Resource	Description
Coarse	Database	Locks an entire database.
	Table	Locks an entire table, including indexes.
	Extent	Locks a contiguous group of eight pages.
	Page	Locks one page (8 KB) of data.
	Key	Locks a key or range of keys in an index.
Fine	Row	Locks a single row within a table.

Description

- SQL Server can lock data at various levels, known as *lockable resources*. The six levels form a hierarchy based on *granularity*, which refers to the amount of data the resource encompasses. A resource that encompasses more data than another resource is said to be less granular, or *coarser*, than the other resource.

- A *coarse-grain lock* affects more data than a *fine-grain lock*. For this reason, more transactions are locked out when the lock is less granular. Since this slows database performance, the server assigns locks of the finest possible granularity.

- Locking is automatically enabled and controlled by a SQL Server application called the *lock manager*. This program generates locking events and handles the setting and releasing of locks.

- Maintaining several fine-grain locks requires greater server resources than maintaining one coarse-grain lock. For this reason, the lock manager will automatically convert multiple fine-grain locks on the same resource into a single coarse-grain lock. This is known as *lock escalation*.

Figure 16-8   Lockable resources and lock escalation

Lock modes and lock promotion

In addition to assigning a resource level, the lock manager also assigns a *lock mode* to your transaction. Figure 16-9 presents the lock modes supported by SQL Server. Although there are nine different lock modes, each mode can be categorized as a either a shared lock or an exclusive lock.

A *shared lock* doesn't prevent other shared locks from being granted on the same resource. For example, if you submit the query

```
SELECT * FROM Invoices
```

the lock manager grants your transaction a Shared (S) lock on the Invoices table. If, while your query is executing, another user submits a query on the same table, your lock doesn't prevent the lock manager from granting a second S lock on the same table.

An *exclusive lock* on a resource, however, is granted exclusively to a single transaction. If another transaction requests a lock on the same resource, it must wait until the transaction that holds the exclusive lock has finished and its lock is released. If you submit an INSERT statement against the Invoices table, for example, the lock manager requests an Exclusive (X) lock on the Invoices table. If no other transaction has an exclusive lock on that table, the lock is granted. While that transaction holds that lock, no other transaction can be granted a lock.

A single transaction can include various SQL statements that each require a different lock mode. In that case, a shared lock may need to be *promoted* to an exclusive lock. If, while the transaction is still executing, an exclusive lock can't be acquired, the transaction must wait until the lock is available. If the lock never becomes available, the transaction can never commit.

To prevent this problem, an Update (U) lock is assigned for some transactions. For example, consider the locks needed for an UPDATE query. First, the query must determine which row or rows are being updated based on the WHERE clause. For this part of the query, only a shared lock is needed. Then, when the actual update takes place, the lock must be promoted to an exclusive lock. Since this kind of lock promotion occurs with virtually every action query, the lock manager first assigns a U lock, which prevents another transaction from gaining a shared lock.

The Schema lock modes place a lock on a table's design. For this reason, it can't be placed at resource levels other than the table level. Interestingly, these lock modes represent both the least restrictive and the most restrictive mode. A Schema Stability (Sch-S) lock is placed when a query is compiling to prevent changes to the table's design. A Schema Modification (Sch-M) lock is placed when a query includes DDL statements that modify a table's design.

If another transaction requests a lock on the same resource but at a lower granularity, your finer-grain lock must still be honored. In other words, if your transaction holds an X lock on a page of data, you wouldn't want the lock manager to grant another transaction an X lock on the entire table. To manage this, the three intent lock modes are used as placeholders for locks on finer-grained resources.

The nine SQL Server lock modes

Category	Lock mode	What the lock owner can do
Shared	Schema Stability (Sch-S)	Compile a query
	Intent Shared (IS)	Read but not change data
	Shared (S)	Read but not change data
	Update (U)	Read but not change data until promoted to an Exclusive (X) lock
Exclusive	Shared with Intent Exclusive (SIX)	Read and change data
	Intent Exclusive (IX)	Read and change data
	Exclusive (X)	Read and change data
	Bulk Update (BU)	Bulk-copy data into a table
	Schema Modification (Sch-M)	Modify the database schema

Description

- SQL Server automatically determines the appropriate *lock mode* for your transaction. In general, retrieval operations acquire *shared locks*, and update operations acquire *exclusive locks*. As a single transaction is being processed, its lock may have to be converted, or *promoted*, from one lock mode to a more exclusive lock mode.

- An Update (U) lock is acquired during the first part of an update, when the data is being read. Later, if the data is changed, the Update lock is promoted to an Exclusive (X) lock. This can prevent a common locking problem called a deadlock.

- An *intent lock* indicates that SQL Server intends to acquire a shared lock or an exclusive lock on a finer-grain resource. For example, an Intent Shared (IS) lock acquired at the table level means that the transaction intends to acquire shared locks on pages or rows within that table. This prevents another transaction from acquiring an exclusive lock on the table containing that page or row.

- *Schema locks* are placed on a table's design. Schema Modification (Sch-M) locks are acquired when the design is being changed with a DDL statement. Schema Stability (Sch-S) locks are acquired when compiling a query to prevent a schema change while the query is compiling.

- The Bulk Update (BU) lock mode is acquired for the BULK INSERT statement and by the bulk copy program (bcp). Since these operations are typically done by DBAs, neither is presented in this book.

Figure 16-9   Lock modes and lock promotion

The three *intent locks* differ based on the portion of the resource and the type of lock that the transaction intends to acquire. An Intent Shared (IS) lock indicates that the transaction intends to acquire a shared lock on some, but not all, of the finer-grained resource. Likewise, an Intent Exclusive (IX) lock indicates an intent to acquire an exclusive lock on some, but not all, of the resource. Finally, a Shared with Intent Exclusive (SIX) lock indicates an intent to acquire both an exclusive lock on some of the resource and a shared lock on the entire resource.

The Bulk Update (BU) lock mode is used exclusively for copying large amounts of data in bulk into a database using either the BULK INSERT statement or the bulk copy program. Since bulk copies are usually done by DBAs to create databases based on other sources, they're not presented in this book.

Lock mode compatibility

Figure 16-10 presents a table that shows the compatibility between the different lock modes. When a transaction tries to acquire a lock on a resource, the lock manager must first determine whether another transaction already holds a lock on that resource. If a lock is already in place, the lock manager will grant the new lock only if it's compatible with the current lock. Otherwise, the transaction will have to wait.

For example, if a transaction currently holds a U lock on a table and another transaction requests a U lock on the same table, the lock manager doesn't grant the second transaction's request. Instead, the second transaction must wait until the first transaction commits and releases its lock.

As you can see, Sch-S lock mode is compatible with every other lock mode except Sch-M. For this reason, the only lock that can delay the compilation of a query is the lock placed by a DDL statement that's changing the table's design.

Notice that the IS and S locks are compatible. This means that any number of SELECT queries can execute concurrently. All of the other locks, however, are incompatible to some extent. That's because each of these other modes indicates that data is already being modified by a current transaction.

Although the intent locks are similar to the standard shared and exclusive locks, they result in improved performance. That's because when the lock manager grants an intent lock, it locks a resource at a higher level than it would if it granted shared or exclusive locks. In other words, it grants a more coarse-grained lock. Then, to determine if a resource is already locked, the lock manager needs to look only at the coarse-grained resource rather than every fine-grained resource it contains.

Compatibility between lock modes

Current lock mode		Sch-S	IS	S	U	SIX	IX	X	BU	Sch-M
		— Requested lock mode								
Schema Stability	**Sch-S**	√	√	√	√	√	√	√	√	
Intent Shared	**IS**	√	√	√	√	√	√			
Shared	**S**	√	√	√	√					
Update	**U**	√	√	√						
Shared w/Intent Exclusive	**SIX**	√	√							
Intent Exclusive	**IX**	√	√				√			
Exclusive	**X**	√								
Bulk Update	**BU**	√								
Schema Modification	**Sch-M**									

Description

- If a resource is already locked by a transaction, a request by another transaction to acquire a lock on the same resource will be granted or denied depending on the compatibility of the two lock modes.

- For example, if a transaction has a Shared (S) lock on a table and another transaction requests an Exclusive (X) lock on the same table, the lock isn't granted. The second transaction must wait until the first transaction releases its lock.

- Intent locks can help improve performance since the server only needs to examine the high-level locks rather than examining every low-level lock.

Figure 16-10   Lock mode compatibility

How to prevent deadlocks

A *deadlock* occurs when two transactions are simultaneously holding and requesting a lock on each other's resource. Since deadlocks can occur more frequently at higher isolation levels, you need to understand how they come about and how you can prevent them.

Two transactions that deadlock

Figure 16-11 presents two transactions that are executed simultaneously. As you can see, transaction A queries the InvoiceLineItems table to determine the sum of all line item amounts for a specific invoice. Then, the WAITFOR DELAY statement causes the transaction to wait five seconds before continuing. (This statement is included only so that you can actually cause the deadlock to occur.) Next, an UPDATE statement updates the InvoiceTotal column in the Invoices table with the value retrieved by the SELECT statement.

When this transaction executes, it requests several different locks. In particular, when the SELECT statement is executed, it requests an S lock on one page of the InvoiceLineItems table. And when the UPDATE statement is executed, it requests an X lock on a page of the Invoices table.

Now take a look at transaction B, which queries the Invoices table and then updates the InvoiceLineItems table for the same invoice as transaction A. In this case, the transaction requests an S lock on the Invoices table when the SELECT statement is executed, and it requests an X lock on the InvoiceLineItems table when the UPDATE statement is executed. Because transaction A has an S lock on the InvoiceLineItems table, however, the X lock isn't granted. Similarly, the X lock on the Invoices table isn't granted to transaction A because transaction B has an S lock on it. Because neither UPDATE can execute, neither transaction can commit and neither can release the resource needed by the other. In other words, the two transactions are deadlocked.

SQL Server automatically detects deadlocks and keeps them from tying up the system. It does this by selecting one of the transactions as the *deadlock victim*, which is rolled back and receives an error message. The other transaction runs to completion and commits. In the example in this figure, transaction B is the deadlock victim, as you can see by the system response.

Note that these two transactions will deadlock only if you set the transaction isolation level to REPEATABLE READ or SERIALIZABLE. Otherwise, the S lock acquired by each transaction is released after the SELECT statement completes. Since this doesn't prevent the other transaction from acquiring an X lock, each transaction can commit but causes the other to suffer from a dirty read.

Two transactions that deadlock

A
```
SET TRANSACTION ISOLATION LEVEL
    REPEATABLE READ
DECLARE @InvoiceTotal money

BEGIN TRAN
    SELECT @InvoiceTotal =
        SUM(InvoiceLineItemAmount)
    FROM InvoiceLineItems
    WHERE InvoiceID = 101

WAITFOR DELAY '00:00:05'

    UPDATE Invoices
    SET InvoiceTotal =
        @InvoiceTotal
    WHERE InvoiceID = 101
COMMIT TRAN
```

B
```
SET TRANSACTION ISOLATION LEVEL
    REPEATABLE READ
DECLARE @InvoiceTotal money

BEGIN TRAN
    SELECT @InvoiceTotal =
        InvoiceTotal
    FROM Invoices
    WHERE InvoiceID = 101

    UPDATE InvoiceLineItems
    SET InvoiceLineItemAmount =
        @InvoiceTotal
    WHERE InvoiceID = 101 AND
        InvoiceSequence = 1
COMMIT TRAN
```

The response from the system

```
(1 row(s) affected)
```

```
Server: Msg 1205, Level 13, State
50, Line 10
Transaction (Process ID 56) was
deadlocked on {lock} resources with
another process and has been chosen
as the deadlock victim. Rerun the
transaction.
```

How the deadlock occurs

1. Transaction A requests and acquires a shared lock on the InvoiceLineItems table.

2. Transaction B requests and acquires a shared lock on the Invoices table.

3. Transaction A tries to acquire an exclusive lock on the Invoices table to perform the update. Since transaction B already holds a shared lock on this table, transaction A must wait for the exclusive lock.

4. Transaction B tries to acquire an exclusive lock on the InvoiceLineItems table, but must wait because transaction A holds a shared lock on that table.

Description

- A *deadlock* occurs when neither of two transactions can be committed because they each have a lock on a resource needed by the other.

- SQL Server automatically detects deadlocks and allows one of the transactions to commit. The other transaction is rolled back and raises error number 1205. This transaction is known as the *deadlock victim*.

Note

- To test this example, you must execute transaction A first and then execute transaction B within five seconds.

Figure 16-11   Two transactions that deadlock

Coding techniques that prevent deadlocks

Deadlocks slow system performance and cause transactions to become deadlock victims. For these reasons, you should try to avoid deadlocks as much as possible. Figure 16-12 presents a summary of the techniques you can use to do that.

First, you shouldn't leave transactions open any longer than is necessary. That's because the longer a transaction remains open and uncommitted, the more likely it is that another transaction will need to work with that same resource. Second, you shouldn't use a higher isolation level than you need. That's because the higher you set the isolation level, the more likely it is that two transactions will be unable to work concurrently on the same resource. Third, you should schedule transactions that modify a large number of rows to run when no other transactions, or only a small number of other transactions, will be running. That way, it's less likely that the transactions will try to change the same rows at the same time.

Finally, you should consider how a program you code could cause a deadlock. To illustrate, consider the UPDATE statements shown in this figure that transfer money between two accounts. The first example transfers money from a savings to a checking account. Notice that the savings account is updated first. The second example transfers money from a checking to a savings account. In this example, the checking account is updated first, which could cause a deadlock if the first transaction already has an X lock on the data. To prevent this situation, you should always update the same account first, regardless of which is being debited and which is being credited. This is illustrated by the third example in this figure.

Use the lowest possible transaction isolation level

• The default level of READ COMMITTED is almost always sufficient.

• Reserve the use of higher levels for short transactions that make changes to data where integrity is vital.

Don't allow transactions to remain open for very long

• Keep transactions short.

• Keep SELECT statements outside of the transaction except when absolutely necessary.

• Never code requests for user input during an open transaction.

Make large changes when you can be assured of nearly exclusive access

• If you need to change millions of rows in an active table, don't do so during hours of peak usage.

• If possible, give yourself exclusive access to the database before making large changes.

Consider locking when coding your transactions

• If you need to code two or more transactions that update the same resources, code the updates in the same order in each transaction.

UPDATE statements that transfer money between two accounts

From savings to a checking

```
UPDATE Savings SET Balance = Balance - @TransferAmt
UPDATE Checking SET Balance = Balance + @TransferAmt
```

From checking to savings

```
UPDATE Checking SET Balance = Balance - @TransferAmt
UPDATE Savings SET Balance = Balance + @TransferAmt
```

From checking to savings in reverse order to prevent deadlocks

```
UPDATE Savings SET Balance = Balance + @TransferAmt
UPDATE Checking SET Balance = Balance - @TransferAmt
```

Figure 16-12   Coding techniques that prevent deadlocks

Perspective

In this chapter, you've learned the ways that SQL Server protects your data from the problems that can occur on a real-world system. Since the failure of one or more related SQL statements can violate data integrity, you learned how to prevent these problems by grouping the statements into transactions. Since multiple transactions can simultaneously modify the same data, you learned how to prevent concurrency problems by setting the transaction isolation level to change the default locking behavior. And since changing the isolation level can increase the chances of deadlocks, you learned defensive programming techniques to prevent deadlocks.

Terms

transaction	dirty read	lock escalation
commit a transaction	nonrepeatable read	lock mode
roll back a transaction	phantom read	shared lock
autocommit mode	transaction isolation level	exclusive lock
nested transactions	lockable resource	intent lock
save point	granularity	schema lock
concurrency	fine-grain lock	lock promotion
locking	coarse-grain lock	deadlock
lost update	lock manager	deadlock victim

17

How to manage database security

If you've been using a stand-alone copy of SQL Server installed on your own computer, the security of the system hasn't been of concern. When you install SQL Server for use in a production environment, however, you must configure security to prevent misuse of your data. In this chapter, you'll learn how to do that using either the Enterprise Manager or Transact-SQL.

How to work with SQL Server login IDs

Before a user can work with the data in a database, he must have a valid *login ID* so that he can log on to SQL Server. Then, he must have access to the database itself. In the topics that follow, you'll learn how to work with login IDs and how to give a user access to a database. But first, I'll present an overview of how SQL Server manages database security.

An introduction to SQL Server security

Figure 17-1 illustrates how a user gains access to a SQL Server database. First, the user must connect and log on to the server using either an application program or one of the SQL Server client tools. As you can see, the login ID can be authenticated in one of two ways, which I'll discuss in a moment.

Once the user is logged on to SQL Server, the data he has access to and the operations he can perform depend on the *permissions* that have been granted to him. You can grant *object permissions* so the user can perform specific actions on a specific database object, or you can grant *statement permissions* so the user can execute specific SQL DDL statements. In addition, you can define a collection of permissions called a *role*. Then, you can assign users to that role to grant them all of the permissions associated with that role. This reduces the number of permissions you must grant each user and makes it easier to manage security. For this reason, roles are used on most systems.

This figure also summarizes the two ways you can manage SQL Server security. First, you can do that by executing SQL statements and system stored procedures from the Query Analyzer or OSQL. Second, you can use the Enterprise Manager. You'll learn how to use both of these techniques in this chapter. The technique you use is mostly a matter of preference. However, even if you intend to use the Enterprise Manager, you should still read the topics on using the SQL statements and stored procedures. These topics will help you understand the underlying structure of SQL Server security, which will help you use the Enterprise Manager better.

Although the Enterprise Manager's interface makes it easier to work with security, it can also slow you down. For example, if you need to set up a new database with hundreds of users, you'll have to create those users one at a time using the Enterprise Manager. On the other hand, if you've read chapter 13 and know how to code dynamic SQL, you can code a script that will manage the entire process. For this reason, many experienced system administrators prefer to manage security using Transact-SQL.

How users gain access to a SQL Server database

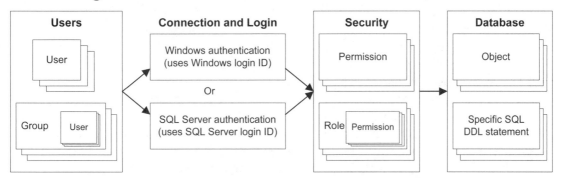

Two ways to configure SQL Server security

Method	Description
Transact-SQL	Use the ANSI-standard GRANT and REVOKE statements to manage permissions for users. Use system stored procedures to manage login IDs and roles.
Enterprise Manager	Use the Enterprise Manager to configure all aspects of system security.

Description

- Typically, a network user must log on to the network at a PC using a *login ID* and password. If the client PC uses Windows, SQL Server can use the Windows login ID defined for the user. If the client PC doesn't use Windows, you can create a separate SQL Server login ID.

- Once a user is logged on to SQL Server, the security configuration determines which database objects the user can work with and which SQL statements the user can execute.

- *Permissions* determine the actions that a user can take. *Object permissions* determine what actions a user can take on a specific database object, such as a database, table, view, or stored procedure. A *statement permission* determines whether or not a user can execute a specific SQL DDL statement.

- A *role* is a collection of permissions that you can assign to a user by assigning the user to that role.

- You can create a collection of users in Windows called a *group*. Then you can assign permissions and roles either to individual users or to a group of users.

- If you need to set up a new system with many users, it's often easier to code SQL scripts using the SQL security statements and system stored procedures. The Enterprise Manager is better for making changes to an existing system or for setting up a small system.

- Even if you use the Enterprise Manager to manage security, you should know how to manage security with Transact-SQL statements and procedures. That will help you understand the underlying structure of SQL Server security.

Figure 17-1   An introduction to SQL Server security

How to change the authentication mode

As you learned in chapter 2, you can log on to SQL Server using one of two types of login authentication: *Windows authentication* or *SQL Server authentication*. To accommodate these two types of authentication, a server can be configured to run in one of two *authentication modes*: Windows authentication mode or Mixed mode. Figure 17-2 summarizes these authentication modes and shows you how you can change from one to the other.

If you install SQL Server on a machine that's running Windows NT, Windows 2000, or Windows XP, Windows authentication mode is the default. Then, when a user logs on to SQL Server, authentication is handled by the security that's integrated into Windows. In other words, the login ID and password that the user enters to log on to Windows are also used to log on to SQL Server.

In contrast, if you install SQL Server on a machine that's running Windows 98, Mixed mode is the default. That means that users can log on using either Windows authentication or SQL Server authentication. When SQL Server authentication is used, the user must enter a SQL Server login ID and password to log on to SQL Server. This login ID and password are separate from the Windows login ID and password, which means that the user must enter two IDs and passwords to access SQL Server.

Since non-Windows clients can't use Windows authentication, it's likely that the only time you'll use SQL Server authentication is to support access by non-Windows clients. However, you must also use SQL Server authentication if the client is running a version of Windows that's older than Windows 95 or if your server is running Windows 98. If your server is running Windows 98, though, it's probably not powerful enough to run a production database anyway.

To change the authentication mode, you use the Security tab of the SQL Server Properties dialog box shown in this figure. The two available options are listed under the Authentication heading. The SQL Server and Windows option corresponds to Mixed mode.

If you change the authentication mode, the Enterprise Manager warns you that the change won't take effect until you stop and restart SQL Server. Before you stop SQL Server, though, you'll want to be sure that there aren't any transactions currently executing. If there are and you stop SQL Server, those transactions won't be committed. If you're working on a desktop server or on a new server with no users, this shouldn't be a problem. If you're working on an active server, however, you shouldn't restart the server until you're sure that no users are connected.

If you switch from Windows authentication mode to Mixed mode, you should realize that the default system administrator login ID, sa, is assigned a blank password. Since this login ID has unrestricted access to all of the database objects on the server, you should immediately change the password for this account. You'll see how to do that in the next topic.

The Security tab of the SQL Server Properties dialog box

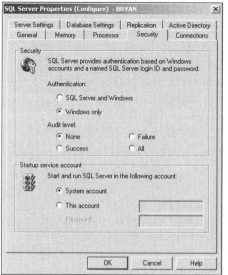

The two SQL Server authentication modes

Mode	Description
Windows authentication mode	Only Windows authentication is allowed. To use this mode, select the Windows only option. This is the default for SQL Server running on Windows NT, Windows 2000, or Windows XP.
Mixed mode	Both Windows authentication and SQL Server authentication are allowed. To use this mode, select the SQL Server and Windows option. This is the default for SQL Server running on Windows 98. If your database needs to be accessed by non-Windows clients or by clients running versions of Windows older than Windows 95, you must use mixed mode.

Description

- To change the SQL Server *authentication mode*, select the server in the console tree of the Enterprise Manager, select Action→Properties to display the SQL Server Properties dialog box, and then select the Security tab.

- When you use *Windows authentication*, access to SQL Server is controlled via the security integrated into Windows. This simplifies login because Windows users only have to log on once.

- When you use *SQL Server authentication*, access to SQL Server is controlled via the separate security built into SQL Server. The user has a login ID and password that are distinct from their Windows login ID and password, so they have to log on twice.

- The Audit level options let you determine how login attempts are tracked. You should set this option to None unless you suspect unauthorized access.

- The Startup service account options specify which login ID is used by the SQL Server Service Manager to connect to the server. The system administrator account is used by default, but you can change to another account if you have administrator privileges.

Figure 17-2   How to change the authentication mode

How to work with login IDs and passwords

When you install SQL Server, it's configured with a single login ID: sa. Then, to add and work with additional login IDs, you can use the system stored procedures shown in figure 17-3. As you can see, you use the first set of procedures to work with login IDs for SQL Server authentication. You use the second set of procedures to work with login IDs for Windows authentication.

The sp_AddLogin procedure creates a new SQL Server login ID. Its only required parameter is the login ID for the new user. In addition, you can include a password for the new login ID. The first statement in this figure, for example, creates a login ID for user "JohnDoe" with the password "pw8806." If you omit the password, the default is null (no password).

You can also code a parameter for this procedure that specifies the default database. If you do that, the user won't have to execute a USE statement to work with that database. If you don't specify a default database, the Master database is the default.

You can use the sp_Password procedure to change the password for a SQL Server login ID as shown in the second statement in this figure. If the current password is null, you must code the NULL keyword as the first parameter, as shown in the third example.

To delete a SQL Server login ID, you use the sp_DropLogin procedure. This is illustrated in the fourth example in this figure.

When you work with login IDs for Windows authentication, you don't explicitly add or delete login IDs. Instead, you use the sp_GrantLogin and sp_DenyLogin procedures shown in this figure to grant or deny a Windows user or group access to the server. Both of these procedures require a single parameter that identifies the Windows user or group. Note that this name must include the Windows domain name along with the user or group name. The next to last statement in this figure, for example, grants access to a Windows user named "JaneSmith" in the Windows domain named "Accounting."

If you're working with MSDE on your own system, the domain name is just the name of your computer. In that case, though, you probably won't need to set up additional login IDs. The exception is if you have more than one user account defined on your system, in which case you can set up a separate login for each account.

When you use the sp_GrantLogin procedure, you should realize that it actually creates a SQL Server login ID with the name and domain you specify. That way, you can use the same system stored procedures to work with these login IDs as you do to work with login IDs you create using the sp_AddLogin procedure. Even so, to distinguish between the login IDs you create using the sp_AddLogin procedure and the ones you create using the sp_GrantLogin procedure, I'll refer to the former as SQL Server login IDs and the latter as Windows user accounts.

System stored procedures for login IDs that use SQL Server authentication

The syntax for sp_AddLogin

```
sp_AddLogin [@loginame = ] 'login_ID'
        [,[@passwd = ] 'password']
        [,[@defdb = ] 'default_database']
```

The syntax for sp_Password

```
sp_Password [@old = ] 'old_password',
        [@new = ] 'new_password'
        [,[@loginame = ] 'login_ID']
```

The syntax for sp_DropLogin

```
sp_DropLogin 'login_ID'
```

System stored procedures for login IDs that use Windows authentication

The syntax for sp_GrantLogin

```
sp_GrantLogin 'Domain_name\User_name'
```

The syntax for sp_DenyLogin

```
sp_DenyLogin 'Domain_name\User_name'
```

Statements that use system stored procedures to work with login IDs

A statement that creates a new SQL Server login ID

```
EXEC sp_AddLogin JohnDoe, pw8806
```

A statement that changes the password for a SQL Server login ID

```
EXEC sp_Password pw8806, reggie49, JohnDoe
```

A statement that changes a null password

```
EXEC sp_Password NULL, newsapw802, sa
```

A statement that deletes a SQL Server login ID

```
EXEC sp_DropLogin JohnDoe
```

A statement that grants SQL Server access to a Windows user account

```
EXEC sp_GrantLogin [Accounting\JaneSmith]
```

A statement that denies SQL Server access to a Windows user account

```
EXEC sp_DenyLogin [Accounting\JaneSmith]
```

Description

- You use the sp_AddLogin, sp_Password, and sp_DropLogin procedures to add a new SQL Server login ID, change the password for a SQL Server login ID, and delete a SQL Server login ID.

- SQL Server login IDs and passwords can contain from 1 to 128 characters, including letters, symbols, and numbers. The backslash character (\) isn't allowed.

- If you don't specify a password for the sp_AddLogin procedure, it's set to null. If you don't specify a default database, it's set to the Master database.

- You use the sp_GrantLogin and sp_DenyLogin procedure to grant or deny SQL Server access to an existing Windows user account or a Windows group. You must specify both the Windows domain name and the Windows user or group name.

Figure 17-3   How to work with login IDs and passwords

How to grant or revoke user access to a database

Each database maintains a list of the users that are authorized to access that database. This list is distinct from the list of login IDs that's maintained by the server. Figure 17-4 presents the system stored procedures you use to maintain the list of users for a database.

You use the sp_GrantDbAccess procedure to grant a user access to the current database. In addition to the login ID that you code in the procedure, you can also code a database alias. If you include this parameter, the name you specify is used as the user name within the database. If you omit this parameter, the login ID is used as the user name.

In most cases, it's not a good idea to use two different names for the same user. For this reason, the database alias parameter is generally omitted. However, since login IDs generated from Windows user names include the domain name, those login IDs can be quite long. If all of your users are on the same Windows domain, then, you may want to use just the user names as aliases. In addition, you should know that if you create a database using the "sa" login ID, the default database owner, dbo, is automatically used as the database alias.

When you grant a user access to a database, it simply means that the user can set the database as the current database using the USE statement. In other words, the user can't submit any queries against the database. To do that, the user must be granted object and statement permissions. You'll learn how to grant these permissions in a moment.

To revoke user access to a database, you use the sp_RevokeDbAccess procedure. In this procedure, you name the user whose access rights you want to revoke. The second statement in this figure, for example, revokes access to the user who was granted access in the first statement. Notice that a SQL Server login ID is used in this example. In contrast, the third and fourth examples grant and revoke access to a login ID that was created from a Windows user account.

If you assigned an alias to the user when you granted access, you must use that alias to revoke access. The next to last statement in this figure, for example, assigns an alias of "Sue" to the database user. Then, the last statement revokes access to this user by specifying this alias.

Note that both of these procedures work with the current database. For this reason, you must be sure to change the database context to the database you want to work with before you execute either of these procedures. If you don't, you may inadvertently grant or revoke access to the wrong database.

System stored procedures for granting and revoking access to the current database

The syntax for sp_GrantDbAccess

```
sp_GrantDbAccess [@loginame = ] 'login_ID'
              [, [@name_in_db  = ] 'database_alias']
```

The syntax for sp_RevokeDbAccess

```
sp_RevokeDbAccess 'name_in_db'
```

Statements that use these procedures

A statement that grants access to a database for a SQL Server login ID

```
EXEC sp_GrantDbAccess JohnDoe
```

A statement that revokes access to a database for a SQL Server login ID

```
EXEC sp_RevokeDbAccess JohnDoe
```

A statement that grants access to a database for a Windows user account

```
EXEC sp_GrantDbAccess [Accounting\SusanRoberts]
```

A statement that revokes access to a database for a Windows user account

```
EXEC sp_RevokeDbAccess [Accounting\SusanRoberts]
```

A statement that grants access to a database and assigns a user alias

```
EXEC sp_GrantDbAccess [Accounting\SusanRoberts], Sue
```

A statement that revokes access to a database using a user alias

```
EXEC sp_RevokeDbAccess Sue
```

Description

- You use the sp_GrantDbAccess system stored procedure to grant access to a specific login ID for the current database. To revoke access to the current database, you use the sp_RevokeDbAccess system stored procedure.

- Since both of these procedures work on the current database, you must change the database context using the USE statement prior to executing the procedure.

- The optional parameter (@name_in_db) of the sp_GrantDbAccess procedure lets you assign an alias for the user. Since aliases can cause confusion, you should generally avoid using them.

Figure 17-4   How to grant or revoke user access to a database

How to work with permissions

Now that you understand how to create a new login ID and grant the new user access to a database, you need to learn how to grant the new user permission to work with the database. That's what you'll learn in the topics that follow.

How to grant or revoke permission to use an object

Figure 17-5 presents the GRANT and REVOKE statements you use to grant or revoke permissions to use an object in the current database. In the GRANT clause, you list the permissions you want to grant. You'll see a list of the standard permissions in the next figure. You can also code the ALL keyword to grant all permissions to the database.

You code the name of the object for which this permission is granted in the ON clause. This object can be a table, a view, a stored procedure or a user-defined function. Note that you can't grant permissions for two or more objects with a single GRANT statement.

In the TO clause, you code one or more security account names to which you're granting the permission. Typically, this is the database user name, which can represent a SQL Server login ID, a Windows user account name, or a database alias. The statement in this figure, for example, grants permission for the user "Accounting\JaneSmith" to select data from the Invoices table. You can also use this statement to assign permissions to a role. You'll learn more about roles later in this chapter.

If you code the GRANT statement with the optional WITH GRANT OPTION clause, you delegate to this user the permission to GRANT this same permission to others. Since it's simpler to have a single person or group managing the security for a database, I don't recommend that you use this option. If you do, however, you should keep good records so you can later revoke this permission if you begin to have security problems.

The syntax of the REVOKE statement is similar to the syntax of the GRANT statement. You code the name of the permission you're revoking in the REVOKE clause, the object name in the ON clause, and the security account name in the FROM clause. The statement in this figure, for example, revokes the SELECT permission for the Invoices table that was granted to user "Accounting\JaneSmith" by the GRANT statement.

You can code two optional clauses in the REVOKE statement. These clauses are related to the WITH GRANT OPTION clause you can code in the GRANT statement. The GRANT OPTION FOR clause revokes the user's permission to grant this permission to others. The CASCADE clause revokes this permission from all of the users to whom this user has granted permission. If you avoid using the WITH GRANT OPTION clause, you won't have to use these clauses.

How to grant object permissions

The syntax of the GRANT statement for object permissions

```
GRANT {ALL|permission [, ...]}
ON object_description
TO security_account [, ...]
[WITH GRANT OPTION]
```

The syntax of the ON clause

```
ON {table[(column [, ...])]|view[(column [, ...])]|sproc|udf}
```

A GRANT statement that grants SELECT permission for the Invoices table

```
GRANT SELECT
ON Invoices
TO [Accounting\JaneSmith]
```

How to revoke object permissions

The syntax of the REVOKE statement

```
REVOKE [GRANT OPTION FOR] {ALL|permission [, ...]}
ON object_description
FROM security_account [, ...]
[CASCADE]
```

A REVOKE statement that revokes SELECT permission

```
REVOKE SELECT
ON Invoices
FROM [Accounting\JaneSmith]
```

Description

- You use the GRANT statement to give a user permission to work with a database object. The REVOKE statement takes permissions away. See figure 17-6 for a list of the standard permissions that can be granted for objects.

- The ON clause specifies the objects for which the permission is being granted or revoked. It can specify a table, a view, a stored procedure, or a user-defined function. If you specify a table or view, you can also list the columns for which permissions are granted or revoked if the permission is SELECT or UPDATE.

- The security_account argument in the TO and FROM clauses can be the name of a database user or a user-defined role.

- The WITH GRANT OPTION clause gives a user permission to grant this permission to other users. Since it is safer and less confusing to have security managed by either a single user or a small group of users, I recommend that you don't use this option.

- The REVOKE statement includes two clauses that undo WITH GRANT OPTION. GRANT OPTION FOR revokes the user's permission to grant the permission to others. CASCADE revokes the permission from any other users who were given the permission by this user.

- Since both the GRANT and REVOKE statements work on the current database, you must first change the database context using the USE statement.

Figure 17-5   How to grant or revoke permission to use an object

The SQL Server object permissions

Figure 17-6 lists the specific object permissions that you can code in either the GRANT or REVOKE statement. The first four permissions allow the user to execute the corresponding SQL statement: SELECT, UPDATE, INSERT, or DELETE. The fifth permission, EXECUTE, lets the user run an executable database object.

Each permission can be granted only for certain types of objects. For example, you can grant SELECT permission only to an object from which you can select data, such as a table or view. Likewise, you can grant EXECUTE permission only to an object that you can execute, such as a stored procedure or a function.

The REFERENCES permission lets a user refer to an object, even if the user doesn't have permission to use that object directly. For example, to create a FOREIGN KEY constraint that refers to another table, the user would need to have REFERENCES permission on that other table. Of course, he'd also need permission to execute the CREATE TABLE statement. You'll see how to grant permission to statements like this in a moment.

You also need to assign the REFERENCES permission to objects that are referenced by a function or view that's created with the WITH SCHEMABINDING clause. Since this permission is only needed for users who'll be creating database objects, you'll probably never assign it individually. Instead, you'll include it with other permissions in a database role as you'll learn later in this chapter.

The standard permissions for SQL Server objects

Permission	Description	Objects
SELECT	Lets the user select the data.	Table, view, table-valued function
UPDATE	Lets the user update existing data.	Table, view, table-valued function
INSERT	Lets the user insert new data.	Table, view, table-valued function
DELETE	Lets the user delete existing data.	Table, view, table-valued function
EXECUTE	Lets the user execute a procedure or function.	Stored procedure, function
REFERENCES	Lets the user create objects that refer to the object.	Table, view, function
ALL	Gives the user all applicable permissions for the object.	Table, view, stored procedure, function

A GRANT statement that grants permission to run action queries

```
GRANT INSERT, UPDATE, DELETE
ON Invoices
TO [Accounting\JaneSmith]
```

A REVOKE statement that revokes the DELETE permission

```
REVOKE DELETE
ON Invoices
FROM [Accounting\JaneSmith]
```

A GRANT statement that grants permission to execute a stored procedure

```
GRANT EXECUTE
ON spInvoiceReport
TO [Payroll\MarkThomas], JohnDoe, TomAaron
```

A REVOKE statement that revokes all permissions for the Vendors table

```
REVOKE ALL
ON Vendors
FROM [Payroll\MarkThomas]
```

A GRANT statement that grants SELECT permission to specific columns

```
GRANT SELECT
ON Vendors (VendorName,VendorAddress1,VendorCity,VendorState,VendorZipCode)
TO TomAaron, [Payroll\MarkThomas]
```

Description

- You can only grant permissions that are appropriate for the object.
- You can grant or revoke SELECT or UPDATE permission to specific columns in a table or view. However, a view is typically a better way to limit access to specific columns.

Figure 17-6   The SQL Server object permissions

How to grant or revoke statement permissions

In addition to the object permissions presented in the last two figures, you can also grant statement permissions. These permissions let a user execute individual SQL DDL statements. Figure 17-7 presents the syntax of the GRANT and REVOKE statements you use to work with these permissions.

In the GRANT clause, you list the statements you want to grant a user permission to execute. Some of the statements you can include in this list are shown in this figure. Then, in the TO clause, you list the users you want to have these permissions. The first GRANT statement in this figure, for example, grants two users permission to create views. The second GRANT statement gives another user permission to use all the DDL statements that can be permitted explicitly.

The syntax of the REVOKE statement is identical except that you code the user names in the FROM clause. The REVOKE statement shown in this figure, for example, revokes permission for the specified user to create databases or tables.

How to grant statement permissions

The syntax of the GRANT statement for statement permissions

```
GRANT {ALL|statement [, ...]}
TO security_account [, ...]
```

A GRANT statement that gives permission to create views

```
GRANT CREATE VIEW
TO JohnDoe, [Accounting\JaneSmith]
```

A GRANT statement that gives permission to use all statements

```
GRANT ALL
TO [Payroll\MarkThomas]
```

How to revoke statement permissions

The syntax of the REVOKE statement for statement permissions

```
REVOKE {ALL|statement [, ...]}
FROM security_account [, ...]
```

A REVOKE statement that revokes permission to create databases and tables

```
REVOKE CREATE DATABASE, CREATE TABLE
FROM [Administration\SylviaJones]
```

Some of the SQL statements that can be explicitly permitted

```
CREATE DATABASE
CREATE TABLE
CREATE VIEW
CREATE PROCEDURE
CREATE FUNCTION
```

Description

- In addition to granting or revoking permissions for objects, you can grant or revoke permissions to execute certain SQL DDL statements.
- This list of SQL statements only includes those discussed in this book. For a complete list, refer to the index entry "GRANT (described)" in Books Online.

Figure 17-7   How to grant or revoke statement permissions

How to work with roles

Now that you've learned how to grant object and statement permissions to a user, you can set up security on your database. If a system has many users, however, granting and revoking all of these permissions one by one would require a lot of coding. To help reduce the amount of coding and to help you keep your database security organized, you can use roles.

As you know, a role is a collection of permissions. When you assign a user to a particular role, you grant them all of the permissions associated with that role. SQL Server supports two different types of roles: fixed roles and user-defined roles. You'll learn how to work with both of these types of roles in the topics that follow.

How to work with the fixed server roles

Fixed roles are roles that are built into SQL Server. These roles can't be deleted and the permissions associated with them can't be modified. SQL Server provides two types of fixed roles: *fixed server roles* and *fixed database roles*. Figure 17-8 shows you how to work with the fixed server roles. You'll learn how to work with the fixed database roles in the next figure.

The fixed server roles typically include users who manage the server. For example, the sysadmin role is intended for system administrators. For this reason, it grants permission to perform any task on any object in the database. If you've been working with the MSDE on your own PC, you've been using the "sa" login ID, which is a member of this role.

The securityadmin role is intended for those users who need to be able to manage security. The members of this role are allowed to work with login IDS and passwords. The dbcreator role is intended for those users who need to be able to work with database objects. The members of this role can create, alter, and drop databases. Although SQL Server provides other server roles, these are the ones you'll use most often.

To assign a user to a server role, you use the sp_AddSrvRoleMember procedure. To remove a user from a server role, you use the sp_DropSrvRoleMember procedure. The two parameters of these procedures specify the login ID of the user you want to add or remove from the role and the name of the server role. The first statement in this figure, for example, adds user "JohnDoe" to the sysadmin server role. The second statement drops this user from that role.

How to assign a user to a server role

The syntax for sp_AddSrvRoleMember

```
sp_AddSrvRoleMember [@loginame = ] 'login_ID',
                    [@rolename = ] 'server_role_name'
```

A statement that assigns a user to a server role

```
EXEC sp_AddSrvRoleMember JohnDoe, sysadmin
```

How to remove a user from a server role

The syntax for sp_DropSrvRoleMember

```
sp_DropSrvRoleMember [@loginame = ] 'login_ID',
                     [@rolename = ] 'server_role_name'
```

A statement that removes a user from a server role

```
EXEC sp_DropSrvRoleMember JohnDoe, sysadmin
```

Some of the SQL Server fixed server roles

Role	Description
sysadmin	Can perform any activity on the server. Equivalent to the "sa" login ID that's automatically created for SQL Server.
securityadmin	Can manage login IDs and passwords for the server.
dbcreator	Can create, alter, and drop databases.

Description

- A role is a collection of permissions you can assign to a user or group of users. By assigning a user to a role, you grant that user all of the permissions of the role.

- SQL Server has built-in, or *fixed*, roles defined at the server level and at the database level. In addition, you can create user-defined roles for your own database.

- Each role is assigned a set of permissions. For example, the dbcreator role can execute CREATE DATABASE, ALTER DATABASE, DROP DATABASE, and RESTORE DATABASE statements. In addition, this role can run the sp_RenameDb system stored procedure to rename an existing database, and it can add new members to this role.

- You use the sp_AddSrvRoleMember system stored procedure to add a user to a server role. You use the sp_DropSrvRoleMember to remove a user from a server role.

- The fixed server roles are intended for users who are involved in the administration of the server. For a complete list of the fixed server roles, see the "roles-SQL Server, fixed server" index entry in Books Online.

Figure 17-8   How to work with the fixed server roles

How to work with the fixed database roles

Figure 17-9 lists the fixed database roles and shows you how to work with them. These roles are added automatically to each new database you create. In addition, when you create a database, you're automatically added to the db_owner database role.

To add a member to a database role, you use the sp_AddRoleMember stored procedure. The first statement in this figure, for example, adds the user named "JohnDoe" to the db_owner database role. The member name you specify can be a SQL Server login ID, a Windows user or group name, or a user-defined role. You'll see how to create user-defined roles in a moment. For now, just realize that the ability to assign user-defined roles as members of fixed database roles makes assigning permissions flexible and convenient.

To delete a member from a database role, you use the sp_DropRoleMember stored procedure. Like the procedure for adding a member to a database role, this procedures identifies the role and the member to be dropped. The second statement in this figure, for example, deletes the member that was added to the db_owner role by the first statement.

In addition to the fixed database roles listed in this figure, SQL Server includes a special fixed database role named "public." This role is included in every database, and every database user is automatically a member of this role. This role has no permissions by default, however, so you don't need to be concerned about security violations due to the existence of this role. You can't add or drop members from this role, nor can you delete the role from a database.

How to assign a user to a database role

The syntax for sp_AddRoleMember

```
sp_AddRoleMember [@rolename = ] 'database_role_name',
                 [@membername = ] 'security_account'
```

A statement that assigns a user to a database role

```
EXEC sp_AddRoleMember db_owner, JohnDoe
```

How to remove a user from a database role

The syntax for sp_DropRoleMember

```
sp_DropRoleMember [@rolename = ] 'database_role_name',
                  [@membername = ] 'security_account'
```

A statement that removes a user from a database role

```
EXEC sp_DropRoleMember db_owner, JohnDoe
```

The SQL Server fixed database roles

Role	Description
db_owner	Has all permissions for the database.
db_accessadmin	Can add or remove login IDs for the database.
db_securityadmin	Can manage object permissions, statement permissions, roles, and role memberships.
db_ddladmin	Can issue all DDL statements except GRANT, REVOKE, and DENY.
db_datawriter	Can insert, delete, or update data from any user table in the database.
db_datareader	Can select data from any user table in the database.
db_denydatawriter	Can't insert, delete, or update data from any user table in the database.
db_denydatareader	Can't select data from any user table in the database.
db_backupoperator	Can backup the database and run consistency checks on the database.

Description

- The *fixed database roles* are added to each database you create. You can add and delete members from these roles, but you can't delete the roles.

- You use the sp_AddRoleMember system stored procedure to assign a user to a database role in the current database. You use the sp_DropRoleMember system stored procedure to remove a user from a database role in the current database.

- The security_account argument can be the name of a database user or a user-defined role. This means that you can create your own role and then assign it as a member of a fixed database role.

- The users you specify are assigned to or removed from the role you name in the current database. Because of that, you should be sure to change the database context before executing one of these stored procedures.

- In addition to the SQL Server fixed database roles, you can create your own user-defined database roles as shown in the next figure.

Figure 17-9   How to work with the fixed database roles

How to work with user-defined database roles

Like the fixed database roles, a *user-defined role* consists of a set of permissions that you can grant to a user by giving them membership in that role. Unlike the fixed database roles, you can create your own user-defined roles, you can modify the permissions associated with those roles, and you can delete the roles when necessary. Figure 17-10 presents the two stored procedures you use to create and delete user-defined roles.

The sp_AddRole procedure creates a new role in the current database. The role name you specify in this procedure must be unique: It can't be the same as another user-defined role, fixed role, or database user name. The first statement in this figure, for example, creates a new role named InvoiceEntry.

Once a role is defined, you can use the GRANT statement to grant permissions to that role. To do that, you simply code the role name in the TO clause instead of a user name. The two GRANT statements in this figure, for example, grant the InvoiceEntry role INSERT and UPDATE permissions to the Invoices and InvoiceLineItems tables in the AP database. (You can assume that AP is the current database for these examples.)

The next two statements in this figure assign two users to the new role. That means that these two users now have the INSERT and UPDATE permissions that were assigned to the role by the previous GRANT statements. In addition, the next statement assigns the new role as a member of the db_datareader role. If you look back to figure 17-9, you'll see that this role grants any member of the role permission to select data from any user table in the database. Since the member itself is a role, that means that any member of that role now has permission to select data from the database.

As you can see, using roles can significantly simplify security management. If you assign roles as members of other roles, however, managing the various roles and permissions can quickly get out of hand. For example, suppose you added a new table to the AP database. Then, the two users that are members of the InvoiceEntry role would automatically be able to select data from that table because the InvoiceEntry role is a member of the db_datareader role. If that's not what you want, you'd need to remove InvoiceEntry from the db_datareader role and then grant SELECT permission to that role for each of the tables in the database that you want the users to have access to. If you plan to assign roles to other roles, then, you'll want to plan it out carefully to avoid having to redesign the security in the future.

To drop a user-defined role, you use the sp_DropRole stored procedure. Before you do that, however, you must delete all of the members of the role. The last three statements in this figure, for example, drop the two members of the InvoiceEntry role and then drop the role.

System stored procedures for creating and deleting user-defined roles

The syntax for sp_AddRole

```
sp_AddRole [@rolename = ] 'role_name'
        [,[@ownername = ] 'owner_login_ID' ]
```

The syntax for sp_DropRole

```
sp_DropRole [@rolename = ] 'database_role_name'
```

Statements that work with user-defined roles

A statement that creates a new user-defined role

```
EXEC sp_AddRole InvoiceEntry
```

Statements that grant permissions to the new role

```
GRANT INSERT,UPDATE
ON Invoices
TO InvoiceEntry
GRANT INSERT,UPDATE
ON InvoiceLineItems
TO InvoiceEntry
```

Statements that assign users to the new role

```
EXEC sp_AddRoleMember InvoiceEntry, JohnDoe
EXEC sp_AddRoleMember InvoiceEntry, [Accounting\JaneSmith]
```

A statement that assigns the new role to a fixed database role

```
EXEC sp_AddRoleMember db_datareader, InvoiceEntry
```

Statements that delete the new role

```
EXEC sp_DropRoleMember InvoiceEntry, JohnDoe
EXEC sp_DropRoleMember InvoiceEntry, [Accounting\JaneSmith]
EXEC sp_DropRole InvoiceEntry
```

Description

- You use the sp_AddRole system stored procedure to create *user-defined roles*. Role names can be up to 128 characters in length and can include letters, symbols, and numbers, but not the backslash (\) character. If you omit the owner ID, the default is dbo.

- You use the sp_DropRole stored procedure to delete user-defined roles. You can't delete a fixed database role or the public role. Once you create a role, you can grant permissions to or revoke permissions from the role. Then, you grant or revoke permissions for every member of the role.

- To add members to a user-defined role or delete members from the role, you use the sp_AddRoleMember and sp_DropRoleMember procedures shown in figure 17-9.

- Before you can delete a database role, you must delete all of its members. To find out how to list the members of a role, see figure 17-11.

- You can use roles to simplify user and security administration. Then, instead of assigning permissions to individual users, you can assign the user to a role that has the appropriate permissions.

- User-defined roles are always database roles. You can't create server roles beyond the SQL Server fixed server roles.

Figure 17-10   How to work with user-defined database roles

How to display information about database roles and role members

As you might expect, most systems have many users and many roles. Some users belong to several roles, and some roles belong to other roles. For this reason, keeping track of security permissions can be a complex task. Since the Enterprise Manager provides an easy way to examine current role settings, most security managers use this tool rather than using Transact-SQL. However, SQL Server provides some system stored procedures that can be helpful for managing roles. Figure 17-11 presents two of these procedures.

The sp_HelpRole procedure returns information about the database roles defined for the current database. If you code a valid role name as a parameter, this procedure returns information about that one role. Otherwise it returns information about all the roles in the database. That includes both user-defined roles and fixed database roles. In most cases, you'll use this function just to list the roles in a database, so you'll omit the role name.

The information that's returned by this procedure includes the role name, the role ID, and an indication of whether or not the role is an application role. The role ID is the internal object identification number that's assigned to the role. An application role is a special kind of role that's typically used to provide secure access to an application program rather than a user. You'll learn more about application roles later in this chapter.

The sp_HelpRoleMember stored procedure returns information about the current members of a database role. If you include a role name as a parameter, it returns information about the members of that role. Otherwise, it returns information about the members in all the roles in the current database that have at least one member.

How to display database role information

The syntax for sp_HelpRole

```
sp_HelpRole [[@rolename = ] 'database_role_name']
```

A statement that lists the roles for the current database

```
EXEC sp_HelpRole
```

The response from the system

	RoleName	RoleId	IsAppRole
1	public	0	0
2	db_owner	16384	0
3	db_accessadmin	16385	0
4	db_securityadmin	16386	0
5	db_ddladmin	16387	0
6	db_backupoperator	16389	0
7	db_datareader	16390	0
8	db_datawriter	16391	0
9	db_denydatareader	16392	0
10	db_denydatawriter	16393	0
11	InvoiceEntry	16400	0

How to display role member information

The syntax for sp_HelpRoleMember

```
sp_HelpRoleMember [[@rolename = ] 'role_name' ]
```

A statement that lists the members of the InvoiceEntry role

```
EXEC sp_HelpRoleMember InvoiceEntry
```

The response from the system

	DbRole	MemberName	MemberSID
1	InvoiceEntry	BRYAN\JaneSmith	0x0105000000000005150000001...
2	InvoiceEntry	JohnDoe	0x3251AB5E12A0254884A756D8B...
3	InvoiceEntry	MartinRey	0xFAC03CC0B422B2478AFF6F24D...

Description

- To display information about the roles defined in the current database, use the sp_HelpRole system stored procedure.
- To display information about the members of a database role, use the sp_HelpRoleMember system stored procedure.

Figure 17-11   How to display information about database roles and role members

How to deny permissions granted by role membership

A user's permissions include those that are granted explicitly to that user plus permissions that are granted by that user's membership in one or more roles. That means that if you revoke a permission from the user but the same permission is granted by a role to which the user belongs, the user still has that permission. Since this might not be what you want, SQL Server provides another statement you can use to deny a user permission that's granted by the user's membership in a role. This statement, DENY, is presented in figure 17-12.

The syntax of the DENY statement is similar to the syntax of the REVOKE statement. To deny object permissions, you specify the permissions you want to deny, the object to which you want to deny permissions, and the users and roles whose permissions you want to deny. To deny statement permissions, you specify the statements to which you want to deny permission and the users and roles whose permissions you want to deny.

The two examples in this figure illustrate how this works. The script in the first example adds the user named MartinRey to the InvoiceEntry role. Since InvoiceEntry is a member of the db_datareaders fixed database role, MartinRey can retrieve data from any table in the database. This is illustrated by the successful completion of the SELECT statement that follows, which retrieves data from the GLAccounts table.

The script in the second example starts by removing MartinRey from the InvoiceEntry role. Then, a DENY statement is used to deny this user SELECT permission to the GLAccounts table. Finally, MartinRey is added back as a member of the InvoiceEntry role. Now, you can see that when this user executes a SELECT statement against the GLAccounts table, the system responds with an error. That's because the DENY statement specifically denied this user permission to retrieve data from this table even though that permission is granted by the db_datareaders role.

The syntax of the DENY statement for object permissions

```
DENY {ALL|permission [, ...]}
ON object_description
TO security_account [, ...]
[CASCADE]
```

The syntax of the DENY statement for statement permissions

```
DENY {ALL|statement [, ...]}
TO security_account [, ...]
```

A script that assigns membership to the InvoiceEntry role

```
EXEC sp_AddRoleMember InvoiceEntry, MartinRey
```

A SELECT statement entered by the user

```
SELECT * FROM GLAccounts
```

The response from the system

	AccountNo	AccountDescription	
1	100	Cash	
2	110	Accounts Receivable	
3	120	Book Inventory	

A script that denies SELECT permission to GLAccounts

```
EXEC sp_DropRoleMember InvoiceEntry, MartinRey
DENY SELECT
ON GLAccounts
TO MartinRey
EXEC sp_AddRoleMember InvoiceEntry, MartinRey
```

A SELECT statement entered by the user

```
SELECT * FROM GLAccounts
```

The response from the system

```
Server: Msg 229, Level 14, State 5, Line 1
SELECT permission denied on object 'GLAccounts', database 'AP', owner 'dbo'.
```

Description

- The permissions granted to individual users are granted by two sources: permissions granted to their login IDs and permissions granted through any roles to which they are members.
- The DENY statement differs from the REVOKE statement in that DENY prevents the permission from being granted by role membership. A denied permission can't be granted by role membership, but a revoked permission can.

Figure 17-12   How to deny permissions granted by role membership

How to work with application roles

An *application role* is a special kind of user-defined database role. Unlike other roles, you can't assign members to an application role. Instead, you activate the role for a connection. Then, the normal security for the login ID that was used to open the connection is replaced by the security that's specified by the application role.

Figure 17-13 presents three system stored procedures for working with application roles. To create a new application role, you use the sp_AddAppRole procedure. As you can see, this procedure requires two parameters: a role name and a password. The first statement in this figure, for example, creates an application role named AppInvoiceQuery that has a password of "appqrypw."

After you create an application role, you can use it in GRANT, REVOKE, or DENY statements just as you would any other role. The second statement in this figure, for example, grants the application role permission to retrieve data from the Invoices table.

To activate an application role, you execute the sp_SetAppRole procedure. Once activated, the permissions associated with the user's login ID and roles are all revoked. Instead, the connection is granted the permissions associated with the application role. Since the connection takes on an entirely new set of permissions, it's almost as if the user logged off and then logged back on under a different login ID.

You can see how this works in the script in this figure. First, assume that the login ID that was used to log on to the server doesn't have SELECT permission for the Invoices table. For this reason, the first SELECT statement in this script fails and returns an error message. Next, the script activates the AppInvoiceQuery application role. Because this role has permission to select data from the Invoices table, the SELECT statement that follows now succeeds.

Application roles are intended for use by application programs that manage their own security. Typically, an application like this will open a limited number of connections to a database and then share those connections among many application users. Then, the application role controls the application's access to the database, and the application controls the users that are allowed to use the connections it establishes.

You can also use application roles to provide for more flexible security. For example, suppose a user needs to access a database both through the Query Analyzer and through an application. Also suppose that the user needs broader permissions to use the application than you want to give him through the Query Analyzer. To do that, you could assign the user standard permissions through his login ID and role memberships, and you could give the application enhanced permissions through an application role.

System stored procedures for working with application roles

The syntax for sp_AddAppRole

```
sp_AddAppRole [@rolename = ] 'role_name',
              [@password = ] 'password'
```

The syntax for sp_DropAppRole

```
sp_DropAppRole [@rolename = ] 'role_name'
```

The syntax for sp_SetAppRole

```
sp_SetAppRole [@rolename = ] 'role_name',
              [@password = ] 'password'
```

Statements that work with application roles

A statement that creates a new application role

```
EXEC sp_AddAppRole AppInvoiceQuery, appqrypw
```

A statement that adds permissions to the new application role

```
GRANT SELECT
ON Invoices
TO AppInvoiceQuery
```

A script that tests the application role

```
SELECT * FROM Invoices
EXEC sp_SetAppRole AppInvoiceQuery, appqrypw
SELECT * FROM Invoices
```

The response from the system

```
Server: Msg 229, Level 14, State 5, Line 1
SELECT permission denied on object 'Invoices', database 'AP', owner 'dbo'.
The application role 'AppInvoiceQuery' is now active.
```

	InvoiceID	VendorID	InvoiceNumber	InvoiceDate	InvoiceTot
1	1	34	QP58872	2002-02-25 00:00:00	116.5400
2	2	34	Q545443	2002-03-14 00:00:00	1083.5800

Description

- An *application role* is a special type of database role. It can't contain any members, but it's activated when a connection executes the sp_SetAppRole system stored procedure.

- Once the connection activates an application role, the normal security for the login ID set by the permissions for the ID and its roles is ignored. Instead, the connection assumes a new security profile as defined by the permissions for the application role.

- Once a connection activates an application role, the role can't be deactivated. Because of that, the application role remains in effect until the connection is closed or until a different application role is activated.

- Application roles are typically used by application programs that manage their own security. Then, those applications can control the users that are allowed to log on to the server.

Figure 17-13   How to work with application roles

How to manage security using the Enterprise Manager

Now that you understand the relationships between the various security objects that exist on your server and in your database, you're ready to learn how to manage those same objects using the Enterprise Manager. You'll find most of these objects in one of two places in the console tree of the Enterprise Manager. To work with login IDS and fixed server roles, you can use the items in the Security node for the server. To work with database security objects, such as database user names, permissions, and database roles, you can use the items in the node for a specific database.

How to work with logins

Figure 17-14 presents the Login Properties dialog box for creating a new login. As you can see, this dialog box has three tabs: General, Server Roles, and Database Access. I'll show how to work with the options in the General tab in this topic, and I'll show you how to work with the options in the other tabs in the topics that follow.

When you create a new login, you can select which type of authentication to use. If you select Windows Authentication, you can click on the button to the right of the Name box with the ellipsis on it (…) to select a domain and user. Alternatively, you can enter a name into the Name box and then select a domain from the drop-down list. You can also select a Security access option when you use Windows authentication. By default, the Grant access option is selected, which means that the user will be allowed to log on to the server. If you select the Deny access option, SQL Server will create the login ID but will not let the user log on. You typically use this option to temporarily disable access for an existing user.

If you select SQL Server authentication, you must enter the new user name in the Name box. In addition, you can enter a password for the user. If you don't, the password will be set to null, which isn't usually what you want.

In addition to setting the authentication mode, you can use this dialog box to set the default database and the default language for the user. If you don't select another database, the Master database is used. And if you don't select a specific language, the default language for the server is used. Unless it's been changed, the server language default is English.

A dialog box similar to the one shown here is displayed for an existing user. This dialog box lets you grant or deny security access for a user that uses SQL Server authentication or change the password for a user that uses Windows authentication. It also lets you change the default database or language. However, it doesn't let you change the type of authentication that's used. To do that, you have to delete the login ID and create a new one with the authentication you want.

The SQL Server Login Properties dialog box

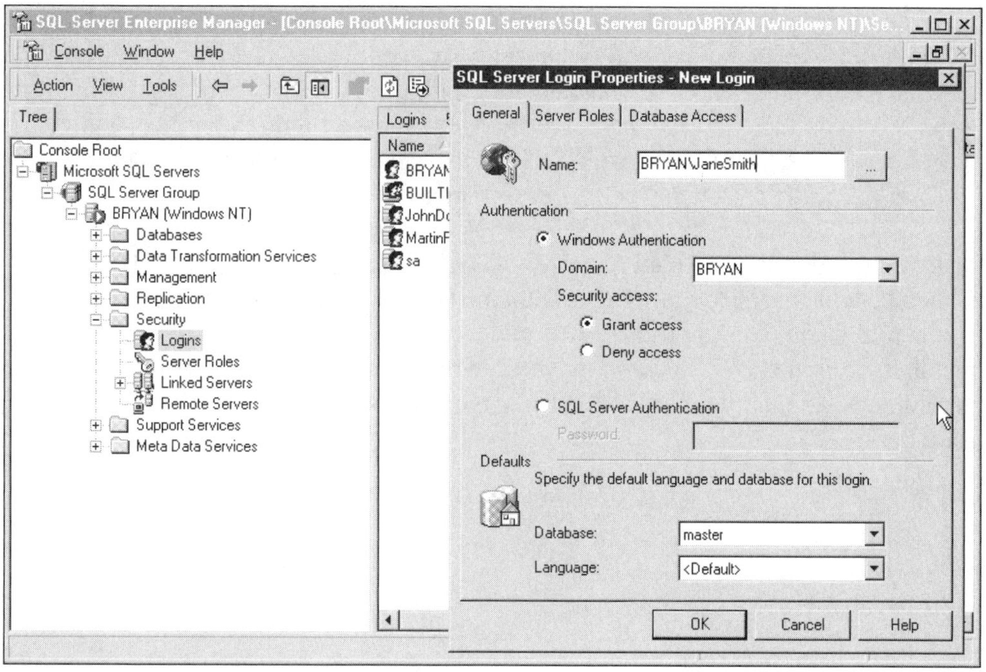

How to create a new login ID

- Expand the Security node for the server in the console tree. Then, highlight the Logins node and select Action→New Login to open the Login Properties dialog box.

- Select the type of authentication you want to use.

- If you select Windows authentication, you can click on the ellipsis button (…) to select the Windows domain and user. You can also specify whether the user will have access to the login by selecting one of the Security access options.

- If you select SQL Server authentication, you must enter a user name and an optional password.

- Select the default database and default language for the login.

How to change properties for an existing user

- Highlight the Logins node in the console tree, select the user name in the right pane, and select Action→Properties to open the Login Properties dialog box.

- If the login ID uses SQL Server authentication, you can reset the user's password from this dialog box. If the login ID uses Windows authentication, you can grant or deny security access. For either type of authentication, you can set the default database and language. You can't switch the authentication of an existing user.

How to delete a login ID

- Highlight the user name in the right pane, select Action→Delete, and then confirm the deletion.

Figure 17-14   How to work with logins

How to work with server roles

Figure 17-15 shows two ways you can work with the fixed server roles from the Enterprise Manager. First, you can work with the server roles for a specific login ID. To do that, you use the Server Roles tab of the Login Properties dialog box shown at the top of this figure. This tab lists all of the fixed server roles and lets you select the ones you want the user assigned to.

Second, you can work with the login IDs for a specific server role. To do that, you use the Server Role Properties dialog box shown in this figure. The General tab of this dialog box lists the login IDs that are members of the selected role. Then, you can use the Add and Remove buttons to add and remove members from this role. In addition, you can use the Permissions tab to view the permissions for the role. You can't change the permissions for a fixed server role, however.

The dialog boxes for working with server roles

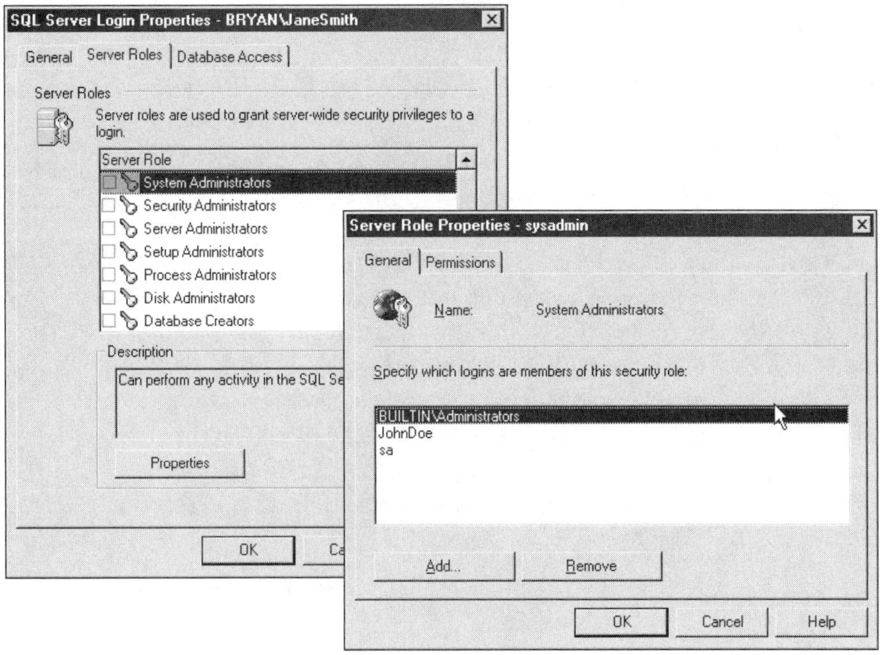

How to work with the server roles for a user

- Display the Login Properties dialog box and then click on the Server Roles tab. The roles that the user is current assigned to are checked in the list that's displayed.

- To add or remove a user from a server role, select or deselect the role.

How to work with the users assigned to a server role

- Highlight a role in the Server Roles tab of the Login Properties dialog box and then click on the Properties button to display the Server Role Properties dialog box. You can also display this dialog box by highlighting the Server Roles node in the console tree, highlighting the role in the right pane, and then selecting Action→Properties.

- To add a member to the role, click the Add button and select the member from the dialog box that's displayed.

- To remove a member, highlight the member and then click on the Remove button.

- To review the permissions for the role, click on the Permissions tab.

Figure 17-15   How to work with server roles

How to assign database access and roles by login ID

Figure 17-16 presents the Database Access tab of the Login Properties dialog box. This tab lists all of the databases on the server and all of the database roles defined for the highlighted database. You can use this dialog box to grant database access to a user and to assign a user membership in one or more database roles.

To grant or revoke database access, simply select or deselect the check box to the left of the database name. If you grant access to a database, you can also assign an alias for the user to be used within the database. To do that, enter the name in the User column. The default is the login ID.

After you grant a user access to a database, you can add that user as a member of any of the database roles defined for the database. That includes both the fixed database roles and any user-defined roles. To do that, just highlight the database and then select the check boxes to the left of the database roles to add the user to those roles.

The Database Access tab of the Login Properties dialog box

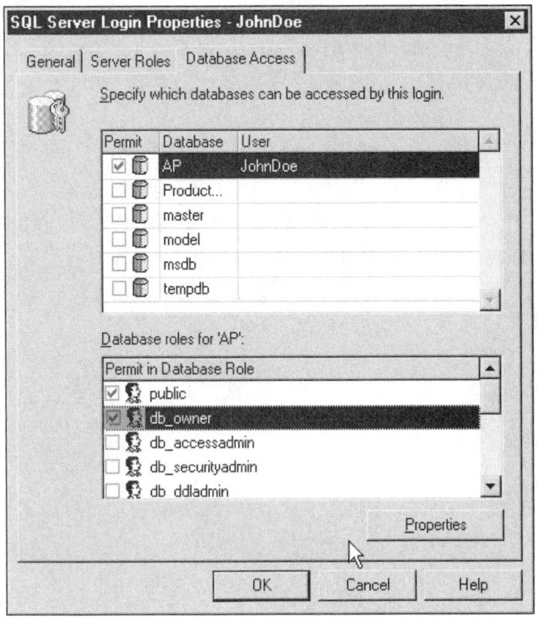

How to grant or revoke database access for a user

- Display the Login Properties dialog box and then click on the Database Access tab.
- To grant or revoke access to a database, select or deselect the Permit check box for that database.
- When you grant access, the user name for the database is automatically set to the login ID. If you want to use an alias for the user name, change the name in the User column.

How to add or remove a user from a database role

- If the user has access to a database, you can add or remove the user from the database roles for that database. To do that, highlight the database to display the database roles in the lower portion of the dialog box. Then, select or deselect the roles.
- You can also set role memberships for a user from the Database User Properties dialog box shown in the next figure.

Figure 17-16   How to assign database access and roles by login ID

How to assign role memberships

You can also assign a user membership in one or more database roles using the Database User Properties dialog box shown in figure 17-17. To do that, just select the check boxes for the roles.

You can also use this dialog box to display two additional dialog boxes. If you click on the Permissions button, a dialog box is displayed that lets you modify the object permissions that are granted to this user. You'll see how to use this dialog box in figure 17-18. If you highlight a database role and then click on the Properties button, a dialog box is displayed that lets you edit the properties of the selected role. You'll see how to use this dialog box in figure 17-19.

The Database User Properties dialog box

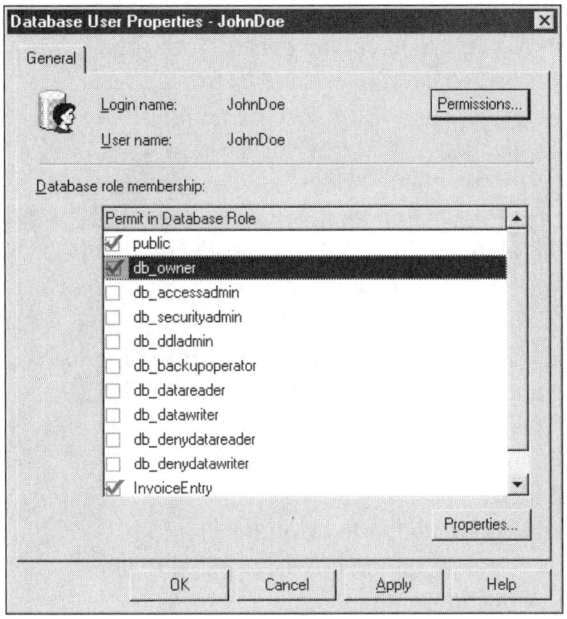

Description

* To display the Database User Properties dialog box, expand the database in the console tree and then highlight the Users node. Highlight the user name in the right pane and then select Action→Properties.

* To add or remove a user from a database role, select or deselect the check box for the role.

* To grant or revoke individual object permissions for the user, click on the Permissions button. See figure 17-18 for details.

* To grant or revoke object permissions for a role, highlight the role and then click on the Properties button. See figure 17-19 for details.

Figure 17-17   How to assign role memberships

How to assign database user permissions

Figure 17-18 presents the dialog box you use to set the permissions for a database user. Although this dialog box is displayed from the Database User Properties dialog box for a specific user, you can use it to set the permissions for any user in the database. To do that, just select the user you want to work with from the drop-down list at the top of this dialog box.

As you can see, this dialog box displays a grid with the object names and owners in the leftmost columns. The six columns to the right correspond to the standard SQL Server object permissions (DRI corresponds to the REFER-ENCES permission). By clicking on a check box for one of these permissions, you can cycle between granting permission to the object, denying permission to the object, and revoking permission from the object. To grant permission, click on the check box until a green check mark is displayed. To deny permission, click on the check box until a red X is displayed. And to revoke permission, click on the check box until it's blank.

If you highlight a table or view, you'll notice that the Columns button becomes available. If you click on this button, a dialog box is displayed that lists the columns in that table or view. You can use this dialog box to set SELECT or UPDATE permissions for those columns.

By default, the permissions for all of the objects in the database are displayed so that you can grant, revoke, or deny permissions to any of these objects. If a database has many objects, however, you may want to display just the objects that the user has permission to use. To do that, select the List only objects with permissions for this user option.

The Permissions tab of the Database User Properties dialog box

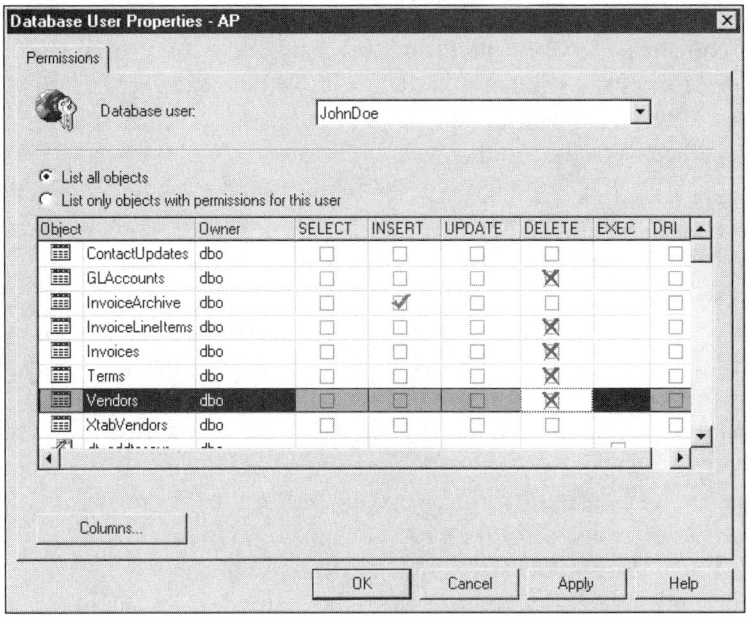

Description

- To display the permissions for a user, click the Permissions button in the Database User Properties dialog.
- To grant the user permission to an object, click in the box for that permission until a green check mark appears.
- To deny the user permission to an object, click in the box for that permission until a red X appears.
- To revoke the user permission to an object, click in the box for that permission until it's blank.
- To set the permissions for the columns in a table or view, highlight the object and then click on the Columns button.
- The five permissions available from this dialog box correspond to the first five standard permissions listed in figure 17-6 that you can assign using the GRANT statement. The DRI option in this dialog box stands for declarative referential integrity, and it corresponds to the REFERENCES permission.

Note

- Only permissions that are granted to the user appear in this dialog box. Permissions that are granted by the user's membership in a role aren't listed.

Figure 17-18   How to assign database user permissions

How to manage user-defined roles

Figure 17-19 presents the Database Role Properties dialog box you use to manage the user-defined roles for a database. In this example, you can see the properties for the InvoiceEntry role that was created in figure 17-10. As you can see, three members have been assigned to this role.

To remove a member from the role, highlight the member and then click on the Remove button. To add new members to the role, click on the Add button. Then, a dialog box is displayed that lists all of the users and roles that aren't currently members of this role.

Although it's difficult to see, you should notice that the Standard role option is selected for this role. That means that it's a standard database role that can contain members. The other option is for an application role. If you display this dialog box for an application role, you can modify the password for the role rather than the members.

To set the permissions for the selected role, you can click on the Permissions button. Then, the Permissions tab of the Properties dialog box for the database is displayed. You'll learn how to use this dialog box in the next topic.

Notice that you can't add a user-defined role from the dialog box shown in this figure. To do that, you highlight the Roles node for the database and then select the Action→New Database Role command. When you do, a dialog box similar to the one shown in this figure is displayed. The differences are that you can enter a name for the role and you can select the type of role you want to create.

The Database Role Properties dialog box for the InvoiceEntry role

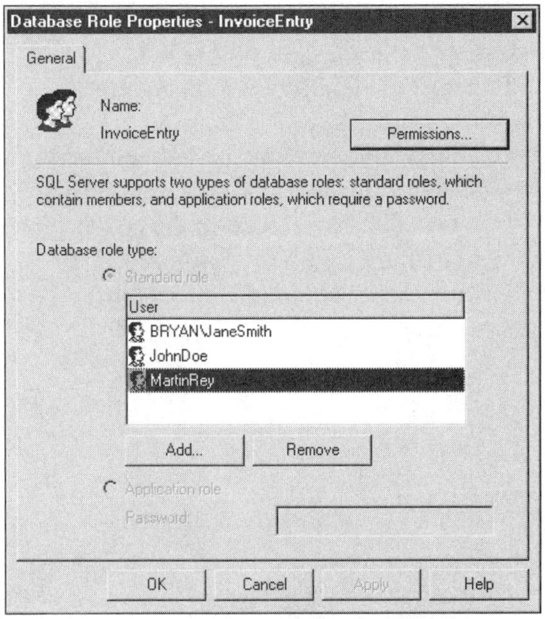

How to modify an existing database role

- To display the Database Role Properties dialog box, highlight the Roles node for the database, select the role name in the right pane, and select Action→Properties. You can also display this dialog box by clicking on the Properties button in the Database User Properties dialog box.
- To add a member to the role, click the Add button and then select the user or role from the dialog box that's displayed.
- To delete a member from the role, highlight the name and then click the Remove button.
- To modify the permissions for the role, click on the Permissions button to display the Database Role Properties dialog box for the role. This dialog box is similar to the Database User Properties dialog box you saw in figure 17-18.

How to delete a database role

- Highlight the Roles node, select the role name, and select Action→Delete. You must remove all members from a role before you can delete it.

How to create a new database role

- Highlight the Roles node, select Action→New Database Role, and enter the name of the new role in the dialog box that's displayed. By default, the new role will be a standard database role. To create an application role, select the Application role option in this dialog box and enter a password for the role.

Figure 17-19   How to manage user-defined roles

How to work with statement permissions

To work with the statement permissions for the users and roles in a database, you use the Permissions tab of the Properties dialog box for the database. This dialog box and tab are displayed in figure 17-20.

The leftmost column of this tab lists the users and roles that are defined for the database. As you can see, a key icon indicates a role and an icon resembling a head indicates a user. The eight columns to the right correspond to the eight DDL statements that you can permit. As with the grid for object permissions, a green check mark means the permission has been granted, a red X means the permission has been denied, and a blank box means the permission has been revoked.

The Permissions tab of the database Properties dialog box

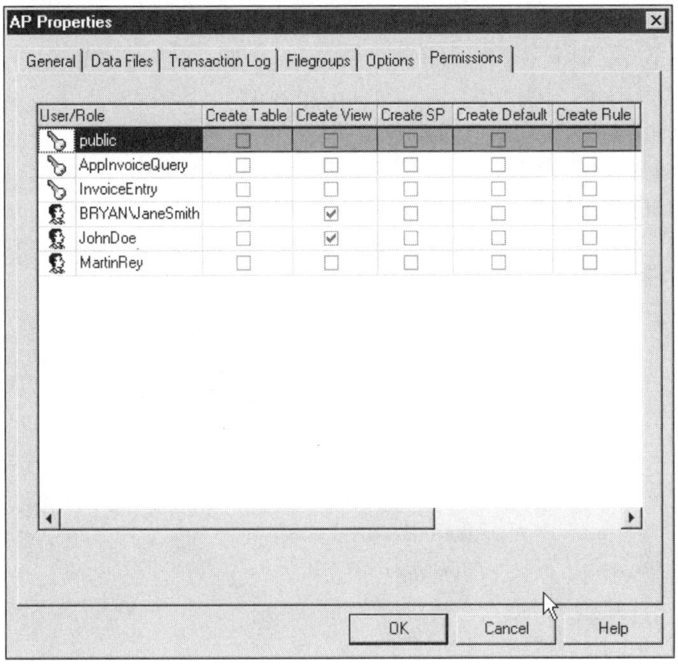

Description

- To display the statement permissions for a database, highlight the Databases node in the console tree, highlight the database in the right pane, select Action→Properties, and then click on the Permissions tab.

- To grant a user or role permission to a statement, click in the box for that permission until a green check mark appears.

- To deny a user or role permission to a statement, click in the box for that permission until a red X appears.

- To revoke a user or role permission to a statement, click in the box for that permission until it's blank.

- You can grant, revoke, or deny permission to any of the eight SQL DDL statements listed in this dialog box.

Figure 17-20   How to work with statement permissions

Perspective

Although managing security on a server can be complex, SQL Server provides useful tools to simplify the job. In this chapter, you've learned how to manage security for your server and database using both Transact-SQL and the Enterprise Manager. Once you're familiar with both of these techniques, you can use the one that's easiest for the security task at hand.

Terms

login ID	Windows authentication
permissions	SQL Server authentication
object permissions	fixed role
statement permissions	fixed server role
role	fixed database role
group	user-defined role
authentication mode	application role

Appendix A

How to install and use the software and files for this book

The best way to learn SQL is by coding and executing SQL statements. Before you can get started, though, you need to have access to a SQL database system. If you install the software that's on the CD in the back of this book, you can work with a copy of SQL Server on your own PC. Then you'll be able to try all of the examples in this book on your own computer. In addition, you'll be able to practice the database administration skills that are presented in sections 3 and 4 of this book.

An overview of the software and files included with this book

Throughout this book, you'll see examples of SQL code and the response you'll get from SQL Server when you execute that code. Although you may be able to learn how to code SQL by simply studying these examples, you'll learn faster and better by entering and executing the code yourself. To do that, however, you must have access to a SQL database system that's running Microsoft SQL Server 2000. You must also have the client tools on your PC that let you connect to the server and submit SQL queries. And a copy of the databases that are used in the examples in this book must be installed on the server.

In the two topics that follow, you'll learn how to install and use the software and files that come on the CD for this book. Figure A-1 presents an overview of the software and files and the installation process. To install Microsoft SQL Server 2000 Desktop Edition (MSDE) on your own PC, for example, you use the files in the MSDE2000 directory. MSDE is a scaled-down version of SQL Server that's 100% compatible with other versions of SQL Server 2000. Although MSDE is only licensed for stand-alone use, it provides a perfect environment for learning SQL Server.

If you already have access to a copy of SQL Server through your school's or company's server, you may be able to use that copy of SQL Server instead of installing MSDE. Keep in mind, however, that the system administrator may restrict what you can do with that server. Because of that, you may not be able to try all the examples in this book. So I recommend you install MSDE on your own system whenever you have that option.

Another option is to install the full Enterprise Edition of SQL Server on your own system. To do that, you can use the files in the SQLEVAL directory. If you install this edition of the server software, the server isn't limited to stand-alone use. However, the edition that's provided on this CD is an evaluation edition that expires 120 days after you install it. Because of that, you're better off installing MSDE.

Although you probably won't use the Enterprise Edition of SQL Server, you will need to use the client tools that come with this edition. You can use these tools to work with MSDE or the Enterprise Edition of SQL Server. These tools include the Enterprise Manager, the Query Analyzer, and Books Online. You'll be introduced to these tools in chapter 2 of this book. Because Books Online, which includes the documentation for SQL Server, has been updated, we've included the updated version on this CD, too. You can install it using the files in the SQL_BOL directory.

Finally, the file named Install.exe is an executable file that you can use to install the databases used in the examples in this book along with some of the SQL code. If you're using MSDE, you can install these databases and files on your own system. If you're using a copy of SQL Server on another server, however, you'll need to have the administrator of that system install the databases for you on that server and then give you access to them.

The files and directories of the CD

File or directory	Description
MSDE2000	A directory that contains the executable file used to install the Microsoft SQL Server 2000 Desktop Edition (MSDE). This is a fully-compatible version of SQL Server 2000 that you can install and run on your own PC.
SQLEVAL	A directory that contains the executable file used to install the Enterprise Evaluation Edition of Microsoft SQL Server 2000. This includes both the client tools you'll use to work with the server as well as a 120-day limited-use license for the Enterprise Edition of the server software.
SQL_BOL	A directory that contains the executable file used to install an updated version of Books Online for SQL Server 2000.
Install.exe	An executable file used to install a copy of the databases used in the examples presented in this book, files you can use to attach the databases to your server, and files containing the SQL code for some of the examples.

An overview of the installation

- If you install the software and files that are available on the CD that comes with this book, you'll be able to work along with the examples presented throughout the book. In addition, you'll be able to create databases of your own and enter and execute queries against those databases.

- Although the CD includes a copy of MSDE that you can install on your own computer, you can also use an existing server if one is available to you. Since you'll have more control over what you can do if you use MSDE, however, I recommend you do that if possible.

- To work with the databases that come with this book and to create databases of your own, you'll need to install the SQL Server 2000 client tools on your PC. These tools include the Enterprise Manager, the Query Analyzer, and Books Online. Because Books Online has been updated since it was released, you'll also want to install the updated copy that's provided.

- If you're going to use the databases and code examples that come with this book, you'll need to install them on your hard drive. Then, you'll need to attach the databases to the server. If you're using MSDE, you can do that by following the steps in figure A-3. If you're using a server that's installed on another machine, however, you'll need to contact the system administrator about getting the databases attached and being granted permission to use them.

Figure A-1   An overview of the software and files included with this book

How to install the software, database files, and code examples

Figure A-2 presents the steps you need to follow to install the software, database files, and code examples from the CD to your PC. As you can see, the first two steps install a copy of MSDE on your PC. If you're going to use an existing server or if you're going to install the Enterprise Evaluation Edition of the server, you can skip these two steps.

The next eight steps install the SQL Server 2000 client tools that you use to work with SQL Server. These tools are part of the Enterprise Evaluation Edition of SQL Server that's on the CD. Although you can also install the server components that come with this edition, I recommend you use MSDE instead. If you want to use the Enterprise Edition, however, you can install it by selecting the Server and Client Tools option in step 8.

The Books Online application contains a complete set of reference documents for SQL Server 2000. As you'll see when you start learning SQL, it's an invaluable resource that you'll refer to often. Because the version that's installed from the Enterprise Evaluation Edition is out of date, however, you'll want to follow steps 11 and 12 to install the updated version.

Most of the examples in this book use an accounts payable database named AP. This is a complete database that contains realistic data. If you understand the examples that use this database, you'll understand how SQL is used in the real world.

The last step in this figure runs an installation program that copies the data file for this database onto your PC. In addition, this program copies files for other databases used in the book examples, along with script files that contain the SQL code for most of the more complex examples presented in the book. It also copies some files you can use to attach the database files to your server as described in the next figure.

All of these files are installed by default in a folder named C:\Murach\SQL for Server. The database files are stored in a subfolder named Databases, the SQL code examples are stored in a subfolder named Scripts, and the files for attaching the database files are stored in a subfolder named OSQL_Batches. To make the code examples you want to use easy to find, the examples for each chapter are stored in a separate folder within the Scripts folder, and the files are named according to the figure number where they're presented.

Install MSDE

1. Put the CD that came with this book into the CD drive and then use the Windows Explorer to navigate to the MSDE2000 directory. Double-click on the Setup.exe file to run it and install MSDE on you system. When the installation is complete, restart your PC.

2. Verify that your server is running by looking at the SQL Server Service Manager icon in the system tray near the right side of the Windows taskbar. If this icon shows a small green arrow, then the server is running. If not, refer to figure 2-1 to learn how to use the Service Manager to start it.

Install the SQL Server 2000 client tools

3. Navigate to the SQLEVAL directory on the CD and then double-click on the Autorun.exe file to start the installer program for SQL Server 2000.

4. Click on the SQL Server 2000 Components option in the first window that's displayed, then click Install Database Server in the second window.

5. If you're running a version of Windows older than Windows NT, the installer displays a warning message that only the client components are available for installation. Click OK.

6. When the Welcome window is displayed, click Next. Then, select Local Computer from the Computer Name window, and choose Create a new instance of SQL Server from the Installation Selection window.

7. Enter your name and an optional company name in the User Information window. Then, review the license agreement in the Software License Agreement window and select Yes to accept this agreement.

8. Choose Client Tools Only from the Installation Definition window. (Depending on your version of Windows, this may not be the default.)

9. Accept the default options in the Select Components window, then click Next in the Start Copying Files window.

10. When the installation is complete, click Finish and then restart your PC.

Install the updated version of Books Online

11. Navigate to the SQL_BOL directory on the CD and double-click on the Setup.exe file to start the installer for the updated version of Books Online.

12. When the Setup Wizard window is displayed, click Next. Then, select I Agree from the License Agreement window. When the Select Installation Folder window is displayed, verify that the Overwrite SQL Server 2000 Books Online option is selected and then click Next. Finally, click Next in the Confirm Installation window. When the installation is complete, click the Close button.

Install the database files and SQL code examples

13. Double-click on the file named Install.exe in the root directory of the CD and respond to the dialog boxes that follow. This installs the database files and SQL code examples on your C drive in folders named Murach\SQL for SQL Server\Databases and Murach\SQL for SQL Server\Scripts.

Figure A-2   How to install the software, database files, and code examples

How to attach the database files to your server

When you attach a database file to SQL Server, the server creates a new database based on the contents of the file. Then, that file is used to store the tables, data, and other objects of the database. In addition, the server maintains a transaction log file for the database that's used to recover your database in the event of a system failure. Figure A-3 presents the steps you need to perform to attach the database files for the databases used by this book.

In the first step, you copy the seven files in the Databases folder to the default database file folder for SQL Server. Then, you can perform the next three steps to attach the database files for the AP and ProductOrders databases. Although files are provided for three other databases, the AP and ProductOrders databases are the ones you'll use most often. So I've tried to make it as easy as possible for you to attach these two databases. If you want to attach any of the other databases, you can do that using SQL as described in chapter 10 or the Enterprise Manager as described in chapter 11.

To attach the AP and ProductOrders databases, you can use one of two DOS batch files. You use the one named Attach_WA.bat if you're using Windows NT, Windows 2000, or Windows XP. If you're using Windows 98 or Windows ME, however, you'll need to use the one named Attach_SSA.bat. Keep in mind that these batch files will work correctly only if you've copied the database files into the default directory.

The database file named AP_AllObjects_Data.mdf contains a copy of the AP database that has many other objects in it, including views, stored procedures, user-defined functions, and triggers. These objects aren't included in the AP database so that you can add them yourself as you read the related chapters in this book. If you'd like to view or work with the complete database, however, you'll be able to do that after reading section 3 of this book.

The database file named Examples_Data.mdf contains several small tables that are used in some of the examples for which the main AP database couldn't be used. And the database file named Test_AP_Data.mdf is an empty database that's used in the example in chapter 10 that shows you how to attach an existing database file.

How to restore the databases to their original states

As you work with the examples in this book, you may make changes to the AP and ProductOrders databases that you don't intend to make. In that case, you may want to restore the original databases. The last procedure in this figure describes how you can do that. Note that to use this procedure, you need to know how to detach a database. You can learn how to do that in chapter 11.

How to copy and attach the database files

Before you can attach the database files to your server, you should copy them to the default SQL Server directory. That way, you can restore the original files later if you need to.

Copy the database files to the default SQL Server directory

1. Use the Windows Explorer to copy the seven database files in the C:\Murach\SQL for SQL Server\Databases folder to the folder named C:\Program Files\Microsoft SQL Server\MSSQL\Data. The seven files are: AP_Data.mdf, AP_Log.ldf, ProductOrders_Data.mdf, ProductOrders_Log.ldf, AP_AllObjects_Data.mdf, Examples_Data.mdf, and Test_AP_Data.mdf.

Attach the AP and ProductOrders databases to your server

2. Use the Windows Explorer to navigate to the C:\Murach\SQL for SQL Server\OSQL_Batches folder. This folder contains two DOS batch files that are installed on your system along with the database files and SQL code examples. You can use one of these files to attach the files for the AP and ProductOrders databases to your server.

3. If your computer is running Windows NT, Windows 2000, or Windows XP, double-click on the file named Attach_WA.bat to execute it. If your computer is running Windows 98 or Windows Me, double-click on the file named Attach_SSA.bat to execute this file.

4. If no error is displayed, the databases were correctly attached and the databases are now ready to use. If an error occurs, it's probably because you didn't copy the database files into the correct folder. To fix this problem, repeat the copy operation shown above.

How to restore the AP and ProductOrders databases to their original states

In the event that you accidentally delete or modify the data in the AP or ProductOrders database, you can restore these databases to their original states.

1. Detach the current copies of the AP and ProductOrders databases from the server. To do that, follow the instructions shown in figure 11-9. Note that you can't detach a database if it's in use, so you'll want close the Query Analyzer if you have it open, and you'll want to close any open queries in the Enterprise Manager.

2. If you want to keep the current copies of the databases, move or rename the AP_Data.mdf, AP_Log.ldf, ProductOrders_Data.mdf, and ProductOrders_Log.ldf files in the C:\Program Files\Microsoft SQL Server\MSSQL\Data folder. Otherwise, delete these files.

3. Copy the AP_Data.mdf, AP_Log.ldf, ProductOrders_Data.mdf, and ProductOrders_Log.ldf files from the C:\Murach\SQL for SQL Server\Databases folder to the C:\Program Files\Microsoft SQL Server\MSSQL\Data folder. Then, use the procedure above to attach these new files to the server.

Note

*   If you want to attach one of the other databases, you can use the Enterprise Manager as described in figure 11-9. You can also restore any of these databases to its original state using a procedure like the one shown above.

Figure A-3   How to use the database files

What about security flaws and service packs

Perhaps you've read that SQL Server 2000 has some security flaws. In particular, you may have read about the SQL Slammer Worm that exploits a security weakness in SQL Server 2000 and MSDE. In that case, you may be wondering whether your system will be safe after you install SQL Server 2000.

If you just install MSDE on your own PC from this book's CD as described in this appendix, you shouldn't have any problems. Because you're using MSDE on your own computer, not on a network, a security breach is unlikely. You should be able to run all of the types of SQL statements that are described in this book without encountering any bugs. And you won't have to worry about the 120-day trial period because that applies to SQL Server itself, not to MSDE or the Client Tools.

However, if you're worried about security problems or you want to make sure that your version of MSDE has as few bugs as possible, you can download the latest service pack from www.microsoft.com/sql/evaluation/trial/default.asp. You may also want to download the evaluation edition of SQL Server 2000 from that site instead of using the one on the CD because it may be a later release than the one on the CD.

On the other hand, if you're using SQL Server 2000 on a network, you should definitely download the latest service packs as soon as they become available. You can also read more about Microsoft's Slammer Worm Resources at www.microsoft.com/sql/techinfo/administration/2000/security/slammer.asp.

Appendix B

Coding and syntax conventions

Throughout this book, you've learned how to code Transact-SQL statements, functions, and procedures. This appendix summarizes the coding rules you have to follow and the syntax conventions that are used in the syntax summaries in the figures. As you enter queries, you'll find that the Query Analyzer color codes different elements, like keywords, which also helps you to pinpoint and resolve syntax problems.

Coding rules and guidelines

General coding rules
1. Use spaces to separate the elements in each statement.
2. Use commas to separate the items in a list.
3. Use single quotes (') to enclose literal values.
4. Line breaks, white space, indentation, and capitalization have no effect on the operation of a statement.

Identifiers
1. The first character of an identifier must be a letter as defined by the Unicode Standard 2.0, an underscore (_), an at sign (@), or a number sign (#).
2. An identifier can contain from 1 to 128 characters. All characters after the first must be a letter, a number, an underscore, an at sign, a number sign, or a dollar sign ($).
3. An identifier can't be a Transact-SQL reserved keyword.
4. An identifier can't contain spaces or special characters other than those already mentioned.
5. If an identifier doesn't follow these rules, it must be enclosed in brackets ([]) or double quotation marks ("") unless it's a column alias. A column alias can also be enclosed in single quotes.

Comments
1. To code a block comment that consists of more than one line, type /* at the start of the block and */ at the end.
2. To code a single-line comment, type -- followed by the comment.

Continuations
No special coding is required to code a statement on more than one line. Simply enter a return at the end of the first line and continue the statement on the next line.

Coding recommendations for more readable code
1. Start each new clause on a new line.
2. Break long clauses into multiple lines and indent continued lines.
3. Capitalize the first letter of each keyword and each word in column and table names.
4. Use comments only for portions of code that are difficult to understand. Then, make sure that the comments are correct and up-to-date.

Syntax conventions

UPPERCASE ELEMENT	Indicates that the element is a keyword that must be entered exactly as shown, except that it doesn't have to be capitalized.
`lowercase element`	Indicates an element that you need to provide.
`[option]`	Indicates an option that may be coded but isn't required.
`[option|option]`	Indicates a set of alternative options, one of which may be coded.
`{option|option}`	Indicates a set of alternative options, one of which must be coded.
`...`	Indicates that the preceding option may be repeated multiple times.
<u>`option`</u>	Indicates the default value for an option.

Coding examples

Syntax:
```
SELECT [ALL|DISTINCT] [TOP n [PERCENT] [WITH TIES]]
    column_specification [[AS] result_column]
    [, column_specification [[AS] result_column]] ...
```

Examples:
```
Select VendorName, VendorCity, VendorState

Select InvoiceNumber As 'Invoice Number',
    InvoiceTotal - PaymentTotal - CreditTotal As BalanceDue

Select Top 5 Percent VendorID, InvoiceTotal
```

Syntax:
```
WHERE test_expression
    [NOT] IN ({subquery|expression_1 [, expression_2]...})
```

Examples:
```
Where VendorState Not In ('CA', 'NV', 'OR')

Where VendorID In
    (Select VendorID
    From Invoices
    Where InvoiceDate = '2002-05-01')
```

Syntax:
```
ORDER BY expression [ASC|DESC] [, expression [ASC|DESC]] ...
```

Examples:
```
Order By VendorName

Order By InvoiceDate Desc, InvoiceNumber, InvoiceTotal
```

Index

G

S

Subquery (continued)
   in HAVING clause, 166, 167
   and IN phrase, 170, 171
   noncorrelated, 178, 179
   predicate, 166, 167
   procedure for coding, 186-189
   search condition, 166, 167, 170-181
   in SELECT clause, 166, 167, 184, 185
   and SOME keyword, 176, 177
   in UPDATE statement, 202, 203
   in WHERE clause, 166, 167, 170-181
Substitute name, 86, 87
SUBSTRING function, 228-231
SUM function, 148-151
Summary query, 148-163
Sybase database system, 20
Symbols (wildcard), 106, 107
Syntax
   explicit cross join, 140, 141
   explicit join, 116, 117
   format for summary, 80, 81
   implicit cross join, 140, 141
   implicit inner join, 128, 129
   implicit join, 116, 117
   implicit outer join, 136, 137
   SQL-92 join, 116, 117
   theta, 128, 129, 136, 137
System catalog, 366, 367
System comparison, 16, 17
System function, 380, 381, 394, 395
System stored procedure, 430, 431
System/R, 18, 19
SYSTEM_USER function, 395, 395

T

Table, 10, 11
   alias, 118, 119
   associate, 266, 267
   attribute, 292, 293
   base, 26, 27
   change, 302-305
   connecting, 266, 267
   create, 292, 293, 334, 335
   data type, 382, 383, 436-439
   database, 10, 11
   delete, 192, 193, 302, 303
   Deleted, 442, 443
   derived, 182, 183, 202, 203, 386, 387
   design, 334, 335
   Inserted, 442, 443

   interim, 126, 127
   linking, 266, 267
   lock, 492, 493
   name, 120, 121, 356, 357
   objects, 386, 387
   property, 50, 51, 336-341
   relationships between, 12, 13
   scan, 272
   table-level constraint, 292, 293, 296, 297
   temporary, 384-387
   user-defined function, 432, 433, 436-439
   variable, 382, 383, 386, 387
Temporal data type, *see Date/time data type*
Temporary
   object, 288, 289
   stored procedure, 412, 413
   table, 384-387
Test for database object, 390, 391
Text data type, 15
Theta syntax, 128, 129, 136, 137
Thin client, 8
Third normal form, 274, 275, 280, 281
Time search, 246, 247
Timestamp data type, 213
Tinyint data type, 15, 214, 215
TO clause
   DENY, 526, 527
   GRANT, 512, 513
Tool (client), 42, 43
TOP clause, 84, 85, 96, 97, 326, 327, 396, 397
   in view, 354-359, 373
@@TRANCOUNT system function, 482, 483
Transaction, 444, 445, 478-485
   when to use, 479
Transaction isolation level, 490, 491, 500, 501
Transaction log file, 290, 291
Transact-SQL, 378, 379
   cursor, 454, 455, 474, 475
   defined, 19
   programming, 408, 409
   and security, 504, 505
   table objects, 386, 387
Transitional (compliance with SQL-92), 18, 19
Transitive dependency, 274, 275
Tree (console), 44, 45
Trigger, 408, 409, 442-451
   AFTER, 442-445
   change, 450, 451
   compared to constraint, 448, 449
   data consistency, 448, 449
   defined, 37

XYZ

What the CD contains

- Microsoft® SQL Server™ 2000 Enterprise Evaluation Edition (this can also be down-loaded for free from Microsoft at www.microsoft.com/downloads)

- Microsoft® SQL Server™ 2000 Desktop Engine (MSDE) (this is also available from Microsoft as part of the free download listed above)

- Microsoft® SQL Server™ 2000 Books Online (updated) (this can also be downloaded for free from Microsoft at www.microsoft.com/downloads)

- A complete accounts payable (AP) database, along with four other databases you can use with this book

- SQL script files that contain the code for some of the examples presented in the book

- Two batch files and a script you can use to attach the AP database to your server

Read appendix A first

- Appendix A describes the software and files that are on the CD and gets you started using them.

How to install MSDE

- Navigate to the directory on the CD named MSDE2000. Then, double-click on the file named Setup.exe. For more information, see figure A-2 on page 549.

How to install the SQL Server client tools

- Navigate to the directory on the CD named SQLEVAL. Then, double-click on the file named Autorun.exe and respond to the dialog boxes that follow. Be sure to select the correct option so that only the client tools are installed, not the server software. For more information, see figure A-2 on page 549.

How to install Books Online

- Navigate to the directory on the CD named SQL_BOL. Then, double-click on the file named Setup.exe. For more information, see figure A-2 on page 549.

How to install the database, script, and batch files

- Navigate to the root directory on the CD and double-click on the file named Install.exe. This copies all the database, SQL, and batch files for use with this book to the C:\Murach\SQL for SQL Server directory.

How to copy and attach the database files

- Use the procedure presented in figure A-3 on page 551.